THE DICTIONARY OF
PUBLIC POLICY AND
ADMINISTRATION

Consulting Editors

THE DICTIONARY OF PUBLIC POLICY AND ADMINISTRATION

Jay M. Shafritz
University of Pittsburgh

Westview
PRESS

A Member of the Perseus Books Group

DEDICATED TO

ALBERT C. HYDE

AND

J. STEVEN OTT

FRIENDS AND MENTORS

Copyright © 2004 by Westview Press, a Member of the Perseus Books Group.

Published in the United States of America by Westview Press, A Member of the Perseus Books Group, 5500 Central Avenue, Boulder, Colorado 80301-2877, and in the United Kingdom by Westview Press, 12 Hid's Copse Road, Cumnor Hill, Oxford OX2 9JJ.

Find us on the world wide web at www.westviewpress.com

Westview Press books are available at special discounts for bulk purchases in the United States by corporations, institutions, and other organizations. For more information, please contact the Special Markets Department at the Perseus Books Group, 11 Cambridge Center, Cambridge, MA 02142, or call (617) 252-5298, (800) 255-1514, or e-mail special.markets@perseusbooks.com.

Library of Congress Cataloging-in-Publication Data

Shafritz, Jay M.
    Dictionary of public policy and administration / Jay Shafritz.
        p.   cm.
    ISBN 0-8133-4260-0 (pbk.); 0-8133-4261-9 (hc)
    1. Policy sciences—Dictionaries.   2. Public administration—Dictionaries.   I. Title.
    H97.S483 2004
    320.6'03—dc22

                                                                            2004008455

The paper used in this publication meets the requirements of the American National Standard for Permanence of Paper for Printed Library Materials Z39.48–1984.

10   9   8   7   6   5   4   3   2   1

Foreword

Jay M. Shafritz, the leading U.S. lexicographer of public policy and administration, has produced another useful volume. The 1,600 or so entries in *Dictionary of Public Policy and Administration* contain an impressive amount of pertinent information, as well as wisdom and insightful humor. This volume will be conveniently located on my desk and consulted often. What distinguishes the *Dictionary* as a most valuable resource in the field is its comprehensive coverage, succinct definitions, remarkable readability, and sophisticated explanations of both classical and contemporary concepts, ideas, and terms. Its coverage extends to public and public service organizations and policies at all levels of government, including multinational and international.

The *Dictionary* is not meant to be read cover to cover, but I did so and learned a great deal from it. Each reader will find a variety of fascinating new facts and observations tucked away in entries throughout the book. For example, I was reminded of "SWOT analysis," defined as "a review of an organization's strengths, weaknesses, opportunities, and threats." Then I learned that a slush fund was originally "money collected by the military services in the nineteenth century by selling grease and other refuse (the slush)." At first, the sixty-two entries beginning with "tax" surprised me. On further reflection, the *Dictionary* is also an invaluable inventory of public policy and administration concepts and activities. I will urge my department to present each of our new Master of Public Administration and Master of Public Policy students with a copy of the *Dictionary*. I cannot think of any book that would be of greater use, value, and longevity to them.

David H. Rosenbloom
Distinguished Professor of Public Administration
American University (Washington, D.C.)

Preface

This *Dictionary* is a tool for all those who must be knowledgeable about the theory, concepts, practices, laws, institutions, literature, and people of the academic discipline and professional practice of public administration. Included are definitions of the major concerns of contemporary public policy and administration: accounting, accountability, administrative management, affirmative action, budgeting, bureaucracy, city/county management, decisionmaking, ethics, federalism, human resources management, implementation, information technology, intergovernmental relations, labor relations, leadership, machinery of government, organization theory and behavior, managerialism, policy analysis, policy studies, privatization, program evaluation, public administration, public finance, public management, public policy, strategic management, and taxation. Also included are brief biographies of major scholars and influential practitioners, summaries of major rulings by the U.S. Supreme Court, overviews of significant laws, descriptions of major government agencies, explanations of historical trends and governing doctrines, and definitions of slang and informal processes.

This *Dictionary* has been created for students, researchers, government officials, and citizens interested in how public policies are evolved, implemented, and administered. It is a ready reference for students and practitioners of public administration—the book that they should keep beside them while they are reading other books in the field. With more than 1,600 entries, it seeks to capture and codify the living language of public affairs. Generally excluded are terms for which the meanings in the context of politics and economics do not differ from definitions to be found in any college-level dictionary of the English language. Terms that once were, but no longer are, part of the language of public affairs are also excluded. A term has to be relevant to current practices for inclusion.

Note that the *Dictionary* is continuously alphabetized. This organization is especially useful for comparing entries that sound similar. It also allows for quick comparison of terms with the same root. For example, the entry for "tax" will be followed by dozens of variants of tax—such as tax avoidance, tax base, and so on. The book follows this format as often as possible; therefore, if the root is known, variants of the term can readily be found. Cross-references are indicated by SMALL CAPITALS within an entry only when reading the cross-reference will significantly enhance the understanding of the original entry.

The *Dictionary* was to be based upon my 1985 *Facts on File Dictionary of Public Administration.* But public policy and administration have changed so much in the last two decades that most of this present work had to be written anew. If you do not find a term that you think should be included, I can only mimic Samuel Johnson's explanation when a woman complained about his 1755 English *Dictionary:* "Ignorance, Madam, pure ignorance." Naturally, all omissions, mistakes, or other flaws to be found herein are solely my responsibility. The consulting editors listed here were just that: consultants. I am grateful for their advice and pleased now to thank them publicly; but all decisions about inclusions and exclusions were mine. I am particularly indebted to David H. Rosenbloom of American University for his extensive review of the manuscript and many helpful recommendations for improvement.

It is still true today, as Johnson wrote in 1755, that although "every other author may aspire to praise; the lexicographer can only hope to escape reproach." Yet I remain hopeful that, as the years go by, this work will warrant subsequent editions. Suggestions for enhancements or new entries will always be welcome.

Jay M. Shafritz
Graduate School of Public and International Affairs
University of Pittsburgh
Pittsburgh, Pennsylvania 15260

A

ability to pay 1. The principle of taxation holding that the tax burden should be distributed according to wealth. It is based on the assumption that, as a person's income increases, that person (whether an individual or a corporation) can and should contribute a larger percentage of income to support government. The first major analysis came from ADAM SMITH's *Wealth of Nations* (1776): "The subjects of every state ought to contribute towards the support of the government, as nearly as possible, in proportion to their respective abilities; that is, in proportion to the revenue which they respectively enjoy under the protection of the state." The progressive income tax is based on the ability-to-pay principle. **2.** A concept from labor relations and collective bargaining that refers to an employer's ability to tolerate the costs of requested wage and benefit increases.

absolute advantage A concept which provides the basis for international economic specialization and division of labor. It was first formulated by ADAM SMITH (1723–1790) who contended that one nation has an absolute advantage over another when, using the same amount of resources, it can produce more of a product than another nation. It should be distinguished from COMPARATIVE ADVANTAGE.

abuse 1. The furnishing of excessive services to the beneficiaries of government programs, violating program regulations, or performing improper practices, none of which involves prosecutable fraud. Fraud, a more serious offense, is the obtaining of something of value by unlawful means through willful misrepresentation. **2.** The use of an existing authority for purposes that extend beyond, or even contradict, the intentions of the grantors of that authority. President James Madison warned in a December 2, 1829, speech that "the essence of Government is power; and power, lodged as it must be in human hands, will ever be liable to abuse."

accountability 1. The extent to which one must answer to higher authority—legal or organizational—for one's actions in society at large or within one's particular organizational position. Elected public officials are theoretically accountable to the political sovereignty of the voters. In this sense, appointed officials—from file clerks to cabinet secretaries—are less accountable than elected officials. The former are accountable mainly to their organizational supervisors, but the latter must answer to their constituents. 2. An obligation for keeping accurate records of property, documents, and funds.

accountability, administrative That aspect of administrative responsibility by which officials are held answerable for general notions of democracy and morality as well as for specific legal mandates. The two basic approaches to administrative accountability were first delineated by the political scientists Carl J. Friedrich (1901–1984) and Herman Finer (1898–1969). Friedrich argued that administrative responsibility can be ensured only internally, through professionalism or professional standards or codes, because the increasing complexities of modern policies require that bureaucrats exhibit extensive policy expertise and specialized abilities. Finer, on the other hand, argued that administrative responsibility could be maintained only externally, through legislative or popular controls, because internal power or control would ultimately lead to corruption. The tension between these two approaches continues today. Thus, the challenge of accountability is to find a balance between trusting government officials to use their best professional judgment in the public's interest and watching them so closely through legislative committees and executive review agencies that their ability to function is inhibited.

accounting The process of classifying, measuring, and interpreting financial transactions to provide management with information upon which to base economic decisions.

accounting, accrual Recording debts owed to and by a company when the debt becomes a legal obligation; this obligation may occur before the money is paid. The widespread adoption of accrual accounting has been a key measure leading to meaningful reporting, financial statements, and asset management in public-sector organizations. Accrual accounting allows for true measures of income and expenditures whether or not the cash payments associated with the earnings and debts have taken place. Without an accrual accounting system, costs and obligations can be taken off financial statements to make results and conditions seem better than they are. Under accrual accounting, government organizations can illustrate their financial status with a BALANCE SHEET, as is done in the private sector.

accounting, cash Recording accounting transactions at the time payment is made. Traditional systems of government accounting were termed *cash accounting* because they sought to control and track the passage of cash funds voted by legislatures as these funds were allocated to, and spent by, the various departments and agencies.

accounting principles The basic premises that govern most accounting theory and practice. Accounting principles are validated by general acceptance within the accounting community; they are not immutable in the sense of scientific laws. They arise from common experiences, historical precedents, and the formulations of professional bodies and governmental agencies. They change over the years as new techniques, business practices, and laws evolve.

accounts payable Money owed by an organization.

accounts receivable Money owed to the organization.

accreditation 1. The formal process by which an individual is invested with credit as a diplomatic representative. Heads of state typically sign a letter of credence, which is personally presented by an ambassador to the head of the receiving state. Lower-ranking diplomats usually present their letters to a foreign minister. 2. The letter of credence itself. 3. The process by which an authoritative organization evaluates and recognizes a program of study or an institution as meeting certain predetermined standards. Similar assessment of an individual is called *certification.*

across-the-board increase An upward adjustment in wages, whether expressed in dollars or percentage of salary, given to an entire workforce.

actionable Something that provides adequate reason for a grievance or lawsuit.

action-reaction 1. An explanation of how states behave during international crises. Because each state responds to the actions of others with preplanned moves, the military and diplomatic actions that are taken do not necessarily reflect motivation or long-term policy goals. The term originated in Isaac Newton's (1642–1727) law of motion stating that "for every action, there is an equal and opposite reaction." 2. The deployment of a new weapons system by one side that leads to the development of an equivalent or superior system by the other side in an arms race.

action plan The specifics involved in achieving a goal.

action research An approach to organizational change that seeks to identify needs for organizational improvement by using external consultants to help create PSYCHOLOGICAL OWNERSHIP of problems and solutions by an organization's members. Action research involves the following: (1) collecting organizational diagnostic data (ascertaining the problem), usually either through written questionnaires or interviews; (2) systematically feeding back information to the organization's members who provided input; (3) discussing what the information means to members and its implications for the organization to be certain whether the "diagnosis" is accurate and to generate psychological ownership of the need to improve the situation; (4) jointly developing an improvement plan that uses both the knowledge and skills of the consultant and the insider perspective of members; and (5) repeating all of the above as needed. The process is called *action research* because the thing being experimented on, the organization, is constantly in action.

active listening A technique by which a counselor or supervisor listens to the facts and also considers the speaker's feelings. This type of listening is considered "active" because the counselor has the specific responsibilities of showing interest, of not passing judgment, and of helping the speaker solve problems.

actor A player in the "game" of politics; for purposes of analysis the word is applied both to individuals and organizations. Actors can be individuals who play their roles as presidents or prime ministers of their states. International organizations such as the United Nations or nongovernmental organizations such as privately controlled multinational corporations may also be actors. While actor is a term that is inherently vague, it is extremely useful to analysts because it furthers a dispassionate systems view of events.

ad hoc A Latin term meaning "temporarily"; "for this one time." It is sometimes used to criticize methods that are substituted for standard procedures.

ad interim A Latin term meaning "in the meantime." A public official is ad interim when serving the unexpired term of a predecessor (who has died, resigned, or been removed) until a permanent official can be appointed or elected.

adjudication 1. The resolution of a dispute by means of judicial or quasi-judicial proceedings in which the parties are able to present evidence and reasoned arguments. 2. The formal pronouncing and recording of the decision of a court or quasi-judicial entity. 3. A loose term that refers to myriad forms of third-party settlements, including ARBITRATION.

administration 1. The management and direction of the affairs of governments and institutions. In ancient Rome, *administrare* meant "to render assistance to" as well as "to run" something, such as an army or the republic itself. 2. A collective term for all the policymaking officials of a government. 3. The execution and implementation of public policy; the realization of legislative intentions. 4. The time in office of a chief executive such as a president, a governor, or a mayor. Thus, "the Reagan administration" refers to those years (1981–1989) when Ronald Reagan was the president of the United States. 5. The supervision of a dead person's estate: paying taxes and assigning assets to the heirs of the deceased. *Compare to* PUBLIC ADMINISTRATION.

administrative agency 1. A government organization set up to implement a law. 2. A civilian government body (board, bureau, department, or individual), other than a court or legislature, that deals with the rights of private parties by adjudicating, rulemaking, investigating, and prosecuting. **3.** An impartial organization that oversees or facilitates labor relations. Although generally headed by a board of from three to five members, these agencies rule on unfair labor practices, on the appropriateness of bargaining units, and sometimes on the interpretation of a contract or the legitimacy of the scope of bargaining. They also oversee authorization elections and certify the winners as the exclusive bargaining agents for the employees in a bargaining unit. The National Labor Relations Board is the prototype for administrative agencies dealing with labor relations. The equivalent agency for federal employees is the Federal Labor Relations Authority. In the states, such agencies are generally called *Public Employee Relations Boards.*

administrative conservatorship A normative approach to public administration that assures a major role in governance for career public officials. They are considered to be conservators because their role is to preserve constitutional values in general and the integrity of bureaucratic institutions in particular.

administrative discretion The power of subjective judgment given to administrative officials by law, practice, and custom. Such discretion ranges from setting overall agency priorities to deciding the worthiness of an individual supplicant's appeal for help.

administrative doctrine The rules, procedures, and ways of doing things that reflect the basic values of an organization. Doctrines and values may be stated or unstated, conscious or unconscious, advertent or inadvertent; but they are always there. No management program can be viable without a guiding doctrine and compatible behavioral techniques for implementing it. The first administrative doctrine was that contained in the brutality of military discipline: "Do this or die." Indeed, one of the main reasons officers traditionally carried pistols was to shoot their own men if they were not sufficiently enthusiastic about obeying an order. A more modern example of a doctrine is Henry Ford's (1863–1947) famous dictum: "All that we ask of the men is that they do the work which is set before them." With Ford there was an underlying assumption that employees who do not respond adequately to the "work which is set before them" should be dismissed. (A much better alternative to being shot!) The behavioral technique used here is the same as that applied to those small experimental animals who have spent generations running through mazes for psychologists. The more work, the more cheese.

administrative law The totality of constitutional provisions, legislative statutes, court decisions, and executive directives that regulate the activities of government agencies. In the U.S. context, administrative law does not deal with the substantive content of agency policies and practices. Instead, it focuses on the procedures that agencies use in exercising their authority. Administrative law is not uniform. Unless U.S. Supreme Court decisions apply to all jurisdictions, considerable variation exists in state, local, and federal requirements.

administrative law judge A "hearing officer" or "hearing examiner" who, functioning much like a judge, hears and decides disputes arising in administrative and independent regulatory agencies.

Administrative Procedure Act (APA) The basic law governing the way federal agencies operate to safeguard agency clients and the general public. The APA specifies the conditions under which administrative agencies (1) publicize information about their operations; (2) make rules; (3) engage in adjudication; and (4) are subject to judicial review. Thus, agencies begin with some form of legislative mandate and translate their interpretation of that mandate into policy decisions, specifications of regulations, and statements of penalties and enforcement provisions. The APA requires that rules be published thirty days before their effective date and that agencies afford interested parties the right to petition for the issuance, amendment, or repeal of a rule. In effect, although the APA establishes a process of notice and time for comment, it accords administrative rulemakers the same prerogatives that legislatures have in enacting statutes, as long as the rule enacted is consistent with the enabling statute.

administrative remedy A means of enforcing a right by appealing to an administrative agency, either for help or for a decision. People are often required to "exhaust all administrative remedies" by submitting their problems to the proper agency before resorting to the courts.

administrative state A government in which bureaucratic institutions and administrative mechanisms have become the dominant feature; the implication is that the sheer size, complexity, and discretion given such institutional powers can threaten or rival traditional constitutional provisions.

administrator 1. A manager. 2. The head of a government agency. 3. Someone appointed by a court to handle a deceased person's estate. 4. Someone entrusted with a FIDUCIARY responsibility.

adversary system Judicial proceedings in which opposing sides have the same opportunity to present their cases by offering evidence and challenging each other's witnesses before an impartial judge.

adverse action 1. An act against someone else's interests. 2. Proceedings by management considered unfavorable to an employee, such as suspension, demotion, or worse. 3. A use of land that harms local property values, such as the construction of a gas station or a prison on land previously zoned for and occupied by single-family homes.

adverse impact A selection process for a particular job or group of jobs that results in the selection of members of any racial, ethnic, or gender group at a lower rate than for members of others groups. Federal EQUAL EMPLOYMENT OPPORTUNITY enforcement agencies generally regard a selection rate for a group that is less than 80 percent of the rate for other groups as constituting evidence of adverse impact.

advice and consent The right of the U.S. Senate, granted in Article II, Section 2, of the U.S. Constitution, to approve or disapprove treaties and major presidential appointments.

advisors 1. Military units or civilians (who may be military experts) from one state sent to "advise" the military forces of another. While such advisors are often limited to training missions, they sometimes become more like "lead workers" and show their "students" how to operate against insurgents or other enemies. 2. A euphemism for the military forces of one country who openly intervene in the affairs of another country. 3. Technical experts. The classic statement on the advice of experts is contained in a letter the British Secretary of India, Lord Salisbury, wrote on June 15, 1877 to Lord Lytton, Viceroy of India: "No lesson seems to be so deeply inculcated by the experience of life as that you never should trust in experts. If you believe the doctors nothing is wholesome; if you believe the theologians nothing is innocent; if you believe the soldiers nothing is safe. They all required to have their strong wine diluted by a very large admixture of insipid common sense."

advocacy organization 1. A lobby. 2. A nonprofit organization created specifically to promote a cause and disseminate information about it.

affirmative action A term first used in President John F. Kennedy's 1961 Executive Order 10925 to mean the removal of "artificial barriers" to the employment of women and minority group members. Today it refers to compensatory opportunities for hitherto disadvantaged groups—specific efforts to recruit, hire, and promote qualified members of disadvantaged groups for the purpose of eliminating the present effects of past discrimination. *Compare to* DIVERSITY; REVERSE DISCRIMINATION.

agency 1. A department, office, commission, authority, administration, board, government-owned corporation, or other independent establishment of a branch of government. 2. A legal relationship whereby one person is authorized to act for another. 3. In intelligence usage, an organization engaged in collecting and/or processing information.

agency shop A union security provision, found in some collective bargaining agreements, requiring that nonunion employees of the bargaining unit pay for the union's representational services as a condition of continuing employment. The agency shop was designed as a compromise between the union's desire to eliminate free riders by means of compulsory membership (the union shop) and management's wish that union membership be voluntary. Its constitutionality was upheld by the U.S. Supreme Court in *Abood v. Detroit Board of Education* (1977). Later, in *Chicago Teachers Union v. Hudson* (1986), the Court held against making nonmembers of the union pay for union activities other than representation.

agency theory An approach to organizational behavior that uses contracts between buyers (the principals) and sellers (the agents) as its mode of analysis. Thus, a principal such as a government agency provides work space, staff support, and a salary to an individual employee agent who is then obligated to carry out the directives of the principal. But because both parties are motivated by self-interest, the contractual arrangements are often less than ideal. Conflict often arises concerning what work should be done and how it is to be performed. Agency theory is a means of analyzing these conflictive relationships so that incentive structures and organizational goals may be harmonized.

agenda setting The process by which ideas or issues bubble up through the various political channels for consideration by a political institution such as a legislature or court. The agenda-setting process often makes extensive use of the mass media to take a relatively unknown or unsupported issue and, through publicity, expand the numbers of people who care about the issue so that an institution, whether it be city hall or the U.S. Congress, is forced to take action. One example occurred in 1955, when Rosa Parks, an African American woman, was arrested for refusing to take a seat in the back of a bus in Montgomery, Alabama. This confrontation sparked the modern civil rights movement. Dr. Martin Luther King Jr. would later use the tactics of nonviolent confrontation with Southern segregationist policies to arouse sympathy and support in the rest of the nation; the strategy would lead to landmark civil rights legislation in Congress. When nonviolent demonstrations turned violent, it was all the better because it made for better TV and thus ensured a bigger audience for the message of the cause. In the 1980s, pro life (meaning "antiabortion") groups began to put demonstrators in front of medical offices providing abortion services to arouse the national consciousness about this issue. These demonstrations, too, often became spontaneously violent and thus made for better TV. The lesson is clear. "Nonviolent" demonstrators that turn violent, or at least contentious once the TV news cameras arrive, are more likely to appear on the six o'clock news. *See also* PSEUDOEVENT.

agent 1. A person authorized to act on behalf of another. **2.** In intelligence usage, a person who is recruited, trained, controlled, and employed to obtain and report information. **3.** An intelligence agent employed in a covert operation; a spy. **4.** A saboteur. *See also* BARGAINING AGENT.

Aid to Families with Dependent Children (AFDC) The program by which the federal government matched state spending on welfare. Beginning in 1935,

AFDC provided federal funds, administered by the states, for children living with a parent or a relative who met state standards of need. The program became controversial because of charges that it not only promoted illegitimacy but also encouraged fathers to abandon their families so that they could become eligible for AFDC. In 1994, more than 14 million people were receiving AFDC, up from just over 2 million in 1955. AFDC was abolished by the 1996 WELFARE REFORM ACT.

alien 1. A legal temporary visitor or permanent resident living in a state of which he or she is not a citizen; a citizen of one state who lives in another. A resident alien is allowed to reside permanently in a nation of which he or she is not a citizen. Because no state can insist that its nationals be allowed to reside in or visit another state, the laws governing the rights and obligations of aliens are internal matters for every state. 2. A creature from another planet; an earthling on another planet.

alien, enemy A national of an enemy state who has encroached upon the territory of, or territory occupied by, a belligerent power.

alien, illegal A person from one country who is living or working in another country unlawfully. Illegal aliens are often called *undocumented workers,* a term that preserves the presumption of innocence and sounds less criminal.

alien, resident One who lives in a country of which he or she is not a citizen. In the United States, resident aliens have the full protection of the laws but do not enjoy all the privileges of citizenship, such as the right to vote, the opportunity to hold selected government jobs, and the right to certain welfare benefits.

alienation 1. A Marxist term for the inevitable dissociation felt by industrial workers because they lack control over their work (and are thus ripe for revolution). 2. Feelings of estrangement from one's work, family, government, and society. In the context of politics and voting behavior, alienation refers to a voluntary dropping out of the political process, to nonvoting, and to feelings of contempt or indifference toward government.

allegiance 1. The loyalty and devotion that citizens owe their country; the customary obligation of citizens to protect the interests of their state. 2. The bond, whether emotional, coercive, or legal, that binds individuals to a sovereign.

Allison, Graham T., Jr. (1940–) The Harvard University professor who wrote a classic study of government decisionmaking, *Essence of Decision: Explaining the Cuban Missile Crisis* (1971). The work showed the inadequacies of the view that policies are made by a "single calculating decisionmaker" who controls the organizational units and individual officials within a government. Instead, Allison demonstrated that differing bureaucratic viewpoints fight over policy. Although Allison's ideas were not new, he helped to crystallize thinking about foreign policy making by dealing with the different approaches through three models. The dominant model, which, he argued, obscured more than it illuminated, he described as the Rational Actor Model or Model One. He argued that this model needed to be replaced by two other models. Allison's Model Two, the Organizational Processes Model, basically argued that government action could be understood as the output of large organizations that operated according to standard operational procedures. Allison described Model Three as a Governmental Politics Model, the essence of which was that decisions were the outcome of a bargaining process between different groups and individuals with different bureaucratic perspectives and different political interests. Allison's thesis first appeared in "Conceptual Models and the Cuban Missile Crisis," *American Political Science Review,* September 1969.

Americans with Disabilities Act *See* DISCRIMINATION, DISABILITIES.

amnesty The act of "forgetfulness" by a government for crimes committed by a group of people. Amnesty is commonly granted after a civil war to help reunite a country. For example, after the American Civil War, President Andrew Johnson granted amnesty to all Confederate soldiers. An amnesty is usually a group action granted for political offenses. President Jimmy Carter granted an amnesty to all Vietnam draft evaders (but not to military deserters) in 1977. *See also* TAX AMNESTY.

annexation 1. A state's formal extension of sovereignty over new territory. Traditionally annexation has been done by force or by the threat of force. Historically, annexations have been generally recognized under the law of war. But after World War I, the right of nations to self-determination became a competing interest in international law. 2. The acquisition of adjacent settlements by a city. After annexation, these settlements are part of the city. Although most cities grew by annexation, it is difficult for most cities to annex now because the suburbs are often incorporated entities that may not be subject to involuntary annexation.

antitrust laws Statutes that limit the ability of businesses and unions to exercise monopoly control and to cause the restraint of trade. They are thought necessary because, as ADAM SMITH observed in *The Wealth of Nations* (1776), "People of the same trade seldom meet together, even for merriment and diversion, but the conversation ends in a conspiracy against the public, or in some contrivance to raise prices." The Sherman Anti-Trust Act of 1890 was the first significant U.S. break with the economic philosophy of LAISSEZ-FAIRE. The act asserted that law could create and control conditions in the marketplace and that it was sometimes in the public interest for government to exercise substantial indirect control over economic conditions. The U.S. policy of antitrust enforcement is in sharp contrast to the practices of most other nations, which encourage and tolerate CARTELS as the normal order of things.

Appleby, Paul H. (1891–1963) A prominent New Deal administrator and dean of the Maxwell School at Syracuse University who wrote a skillful polemic asserting that the theoretical insistence on apolitical governmental processes went against the grain of the American experience. In his book *Big Democracy* (1945), Appleby emphatically shattered public administration's self-imposed demarcation between politics and administration. He held as myth that politics was separate and could somehow be taken out of administration. This was good, not evil as many of the progressive reformers had asserted, because political involvement in administration acted as a check on the arbitrary exercise of bureaucratic power. In the future those who would describe the political ramifications and issues of administration would not begin by contesting the POLITICS-ADMINISTRATION DICHOTOMY as incorrect or irrelevant—they would begin from the premise, as Appleby put it so succinctly, that "government is different because government is politics."

appropriate technology A concept that rejects centralized control or direction for the use of technology, and replaces it with local determination of which technologies best fit the local environment. Proponents stress the democratizing, populist thrust of appropriate/alternative technology, as opposed to centralized decisionmaking. According to the proponents of the growing appropriate technology movement, the technology developed during periods when unemployment was low and natural resources were considered unlimited is not necessarily the right technology when resources are scarce and unemployment is high, especially if the technology is to be transferred to developing countries. Other terms used synonymously with *appropriate technology* and *alternative technology* are *intermediate technology* and *soft technology*. E. F. Schumacher's *Small Is Beautiful* (1973) has popularized the concept in the United States. *See also* TECHNOLOGY TRANSFER.

appropriation 1. Funds set aside by a legislature to pay for something authorized by law. **2.** An act of the U.S. Congress that permits federal agencies to incur obligations and to make payments out of the U.S. Treasury for specified purposes. An appropriation usually follows the enactment of authorizing legislation and is the most common form of budget authority, but sometimes the authorizing legislation also provides the budget authority. Appropriations are categorized in a variety of ways, such as by their period of availability (one-year, multiple-year, no-year), the time of congressional action (current, permanent), and the manner of determining the amount of the appropriation (definite, indefinite).

approximation of laws The process whereby governments align their laws concerning commercial transactions to facilitate international trade. The goal of approximation is to bring similarity to laws, but not to make them identical, as in HARMONIZATION.

arbitrary An action decided according to individual judgments that do not meet the commonly understood rules of procedure and hence may not appear justifiable to those seeking to explain them to others or to replicate them in similar circumstances.

arbitration 1. Settling a dispute by having an impartial third party (the arbitrator) hold a formal hearing and render a decision that may or may not be binding on both sides. The arbitrator may be one person or a board of three, five, or more (usually an uneven number). When boards are used, they may include, in addition to impartial members, representatives from both of the disputants. In the context of labor relations, arbitrators are selected jointly by labor and management, recommended by the Federal Mediation and Conciliation Service, by a state or local agency offering similar referrals, or by the private American Arbitration Association. 2. A process sometimes used to bring peaceful resolve to a dispute between two (or more) states. The parties agree to submit their case to a third party for resolution and at the same time agree to be bound by the decision. The formal agreement to use arbitration is called the *compromis* or *compromis d'arbitrage*. The decision or verdict in the case is called the *award*. Arbitration has been much discussed as a conflict resolution technique in international affairs, but it is seldom used for truly important issues.

arbitration acts Laws that help (and sometimes require) the submission of certain types of problems (often labor disputes) to an arbitrator.

arbitration, compulsory A negotiating process whereby the parties are required by law to arbitrate their dispute. Some state statutes concerning collective bargaining impasses in the public sector mandate that parties who have exhausted all other means of achieving a settlement must submit their dispute to an arbitrator. The intent of requirements for compulsory arbitration is to induce the parties to reach agreement by presenting them with a definite, if somewhat unpleasant, alternative.

arbitration, final offer A negotiating stratagem that has an arbitrator choose from among the disputing parties' final or last offers.

area studies Social science analyses of a given geographical area that explores its history, economy, political institutions, and culture.

aristocracy 1. Rule by a relatively small, elite group. Aristotle in ancient Greece believed aristocracy to be rule by the most virtuous of a society. By medieval times, the concept had degenerated to mean rule by the upper classes—those, it was thought, who were chosen by God to lead. Thomas

Jefferson returned to the Aristotelian notion when he spoke of rule by a "natural aristocracy," people whose talent entitled them to govern. Article I, Section 9, of the U.S. Constitution sought to inhibit traditional aristocracies when it proclaimed that "no Title of Nobility shall be granted by the United States." **2.** A group with great (usually hereditary) wealth and influence.

Aristotle (384–322 B.C.E.) The philosopher in ancient Greece who is perhaps the world's best example of a student's exceeding his illustrious teacher—and then having his student exceed him in accomplishment. In *Politics,* Aristotle, a student of Plato, presented the first comprehensive analysis of the nature of a state and of a political community. To Aristotle, the state was a natural development because "man is by nature a political animal." The state was even more important than family because a family exists only for comfort, but the state can be a vehicle for glory and the good life. Perhaps Aristotle's most well-known analytical construct is his TYPOLOGY of the three basic forms of government. He found that every political community had to be governed by either the one, the few, or the many. This corresponds to his three governing types: kingship, aristocracy, and polity (majority rule). Unfortunately, each of these had its perversions, the conditions to which it degenerated when the rulers ceased ruling in the interests of the entire community. Kingship often degenerated into tyranny; aristocracy (rule by a talented and virtuous elite) into an oligarchy (rule by a small group in its own interest); and a polity or constitutional system (where a large middle class rules for the common interest) into democracy (mob rule in the interests of the lower classes). Aristotle favored a mixed constitution—one in which all citizens "rule and are ruled by turn," no class monopolizes power, and a large middle class provides stability. Aristotle's most famous student was Alexander the Great (356–323 B.C.E.). He did not write any books; he just used what Aristotle had taught him about logic. Then, using the superb army he inherited from his father, he went on to conquer the known world.

assessment 1. Analysis of the security, effectiveness, and potential of an existing or planned intelligence activity. **2.** Judgment of the motives, qualifications, and characteristics of present or prospective employees or "agents." **3.** Financial contributions made by a government (such as the United States) to the regular budget of an international organization (such as the United Nations) to which it belongs. **4.** Contributions to political parties that are determined according to a schedule of rates and made to retain a civil service or patronage appointment. **5.** Analysis of a tactical or strategic problem by a military or intelligence staff. **6.** The valuation of property for the purposes of TAXATION. **7.** Amounts paid by labor union members in addition to the regular dues when a union needs funds urgently to support a strike or some other union-endorsed cause. The amount of these assessments is usually limited by a union's constitution or bylaws.

assessment centers Not a particular place but a process consisting of the intense observation of a person undergoing a variety of simulations and stress situations over several days. The assessment-center concept is far from new. Assessment-center techniques were used by the German army for selecting officers in World War I, and the Office of Strategic Services used them for selecting secret agents in World War II. The assessment-center concept did not reach U.S. industry until the mid-1950s when AT&T pioneered a program. The practice spread during the 1960s, but it was not until 1969 that a U.S. government agency, the Internal Revenue Service, used assessment-center methodology on a large scale. Today, these techniques are commonly adopted by government agencies at all jurisdictional levels.

assessment ratio A property tax computation; the ratio between market value and assessed value. Assessment ratios vary tremendously because some jurisdictions value property at or close to market value and others use formulas calling for assessed values to be various fractions of market value.

assessor 1. In ancient Rome, a legal expert who advised the governor of a province on the technical details of the law. 2. An official of a jurisdiction who determines the value of property for the purpose of taxation. 3. An expert who sits with a court to provide technical advice but has no right to decide issues. 4. An insurance investigator who determines the amount of a loss and decides whether the loss is genuine.

assets All money, property, and money-related rights (such as money owed) owned by a person or an organization. Assets that cannot be turned into cash easily (e.g., buildings) are called *capital assets* or *fixed assets*. Assets that can be turned into cash easily (e.g., cash or goods for sale) are called *current assets* or *liquid assets*. Assets that are tied up (for instance, because of a pending lawsuit) are called *frozen assets*.

attrition 1. Reducing the effectiveness of something by constantly wearing it down. 2. The reduction of a workforce that occurs through voluntary resignations, retirements, and deaths. 3. A military tactic of gradually wearing down the enemy's forces. All wars are wars of attrition in that each side seeks to destroy soldiers of the other side. But a "war of attrition" implies that one side is wearing down the enemy at roughly equal expense as its own.

audit 1. An independent examination, an objective assessment of something; typically the financial reports of an individual or organization to determine whether they accurately represent expenditures and are in compliance with accounting standards and laws. 2. The final phase of the government budgetary process during which the operations of an agency, especially its financial transactions, are reviewed to determine whether the agency has spent its money in accordance with the law, in the most efficient manner, and with the desired results.

audit, compliance This, the oldest and most traditional form of auditing, has the auditor looking for the extent to which, in the financial management of an organization, financial inputs have been managed in compliance with the law and accepted standards and conventions for the treatment of accounting information. In the past, a traditional compliance audit was embodied by the annual visit of the auditor to remote parts of the organization, where he would check each entry in financial journals and ledgers to make sure that the arithmetic and balances were correct. At the end of this process, the auditor would certify that the financial records were in order. The value of this traditional form of audit is clear. Officials dealing with funds could not simply dispose of them as they wished, nor could they keep records that could not be understood or fail to keep records at all. The advent of traditional auditing meant that every public official had to expect and prepare for a regular visit by the auditor, had to keep accounts in a manner officially prescribed (often by regulations), and had to make those records available for the auditor's scrutiny. In some jurisdictions, the audit might be accompanied by an inventory of stores and equipment, hence the derisive references at times to the compliance audit as involving the counting of paper clips. In fact, the compliance audit was and remains a powerful primary tool for preventing many types of corruption.

audit, comprehensive An audit program that typically includes three types of audit: (1) financial and compliance, which determines whether the funds were properly spent and whether the law was complied with; (2) economy and efficiency, which determines whether resources have been used economically and efficiently; and (3) program results, which determine whether desired results have been achieved.

audit, performance A review of the efficiency and/or effectiveness of an organization. An efficiency audit compares the activities of an organization with the objectives that have been assigned to it. In a sense, an efficiency audit still entails a compliance notion—though it is now the extent to which the organization has complied with and realized its objectives that is being examined. This extension of the auditor's role is compatible with an instrumental view of administration because the implementation of the objectives set by political leaders is being reviewed. They and their constituents want to know how responsive the organization has been to their will, how effective they have been in playing the instruments of state. When the scope of audit is extended beyond the efficiency of an organization to its effectiveness, attention turns from the extent to which politically set objectives have been achieved to the broader question of whether the objectives themselves were correct in the first place. This further extension of scope has been controversial because it places the auditor firmly in the role of policy evaluator.

audit program The detailed steps and procedures to be followed in conducting an audit and preparing a report. A written audit program should be prepared for each audit and should include the purpose and scope, the background information needed to understand the audit objectives and the entity's mission, and the definition of unique terms, objectives, and reporting procedures.

authority 1. The right to exercise influence over others. Authority is exercised within states by a legitimate government. In the international system, authority is far less evident; this helps to explain why relations among states have so much to do with strict power relations rather than with notions of legitimacy and authority. 2. A government-owned corporation. 3. The power inherent in a specific government position that allows an incumbent to perform assigned tasks.

authorization election Polls conducted by the National Labor Relations Board (or other ADMINISTRATIVE AGENCY) to determine whether a particular group of employees will be represented by a particular union. Authorization election is used interchangeably with certification election (because, if the union wins, it is certified as the representative of the workers by the administrative agency) and representative election (because a winning union becomes just that, the representative of the workers).

automatic stabilizers Preset or built-in FISCAL POLICIES.

autonomy 1. Political independence; a sovereign state is said to have autonomy. Because of the interdependent nature of the modern world economies, autonomy in a pure sense is no longer viable. Autonomy is always relative. 2. Less than full political independence; a situation in which a region within a larger sovereign state has a limited measure of authority in the conduct of its internal affairs. 3. Local control over nonpolitical affairs; for example, a region could be granted cultural or religious autonomy.

auxiliary agency An administrative unit having the prime responsibility to service other agencies of the greater organization. For example, in the federal government, the Office of Personnel Management and the General Services Administration are auxiliary, or overhead, agencies.

B

back channel An informal method for government-to-government and sensitive leadership communications as opposed to normal or routine diplomatic methods. The use of a back channel can be effective in making breakthroughs in negotiations or in implementing new departures in policy. At the same time, it can be confusing because it creates a second level and undercuts more formal negotiations that may be taking place simultaneously.

bailout A government-sponsored rescue of a failing private-sector enterprise. The best-known bailout of an individual business is the Chrysler Corporation Loan Guarantee Act of 1979. The act authorized the federal government to guarantee up to $1.5 billion in loans to the Chrysler Corporation to prevent the bankruptcy of the company and the widespread negative impacts on the economy that would have resulted. Within four years, Chrysler became profitable again and repaid all its federally guaranteed loans—seven years ahead of schedule.

balance of payments 1. A tabulation of a nation's debt and credit transactions with foreign countries and international institutions. A favorable balance, more money coming in from other countries than going out, is an economic advantage. An unfavorable balance over a significant time is one indication of problems within a nation's economy. The balance of payments is broader then the balance of trade because it also includes invisible exports such as insurance and shipping. 2. In the United States, a tabulation of what a state as a whole pays in taxes to the federal government compared to what it as a whole receives back from the federal government.

balance of power 1. The foreign policy taken by rival states to prevent any one state or alliance from gaining a preponderance of power in relation to rivals; thus a military balance (and therefore peace) is maintained. 2. A principle of international relations that asserts that when any nation seeks to increase its military potential, neighboring or rival nations will take similar actions to maintain the military equilibrium. 3. A purely descriptive way to describe the actual distribution of power in the world—economic, political, and military—without implying that an equally "balanced" distribution exists.

balance of trade The amount by which the value of merchandise exports exceeds (trade surplus) or falls short of (trade deficit) the value of merchandise imports. The balance of trade is the visible element of a nation's balance of payments; it excludes payments for service and transfers of funds.

balance sheet A summary showing the financial worth of an individual or organization broken down by assets (what is owned) and liabilities (what is owed). It is called *a balance sheet* because total assets balance with, or are equal to, total liabilities, plus net worth.

bar 1. The once real but now imaginary partition across a court: lawyers stood at this bar to argue their cases. Thus, to be "called to the bar" meant that you were thought to be enough of a lawyer to plead a case in court. 2. The legal profession; a jurisdiction's community of lawyers.

bargaining agent The union organization (not an individual) that is the exclusive representative of all the workers, union as well as nonunion, in a bargaining unit. Employers may voluntarily agree that a particular union will serve as the bargaining agent for their employees, or the decision on representation can be settled by secret ballot election conducted by the Federal Labor Relations Authority, the National Labor Relations Board, or a counterpart state agency.

bargaining strength The relative power each party holds during negotiation. One government has great bargaining strength vis-à-vis another if both sides know that it has the military power to impose its will regardless of the outcome of negotiations; management has great bargaining strength over labor if it has so much excess inventory that a short strike would be desirable. The final settlement often reflects the bargaining power of each side. The most famous statement on a bargaining position backed by force comes from Mario Puzo's novel *The Godfather* (1969): "I'll make him an offer he can't refuse."

bargaining unit A group of employees, both union members and others, that an employer has recognized and/or an administrative agency has certified as appropriate for representation by a union for purposes of collective bargaining. All the employees in a bargaining unit are subsequently covered in the labor contract that the union negotiates on their behalf. Bargaining units may be as small as the handful of workers in a local shop or as large as the workforce of an entire industry. The size of a bargaining unit is important in that it significantly affects the relative bargaining strength of both sides.

Barnard, Chester I. (1886–1961) A Bell System executive closely associated with the Harvard Business School, best known for his sociological analyses of organizations that encouraged and foreshadowed the post–World War II behavioral revolution. In *The Functions of the Executive* (1938), Barnard viewed organizations as cooperative systems where "the function of the executive" was to maintain the dynamic equilibrium between the needs of the organization and the needs of its employees. To do this, management had to be aware of the interdependent nature of the formal and informal organization. Barnard's analysis of the significance and role of informal organizations provided the theoretical foundations for a generation of empirical research.

barriers to entry 1. Impediments to business competition whether they be legal (critical patents owned by others), economic (start-up costs too high), political (unstable government), or social (the market has established brand preference). **2.** Impediments to participation in the public policymaking process.

baseline 1. A specific value used for purposes of comparison; beginning data. **2.** Budget estimates at current levels of expenditure, sometimes adjusted for inflation.

beggar-thy-neighbor policy Action through which a country tries to reduce unemployment and increase domestic output by raising tariffs and instituting measures that impede imports. Countries that pursued such policies in the early 1930s found that other countries retaliated by raising barriers against the first country's exports; this, in turn, tended to worsen the economic difficulties that precipitated the initial protectionist action. Such actions are the equivalent in the economic sphere of actions that trigger and fuel arms races in the security sphere. *Compare to* PROTECTIONISM.

behavioral sciences A general term for the academic disciplines that study human and animal behavior by means of empirical research. The phrase was first put into wide use in the early 1950s by the Ford Foundation to describe its funding for interdisciplinary research in the social sciences; and by faculty at the University of Chicago seeking federal funding for research—and concerned in an era of McCarthyism that their social science research might be confused with socialism.

behavioralism 1. A philosophic disposition toward the study of people's behavior in political situations as opposed to studying the institutional structures of politics. Thus, for example, one should not study the structure of a government organization because what is really important is the behavior of its officials. **2.** The scientific study of politics that emphasizes the use of the scientific method for empirical investigations and the use of quantitative techniques. **3.** An approach to political science and international politics that developed in the 1950s. Behavorism challenged the realist domination of the study of international politics on the grounds that realists had failed to define their central concepts, were overly deterministic in their approach, and had not produced theories that were empirically testable. The main objective of the behavioralists was to develop rigorous and systematic approaches and methods that would explain behavior and provide the basis for generalizations about political phenomena.

behavioralism, post The critical response to behavioralism. Post-behavioralism complained that, as political science adopted the orientation of behavioralism, it became less relevant to the study of politics. Because of the overemphasis on being empirical and quantitative, too much attention was being devoted to easily studied trivial issues at the expense of important topics. Post-behavioralism as a movement within political science does not advocate the end of the scientific study of politics; it mainly suggests that there is more than one way of advancing knowledge and that methodologies should be appropriate to the issue under study.

benchmark 1. A standard. 2. The systematic comparison of work processes with those of competitors or with BEST PRACTICES in an industry. The process may be carried out internally within an organization (perhaps comparing how regional offices in different districts perform); it may be carried out externally (e.g., a study of local tax collection efficiency between two municipalities); or it may involve like functions (such as customer service) in unlike organizations.

benefit district A method for financing the construction of public works in which those who directly benefit are charged for the construction costs. For example, sidewalks are often financed by increasing the property taxes of residents through whose property the sidewalk passes; that is, those owners are members of a sidewalk benefit district that levies a tax; when the construction costs have been recovered, the tax is dissolved.

benefit theory The belief that those who gain from a government action should pay for it. Thus, gasoline taxes paid by drivers help pay for highway repair and construction; and fees for fishing licenses help pay for restocking lakes.

benefit-cost analysis The process by which organizations seek to determine the effectiveness of their spending, in relation to costs, in meeting policy objectives.

Bentham, Jeremy (1748–1832) A British philosopher who held that self-interest was the prime motivator and that a government should strive to do the greatest good for the greatest numbers. He wanted institutions to justify themselves on practical grounds at the level of useful welfare achieved. He was thereby the prophet of utilitarianism, which he preached from the 1770s but did not become prominent until the 1810s. Bentham held that governments were created not by divine intervention but because of man's desire for happiness. His beliefs, writings, and actions make Bentham the major social reformer of nineteenth-century England. The difference between Bentham and other would-be reformers was that Bentham sought to develop techniques to deal with policy questions—techniques that others could use to apply to yet unknown problems. In effect, Bentham's patrimony is so great because he was the first methodologist in policy analysis. He showed the way to find a way. Bentham demanded that all laws and policies answer the question, who benefits? And if the proposal didn't meet his test of the "greatest happiness for the greatest number," then it was not deserving of enactment. Above all, Bentham urged practical, pragmatic solutions to the problems of crime, education, welfare, and public health, among others. He felt that he had a genius for legislation, for recommending new policies that should be enacted into law, exactly what he spent his life doing. And Bentham demanded that legislators be guided not by their respective parties but by his principle of utility; to do otherwise is to be dishonorably immoral. That is why his most influential work is called *An Introduction to the Principles of Morals and Legislation* (1780).

Bentley, Arthur F. (1870–1957) The political scientist who was one of the pioneering voices in the behavioral analysis of politics and the intellectual creator of modern interest group theory. In *The Process of Government* (1908), Bentley argued that political analysis has had to shift its focus from forms of government to the actions of individuals in the context of groups. Groups are the critical action mechanisms that enable numbers of individuals to achieve their political, economic, and social desires. Bentley's work was effectively "lost" until it was rediscovered and publicized by David B. Truman.

best and the brightest A description of the intellectual and managerial talent each new presidential administration claims it will bring to Washington to solve the nation's problems. The phrase has been used almost cynically since David Halberstam, in his book *The Best and the Brightest* (1972), showed how all that talent still managed to lead the nation into the morass of Vietnam in the 1960s. The story is often told of Speaker of the House Sam Rayburn's response when Vice President Lyndon B. Johnson mentioned the great brilliance and tremendous intellects enjoyed by the new leaders of the Kennedy administration in the early 1960s. Rayburn responded: "That may be true, but I'd feel a helluva lot better if just one or two of them had ever run for sheriff."

best practices 1. The generally recognized optimal ways of performing a task; ideal management standards; the state of the art in any given area of management. 2. Using exemplary programs in one organization as a model to be adopted by other organizations.

big brother 1. An artificial form of familial protection, as in the charitable Big Brother Association, created to offer substitutes for a missing father figure.

2. George Orwell's (1903–1950) symbolization, from his novel *1984* (1949), of government so big and intrusive that it literally oversaw and regulated every aspect of life. The term has evolved to mean any potentially menacing power constantly looking over one's shoulder in judgment.

bill 1. A legislative proposal formally introduced for consideration; unfinished legislation. After a bill is passed and signed into law, it becomes an act. 2. A law passed by a legislature when it is functioning in a judicial capacity; for example, a bill of impeachment. 3. A negotiable instrument; for example, a dollar bill. 4. A statement of details in a legal proceeding; for example, a bill of indictment. 5. A petition or statement to an appellate court; for example, a bill of exceptions. 6. An important listing; for example, the Bill of Rights—the first ten amendments to the U.S. Constitution.

bipartisan 1. A policy or initiative that has the support of both major political parties. 2. A synonym for a lack of partisanship as, for example, when a bipartisan or nonpartisan COMMISSION is formed to deal with a particularly intractable problem.

bipartisanship 1. Cooperation by usually differing political parties and institutions on political issues. Bipartisanship occurs when the party leaders wish to assure that a given topic will not become the subject of partisan disputes. 2. Consultation and cooperation between the president and the leaders of both parties in the U.S. Congress on major policy issues.

black 1. Bad; for example, black Friday was the day the stock market crashed in 1929; and no one wants to be on a BLACKLIST. 2. In intelligence operations, *black* is a term used in certain phrases (e.g., living black, black border crossing) to indicate reliance on illegal concealment rather than on cover. 3. Secret; for example, a black economy is a hidden (from tax collectors) underground economy. Black operations are the most secret and possibly illegal covert operations of an intelligence agency or special operations military unit. 4. A reference to someone of African ancestry. Because this usage was related to slavery, it fell out of fashion in favor of "colored" or "Negro." But beginning in the 1960s as part of the CIVIL RIGHTS MOVEMENT, a companion black pride movement asserted that "black is beautiful." Very quickly, *black* became the preferred term of reference. The black pride movement removed the negative connotations from the word. However, beginning in the late 1980s, some black leaders began objecting to the word *black* and asserting that *African American* is the correct term of reference.

blacklist A listing of individuals or organizations that are banned, boycotted, or disapproved. Originally, they were lists prepared by merchants containing the names of men who had gone bankrupt. Later, employers used them for lists of men who had joined unions. Blacklists generally carry no legal authority, though they have been issued by governments in an effort to silence or preclude opposition. Although blacklists are not necessarily associated with terrorism, all blacklists are designed to intimidate.

bloc 1. A group or coalition of groups organized to further an interest. For example, there is a farm bloc, a civil rights bloc, and so forth. 2. An ad hoc coalition of legislators that transcends party lines to further or obstruct a legislative proposal. 3. A combination of states that supports or opposes a given issue or interest. By their very nature, all alliances are blocs. But the word is also used to describe voting coalitions in international organizations such as the United Nations, and as a shorthand way of referring to segments of the world such as the African bloc or the THIRD WORLD bloc.

board 1. A group charged with directing a government function such as a county government or school district. 2. An administrative body within a larger organization appointed to act as a fact finding or advisory body. For example, a selection board may make recommendations on merit system promotions. Boards, also known as "commissions," are used when their functions are of a quasi-judicial nature or when bipartisan leadership is desirable. 3. A group of individuals elected by stockholders, who, as a body, manages and makes policy for a corporation.

bolstering A term developed by Irving Janis and Leon Mann in *Decision Making: A Psychological Analysis of Conflict, Choice and Commitment* (1977), and that is used to identify ways in which policymakers convince themselves that the action they choose will yield a favorable outcome. Bolstering tends to be used when policymakers do not have an ideal solution at hand yet, for one reason or another, cannot avoid making a decision. Rather than admit that the benefits from this decision are likely to be limited and the costs rather higher than they would like, policymakers engage in bolstering by emphasizing the positive and downplaying the negative.

bond A certificate of indebtedness issued by a borrower to a lender that constitutes a legal obligation to repay the principal of the loan plus accrued interest.

bond anticipation notes (BANs) A form of short-term borrowing used to accelerate progress on approved capital projects. Once the revenues for a project have been realized from the sale of long-term bonds, the BANs are repaid. BANs may also be used to allow a jurisdiction to wait until the bond market becomes more favorable for the sale of long-term securities.

bond bank An arrangement whereby small units of government within a state are able to pool their long-term debt and so create a larger bond issue at more advantageous rates.

bonds, callable Bonds that can be repaid totally or in part prior to the maturity date. For this reason, callable bonds ordinarily carry higher interest rates.

Noncallable bonds, on the other hand, may not be repurchased until the date of maturation.

bonds, general obligation Bonds backed by the jurisdiction's FULL FAITH AND CREDIT with repayment, usually, from general revenues.

bonds, industrial development State or local government bonds issued to finance the building of a factory or installation that will be used by a private company. Although such bonds are popular as a means of attracting new industry to a community, they are essentially fronts for private borrowing. The U.S. Congress, sensing the loss of tax revenue from these fronts, has in recent years put a variety of constraints on their use.

bonds, junk Bonds that are issued by a company or government with a poor credit rating; thus it pays higher than normal interest to compensate for the additional risk.

bonds, moral obligation State or local government bonds that are backed only by the jurisdiction's promise to repay; they are specifically not backed by a jurisdiction's full faith and credit. Moral obligation bonds often carry a higher interest rate than other municipal bonds because full faith and credit bonds will always be paid first.

bonds, municipal The debt instruments of subnational governments, a cause of some confusion because they appear to refer only to bonds issued by a local government. Yet bonds issued by states, territories, and possessions of the United States, or by municipalities, political subdivisions (including cities, counties, school districts, and special districts for fire prevention, water, sewer, irrigation, and other purposes), or public agencies or instrumentalities (such as authorities or commissions) are subsumed under the rubric municipal bonds. Although the interest on municipal bonds is exempt from federal taxes, state and local exemptions may vary. Tax-exempt bonds allow jurisdictions to borrow money at lower than commercial market interest rates. The buyers of the bonds find them an attractive investment because their high marginal tax rates make a tax-free investment more advantageous than a taxable one paying even higher interest.

bonds, revenue Municipal bonds whose repayment and dividends are guaranteed by revenues derived from the facility constructed from the proceeds of the sale of the bonds (e.g., stadium bonds, toll road bonds). As revenue bonds are not pledged against the tax base of the issuing jurisdiction, they are usually not regulated by the same debt limitations imposed by most states on the sale of general obligation bonds. Additionally, revenue bond questions usually do not have to be submitted to the voters for approval because they do not commit the full faith and credit of the jurisdiction.

bonds, serial Bonds that are sold in such a way that a certain number of them are retired (paid off) each year.

bonds, term Bonds that all mature (must be paid off) on the same date.

bossism An informal system of local government in which public power is concentrated in the hands of a central figure, called a *political boss,* who may not hold a formal government position. The power is concentrated through a POLITICAL MACHINE, whereby a hierarchy is created and maintained through PATRONAGE and government largesse to assure compliance with the wishes of the boss. Bossism was a dominant system in city government after the American Civil War and was the main target of the U.S. urban reform effort.

bottom line The profit or loss for an activity; the final result of an activity; a final conclusion or responsibility.

bottom-up development Creating new economic opportunities for the poor masses in a developing country in the expectation that their increasing prosperity will eventually offer economic benefits to the middle and upper classes.

bounded rationality Herbert Simon's term from *Administrative Behavior* (1947) for the "bounds" that people put on their decisions. Because truly rational research on a problem can never be complete, humans make decisions on satisfactory information as opposed to optimal information.

boycott 1. Ostracize. In the nineteenth century, Charles C. Boycott, a former English army officer, managed the Irish estate of an absentee owner. Because his methods were so oppressive, the local citizens as a group refused to deal with him in any manner. When he was forced to flee to England, the first "boycott," or nonviolent intimidation through ostracism, was a success. 2. In the context of labor relations, a refusal to deal with or buy the products of a business as a means of asserting pressure in a labor dispute. 3. A tactic in diplomacy wherein one nation or group of nations pointedly ignores the diplomatic efforts of another. 4. A state's deliberate policy of not buying the products of or doing business with another state—hostile or nonhostile—as a means of influencing the domestic or foreign policies of the state being boycotted. For example, the boycott of exports from South Africa, and sometimes of companies significantly invested in that country, exerted so much pressure that the regime revised its racial policies. 5. A national policy of refusing to do business with companies that also do business with a specified country. This is a kind of economic warfare. 6. A mass consumer tactic to force companies to change a particular policy. For example, a two-year boycott on canned tuna fish was successful in forcing the major producers to announce that they would buy only "dolphin-safe" tuna in the future: tuna that was caught without inadvertently killing dolphins. 7. A political tactic to change or influence a government policy. For example, when the Idaho legislature in 1990 passed a bill severely restricting abortion, prochoice groups threatened to boycott Idaho potatoes if the governor signed the bill. The governor then found "other" reasons to veto it.

brain drain A reference to a perceived unfortunate flow of human capital—talent—from a country or an organization. Although historically used to describe the exodus of physicians, scientists, and other professionals from a particular country, it is also colloquially used to refer to the departure of a valued employee or group of employees. Brain drains are especially acute problems for developing countries. Too often their nationals go abroad to take advanced training and earn degrees and then refuse to return home because of the greater professional opportunities and lifestyle offered by the developed world.

brainstorming The term often used to describe a freewheeling group session designed to generate new ideas and approaches. Brainstorming originated as a formal system for idea generation devised by Alex Osborn in his book *Applied Imagination* (1953). Osborn's system provides order and structure, shelters fragile ideas, protects creativity from the tyranny of groupthink, and ensures a prolific output of options.

brainwashing The altering of a person's social and political views by severe physical and psychological conditioning. The phrase came into English to describe the way the North Koreans "reeducated" U.S. prisoners during the Korean War of 1950–1953. The term is now applied to the techniques used by religious cults to indoctrinate new converts. Brainwashing is countered by "deprogramming."

breaking relations One state's formally severing diplomatic contact with another to demonstrate disapproval of actions or policies. Because this is often a "cut off your nose to spite your face" tactic, a more common resort is to recall publicly the ambassador for consultations. This action expresses disapproval but retains the diplomatic mission.

bribery 1. A public official's receiving of or asking for something of value with the intent to be unlawfully influenced. Viewed systemically, bribery is an important element in all political systems. Systematic bribery allows business operators, dependent upon the discretionary powers of public officials for their livelihoods, to stabilize the relationships essential for the smooth functioning of their businesses. After all, many regulations that govern safety or conditions of business operation may not be universally applicable, reasonably enforceable, or economically feasible. Bribery's occasional exposure by the press serves to foster the political alienation of the electorate, which in turn encourages cynicism and reduces support for the democratic processes of government. Although it is possible to quibble over the particulars of a given instance or noninstance of bribery, its pervasiveness in too many com-

munities is generally contested only by the most naive or the most corrupt.
2. An important and time-honored tool of foreign policy. Of course, the
United States does not have to bribe a foreign government to influence its
support on some international issue; it can achieve the same effect by granting or withholding military or economic aid.

broken windows doctrine The belief that crime is best deterred by extremely aggressive policing; tending to the smallest as well as the more serious crimes.
James Q. Wilson and George L. Kelling in "Broken Windows," *The Atlantic
Monthly* (March 1982) expanded upon the theory of community policing by
first articulating the notion that a link exists between petty disorders and major crimes in a community. Police officers, they suggested, should be as concerned about maintaining order as they are about preventing crime. The
authors draw on the argument that when a community permits a few broken
windows to remain unrepaired and a few unsightly instances of graffiti to remain unpainted, more broken windows and more graffiti are inevitable. By
analogy, Wilson and Kelling suggest that the police should pay more attention
to the small disruptions in communities: "the ill-smelling drunk, the rowdy
teenager, or the importuning beggar." According to the theory, by "repairing"
these "broken windows," the police will create an atmosphere in which criminals and mischief makers feel uncomfortable and move on to other places.

Brown v. Board of Education of Topeka, Kansas (1954) The U.S. Supreme
Court decision on whether black and white children should attend the same
schools. Prior to *Brown*, the prevailing doctrine on civil rights was "separate
but equal." This meant that blacks did not suffer an infringement of their
constitutional rights as citizens if they were not allowed to use the same facilities as whites—so long as "separate but equal" facilities were also provided. Although this doctrine sounded fair on the surface, there were two
insurmountable arguments against it. First, there was the simple reality that
what was provided separately was hardly ever equal. Second, there was the
inherent stigma of being treated differently. How could you be equal if you
were not treated equally? There was no doubt that this made African Americans second-class citizens. In *Brown,* the Court decided that the separation
of children by race and according to law in public schools "generates a feeling of inferiority as to their [the minority group's] status in the community
that may affect their hearts and minds in a way unlikely ever to be undone."
Consequently, the Court held that "separate educational facilities are inherently unequal" and therefore violate the equal protection clause of the Fourteenth Amendment. Chief Justice Earl Warren, in delivering the unanimous
opinion of the Court, stated that public education "is the very foundation of
good citizenship." It was so important to the nation that considerations of

the original intent of the Fourteenth Amendment were less important than remedying the present situation. The schools are often the battlefield for fights over policy issues that have wider impact. The *Brown* decision was not just about segregation in education; it was an invaluable precedent in the subsequent fostering of integration in employment and housing by legislative and judicial means.

Brownlow Committee A committee appointed by President Franklin D. Roosevelt in 1936 for the purpose of diagnosing the staffing needs of the president and making appropriate recommendations for the reorganization of the executive branch. The advent of the reinventing government movement in the 1990s has once again made reorganization a fashionable theme in the practice and literature of public administration in the United States. However, the classic example of government reorganization, the one that to this day is still the most significant, is the structuring of the executive branch recommended by the President's Committee on Administrative Management in 1936–1937. This committee was popularly known as the "Brownlow Committee," named after its chairman, Louis Brownlow (1879–1963), a major figure in the development of city management as a profession. The two other members of the committee were Charles Merriam (1874–1953), of the University of Chicago, and LUTHER GULICK, of Columbia University and the Institute of Public Administration in New York City. Because government grew rapidly during the New Deal, there was little time or inclination for planning. It was largely believed that there existed many poorly conceived and poorly implemented organizational designs that were neither economical nor effective. These inferior designs were often a reflection of the considerable political conflict between the executive and legislative branches. The president's office and the U.S. Congress had deliberately contributed to this problem by catering only to political objectives and failing to take managerial considerations into account when establishing programs in new organizations and agencies. The Brownlow Committee would address this persistent struggle over organizational control and provide the first formal assessment of government organization from a managerial perspective. The Brownlow Committee submitted its report to President Roosevelt in January 1937. The core proposals of the committee were simple enough. Essentially the report indicated that "the president needs help"; that he needs professional staff members around him who possess a "passion for anonymity." This particular passion seems to have faded in recent years, along with the public's belief that a modern president writes his own speeches. Overall, the committee recommended a major reorganization of the executive branch. The president agreed and appropriate legislation was submitted to Congress in 1938. But the Congress, in the wake of the president's efforts to "pack"—to enlarge and thus control—the U.S. Supreme Court, and fearful of too much power in the presidency, killed the bill. When the president resubmitted a considerably modified reorganization bill the following year, the Congress passed the Reorganization Act of 1939. This law created the Executive Office of the President, brought into it the Bureau of the Budget (later to be the Office of Management and Budget) from the Department of the Treasury, and authorized the president to prepare future reorganization plans subject to an after-the-fact congressional veto.

buck Responsibility. To avoid a problem or a responsibility is to *pass the buck*. President Truman was famous for having a sign on his desk that read "The Buck Stops Here." *Buck,* a term from poker, refers to the marker put in front of the player who next has to deal. Bureaucrats in many jurisdictions refer to the form memos they use to direct paper from one to another as "buck slips."

budget A financial plan serving as a pattern for and control over future operations—hence, an estimate of future costs or a systematic plan for using the workforce, material, or other resources. The budget itself is also a jurisdiction's most important reference document. In their increasingly voluminous formats, budgets simultaneously record policy decision outcomes, cite policy priorities as well as program objectives, and delineate a government's total service effort. A public budget has four basic dimensions. First, it is a political instrument that allocates scarce public resources among the social and economic needs of the jurisdiction. Second, a budget is a managerial or administrative instrument: It specifies the ways and means of providing public programs and services; it establishes the costs of programs and the criteria by which these programs are evaluated for efficiency and effectiveness; and it ensures that the programs will be reviewed or evaluated at least once during the budget year or budget cycle. Third, a budget is an economic instrument that can direct a jurisdiction's economic growth and development. Certainly at the national level—and to a lesser extent at the state and regional levels—government budgets are the primary instruments for redistributing income, stimulating economic growth, promoting full employment, combating inflation, and maintaining economic stability. Fourth, a budget is an accounting instrument that holds government officials responsible for the expenditure of the funds with which they have been entrusted. Budgets also hold governments accountable in the aggregate. The very concept of a budget implies a ceiling, or a spending limitation, that literally (but theoretically) requires governments to live within their means.

Budget and Accounting Act of 1921 The law that authorized a Bureau of the Budget within the Department of the Treasury to prepare an executive budget annually; the law also authorized additional staff to conduct continuing studies of efficiency. Therefore, long before the Bureau of the Budget was renamed the Office of Management and Budget in 1970, it enjoyed a significant management role. But because the U.S. Congress was institutionally suspicious of presidential power, the second half of the act (the "accounting") created the General Accounting Office (GAO) as a congressional support agency to audit federal government expenditures and to assist the Congress with its legislative oversight responsibilities.

budget, balanced A budget in which receipts are equal to or greater than outlays. A government that has one is financially healthy. The advantages of a balanced budget, not spending more than you take in, are obvious. But there are also advantages to "unbalanced" budgets, those that require public borrowing. The "extra" spending can stimulate the economy during economic downturns and provide needed public works and public support for the less fortunate. But these considerations must be weighed against the danger that large deficits over a significant period can devalue the currency, kindle inflation, and have such a crowding-out effect on capital markets that an economic depression (or recession) occurs. Note that only the federal government has the option of long-term deficit spending. The states all have constitutional or statutory provisions mandating balanced budgets (at least at the beginning of each year). A balanced budget amendment to the U.S. Constitution is an oft suggested proposal to force an end to deficit spending by the federal government. Many critics see this as an exercise in futility because the U.S. Congress could easily create any number of mechanisms to meet the letter, but violate the spirit, of such an amendment. Others think the amendment is absolutely essential because it is the only way the Congress will make the hard decisions needed to get there.

budget, biennial A budget for a two-year period, as opposed to a single-year period.

budget, black The classified (secret) portion of the federal budget that hides sensitive programs involving high technology military and covert operations.

budget, capital The budget process that deals with planning for large expenditures for capital items. Capital expenditures should be for long-term investments (such as bridges and buildings), which yield returns for years after they are completed. Capital budgets typically cover five- to ten-year periods and are updated yearly. Items included in capital budgets may be financed through borrowing (including tax-exempt municipal bonds), savings, grants, revenue sharing, and special assessments. A capital budget provides for separating the financing of capital, or investment, expenditures from current, or operating, expenditures. The federal government has never had a capital budget in the sense of financing capital programs separately from current expenditures.

budget cycle The timed steps of the budget process, which includes preparation, approval, execution, and audit.

budget deficit Amount by which a government's budget outlays exceed its budget receipts for a given period. Deficits are financed primarily by borrowing from the public.

budget, executive 1. The budget document for an executive branch of government that a jurisdiction's chief executive submits to a legislature for review, modification, and enactment. 2. Both a technical process and a physical entity. First, it is the process by which an agency's requests for appropriations are prepared and submitted to a budget bureau under the chief executive for review, alteration, and consolidation into one budget document that can be compared to expected revenues and executive priorities before submission to the legislature. Then it becomes a tangible document, the comprehensive budget document for an executive branch of government that a jurisdiction's chief executive submits to a legislature for review, modification, and enactment. The president's budget is the executive budget for a particular fiscal year transmitted to the U.S. Congress by the president in accordance with the Budget and Accounting Act of 1921, as amended. Some elements of the budget (such as the estimates for the legislative branch and the judiciary) are required to be included without review by the Office of Management and Budget or approval by the president (note that the president has no say in the budgets of the other branches of government). It is convenient to include the comparatively small budgets of other branches in the overall document. The president's budget is the president's "wish list"— his suggestions to Congress. Every president's budget is "dead on arrival" the moment it is formally sent to the HILL because Congress always makes extensive changes. The same considerations apply to state governors. Thus, a governor's budget is an executive budget prepared by a state governor.

budget guidance The direction given by a jurisdiction's budget bureau or equivalent unit at the time of the call for budget estimates for the forthcoming budget period. Guidance frequently includes specific instructions regarding the format and timing of the budget submissions as well as statements of executive policy concerning the scope of requests and program emphasis for the coming year.

budget, line-item The original budget format in which each item of expense had a literal line in a ledger book. It classified budgetary accounts according to narrow, detailed objects of expenditure (such as motor vehicles, clerical workers, or reams of paper) used within each particular agency of government, generally without reference to the ultimate purpose or objective served by the expenditure. It was useful as a record of expenditures and the criteria against which audits could measure compliance. The line-item budget is still widely used. Most local governments use it either as their basic budget format or as a supplement to more sophisticated formats. Because the line-item budget offers such comprehensive details on proposed expenditures, legislators interested in fine-tuning executive budget recommendations are particularly partial to it because it allows for greater control and oversight.

budget, operating A short-term plan for managing the resources necessary to carry out a program. *Short term* can mean anything from a few weeks to a few years. Usually an operating budget is developed for each fiscal year, changes being made as necessary.

budget, performance The first major step beyond the line-item budget. Performance budgeting requires a performance measure to be stated alongside each line item so that elementary calculations of unit cost and efficiency can be made. Line items are grouped, or categorized, according to their function. For example, a sanitation (trash collection) department's workload can be determined on the basis of the number of houses and businesses served, which makes it relatively easy to calculate how much trash is generated each week, month, or year. This measure allows the efficiency of collection to be measured against a base period and a base cost. At this elementary level, comparisons in relative efficiency can be made from year to year.

budget, planning programming *See* PLANNING PROGRAMMING BUDGETING SYSTEM.

budget process The total system a jurisdiction uses to make decisions on government spending needs and how to pay for them. The main difference between federal, state, and local budget processes is that the state and local jurisdictions must present balanced budgets each year.

budget, program A budget process that consolidates spending into "programs"; because the total resources directed to a purpose should now be more readily apparent, this process provides the foundation for a focus on effectiveness. When a budget comprises large slabs of spending, called *programs,* directed toward particular objectives, the disaggregation problem common to line-item and performance budgeting can be overcome. Compliance can still be monitored, but the monitoring of efficiency and effectiveness is also facilitated. Instead of being primarily an instrument of control and management information, the budget would become not only a planning document but also a document supporting the comparison of alternative expenditures at some meaningful level of aggregation.

budget surplus The amount by which a government's budget receipts exceed its budget outlays for a given period.

budget, target-based A budgeting process by which a central budget office gives targets (maximum amounts) to the departments before they draw up and submit their budgets.

budget, zero-based (ZBB) A budgeting process that is foremost a rejection of the incremental decisionmaking model of budgeting. It demands a rejustification of the entire budget submission (from ground zero), whereas incremental budgeting essentially respects the outcomes of previous budgetary decisions (collectively referred to as the "budget base") and focuses examination on the margin of change from year to year. Therefore, under ZBB, an agency has to rank each of its programs according to importance and face the possibility that those of the least importance will be discontinued. In large part, ZBB failed because the conditions that prevailed for most of the previous budgeting systems reforms have changed. In an era of acute resource scarcity, ZBB had little utility because there was little real chance that funding could be provided for program growth. Critics assaulted ZBB as a fraud; some called it a *nonsystem of budgeting*. ZBB's fate in the federal government was tied to the Carter presidency. After the inauguration of a new president (Reagan) in 1981, the method was quietly rescinded. Still, numerous state and local governments use ZBB techniques or some adaptation of it. Now that the hype has subsided, ZBB remains an important part of public budgeting.

build-down 1. A reduction in nuclear arsenals by destroying more old warheads than new ones are built. A build-down does not necessarily change strategic relationships, because the fewer new weapons may be more accurate and powerful than the more numerous older ones. 2. A gradual budget cutback in a government program. 3. The exact amount of a budget cut; for example, as in "there was a build-down of $2 million."

bully pulpit 1. President Theodore Roosevelt's definition of the U.S. presidency, because the office provided its occupant an unparalleled opportunity to preach to and inspire the national congregation. With the exception of those who do impersonations of Teddy Roosevelt, bully is an informal interjection of approval that has fallen into disuse. 2. By analogy, a highly visible public office whose incumbent uses it as a platform to influence public opinion.

burden-sharing 1. The issue of how the costs and benefits of a military alliance are borne and shared. In the context of NATO (North Atlantic Treaty Organization), this refers to the periodically asked question of who (which of the allies) should bear what expenses for the alliance. Burden-sharing sometimes refers to the relative share of total NATO defense expenditures paid by Europeans as opposed to those paid by the United States. 2. The mutually self-imposed obligation on the part of the developed world to help the underdeveloped world better itself. 3. The question of who shall bear the burden of social security payments as the nation grows increasingly older. Some suggest that older Americans should bear more of the burden by having social security benefits MEANS TESTED or taxed.

bureau movement The efforts of progressive reformers early in the twentieth century to apply scientific methods to municipal problems. Their efforts led to the creation of research bureaus; these, in turn, created the academic field of public administration.

bureaucracy 1. The totality of government offices or bureaus (from a French word meaning "office") that constitute the permanent government of a state; that is, those public functions that continue regardless of changes in political leadership. 2. A general invective to refer to inefficient organizations encumbered by RED TAPE. 3. A specific set of structural arrangements in which workers are organized into hierarchical ranks and must obey numerous rules. 4. All the public officials of a government, high and low, elected and appointed. Thus the secretary of the treasury is a bureaucrat, but so is a lowly secretary in the Department of the Treasury. We typically think of a bureaucrat as someone who sits at a desk and shuffles papers on behalf of the citizenry. But most bureaucrats lead far more active lives. They are police officers, teachers, firefighters, scientists, and astronauts. Although many fit the image and do sit behind a desk all day, the paper-shufflers are no more representative of bureaucrats as a whole than are those in other major categories, such as trash collection and street maintenance.

bureaucracy, ideal type German sociologist MAX WEBER's extrapolation from the real world of the central core of features that characterize the most fully developed bureaucratic form of organization. This ideal type is neither a description of reality nor a statement of normative preference; it is merely an identification of the major variables or features that characterize bureaucracy. The absence of such features in a given organization does not necessarily imply that the organization is not bureaucratic; it may be an immature rather than a fully developed bureaucracy. At some point, however, the characteristics of bureaucracy may be so lacking in an organization that it can no longer reasonably be considered bureaucratic nor can it be expected to produce patterns of bureaucratic behavior. Weber's ideal type of bureaucracy possesses the following characteristics: (1) The bureaucrats must be free as individuals; they can be bossed around only with respect to the impersonal duties of their offices. (2) The bureaucrats are arranged in a clearly defined hierarchy of offices, the traditional scalar chain wherein bureaucrats have their own unambiguous places—and know what they are! (3) The functions of each office are clearly specified in writing. (4) The bureaucrats accept and maintain their appointments freely—without duress. Slave bureaucrats, although once fashionable during the Ottoman Empire and in Imperial China, are an inherent contradiction, the exception being within military and penal organizations. (5) Appointments to office are according to technical qualifications, which ideally are substantiated by examinations administered by the appointing authority, a university, or both. (6) The bureaucrats receive salaries and pension rights that reflect the varying levels of the hierarchy. Although the bureaucrats are free to leave the organization, they can be removed from their offices only under previously stated, specific circumstances. (7) The office must be the bureaucrat's sole, or at least major, occupation. (8) A career system is essential; although promotion may result from seniority or merit, it must be premised on the judgment of hierarchical superiors. (9) The bureaucrats do not enjoy property rights to their office, nor can they make personal claims to the resources that go with it. (10) The bureaucrat's conduct must be subject to systematic control and strict discipline.

bureaucracy, life cycles of Anthony Downs's application of SYSTEMS THEORY to bureaucracy from *Inside Bureaucracy* (1967), in which he posited that there are stages of bureaucratic growth and stagnation along with associated repercussions on administrative performance. Even the death of a bureaucracy had to be seen as part of the life cycle.

bureaucrat bashing Either justified criticism or inappropriate condemnation of public employees. During the 1980s, the constant complaints and jokes about the competence of government employees—led by President Ronald "Government Is the Problem" Reagan—helped to create an acceptance of bureaucrat bashing. Following his 1964 campaign for governor of California, Reagan was constantly complaining that "government is like a big baby—an alimentary canal with a big appetite at one end and no sense of responsibility at the other." The term *bureaucrat bashing* has been used so frequently and in so many contexts that it has taken on two meanings that are the opposite of each other. Those on the ideological right who tend to oppose big government use it to refer to justified criticism of "lazy and incompetent" government employees. At the same time, those on the ideological left, who tend to be more supportive of big government, use it to refer to the political right's "unnecessary and inappropriate" condemnation of public employees.

bureaucrat, budget maximizing Agency managers who seek enhanced funding for their programs more for purposes of personal power and prestige than for genuine public need. In the often perverted world of government, one may be only as important as the size of one's budget. The bureaucratic battle cry of "mine is bigger than yours" is heard often during the perennial budget wars. This phenomenon is universal. As Sir Humphrey Appleby in *The Complete Yes Minister* (1988) explains to a British civil service colleague, "We measure success by the size of our staff and our budget. By definition a big department is more successful than a small one."

bureaucratic dysfunctions The pathological elements of bureaucratic structures that often make them inefficient in operation; the pressures on workers to conform that causes them to adhere to rules as an end rather than a means. *See* CATCH-22.

bureaucratic incapacity Sociologist Robert Merton's (1910–2003) "discovery" in *Bureaucratic Structure and Personality* (1957) that bureaucracies have a "trained incapacity." This term refers to a "state of affairs in which one's abilities function as inadequacies or blind spots. Actions based upon training and skills which have been successfully applied in the past may result in inappropriate responses under changed conditions." According to Merton, bureaucracy exerts constant pressures on people to be methodical and disciplined, to conform to patterns of obligations. These pressures eventually cause people to adhere to rules as an end rather than a means—as a matter of blind conformance. Bureaucratic structure also stresses depersonalized relations as well as power and authority gained by virtue of organizational position rather than by thought or action. Thus, ideas and opinions are valued not according to their intrinsic merit but according to one's rank. *See also* CATCH-22.

bureaucratic impersonality The dehumanizing consequences of formal organizational structures that eliminate personal and emotional consideration from organizational life so that the individual bureaucrat functions only as a cog in an ever-moving machine. Bureaucratic impersonality increases organizational effectiveness by enabling administrators to do things that are otherwise difficult for people to accomplish alone. In the course of their normal functioning, organizations may create considerable hardships for individuals. This is especially true of public organizations, which are often engaged in punishment, taxation, and the withholding of benefits such as food stamps, unemployment compensation, and welfare funds. Impersonality creates a desirable moral insensitivity. For example, it is much easier—emotionally—for military planners on a general staff to select targets for bombardment than it is for a rifleman to shoot an enemy soldier who is a few yards ahead of him and whose face is clearly visible. Similarly, it is far easier for welfare agency budget analysts to cut school lunch funding for poor students than for a food service worker at a school cafeteria to see children go hungry when they cannot pay for lunch.

bureaucrats, street level Government employees who, in delivering goods and services to the public, have a range of discretion that effectively makes them policymakers. Michael Lipsky (1940–) "discovered" these street-level bureaucrats in *Street-Level Bureaucracy* (1980), wherein he assessed the implication of their discretion for accountability, equity, and management control.

bureaupathology Victor A. Thompson's term from *Modern Organization* (1961), wherein he combined "pathological" with "bureaucracy" to describe the all-too-familiar "bureaupathic official." Such a person "usually exaggerates the official, nontechnical aspects of relationships and suppresses the technical and the informal." Being insecure, he or she "may be expected to insist on petty rights and prerogatives, on protocol, on procedure—in short, on those things least likely to affect directly the goal accomplishment of the organization." This is the classic stereotype of "the bureaucrat." Thus, an otherwise "functionless reviewing officer will often insist most violently on his right to review and scream like an injured animal if he is bypassed." Moreover, "if he has a counterpart at a higher organizational level, he will probably insist on exclusive contact with that higher clearance point. By controlling this particular communication channel, he protects his authority and influence." This stereotype has been around, quite literally, for ages. In *Measure for Measure* (2.2), Shakespeare wrote of the "petty officer," the "proud man, dress'd in a little brief authority, most ignorant of what he's most assur'd." This "petty officer" clothed in a "little brief authority" is also probably performing at a bureaucracy near you—right now!

Burke, Edmund (1729–1797) The British political philosopher and member of Parliament who is often referred to as the father of modern conservative thought. Burke, in his 1770 pamphlet "Thoughts on the Cause of the Present Discontents," provided the first modern definition of a political party as a group united on public principle that could act as a link between the executive branch (the king) and the legislative branch (Parliament), providing consistency and strength when in power and principled criticism when out of power. But Burke is best known for his 1774 "Speech to the Electors of Bristol," in which he asserted that the role of an elected member of a legislature should be that of a representative or trustee (free to exercise his own best judgment) rather than that of a delegate (bound by prior instructions from a constituency).

burnout A worker's mental and physical fatigue; this condition causes indifference and emotional disengagement from the job.

business improvement district A special purpose NEIGHBORHOOD ASSOCIATION, usually chartered under state law, which uses its power of taxation (typically special assessments on real estate) to raise money to pay for higher levels of services (such as additional police and trash collection) and infrastructure (more street lighting and parks) than are available from the overall local jurisdiction.

busing The transporting of children to schools at a greater distance from their homes than those they would otherwise attend to achieve racial desegregation. Busing has often been mandated by the federal courts as a remedy for past practices of discrimination. Parents who want their children to attend neighborhood schools have strongly objected to it and it has, in consequence, been a major factor in white flight from central cities. Busing is often used as an example of government by the judiciary, because even though it has been one of the most controversial domestic policies in the history of the United States, it has never been specifically sanctioned by the U.S. Congress. But it was sanctioned by the U.S. Supreme Court in *Swann v. Charlotte-Mecklenburg Board of Education* (1971).

C

cabinet The heads of the executive departments of a jurisdiction who report to and advise its chief executive; for example, the president's cabinet, the governor's cabinet, the mayor's cabinet.

cabinet government 1. The British parliamentary system, whereby the cabinet as a whole, rather than the prime minister who heads it, is considered the executive, and the cabinet is collectively responsible to Parliament for its performance. In addition, whereas in the United States the cabinet secretaries are only of the executive branch, in Britain, the cabinet ministers are typically drawn from among the majority party's members in Parliament. 2. A concept informally applied to a U.S. president's assertion that he and his cabinet are going to work together as a team.

cabinet, inner The federal departments of State, Defense, Treasury, and Justice—because they (and their secretaries) tend to be more prominent and influential in every administration than the rest of the (or outer) cabinet. Although all cabinet secretaries are equal in rank and salary, the missions of those in the inner cabinet give them an advantage in prestige, access, and visibility.

cabinet, kitchen The informal advisors of a chief executive. First used derisively for some of President Andrew Jackson's advisors: *kitchen* implying they were not respectable enough to meet in the more formal rooms of the White House. Over the years, the term has lost its derisive quality.

cabinet, war An informal term for those cabinet secretaries, agency heads, and officials who are the president's primary source of policy advice and military action during wartime.

cadre 1. The most dedicated members of a political party. 2. The founding members of a political organization who thereupon expand the organization by enlisting new members. 3. A detachment from an existing organization capable of being the training nucleus about which a new organizational unit can be built. In a military context, cadres of commissioned as well as noncommissioned officers have always been critical for rapidly expanding an army.

camel's nose One of the principal strategies bureaucrats use to obtain funding for a new program. They begin with an appropriation request that appears insignificant until it becomes part of the agency's base and must be funded at a much higher level if the program is to be completed.

capacity building 1. All systems, efforts, and processes that strengthen the capability of government officials to better plan, implement, manage, and evaluate programs. 2. The development of the physical and human infrastructure for economic advancement. The term is used in the context of the THIRD WORLD to refer to the needs for better ports, bridges, and roads, as well as for a highly trained and well-educated workforce.

capital 1. The city in which a central government is located. New York City became the first capital of the United States (1789); Philadelphia became the capital in 1790; since 1800, the capital has been Washington, D.C. *Compare to* CAPITOL. 2. Wealth; one of the three traditional factors of production, the others being land and labor. *See* HUMAN CAPITAL.

capital campaign A nonprofit organization's fund-raising effort that focuses on raising money for major projects; for example, a new building, the repair or expansion of an old one, or an increase in an endowment.

capital flight 1. The removal of financial capital from a state to safer places where interest rates are higher and inflation is lower, or to escape confiscation by a government. 2. The illegal movement of stolen funds across international borders to escape taxation or other unpopular economic conditions.

capital intensive A production process requiring a large proportion of capital relative to labor.

capital investment 1. Generally, new plants and equipment. 2. In the public sector, a major expense that provides benefits beyond a single budget cycle, such as bridges and buildings. Less clear is whether intangible investments in education and training programs, for example, should be classified as a capital investment. This is a significant issue because capital spending is often financed by borrowing. *See also* BUDGET, CAPITAL.

capital punishment The death penalty. The word *capital* is derived from *caput,* the Latin word meaning "head"; thus, the term *head punishment* once meant that you had to give up your head—that it would be cut off.

capital sector The international economy as a whole wherein investment funds flow relatively unobstructed across national borders.

capitalism An economic system characterized by a combination of private ownership of most means of production and trade, a generally unrestricted marketplace of goods and services, and a general assumption that the bulk of the workforce will be engaged in employment by private (nongovernmental) companies engaged in producing goods and providing services to sell at a profit. The Scottish economist ADAM SMITH (1723–1790) provided the first systematic analysis of the economic phenomena of laissez-faire capitalism. In *The Wealth of Nations* (1776), Smith discovered an "invisible hand" that automatically promotes the general welfare as long as individuals are allowed to pursue their self-interest. To believers in capitalism, this form of economic organization provides the greatest chance of maximizing economic performance and defending political liberty while securing something approaching equality of opportunity. However, classic unrestrained laissez-faire capitalism is today only a theory because all modern capitalistic societies have mixed economies that temper capitalism with government regulation and social welfare measures. *Compare to* MARXISM.

Capitol 1. The domed building in which the Congress of the United States meets. 2. The building in which a state legislature meets; also called a *statehouse*. *Compare to* CAPITAL.

capture theory The argument that when public services become "captured" by special constituencies, the end result is a suboptimal allocation of resources in the interests of those constituencies. This means that public funds will tend to be spent in the interests of those constituencies—and not in the interests of the general public.

cartel 1. An alliance or arrangement among industrial, commercial, or state-controlled enterprises in the same field of business aimed at securing a monopoly. A cartel usually seeks to control production so as to raise prices and maximize profits. Cartels almost always fail in their goals if there are ample supplies of the commodity or available substitutes. In the end even temporarily successful cartels fail because they often drive prices up to where new sources enter the market. 2. An agreement between belligerents to arrange for specified non-hostile relations such as an exchange of wounded.

case 1. A legal dispute, whether criminal or civil, that goes to court. 2. A court's opinion deciding a case. 3. The evidence and arguments presented by each side in a legal dispute. 4. A systematic presentation of arguments in favor of, or in opposition to, a position or circumstances.

case law All recorded judicial and administrative agency decisions.

case study A research design that focuses upon the indepth analysis of one subject. It is particularly useful for the understanding of dynamic processes over time. Most traditional news stories use the case study approach. Note that aspiring journalists are taught that a story should contain all the essential elements of a case study: "who, what, why, when, where, and how." The first case studies examined battles and wars. Thucydides's *History of the Peloponnesian War* (404 B.C.E.) is the progenitor of these military case studies. Military colleges—and general staffs—have long used the case study method to review battles and study generalship. This same technique is now widely used in a civilian context to examine how policy proposals become law, how programs are implemented, and how special interests affect policy development. College courses in business and public administration often use a case study approach. An entire course may consist of case studies (frequently combined into a casebook) of management situations that are to be reviewed. The goal is to inculcate experience artificially. A manager rich in years of service will have lived through a lifetime of "cases." By having students study many cases, each of which may have extended over many years, the case study course compresses time and experience. The relatively young student should then gain the insight and wisdom of an experienced manager.

casework 1. The services performed by legislators and their staffs at the request of and on behalf of constituents. For example, a U.S. senator may be asked to discover why a social security check has been delayed or why a veteran's claim for benefits has been denied. Casework is an important means by which legislators maintain oversight of the bureaucracy and solidify their political base with constituents. **2.** Generally, a method of providing services through a case-by-case treatment of individuals or groups, as in social work or medicine.

caseworker An employee of a government welfare agency resposible for determining and administering individual ENTITLEMENT BENEFITS.

catch–22 Contradictory bureaucratic requirements. This "catch" from Joseph Heller's 1961 novel of the same name about U.S. bomber crews during World War II meant that you could avoid flying combat missions if you were insane. All you had to do was ask. But if you asked, you were not insane, because seeking to avoid combat was a rational, not an insane, act. In Heller's words, a pilot "would be crazy to fly more missions and sane if he didn't, but if he was sane, he had to fly them. If he flew them he was crazy and didn't have to, but if he didn't, he was sane and had to." The "catch" is beautifully circular in its perversity. Because the book was such an enormous bestseller, catch-22 entered the language as the code word for the essence of bureaucratic dysfunctionalism, for being trapped between contradictory bureaucratic regulations. A common example of catch-22 is this double bind: A person can't get a job without having experience but can't get experience without first having a job. *See also* BUREAUCRATIC INCAPACITY.

cause The reason given for removing someone from an office or job (short for just cause). The cause cited may or may not be the real reason for the removal.

CBO *See* CONGRESSIONAL BUDGET OFFICE.

CEA *See* COUNCIL OF ECONOMIC ADVISERS.

cease-and-desist order A ruling, frequently issued in unfair labor practice and regulatory cases, that requires the charged party to stop conduct held to be illegal and to take specific action to remedy the unfair or illegal practice. *Compare to* CONSENT ORDER.

census In ancient Rome, the registration of citizens and their property to determine who owed what taxes and who was entitled to vote. The modern census seeks a vast array of statistical information and is not directly concerned with taxation or suffrage. Article I, Section 2, of the U.S. Constitution requires that a census be conducted every ten years so that seats in the U.S. House of Representatives can be appropriately apportioned among the states.

census undercount The contention that people are missed by the census count because they move, are fearful of filling out government forms, are illiterate, or other reasons. Because the count is critical for congressional districting and for the funding level of many intergovernmental grant programs, jurisdictions are apt to make an issue of what they consider to be an undercount.

central bank In most countries, the central monetary authority. Functions may include issuing a country's currency, carrying out a nation's monetary policy, and managing the country's foreign exchange reserves and the external value of its currency. In the United States, the Federal Reserve System functions as the nation's central bank, although it is not formally a central bank and is subject only to limited influences by the executive and legislative branches.

central clearance The Office of Management and Budget's (OMB) coordination and assessment of recommendations and positions taken by the various federal departments and agencies on legislative matters as they relate to a president's program. The first form of central clearance is substantive bill clearance. Drafts of bills from departments and agencies must clear the OMB before going to the U.S. Congress. Congressional committees also solicit views from interested agencies on substantive legislative bills emanating from sources other than the executive branch; however, executive agency responses are expected to be cleared by the OMB. The second form of central clearance is financial bill clearance. Since the Budget and Accounting Act of 1921, federal agencies have not had the authority to decide what appropriations to ask of the Congress. Instead, their proposed spending measure must clear the OMB. The third form of central clearance is enrolled bill clearance. When enrolled bill enactments come from the Congress to the president for signature or veto, the OMB solicits agency opinion on the merits of the congressionally approved legislation, evaluates these opinions, and prepares its own report to the president recommending either approval or veto and the reasons.

centrally planned economy A socialist or communist economic system wherein the government owns most means of production (factories) and makes all significant economic decisions.

certification of eligibles The procedure whereby those who have passed competitive civil service examinations have their names ranked in order of score and placed on a list of those eligible for appointment. When a government agency has a vacancy, it requests its personnel arm to provide a list of eligibles for the class to which the vacant position has been allocated. The personnel arm then certifies to the appointing authority the names of the highest-ranking eligibles. Usually, only a few of the qualified eligibles are certified. An agency requirement that three eligibles be certified to the appointing authority is called the *rule of three.*

certification proceeding A process by which the National Labor Relations Board and other administrative agencies determine whether a particular labor union is the majority choice and thus the exclusive bargaining agent for a group of employees in a given bargaining unit. Decertification is the opposite process.

certify To attest to the truth or accuracy of something; to guarantee that a standard on quantity or quality has been met; to make a legal determination. Some examples of things that are certified: a certified financial statement has been examined and reported upon with an opinion expressed by an independent public accountant; certified funds are bank deposits held in suspension and awaiting claims by a certified check; certified mail is ordinary mail that provides a receipt to the sender attesting to delivery; and a certified public accountant (CPA) is an accountant certified by a state government as having met specific educational and experiential requirements.

certiorari An order or writ from a higher court demanding that a lower court send up the record of a case for review. Except for a few instances of original jurisdiction, most cases that reach the U.S. Supreme Court do so because the Court itself has issued such a writ, or has granted certiorari. If certiorari is denied by the Court, it means that the justices are content to let the lower court's decision stand. Frequently, a U.S. court of appeals case citation will include "cert. denied," meaning that certiorari has been denied by the Court, which has reviewed the case to the extent that it has made a judgment not to review the case further. The votes of four justices are needed to grant certiorari; however, at least five votes are normally needed for a majority opinion on the substance of a case.

chain of command The succession of commanders from a superior to a subordinate through which command is exercised or policies implemented. Chains of command exist in civilian and military organizations.

channel The route of official communication between headquarters and field offices of military or bureaucratic units. "To go through channels" is to follow the regularly established means for getting things done. *Compare to* BACK CHANNEL.

chaos theory The contention that all large organizations contain a variety of capabilities for renewal and revitalization if allowed to evolve. Chaos theory seeks to explain how the smallest elements of a system, whether weather or organizational, can have the greatest consequences.

charisma Leadership based on the compelling personality of the leader rather than upon formal position. The word *charisma* is derived from the Greek word for divine grace. The concept was first developed by MAX WEBER, who distinguished charismatic authority both from the traditional authority of a monarch and the legal authority given to someone by law. Charismatic leadership, if it is to survive, must eventually be institutionalized or routinized. Thus the founder of a movement or organization may be a charismatic spellbinder, but those who come later are often, of necessity, comparatively dull bureaucrats. Political leaders in the United States didn't have charisma until Daniel Bell applied it to the labor leader John L. Lewis (1880–1969) in a 1949 article in *Fortune*.

charter 1. Originally a document issued by a monarch granting special privileges to groups and individuals, as in the Magna Carta of 1215. Some of the original American colonies were created by such charters. 2. A document that spells out the purposes and powers of a municipal corporation. The municipality can perform only those functions and exercise only those powers that are named in the charter. *See* HOME RULE. 3. The constitution of an international body, such as the United Nations. 4. The government document that allows a group of people to create a corporation.

charter member One of the founding members of an organization. For example, the United States is a charter member of the United Nations.

checkoff 1. A union security provision, commonly provided in collective bargaining agreements, that allows union dues to be deducted from the employee's pay. 2. A taxpayer's designation (or checkoff) of a dollar of his federal income tax payment to be used for presidential campaign expenses. Some states have similar checkoff programs to finance gubernatorial elections.

checks and balances The notion that constitutional devices can prevent a power within a nation from becoming absolute by being balanced against, or checked by, another source of power within that same nation. First put forth by the French philosopher Charles de Montesquieu (1689–1755) in his *Spirit of the Laws* (1734), this notion was further developed by Thomas Jefferson (1743–1826) in his *Notes on the State of Virginia* (1784), in which he asserted that "the powers of government should be so divided and balanced among several bodies of magistracy, as that none could transcend their legal limits, without being effectively checked and restrained by the others." The U.S. Constitution is often described as a system of checks and balances. For example, it allows the president to check the U.S. Congress by vetoing a bill, and the Congress to check the president by overriding a veto or refusing to ratify treaties or confirm nominees to federal office; the U.S. Supreme Court can check either by declaring law passed by the Congress or actions taken by the president to be unconstitutional. *Compare to* FEDERALIST NO. 51; SEPARATION OF POWERS.

Chicago school 1. A loose term for economists associated with the University of Chicago who strongly advocate a return to LAISSEZ-FAIRE capitalism. The Nobel Prize–winning economists Milton Friedman (1912–) and George Stigler (1911–) were leading members. The current wave of government DEREGULATION and government efforts at PRIVATIZATION are two examples of the school's influence. 2. A loose term for political scientists associated with or influenced by the University of Chicago's Department of Political Science's advocacy of BEHAVIORALISM as the best approach to the study of political phenomena.

chief executive The individual personally accountable to a board of directors or an electorate for the activities of an organization or jurisdiction.

chief of mission The ambassador or other diplomat formally in charge of a diplomatic mission.

chief of state The ceremonial head of a government, such as a king, queen, or president; this is in contrast to the chief executive of a government, such as a prime minister, chancellor, or president. The U.S. presidency combines in one office, one person, the roles of chief of state and chief executive. According to Howard K. Smith (*Time,* January 18, 1971), "The 'chief of state' is like the flag—you have to be deferential. The 'head of government' is nothing but a politician—and you can be rough and relentless with him. We [the United States] combine the two in one person . . . and suffer all the psychological stresses usual when you adopt two contradictory attitudes. [In England] you bow and scrape to the monarch—but you raise hell with the Prime Minister." Jimmy Breslin in *How the Good Guys Finally Won* (1975) put it differently: "The Office of President is such a bastardized thing, half royalty and half democracy, that nobody knows whether to genuflect or spit." *Compare to* COMMANDER IN CHIEF.

child labor Originally, the employment of children in a manner detrimental to their health and social development. Now that the law contains strong child labor prohibitions, the term refers to the employment of children below the legal age limit. Efforts by the labor movement and social reformers to prevent the exploitation of children in the workplace date back well into the nineteenth century. As early as 1842, some states (Connecticut and Massachusetts) legislated a maximum ten-hour workday for children. In

1848, Pennsylvania established a minimum working age of twelve years for factory jobs. But it would be twenty years more before states used inspectors to enforce child labor laws. And it would not be until the late 1930s that federal law would outlaw child labor through the FAIR LABOR STANDARDS ACT OF 1938.

chilling 1. Policies or practices that inhibit others from exercising legal rights or professional responsibilities. In *Dombrowski v. Pfister* (1965), the U.S. Supreme Court first used the phrase "chilling effect" to describe the inhibition of First Amendment rights. Then in *United States v. Jackson* (1968), the Court asserted that "if the provisions had no other purpose or effect than to chill the assertion of Constitutional rights by penalizing those who choose to exercise them, then it would be patently unconstitutional." 2. Employment practices, government regulations, court decisions, and legislation (or the threat of these) that inhibit the free exercise of individual employment rights. A chilling effect tends to keep minorities and women from seeking employment and advancement in an organization even in the absence of formal bars. Other chilling effects may be positive or negative, depending upon the "chillee's" perspective. For example, even discussion of proposed regulations could chill employers and unions into compliance. 3. Political activities that consciously or unconsciously inhibit judges from dealing with some cases fairly and impartially. 4. The effect of legislative redistricting that so weakens one party that it is discouraged from even trying to win the district in the next election.

chop 1. Bureaucratic or political clearance or approval on something; the right to participate in a policy's development. 2. To sign off on a policy or document to indicate approval.

circuit rider A government official who travels from jurisdiction to jurisdiction providing a variety of technical services. The term originates from the days before modern transportation when judges, preachers, and others with occupational specialties would travel a circuit from a home base to clients in various locations and back home again.

citizen 1. A person who owes allegiance to a nation and in turn receives protection from it. 2. A person born or naturalized in the United States. All U.S. citizens are also citizens of the state in which they permanently reside; corporations, which are artificial persons, are citizens of the state in which they were legally created. Citizens may take active or passive roles in the government process. The right to vote gives them the opportunity to help select those who will determine public policy. Beyond simply voting, citizens can assist in electoral campaigns, lobby their representatives, and join with others to form interest groups—all to advance personal interests or to further conceptions of the public interest. 3. A person enjoying special privileges. Roman citizens in their ancient empire had special legal rights. That is why President John F. Kennedy, in his speech in Berlin on June 26, 1963, said, "Two thousand years ago the proudest boast was *civis Romanus sum* [I am a Roman citizen]." 4. A person who is a normal resident of a country in which sovereignty is supposed to belong to the people. This is in contrast to a monarchy, in which a normal resident is a subject owing allegiance to a king or queen.

citizen participation A means of empowering individuals or groups with bargaining power to represent their own interests and to plan and implement their own programs with a view toward social, economic, and political power and control. Some government programs have enabling legislation specifically requiring that citizens affected by the program be involved in its administrative decisions. Presumably, the greater level of citizen participation in a program, the more responsive the program will be to the needs of the community and the more responsive the community will be to the needs of the program. *See also* INTEREST GROUP THEORY; LOBBY.

citizenship The dynamic relation between a citizen and the nation. The concept of citizenship involves rules of what a citizen might do (such as vote), must do (pay taxes), and can refuse to do (pledge allegiance). Increasingly, the concept involves benefits or entitlements that a citizen has a right to demand from government. In some jurisdictions, citizenship is a requirement for public employment.

citizenship, dual 1. Having citizenship in two jurisdictions at the same time. For example, all citizens of the United States are citizens not only of the United States but also of the state in which they reside. 2. Having citizenship in two separate nations at the same time. This is not uncommon. For example, the children of U.S. citizens born abroad are usually considered citizens of the countries in which they were born as well as of the United States.

city A municipal corporation chartered by its state. A central city is the core of a metropolitan area, and an independent city is outside of, or separate from, a metropolitan area. *Compare to* MUNICIPAL CORPORATION. A political subdivision must meet various state requirements before it can qualify for a city charter; for example, it must usually have a population that is larger than a state-established minimum. There has long been a bias against cities in U.S. government and political thought. For example, Thomas Jefferson expressed a common opinion in a December 20, 1787, letter to James Madison: "I think our governments will remain virtuous for many centuries; as long as they are chiefly agricultural; and this will be as long as there shall be vacant lands in any part of America. When they get piled upon one another in large cities, as in Europe, they will become corrupt as in Europe." But the real harm to cities was not in thinking ill of them but in state and federal policies of denying them their fair share of representatives in the U.S. Congress and in state legislatures. This bias existed until the U.S. Supreme Court, beginning in 1962 with *Baker v. Carr,* issued a series of decisions that finally ended malapportionment in favor of rural areas. The cities were finally politically equal.

city beautiful movement The late nineteenth- and early twentieth-century city-planning influence, which emphasized neoclassical architecture, parks, open spaces, monuments, boulevards, and other structures that would create a more benign urban environment.

city clerk A title for a municipal administrator. The duties and responsibilities of a city clerk vary tremendously from recording minutes at council meetings to carrying out many of the duties of a city manager.

city council The legislative branch, typically unicameral, of a municipal government. The duties of city council members vary greatly; but in general the most significant functions include passing ordinances (local laws) and controlling expenditures. *Compare to* COMMISSION FORM OF GOVERNMENT; COUNCIL-MANAGER PLAN/COUNTY-MANAGER SYSTEM; MAYOR-COUNCIL SYSTEM.

city manager The chief executive of the council-manager (originally commission-manager) system of local government; appointed chief executive serving at the pleasure of the council. The concept was created by Richard Childs (1882–1978), an urban reformer, who wanted to replace political bosses with municipal experts. To do this effectively, he created the concept of an administrative chief executive armed with critical administrative powers, such as the appointment and removal of administrative officials, but denied political powers, such as the veto. The dichotomy between administration and politics upon which the system was premised was implemented by putting all the policymaking and political functions into the city council, essentially abolishing a separation of powers in the traditional sense at the local level. The decisionmaking ability of the council was assured by (1) creating a small council, typically from five to nine members, elected through at-large, nonpartisan elections; and (2) permitting the council to hire and fire the city manager, their expert in implementing community policies. Present council-manager systems, found in about half of all U.S. cities, often deviate from this traditional model. Many have large councils, partisan elections, and separately elected mayors, and some of the council members, if not all, are elected from wards or districts; indeed, some recent federal court decisions have required ward elections in some cities. The council-manager system has been criticized by some political scientists as being unresponsive to certain elements of the community, but it has been supported by public administration experts for its effective management in the public interest. In some large cities, a variant of the system uses a chief administrative officer generally appointed by the mayor.

city upon a hill An ideal political community thoroughly fit for others to observe as an example. It comes from a discourse written by John Winthrop, governor of the Massachusetts Bay Colony, in 1630. Robert C. Winthrop, in *Life and Letters of John Winthrop,* reprints the full text, which says in part: "For we must consider that we shall be as a city upon a hill. The eyes of all people are upon us." This is a famous quote in Massachusetts history and presidents Kennedy and Reagan favored using it in speeches.

city-county consolidation The merger of several governments within a county to form one new government unit. Consolidation offers considerable cost savings by reducing overlap. Many consolidated cities and counties have the same name; for example, the City and County of Los Angeles, the City and County of Philadelphia.

civic Belonging to citizens as a whole.

civic action 1. The use of military forces for projects useful to a local population. This has the dual effect of (1) providing needed services in areas such as education, transportation, health, and sanitation, and (2) improving the standing of the military forces with the population. 2. The use of organized volunteers to provide certain community services.

civic center 1. An amorphous term for the location of a city's major public buildings and cultural institutions. 2. A specific grouping of municipal and other public buildings.

civic culture A political culture.

civic organization A formal association of local citizens that works to further its concept of the public interest. Such groups may be purely local, such as a parent-teacher association, or a chapter of a national organization, such as the Rotarians or the League of Women Voters.

civic virtue A demonstrable pride in a city by its citizens, evidenced by their willingness to take responsibility for its public affairs, its physical development, and its cultural activities.

civics 1. That part of political science that deals with the rights and responsibilities of citizenship. 2. The study of the U.S. government.

civil affairs 1. Military government; the administrative process by which an occupying power exercises executive, legislative, and judicial authority over occupied territory. 2. A general term for all those matters concerning the relations between military forces and the surrounding civil authorities.

civil defense 1. The mobilization, organization, and direction of the civilian population, designed to minimize, by passive measures, the effects of enemy action against all aspects of civilian life. 2. The emergency repair or restoration of vital utilities and facilities destroyed or damaged by enemy action.

civil disobedience Henry David Thoreau's (1817–1862) notion from his essay *On the Duty of Civil Disobedience* (1849) that one should not support a government (by paying taxes) if it sanctions policies (slavery) with which one disagrees. Thoreau's civil disobedience implied a willingness to stand up in public and accept the consequences (such as going to jail) of one's disobedience. Now the phrase is used to refer to acts of lawbreaking designed to bring public attention to laws of questionable morality and legitimacy. The most famous practitioners of civil disobedience in the twentieth century were Mohandas K. Gandhi (1869–1948) in India and Martin Luther King, Jr. (1929–1968) in the United States. Those who practice civil disobedience often cite a HIGHER LAW as their reason.

civil liberty 1. A freedom to which an individual has a right, such as the right to personal security, the right to own property, and the right to have children. 2. Freedom from government interference that violates the law.

civil religion 1. A belief in the "American way of life" and an acceptance of and reverence for its sacred icons (such as the flag), symbols (such as the U.S. Constitution), rituals (such as the pledge of allegiance), and secular saints (such as George Washington and Abraham Lincoln). Civil religion, which exists in parallel harmony with traditional religious beliefs, provides a society with a common set of unifying ideals that give the overarching political culture cohesiveness and form. 2. A state-sponsored secular religion designed to replace the "corrupting" aspects of traditional religious practices, such as that implemented after the French Revolution of 1789 and the Russian Revolution of 1917. In neither case did this kind of civil religion "take."

civil rights 1. The protections and privileges given to all U.S. citizens by the U.S. Constitution; for example, freedom of assembly and freedom of religion. 2. The positive acts of government that seek to make constitutional guarantees a reality for all citizens; for example, the Civil Rights Act of 1964. 3. Whatever rights a citizen possesses, even if those rights are slight.

Civil Rights Act of 1866 The first civil rights law after the American Civil War and the adoption of the Thirteenth Amendment, which outlawed slavery. It granted citizenship to all people (former slaves) born in the United States and granted these new citizens the same rights "enjoyed by white citizens."

Civil Rights Act of 1870 The reenactment of the Civil Rights Act of 1866 (with minor changes in wording), following the ratification of the Fourteenth Amendment, to allay doubts about the act's constitutionality.

Civil Rights Act of 1871 A law enacted to enforce the Fourteenth Amendment's equal protection concerns against secret, conspiratorial, and terrorist organizations, such as the Ku Klux Klan, which were thwarting black registration, voting, jury service, and officeholding after the American Civil War. The act also provided civil remedies for the denial of constitutional rights and provided for damages or injunctive relief against any person who "under color of law" deprives another of a right, a privilege, or an immunity secured by federal law or the U.S. Constitution. Thus, it has become the basis for lawsuits by those who feel their constitutional rights have been violated by government officials at any level. This act is often called *Section 1983,* after its numerical designation in Title 42 of the United States Code.

Civil Rights Act of 1875 The civil rights law that first provided for equality in public accommodations. The U.S. Supreme Court declared the act unconstitutional in *Civil Rights Cases* (1883), and no subsequent civil rights legislation was passed until 1957. Yet the essence of the 1875 act was incorporated into the Civil Rights Act of 1964, which was later held constitutional by HEART OF ATLANTA MOTEL V. UNITED STATES.

Civil Rights Act of 1957 The first federal civil rights legislation enacted since the post–American Civil War Reconstruction period; significant primarily as an indication of renewed federal legislative concern with the protection of civil rights. The act accomplished essentially three things: (1) it established the U.S. Commission on Civil Rights to investigate civil rights violations and make recommendations; (2) it created the Civil Rights Division in the Department of Justice; and (3) it enacted limited provisions to enforce the Fifteenth Amendment guarantee of the right to vote.

Civil Rights Act of 1960 The twentieth century's second installment of federal civil rights legislation. The act reinforced certain provisions of the 1957 law, but it also included limited criminal provisions related to racially motivated bombings and burnings and to the obstruction of federal court orders; a clause to enlarge the powers of the Civil Rights Commission; and a section providing for the desegregated education of children of U.S. military personnel. The most important new provision made a remedy available to those improperly denied the right to vote: a voter-referee procedure enforced by the federal courts.

Civil Rights Act of 1964 By far the most significant civil rights legislation in U.S. history, with the possible exception of the Voting Rights Act of 1965. The act consists of eleven titles, of which the most consequential are titles II, VI, and VII. Title II bars discrimination in all places of public accommodation the operations of which affect commerce (including hotels and other places of lodging of more than five rooms, restaurants and other eating places, gasoline stations, theaters, motion picture houses, stadiums, and other places of exhibition and/or entertainment). In Title VI, the U.S. Congress made broad use of its spending power to prohibit racial discrimination in programs or activities receiving federal financial assistance. More important, Title VI goes on to provide that compliance with the nondiscrimination requirement is to be effected by the withholding or termination of federal funds to recipients who have been found guilty of racial discrimination. Title VII makes it an unfair employment practice for an employer or labor organization to refuse to hire, or to discriminate against otherwise, any person because of race, religion, sex, or national origin. Title VII is enforced by the Equal Employment Opportunity Commission, which was also created by the act. *Compare to* AFFIRMATIVE ACTION; EQUAL EMPLOYMENT OPPORTUNITY.

Civil Rights Act of 1968 A law that prohibited discrimination in housing rentals and sales, defined the rights of American Indians, and prescribed penalties for interfering—through violence, intimidation, or other means—with any person's enjoyment of federally protected rights.

civil rights clause That portion of the Fourteenth Amendment that reads: "No State shall make or enforce any law which shall . . . deny to any person within its jurisdiction the equal protection of the laws."

civil rights movement The continuing effort of minorities and women to gain the enforcement of the rights guaranteed by the U.S. Constitution to all citizens. The modern civil rights movement is often dated from 1955, when Rosa Parks, a black seamstress, refused to sit in the back of a bus (where blacks were required by local law to sit) and was arrested. MARTIN LUTHER KING, JR., then led the Montgomery, Alabama, bus boycott, the first of a long series of nonviolent demonstrations that eventually led to the passage of the civil rights acts of 1957, 1960, and 1964. The civil rights movement, although still a major force in U.S. politics, has lost much of the energy, support, and organization that it had in the 1960s.

Civil Rights Restoration Act of 1988 The law that reversed the U.S. Supreme Court decision in *Grove City College v. Bell* (1984), which held that laws prohibiting discrimination in school programs financed in part by federal aid apply only to the specific program and not to the entire school. The new act bans federal funds to an entire institution if even one of its programs or units is guilty of illegal discrimination.

civil servant A government employee; a member of a civil service.

civil service A collective term for all nonmilitary employees of a government. Paramilitary organizations, such as police and fire departments, are always included in civil service counts in the United States. Civil service employment is not the same as merit system employment because all patronage positions (those not covered by merit systems) are included in civil service totals. *Compare to* MERIT SYSTEM.

civil service commission A government agency charged with the responsibility of promulgating the rules and regulations of the civilian personnel management system. Depending upon its legal mandate, a civil service commission may hear employee appeals and take an active or a passive role in personnel management. The commission format was mandated by political, not administrative, considerations. Then, as now, the illogic of divorcing the control of personnel from programmatic authority was recognized. Nevertheless, the more immediate goal of defeating the influences of spoils was paramount, a reasonable rationale for the commission device. Not only would the commission be independent from the party-controlled government, but its three- or five-part membership would be in a better position to resist political pressures than could one administrator. Appellate functions, especially, are better undertaken by a tribunal than by a solitary judge. Not insignificantly, a commission provides a political safety valve by making room for representatives of special interests such as racial or employee groups. It was not very long before the rationale for the independent commission was seriously challenged. As the city manager movement developed early in the twentieth century, managers—nonpartisan reform-type managers at that—found themselves burdened with the same kinds of restrictions upon their authority over personnel that had been designed to thwart the spoilsmen. They felt, quite reasonably, that the personnel function should be integrated with the other administrative functions under the executive. Unlike its private-sector counterpart, the personnel function in government has two frequently conflicting roles. Of necessity, it must attend to service and to control. Is it possible to be an integral member of the management team and the organization's policeman at the same time? In its various manifestations, this is the central dilemma of public personnel administration today. *See* UNITED STATES CIVIL SERVICE COMMISSION.

civil service reform 1. Efforts to improve the status, integrity, and productivity of the civil service at all levels of government by supplanting the SPOILS SYSTEM with the MERIT SYSTEM. 2. Efforts to improve the management and efficiency of the public service. 3. The historical events, the movement, leading up to the enactment of the PENDLETON ACT OF 1883. Depending upon your point of view, modern merit systems are an economic, a political, or a moral development. Economic historians would maintain that the demands of industrial expansion—for example, a dependable postal service and a viable transportation network—necessitated a government service based upon merit. Political analysts could argue rather persuasively that it was the demands of an expanded suffrage and democratic rhetoric that sought to replace favoritism with merit. Economic and political considerations are so intertwined that it is impossible to say which factor is the true midwife of the merit system. The moral impetus behind reform is even more difficult to define. As moral impulses tend to hide economic and political motives, the weight of moral concern undiluted by other considerations is impossible to measure. Nevertheless, the cosmetic effect of moral overtones was of significant aid to the civil service reform movement because it accentuated the social legitimacy of the reform proposals. With the ever-present impetus of achieving maximum public services for minimum tax dollars, business interests were quite comfortable in supporting civil service reform, one of a variety of strategies they used to have power pass from the politicos to themselves. The political parties of the time were almost totally dependent for financing upon assessments made on the wages of their members in public office; with the decline of patronage, the parties had to seek new funding sources, and U.S. business was more than willing to assume this new financial burden—as well as its concomitant influence. There is no doubt that civil service reform would have come about without the 1881 assassination of President James A. Garfield by a disappointed office seeker; there is also no doubt that the assassination helped. Although Garfield's death was certainly instrumental in creating the appropriate climate for the passage of the Pendleton Act, historians maintain that the Republican reversals during the midterm elections of 1882 had the more immediate effect on enactment. Civil service reform had been the deciding issue in various congressional contests. Thus, when President Chester A. Arthur signed the Pendleton Act into law on January 16, 1883, and created the UNITED STATES CIVIL SERVICE COMMISSION, it was essentially a gesture by reluctant politicians to assuage public opinion and the reform elements.

Civil Service Reform Act of 1883 *See* PENDLETON ACT.

Civil Service Reform Act of 1978 The law mandating that (in January 1979) the U.S. Civil Service Commission would be divided into two agencies: an Office of Personnel Management (OPM) to serve as the personnel arm of the chief executive; and an independent Merit Systems Protection Board (MSPB) to provide recourse for aggrieved employees. In addition, the act created the Federal Labor Relations Authority (FLRA) to oversee federal labor management policies. On March 2, 1978, President Jimmy Carter, with the enthusiastic support of his Civil Service Commission leadership, submitted his civil service reform proposals to the U.S. Congress. On that same day, before the National Press Club, he further called his proposals to the attention of the Congress by charging that the present federal personnel system had become a "bureaucratic maze which neglects merit, tolerates poor performance, and permits abuse of legitimate employee rights, and mires every personnel action in red tape, delay, and confusion." The reform bill faced considerable opposition from federal employee unions (which thought the bill was too management oriented) and from veterans' groups (which were aghast at the bill's curtailment of veterans' preferences). The unions lost. The veterans won. The bill passed almost intact thanks in great measure to the efforts of Alan K. "Scotty" Campbell (1923–1998), the last chairman of the U.S. Civil Service Commission, who was the architect of the reform act and its most fervent advocate before Congress. Campbell served as the first director of the new Office of Personnel Management during 1979–1980. *See also* FEDERAL LABOR RELATIONS AUTHORITY; MERIT SYSTEMS PROTECTION BOARD; OFFICE OF PERSONNEL MANAGEMENT; SENIOR EXECUTIVE SERVICE.

civilian control The subordination of a nation's military to its civil authorities. The U.S. Constitution (Article II, Section 2), by making the U.S. president "commander in chief of the army and the navy," mandates civilian control in the United States. Even though some generals have become president of the United States, they were elected as civilians.

class 1. A grouping of people or things. 2. A stratum in a hierarchical social structure. 3. A social rank. The United States has often been referred to as a classless society because there are no formal, legal class distinctions even though there are many informal, subtle ones. The most famous pronouncement on class in the United States was made by U.S. Supreme Court Justice John Marshall Harlan in a dissenting opinion in *Plessy v. Ferguson* (1896): "There is in this country no superior, dominant, ruling class of citizens. There is no caste here. Our Constitution is color-blind, and neither knows nor tolerates classes among citizens."

class action A search for a judicial remedy that one or more persons may undertake on behalf of themselves and all others in similar situations. Class action suits are common against manufacturers who have sold defective products that have later harmed significant numbers of unsuspecting people.

class struggle The conflict between competing economic groups in a capitalist society; the continuous competition between social classes over resources and power. In their 1848 *Communist Manifesto,* Karl Marx and Friedrich Engels wrote that "the history of all hitherto existing society is the history of class struggles." Marxists believe that the tension between the exploiting bourgeoisie and the exploited working-class masses (the proletariat) eventually leads to revolution. This has not happened in U.S. society, in large measure because the economic system has made most working-class people middle class in income and outlook.

class warfare 1. Conflict between social classes; classically, the peasants against the aristocracy. 2. A Republican Party term for criticism of their domestic policies; its clever allusion to the Marxist class struggle implies that their critics are communist dupes or worse.

classified information 1. Secrets, usually military. 2. A matter in any form that requires protection in the interests of national security. There is constant discussion, sometimes classified, that too much information is classified for too long.

classified service Positions in a governmental jurisdiction that are included in a formal merit system. Excluded from the classified service are all exempt appointments. The term *classified service* predates the concept of position classification and has no immediate bearing on POSITION CLASSIFICATION concepts or practices.

classify 1. To group bureaucratic positions according to their duties and responsibilities and to assign a class title. *See* POSITION CLASSIFICATION. 2. To make secret; to determine that official information requires, in the interests of national security, a certain level of protection against unauthorized disclosure. 3. To categorize as an analytical technique.

Clausewitz, Karl Maria von (1780–1831) The Prussian general who wrote *On War* (1832), the most famous book on military strategy and tactics; the father of modern strategic thought. Clausewitz developed the concept of absolute war, which he saw as the total defeat of the enemy and as having no limits. Yet, for Clausewitz, this was a theoretical abstraction; he saw real war as differing from the absolute in several ways. Not only was real war full of FRICTION, but it was also determined by the political context; that is, it was "a continuation of politics by other means" and democracy and nationalism would have a profound impact on future wars. His notion of the political control of military actions endeared Clausewitz to strategic analysts, often described as neo-Clausewitzians, in the nuclear age. *See also* FOG OF WAR.

clean hands A legal phrase meaning "free from guilt or dishonesty." A legal maxim holds: "He who comes to equity must come with clean hands." Thomas Jefferson wrote in a March 29, 1807, letter to Count Diodati: "I have the consolation . . . of having added nothing to my private fortune during my public service, and of retiring with hands as clean as they are empty."

clear 1. To approve or authorize or to obtain approval or authorization. For example, a bill may clear one house of a legislature, meaning that it has been approved by that house. 2. To be no longer suspected of committing a crime. 3. To pass a security clearance. 4. The final approval of a check by the bank upon which it was drawn. 5. Free of taxes; a house may be clear for sale after its back taxes have been paid.

clear and present danger The U.S. Supreme Court's test on whether the exercise of the First Amendment's right of free speech should be restricted or punished. This was first articulated by Associate Justice Oliver Wendell Holmes in *Schenck v. United States* (1919), when he wrote that "the most stringent protection of free speech would not protect a man in falsely shouting 'fire' in a theatre and causing a panic." Holmes created the test that has often been used in free-speech cases: "The question in every case is whether the words used are used in such circumstances and are of such a nature as to create a clear and present danger that they will bring about the substantive evils that Congress has a right to prevent."

client state 1. A state the interests of which are subordinated to another state's foreign or domestic policies. For example, during the COLD WAR, many of the states of Eastern Europe were client states of the Soviet Union. 2. A state involved in a relationship with a stronger power or patron. Although client states are often crucially dependent upon their patrons, on occasion they are still able to exercise what is sometimes described as "reverse influence." Some of this influence results from the stake a patron often has in the continued existence or success of the client.

clientele Individuals or groups who benefit from the services provided by an agency.

clientele agency A loose term for a government organization of which the prime mission is to promote, serve, or represent the interests of a particular group.

closed shop A union security provision that would require an employer to hire and retain only union members in good standing. The Labor-Management Relations (Taft-Hartley) Act of 1947 made closed shops illegal.

clout To hit someone with your fist. It has grown to be a slang term for influence or power; it implies an ability to get things done through informal, sometimes nonlegal, personal (as opposed to official) channels, whether the thing is the passage of a bill, a patronage job for a constituent, or the getting of some important person on the phone.

coaching Face-to-face discussions with a subordinate, the purpose being to effect a change in the subordinate's behavior.

coalition 1. A temporary joining of political actors to advance legislation or to elect candidates. The actors in a coalition are often poles apart on many issues but are able to put their continuing differences aside in the interest of joining to advance (or defeat) the issue at hand. Legislative coalitions tend to form around specific issues as the legislators sort themselves out, whether for or against a bill or policy. The leaders of a coalition may or may not occupy formal leadership positions in the legislature or their party. 2. An agreement between political parties in a parliamentary system to form a government. 3. A group of U.S. Supreme Court justices who tend to take the same philosophic approach to judicial decisionmaking. 4. A group of international actors who temporarily combine to further a common interest such as the waging of war against a common enemy or the passing of a proposal in an international conference. 5. A loose synonym for an alliance.

code A comprehensive collection of statutory laws or agency regulations. For example, the U.S. Code is the official compilation of federal laws. A code differs from a collection of statutes in that codes are organized by topics for easy reference rather than in the chronological order in which the various laws were passed.

code, building A usually local, legislatively enacted regulation prescribing construction standards.

code, housing A local, legislatively enacted regulation establishing the minimal conditions under which dwellings are fit for humans to live in.

code law Law found in law books, as opposed to equity law, which a judge makes up (based on related precedents) to deal with a new situation.

code name A word used to refer to a military, intelligence, or diplomatic initiative that must be kept secret until the operational aspects of the event can be announced. Many code words are used well after the operation is over. For example, "Overlord" is still used by historians to refer to the Allied preparations for the June 6, 1944, D-Day invasion of France.

code of conduct 1. The rules governing how soldiers should conduct themselves if captured by the enemy. These vary from nation to nation but usually imply a duty to try to escape, a refusal to make disloyal statements, and a refusal to give information beyond personal identification. 2. An international instrument that specifies acceptable international behavior by nation states or multinational corporations. 3. A compendium of ethical norms promulgated by an organization to guide the behavior of its members. Many government agencies have formal codes or STANDARDS OF CONDUCT for their employees. 4. Rules of behavior that may be tacit rather than explicit and tend to be based upon prudence rather than upon law or morality.

code of ethics A statement of professional standards of conduct to which the practitioners of a profession say they subscribe. Codes of ethics are usually not legally binding, so they should not be taken too seriously as constraints on behavior. They sometimes become significant factors in political campaigns when questionable behavior by one side or the other is attacked or defended as being within or without a professional code. Professional groups also hide behind codes as a way of protecting (or criticizing) a member subject to public attack. President Ronald Reagan took the attitude "that people shouldn't require a code of ethics if they're going to be in government. They should be determined, themselves, that their conduct is going to be beyond reproach" (*U.S. News and World Report,* January 19, 1981). Nevertheless, the problem remains that some people need help in determining just what constitutes ethical behavior. *Compare to* STANDARDS OF CONDUCT.

code word 1. A word or phrase whose use in a political context alters its meaning. Code words are often used when it is not politic or respectable to address an issue directly. For example, in the early days of the civil rights movement, many Southern politicians emphasized that they were in favor of "states rights," a code word for opposition to full civil rights for blacks. Whenever world oil prices start to fall dramatically, politicians from oil-producing states start talking about the need for stable oil prices. In this context, "stable" becomes a code word for higher prices. 2. A word or phrase in another language that means one thing literally but has a different meaning to most of its native speakers. For example, the Japanese phrase *zensho shimasu* literally means "I will do my best," and as such it sounds like an accommodating answer during diplomatic negotiations. But to many Japanese, the phrase really means "no way," which is quite a different answer. Code words should be distinguished from buzz words, which merely refer to the technical vocabularies of various occupational specialties. 3. A CODE NAME.

coercion 1. The exertion of influence through threats to inflict harm or costs unless the target behaves in the desired fashion. Coercion is often contrasted with brute force, and it is generally agreed that coercion is far more cost effective. Thomas Schelling in *Arms and Influence* (1966) describes the difference as one between taking something and making someone give it to you. 2. The use of threats by a government for the purpose of intimidating the population and maintaining its position.

coexistence 1. An international situation wherein nations embracing differing social systems and conflicting ideologies refrain from war. Coexistence is less than peace, but preferable to war. 2. A contentious relation in which genuine rivals (political, organizational) purposely refrain from the direct confrontation that might otherwise be expected of them.

COG *See* COUNCIL OF GOVERNMENT.

cognitive dissonance A theory developed by Leon Festinger in *A Theory of Cognitive Dissonance* (1957) that is based on the assumption that people like balance or consistency between their beliefs and their perceptions. A disconnection between these two things is highly disconcerting for an individual, the result being that efforts are generally made to keep the two things in accord. Because belief systems tend to have an overall cohesion and information comes in discrete bits, it is therefore often easier to downgrade or ignore the information than to change the beliefs—thereby seeing simply what one expects to see. When it is no longer possible to ignore information that contradicts beliefs, a major shift occurs in belief systems. Too often, however, such a transformation comes only after traumatic events have highlighted the gap between the beliefs and reality.

cohort 1. One-tenth of a Roman legion. 2. In the social sciences, a group identified as having common characteristics for the purposes of study, usually over time. Cohorts can be identified by the age of the year they first had a common experience, such as graduating college, entering the military, or winning election to the U.S. Congress.

COLA *See* COST-OF-LIVING ADJUSTMENT.

cold war 1. War by other than military means (a "hot war") and that emphasizes ideological conflict, brinksmanship, and consistently high international tension. This concept is not new. As Thomas Hobbes wrote in *Leviathan* (1651): "War consist not in battle only, or the act of fighting; but in a tract of time, wherein the will to contend by battle is sufficiently known: and therefore the notion of time, is to be considered in the nature of war; as it is in the nature of weather. For as the nature of foul weather, lyeth not in a shower or two of rain; but in an inclination thereto of many days together; so the nature of war, consists not in actual fighting; but in the known disposition thereto, during all the time there is no assurance to the contrary. All other time is peace." 2. The hostile but nonlethal relations between the United States and the Soviet Union that began in 1945 after World War II and ended in 1989 when the Soviet Union disintegrated. Herbert Bayard Swope (1882–1958) first used this phrase in speeches he wrote for Bernard Baruch (1870–1965). After Baruch told the Senate War Investigating Committee on October 24, 1948, "Let us not be deceived—today we are in the midst of a cold war," the press picked up the phrase, and it became part of everyday speech. *Compare to* CONTAINMENT. 3. Behind-the-scenes tension between two parties who cannot openly confront each other.

collateral damage The unintended or incidental destruction that occurs during a military attack. For example, a school or hospital that is bombed by an air raid directed against a nearby enemy airfield can be said to have suffered collateral damage. Such excuses are usually not much consolation to the victims and their families.

collective bargaining Bargaining on behalf of a group of employees as opposed to individual bargaining where workers represent only themselves. *Collective bargaining* is a comprehensive term that encompasses the negotiating process that leads to a contract between labor and management on wages, hours, and other conditions of employment, as well as the subsequent administration and interpretation of the signed contract. Collective bargaining is, in effect, the continuous relation between union representatives and employers. These are four basic stages of collective bargaining: (1) the establishment of organizations for bargaining, (2) the formulation of demands, (3) the negotiation of demands, and (4) the administration of the labor agreement. *See also* ABILITY TO PAY; EXECUTIVE ORDER 10988; EXECUTIVE ORDER 11491; FEDERAL LABOR RELATIONS AUTHORITY; LABOR-MANAGEMENT RELATIONS ACT OF 1947; NATIONAL LABOR RELATIONS ACT OF 1935; POSTAL REORGANIZATION ACT OF 1970.

collective good Anything of value (such as clean air, safe streets, and tax loopholes) that cannot be denied to a group member. A group can vary from an entire society to a subset of it. Mancur Olson in *The Logic of Collective Action* (1965) finds that small groups are better at obtaining collective goods. The larger the potential group, the less likely it is that most will contribute to obtain the "good." Just as in military strategy, concentration is the key. Thus, a particular industry is better able to obtain tax loopholes for itself than the general public is able to obtain overall tax equity.

collective negotiations An alternate term for collective bargaining, which, for the public sector, may sometimes be legally or semantically unacceptable.

color 1. Having the appearance as opposed to the reality of something. For example, "color of law" means an action has the mere semblance of legality. An illegal act done under color of law may have the apparent authority of the law behind it but is, nevertheless, illegal. **2.** The general background and human interest aspects of a press report on a candidate, policy, or party that makes it more interesting to read; information that brightens up and makes bare facts come alive.

comity 1. The constitutional provision that "the citizens of each state shall be entitled to all privileges and immunities of citizens in the several states." **2.** A courtesy by which one nation, court, or house of a legislature defers the exercise of some authority to some other nation, court, or house.

commander in chief 1. The military or naval officer in charge of all allied forces in a theater of operations. **2.** The authority granted under Article III, Section 2, of the U.S. Constitution that "the president shall be commander in chief of the army and the navy of the United States and of the militia of the several states when called into the actual service of the United States." The last president to exercise his authority as commander in chief to command troops in the field was James Madison during the War of 1812. At Bladensburg, Maryland, the Americans under their president met the British and were soundly defeated. The British then marched on Washington, D.C., to burn the White House and other public buildings. No subsequent president, while in office, has sought to lead men in battle. **3.** The officer in charge of a branch of a service, or of all services in a given area. *See also* CIVILIAN CONTROL.

commerce clause The commerce power (Article I, Section 8, of the U.S. Constitution) that allows the U.S. Congress to control trade with foreign countries and among the states. If something "affects interstate commerce" (such as labor unions and product safety), it is fair game for federal government regulation.

commercial market strategy A programmatic approach whereby government subsidizes the delivery of goods or services to a target group by serving as bill payer as clients seek designated benefits from existing market outlets. For example, beneficiaries of Medicare seek medical care from a broad range of physicians and hospitals and government pays a portion of their bills.

commission 1. A group charged with directing a government function, whether on an ad hoc or a permanent basis. Commissions tend to be used (1) when it is desirable to have bipartisan leadership, (2) when their functions are of a quasijudicial nature, or (3) when it is deemed important to have a wide representation of skills, ethnic groups, and regions. 2. In the international context, a United Nations group charged with a particular subject, such as human rights. 3. A written authorization assigning rank or authority either to a civilian or to a military officer. 4. To put into use, as when the navy commissions a ship. 5. A payment based on a percentage of sales or profit.

commission form of government The original reform structure of urban governance that replaced the city council. It put all the executive, legislative, and administrative powers into one commission. As a collective group, the commission is the local legislature, each member serving individually as an administrator of a department or a set of departments. The obvious problem of coordinating administration in such a system led to its decline. It was first used in 1900 in Galveston, Texas, following a devastating hurricane; many of these commissioners were appointed by the governor. The commission form of local government has suffered a steady decline in popularity in recent decades.

Commission on Civil Rights A federal agency the role of which is to encourage constructive steps toward equal opportunity for all. The commission, created by the CIVIL RIGHTS ACT OF 1957, investigates complaints, holds public hearings, and collects and studies information on denials of equal protection under the law because of race, color, religion, sex, and/or national origin. The commission can make findings of fact in cases involving, for example, voting rights, the administration of justice, and the equality of opportunity in education, employment, and housing; but it has no enforcement authority.

commission, presidential A committee sanctioned by the president of the United States to investigate a matter of public concern and to issue recommendations for improvement. The modern presidential commission can be traced back to the British Commission of Inquiry. Ever since the American

Civil War, Americans have found the presidential commission a useful means of dealing with important national issues. There is great public satisfaction to be had in bringing together a group of responsible, respected, supposedly objective but knowledgeable citizens to examine and report upon a national problem or major disaster. These commissions have proven to be handy devices for modern presidents who, when faced with an intractable problem, such as crime, pornography, or urban riots, can, at slight expense, appoint a commission as a gesture to indicate their awareness of constituent distress. Whether that gesture has meaning or sincerity beyond itself is inconsequential for its immediate effect. By the time a commission makes its report, six months to a year later, attention will have been diverted to other issues, and the recommendations can be safely pigeonholed or curtailed.

commissioner 1. A member of the governing board of a government regulatory agency such as the Federal Trade Commission. 2. One member of a multiheaded executive in some local governments, especially counties.

committee 1. One part of a larger group appointed to perform a specialized service on either a one-time or a continuing basis. 2. A subdivision of a legislature that prepares legislation for action by the respective house or that makes investigations as directed by the respective house. Most standing (full) committees are divided into subcommittees that study legislation, hold hearings, and report their recommendations to the full committee. Only the full committee can report legislation for action by the entire legislature.

committee staff Legislative aides employed by legislative committees as opposed to the personal staff of the legislators.

committee system The means by which legislatures organize themselves; all proposed policies and laws are reviewed by various committees before formal consideration by the entire body. The committee system allows legislators to develop expertise and influence in particular areas. Woodrow Wilson wrote in *Congressional Government* (1885) that "Congress in session is Congress on public exhibition, whilst Congress in its committee-rooms is Congress at work."

committee, conference A meeting between the representatives of the two houses of a legislature to reconcile the differences about the provisions of a bill. The most usual occurrence is when a bill passes one house but the amendments are unacceptable to the other house. After attempting to resolve the points in disagreement, the conference committee issues a report to each house. If the report is accepted by both houses, the bill is then passed and sent to the president. If rejected by either house, the matter in disagreement comes up for disposition anew, as if there had been no conference. Unless all differences between the houses are finally adjusted, the bill fails. The conference committee can sometimes have a dramatic effect on a bill. As President Ronald Reagan once said, "You know, if an orange and an apple went into conference consultations, it might come out a pear" (*New York Times,* December 18, 1982).

committee, select A committee established by the U.S. House of Representatives or the U.S. Senate, usually for a limited period and generally for a strictly temporary purpose, usually investigative. When that function has been carried out, the select committee automatically expires. A select committee is also known as a "special committee."

committee, standing A regular committee of a legislature that deals with bills within a specified subject area. In the U.S. Congress, each of the two principal parties has a committee on committees; this committee recommends assignments subject to caucus or conference approval.

common law The totality of judge-made laws that initially developed in England and continued to evolve in the United States. Whenever this kind of law, which is based on custom, culture, habit, and previous judicial decisions, proved inadequate, it was supplanted by statutory laws made by legislatures. But the common law tradition, based upon PRECEDENT, is still the foundation of the U.S. legal system, even though much of what was originally common law has been converted into statutes over the years.

commonwealth The notion of Thomas Hobbes (1588–1679) and other philosophers of his era that the members of a social order have a common weal that it is in their collective interest to preserve and protect. Common weal evolved into commonwealth, which came to mean the modern, centralized state. Thus the republic established in Britain under Oliver Cromwell from 1649 to 1660 was called the *Commonwealth.* Four U.S. states (Pennsylvania, Virginia, Massachusetts, and Kentucky) are formally commonwealths rather than states.

communique 1. A formal announcement by a government. **2.** Joint statements made by parties during or after diplomatic sessions.

communitarianism An overarching philosophy of public-spiritedness, moral commitment to one's neighbors (expansively defined), and greater civic engagement through democratic participation and volunteerism.

community 1. A group of people living in an identifiable area. This can range from the community of man, which occupies the Earth, to the Hispanic community of San Antonio, Texas, or to the Jewish community of Miami, Florida. **2.** A group having common interests, such as the medical community, and the Catholic community. **3.** All the people living in a particular locality. **4.** A housing development. **5.** Descriptive of shared goods, such as a community swimming pool in a city, or community property in a marriage. **6.** A euphemism for the vote. Thus if a candidate asks the campaign manager, "How is the Hispanic community today?" the question does not inquire about their general health or economic welfare; it merely asks, "How many of them plan to vote for me today?" 7. A recognized ESTABLISHMENT of influential individuals or organizations; for example, *see* INTELLIGENCE COMMUNITY.

community control An extreme form of citizen participation in which democratically selected representatives of a neighborhood-sized government jurisdiction are given administrative and financial control over such local programs as education, land use, and police protection.

community development 1. An approach to the administration of social and economic development programs in which government officials are dispatched to the field to act as catalysts at the local level who encourage local residents to form groups, to define their own needs, and to develop self-help projects. The government then provides technical and material assistance and helps the community establish institutions (such as farm cooperatives) to carry on the development programs after the officials have left. 2. Local government efforts to plan for and finance the physical development of the jurisdiction. In this context, community development block GRANTS have been available from the Department of Housing and Urban Development for a variety of activities, such as land acquisition, new parks and playgrounds, historic preservation, and street and drainage improvements.

community policing Creating a problemsolving partnership between the citizens of a locality and their police; thus they work together to improve the quality of life in their community.

community power Usually, the study or description of the political order, formal and informal, of a segment of U.S. local governance.

community relations program The totality of efforts by military and paramilitary organizations (such as local police) to create better understanding and acceptance of their missions in their local communities.

community service A punishment mandated by a court for people convicted of crimes that do not warrant a prison sentence. These are usually nonviolent offenders who at their own expense must work in, for example, nursing homes or drug rehabilitation programs for a given amount of time. Community service often becomes controversial when high-profile figures in politics and entertainment receive what some consider to be very lenient sentences.

comparable worth Equitable compensation for doing a job; comparable worth is determined by judging a job's value to an organization compared to that of other jobs in the organization. The basic issue of comparable worth is whether Title VII of the Civil Rights Act of 1964 makes it unlawful for an employer to pay one sex at a lesser rate than the other when the job is of comparable worth or value. For example, should a graduate nurse be paid less than a gardener? Or should a beginning librarian who has a master's degree be paid less than a beginning manager who has a master's degree? Historically, nurses and librarians have been paid less than those in occupations of comparable worth because they were considered women's jobs. Comparable worth as a legal concept and as a social issue directly challenges traditional and market assumptions about the worth of a job.

comparative advantage The position a country or a region has in the production of those goods it can produce relatively more efficiently than other goods. Modern trade theory says that, regardless of the country's productivity or labor costs relative to those of other countries, it should produce for export those goods in which it has the greatest comparative advantage and import those in which it has the greatest comparative disadvantage. The country that has few economic strengths will find it advantageous to devote its productive energies to those lines in which its disadvantage is least marked, provided the opportunity to trade with other areas is open to it. The comparative advantage theory was first proposed by the English economist David Ricardo (1772–1823) in 1817. *Compare to* ABSOLUTE ADVANTAGE.

compassionate conservatism President George W. Bush's phrase for his administration's policies to help the poor; in Bush's own words (from the foreword to Marvin Olasky's 2000 *Compassionate Conservatism*), "a concerted effort to help [the poor] bring lasting change into their lives."

competitive service A general term for civilian positions in a government jurisdiction that are not specifically excepted from MERIT SYSTEM regulations. Employees in the competitive service would have competed for their jobs by sitting for competitive examinations.

compliance 1. Acting in accordance with the law. Voluntary compliance is the basis of a civil society. No government has the resources to force every citizen to comply with every criminal and civil law. Consequently, all governments are more dependent upon compliance than they would like to admit. The best example of massive voluntary compliance is the U.S. federal income tax system, which is essentially administered by self-assessment and voluntary payment. **2.** A technical term used by funding agencies as a criterion to judge whether a grantee is acting (i.e., spending grant funds) in accordance with the grantor's policies or preset guidelines.

comprehensive plan/master plan A local government document that establishes long-term policies for the physical development of the jurisdiction. These documents are often required by funding agencies, such as the federal government or the states, that want to see where a proposed funding request fits into the "big picture" before they make a grant.

conciliation 1. The process of bringing together two sides to agree upon a voluntary compromise. **2.** An international dispute-settling process whereby a disagreement is submitted to a standing or ad hoc independent commission that examines the facts of the case and makes a recommendation for settlement. However, this recommendation is merely advisory and the parties, unlike those undergoing a similar process in ARBITRATION, are under no formal obligation to accept it.

conclusum 1. A diplomatic note that sums up international negotiations. **2.** A joint memorandum by two or more parties to a negotiation that summarizes agreements to date.

concurrent jurisdiction A legal situation in which two or more court systems (such as state and federal) or two or more agencies (such as the local police and the Federal Bureau of Investigation) have the power to deal with a problem or case.

concurrent power A power held jointly by both federal and state governments. Taxation is a major example.

condemn 1. To pronounce a negative judgment on an individual, an action, or an event. **2.** To pronounce a negative judgment in a criminal case. **3.** To impose the death penalty. **4.** To exercise public domain by taking over private property with payment to the owner, who may or may not have been willing to sell. **5.** To declare that a property is unfit for use or occupancy. This usually means that it must be vacated, renovated, or torn down.

conditionality An economic policy demanded of a THIRD WORLD borrower by the International Monetary Fund or other lender as a condition of a loan. Typical conditionalities are austerity measures taken to reduce inflation, currency devaluations, and food subsidies. Some Third World analysts consider conditionalities a new form of colonialism: another means by which the West seeks to continue dominating its former colonies.

conflict of interest 1. The classic conflict facing a member of a national legislature when the narrow interests of constituents conflict with the broader interests of the nation as a whole. *See* EDMUND BURKE. **2.** A situation in which the personal interest of an officeholder may influence or appear to influence that officeholder's decision on a matter of public interest. Many high-level officials avoid questions of conflicting interests by putting their investments into blind trusts. Officeholders are wise to avoid conflict as well as appearance of it. A common means of avoiding conflict is for the officeholder to abstain from voting or acting on an issue in which a personal benefit may exist. Thus judges and administrators may withdraw from situations where their stock ownership or other interests might be perceived as being benefited. The ETHICS IN GOVERNMENT ACT OF 1978 seeks to avoid conflict of interest by high-level federal employees even after they leave government employment by putting postemployment restrictions on their relations with the agencies they once worked for.

conflict of laws 1. Having the laws of more than one jurisdiction apply to a case. The judge must then choose which jurisdiction's laws are most applicable. This problem is particularly thorny when a state law precedes federal legislation; the conflict comes after the federal legislation takes effect. 2. Having the laws of more than one nation apply to a case involving private parties (as opposed to the nations themselves); the problem then becomes one of international law.

conflict resolution 1. The settlement of disputes by nonviolent and usually nonjudicial methods. 2. The professional practice of negotiation in a generic sense. 3. Organizational efforts to deal with conflict in a constructive sense as opposed to viewing it as a deviancy to be crushed.

conflict theory 1. Theories about the causes and course of military, diplomatic, and interpersonal conflicts. 2. An explicitly methodological approach to conflict that sets out to develop hypotheses about the causes of conflict and then systematically examines the empirical evidence in an effort either to verify or to refute these hypotheses. 3. An approach to conflict that is interested in all manifestations of conflict, whether at the domestic or international level, and that tends to see similar dynamic processes at work in all conflicts.

congressional budget The U.S. budget as set forth by the U.S. Congress in a concurrent resolution on the budget. These resolutions include (1) the appropriate level of total budget outlays and of total new budget authority; (2) an estimate of budget outlays and new budget authority for each major functional category; (3) the amount, if any, of the surplus or deficit in the budget; (4) the recommended level of federal revenues; and (5) the appropriate level of the public debt.

Congressional Budget and Impoundment Control Act of 1974 A major restructuring of the congressional budgeting process. The act's Declaration of Purposes states that it is essential (1) to assure effective congressional control over the budgetary process; (2) to provide for yearly congressional determination of the appropriate level of federal revenues and expenditures; (3) to provide a system of impoundment control; (4) to establish national budget priorities; and (5) to provide for the furnishing of information by the executive branch in a manner that will assist the U.S. Congress in discharging its duties. The significant features of the act are (1) the creation of the House and Senate budget committees; (2) the creation of the CONGRESSIONAL BUDGET OFFICE; (3) the adoption of a new appropriations process for the Congress; (4) the adoption of a new budget calendar for the Congress;

(5) the establishment of a new fiscal year (October 1 through September 30) to deal more rationally with the timing of the budget cycles; (6) the creation of a current services budget; and (7) the creation of two new forms of impoundments—recisions and deferrals—both of which must be submitted to the Congress. *Compare to* IMPOUNDMENT.

Congressional Budget Office (CBO) A support agency of the U.S. Congress created in 1974 by the Congressional Budget and Impoundment Control Act to provide the Congress with basic budget data and with analyses of alternative fiscal, budgetary, and programmatic policy issues, independent of the executive branch. The misrepresentation of budget estimates is a tool used by program advocates as well as by program opponents. An executive branch may seek to overestimate or underestimate expenditure or revenue and thus provide an excuse for cost cutting or for minimizing the perceived budget deficit. For this reason, Congress obtains its own estimates from the Congressional Budget Office, which it regards as more reliable than the president's Office of Management and Budget.

congressional government 1. A government dominated by the legislature. This was the condition of U.S. government during most of the nineteenth century (the American Civil War being the major period of exception). 2. A government in which the legislature is separate from the executive and independent of it. This is in contrast to a cabinet form of government, in which an executive is chosen by a legislature and made responsible to it. WOODROW WILSON published the classic account of congressional government, *Congressional Government: A Study in American Politics* (1885), in which he observed that authority "is perplexingly subdivided and distributed, and responsibility has to be hunted down in out-of-the-way corners."

congressional oversight *See* OVERSIGHT.

congressional veto *See* VETO, LEGISLATIVE.

conscription The authority of the U.S. Congress to demand the enrollment of men in military service. The U.S. Supreme Court held in *Selective Draft Law Cases* (1918) that the power of conscription is implied by the constitutional power to raise armies. When the U.S. Constitution was written, it was understood that the assembling of state militias was to be the basis of all significant military forces; therefore, conscription was never directly addressed in the document. The founders were concerned that a national army raised the threat of "royal" forces under the command of a "king." The story goes that at the Constitutional Convention one of the delegates moved that "the standing army be restricted to five thousand men at any one time." George Washington, as chairman of the convention, could not offer an amending motion himself, so he asked another delegate to suggest an amendment stating that "no foreign army should invade the United States at any time with more than three thousand troops." Although the last period of conscription in the United States ended in 1973, eighteen-year-old males are still required to register for it—just in case Congress suddenly decides to reinstate it.

consent order A regulatory agency procedure to induce voluntary compliance with its policies. A consent order usually takes the form of a formal agreement whereby an industry or company agrees to stop a practice in exchange for the agency's cessation of legal action against it. *Compare to* CEASE-AND-DESIST ORDER.

conservation The protection, preservation, replenishment, and prudent use of natural resources, which indicates the planned use of public lands, forests, wildlife, water, and minerals. Theodore Roosevelt was the first president who was serious about conservation. In *The Outlook* (August 27, 1910), he wrote that "here in the United States we turn our rivers and streams into sewers and dumping-grounds, we pollute the air, we destroy forests, and exterminate fishes, birds, and mammals—not to speak of vulgarizing charming landscapes with hideous advertisements. But at long last it looks as if our people . . . are doing all they can for the Conservation movement." Not quite all! This was the same era when Joseph G. Cannon, the Speaker of the House (from 1903–1911), had a policy of "not one cent for scenery." Federal conservation programs and policies have a long history: The greatest efforts at conservation in the continental United States were made during the administrations of Theodore Roosevelt (1901–1909) and Franklin D. Roosevelt (1933–1945). The Department of the Interior, established in 1849, is the custodian of the national government's natural resources. Conservation policy over the years has tended to be a fight for the soul—or control—of that department. Since the 1970s, conservation groups, such as the Sierra Club and the National Audubon Society, have joined with other groups interested in environmental policy to take a more active role in lobbying for conservation issues. The basic policy issue in conservation has always been whether preservation or controlled use would win out over industrial exploitation, or vice versa.

consolidated government *See* METROPOLITAN GOVERNMENT.

constable A law enforcement officer in a town or township. The word comes from the Latin *comes,* meaning "companion," and *stabulum,* meaning "stable." So the first constables were stable attendants. Over the centuries, they worked themselves up to be guards; thus the modern meaning.

constant dollar A dollar value adjusted for changes in prices. Constant dollars are derived by dividing current dollar amounts by an appropriate price index, a process generally known as "deflating." The result is a constant-dollar series as it would presumably exist if prices and transactions were the same in all subsequent years as in the base year. Changes in such a series would reflect only changes in the real volume of goods and services. Constant-dollar figures are commonly used for computing the gross national product and its components and for estimating total budget outlays. *Compare to* CURRENT DOLLAR.

constitution 1. The basic political and legal structures prescribing the rules by which a government operates. Thomas Paine in *The Rights of Man* (1792) correctly noted that "a constitution is a thing antecedent to a government, and a government is only the creature of a constitution. The constitution of a country is not the act of its government, but of the people constituting a government." There are three kinds of constitutions: (1) written, based upon a specific document supplemented by judicial interpretations and traditional practices; (2) unwritten, where there is no specific document but many laws, judicial decisions, and accepted practices that in their totality establish the principles of governance; and (3) autocratic, where a dictator or an elite holds all power and defines governance at will—even though the state may have a legal document, called a *constitution,* that calls for democratic governance. James Madison wrote in *Federalist* No. 57 that "the aim of every political constitution is, or ought to be, first to obtain for rulers men who possess most wisdom to discern, and most virtue to pursue, the common good of the society; and in the next place, to take the most effectual precautions for keeping them virtuous whilst they continue to hold their public trust." 2. The Constitution of the United States. It is the oldest written constitution for a national government continuously in force and a constant example to the rest of the world of the benefits and effectiveness of such a well-crafted document. Its famous beginning, "We the people," asserts that the source of its authority is the people as opposed to the states. It then assigns powers to the various branches of government and in doing so structures the government. It limits the powers that any branch may have and allows each branch to CHECK AND BALANCE the others. Most significantly it denies certain powers to the national government and reserves them for the states and the people. But aside from its force as law, the U.S. Constitution is more than just a piece of fading parchment in the National Archives—it is the national icon, the premier symbol of U.S. freedom and governance; above all, it represents the collective political will of the American people over more than two centuries to maintain their republican form of government. Nevertheless, because of the nature of JUDICIAL REVIEW, the Constitution is ultimately, as Chief Justice Charles Evans Hughes asserted in a speech on May 3, 1907, "what the judges [of the U.S. Supreme Court] say it is." It is, as Thomas Jefferson wrote in a September 6, 1819, letter to Spencer Roane, "a mere thing of wax in the hands of the judiciary, which they may twist and shape into any form they please." 3. The constitution of a U.S. state. These constitutions tend to parallel the national constitution in that they declare what powers the state does and does not enjoy, provide for three branches of government, and have a bill or declaration of rights. 4. The POLITICAL CULTURE of a community or nation. 5. The formal rules prescribing the governance practices of, for example, a club, an association, a union, or a political party, even though the rules may be called *charters, bylaws,* or *articles of association.*

Constitution, economic interpretation of A reference to Charles A. Beard's (1874–1948) contention, in *An Economic Interpretation of the Constitution of the United States* (1913), that the founders wrote the U.S. Constitution in large measure to protect their economic interests and that it is "an economic document drawn with superb skill by men whose property interests were immediately at stake."

constitutional Consistent with and reflective of the U.S. Constitution, which lies at the very heart of the U.S. political system and establishes the framework and rules of the game within which that system operates. U.S. politics have grown up around the Constitution and have been, thereby, constitutionalized. Many domestic political issues are treated in constitutional terms; for example, civil rights, crime, pornography, and abortion. In addressing matters of government and politics, Americans are first likely to ask, "Is it constitutional?" Only afterward are policies considered on their own merits. In the 1819 case of *MCCULLOCH V. MARYLAND,* the U.S. Supreme Court explained how to tell whether something is constitutional: "Let the end be legitimate, let it be within the scope of the Constitution, and all means which are appropriate, which are plainly adapted to that end, which are not prohibited, but consist with the letter and spirit of the Constitution, are constitutional."

constitutional architecture The administrative arrangements created by a government's constitution—from the separation of powers to the requirement that specific departments be created or services performed.

constitutional law That area of the law concerned with the interpretation and application of the nation's highest law—the U.S. Constitution.

constitutional officers Positions in a government specifically established by its constitution (such as president or governor) as opposed to positions created by subsequent legislation or executive order.

construct An idea or concept created or synthesized ("constructed") from available information and refined through scientific investigation. In psychological testing, a construct is usually dimensional, an attribute of people that varies in degree from one person to another. Tests are usually intended to be measures of intellectual, perceptual, psychomotor, and personality constructs (e.g., a clerical test may measure the construct known as "perceptual speed and accuracy," or the performance of invoice clerks may be measured in their "ability to recognize errors").

constructive engagement A diplomatic phrase for maintaining political and economic ties with regimes with which a nation has many disagreements in the hope that the ties will gradually lead to changes in the regime's objectionable policies and practices.

consumer price index (CPI) The Bureau of Labor Statistics' cost-of-living index, the monthly statistical measure of the average change in prices over time in a fixed market basket of goods and services. The CPI is one of the nation's most important measures of inflation/deflation. Many employment and labor union contracts relate wage increases directly to changes in the CPI.

containment The underlying basis of U.S. foreign and military policy to contain the expansion of communist influence during the Cold War that followed World War II. First espoused by George F. Kennan in a July 1947 *Foreign Affairs* article, "The Sources of Soviet Conduct," in which he asserted that "Soviet pressure against the free institutions of the Western World is something that can be contained by the adroit and vigilant application of counterforce." (The official author of this article was X because Kennan wrote it while serving as a Foreign Service Officer (FSO); but the author's identity was never a secret.) Kennan made the important point that the source of Russian behavior was not a feeling of recent injustice by others but a long-term push to expand, dating back centuries. There was broad agreement on the objective of containment, at least until the reaction against U.S. involvement in Vietnam in the late 1960s. The first Bush administration saw containment come to an end with the demise of the Soviet Union in 1991—a development that vindicated the logic of it. *See also* TRUMAN DOCTRINE.

content analysis A methodology that examines the frequency of particular words and phrases in the statements of a person or government and draws certain conclusions from this. Content analysis has been used to examine the decisions and actions of major public policy decisionmakers.

contingency theory An approach to leadership asserting that leadership styles will vary in their effects in different situations. The situation (not the traits or styles themselves) determines whether a leadership style or a particular leader will be effective. Thus there is no one best way to be an effective leader.

continuing appropriations The means by which the U.S. Congress allows federal agencies to continue operations when the usual political crisis over the budget delays their annual budget appropriations. When a fiscal year begins and the Congress has not yet enacted all the regular appropriation bills for that year, it passes a joint resolution continuing appropriations at rates generally based on the previous year's appropriations for government agencies not yet funded.

continuing campaign Governing as if you were still running for election; using all the public relations tools of an administration to maintain and enhance political support for the administration's personalities and policies.

contract An agreement that affects the legal relationships between two or more persons. To be a contract, an agreement must involve at least one promise, consideration (something of value promised or given), persons legally capable of making binding agreements, and a reasonable amount of agreement between the persons as to what the contract means. A contract is bilateral if both sides expressly make promises (such as the promise to deliver a book on one side and a promise to pay for it on the other); or unilateral if the promises are on one side only (usually because the other side has already done its part).

contract administration The essence of labor relations; the implementation of a collective bargaining contract. This contract is, in effect, the law of the workplace for its stipulated term.

contract authorizations Stopgap provisions, found in authorization as well as appropriation bills, that permit government to let contracts or to obligate itself for future payments from funds not yet appropriated. The assumption is that funds will be available for payment when contracted debts come due.

contracting out Having work performed outside an organization's own workforce. Contracting out is often an area of union-management disagreement, especially in the public sector. Although many unions recognize management's right on occasion to subcontract a job requiring specialized skills and equipment not possessed by the organization or its employees, they oppose the letting of work that could be done by the organization's own workforce. In particular, unions are concerned if work normally performed by its members is contracted out to firms that pay inferior wages and/or provide substandard working conditions, or if such action may result in reduced earnings or layoffs for regular employees. Contracting out is one of the major means of privatizing and thus reducing the size of the public sector.

control *See* MANAGEMENT CONTROL.

control group In a research design, a group exhibiting characteristics similar to those of the experimental or subject group. The control group is not exposed to the experimental treatment and is used for comparative purposes.

controllability The ability of the U.S. Congress or the president under existing law to control spending during a given fiscal year. Uncontrollable spending—spending that cannot be increased or decreased without changes in existing substantive law—is usually the result of open-ended programs and fixed costs, such as social security and veterans' benefits (sometimes called

ENTITLEMENTS), but also includes payments due under obligations incurred during previous years.

controller/comptroller The financial officer of a company or a government agency. For example, the comptroller general of the United States heads the GENERAL ACCOUNTING OFFICE, which audits government agencies. Normally, a controller employs the technical skills of an accountant. The basic functions of the office are to supervise accounting and to make sure that funds are spent for acceptable purposes. The AUDIT function comes afterward.

cooling-off period 1. A legal provision that postpones a labor strike or lockout for a specific time to give the parties an additional opportunity to mediate their differences. Although the device has great popular appeal, it is of doubtful value because more time will not necessarily resolve a labor dispute. The first federal requirements for a cooling-off period were set forth in the War Labor Disputes Act of 1943. This act was superseded by the national emergency provisions of the Labor-Management Relations (Taft-Hartley) Act of 1947, which called for an eighty-day cooling-off period in the event of a national emergency. 2. A legally mandated period of time before a person seeking to buy a rifle or pistol can gain possession of it; the "cooling off" period (1) allows police to perform a background check on the purchaser and (2) allows the purchaser to "cool off" if he or she is buying the weapon in anger.

co-optation The inclusion of new potentially dissident group members into an organization's policymaking process to prevent such elements from becoming a threat to the organization or its mission. The classic analysis of co-optation is found in Philip Selznick's *TVA and the Grass Roots* (1949).

co-optive power A concept developed by Joseph Nye in *Bound to Lead* (1990), which refers to the ability of a state to structure a situation in ways that lead others to define their interests or preferences in ways that are compatible with the state's interests. Sources of co-optive power are culture and ideology. The ability to structure a regime in ways that bring about desired behavior can also be understood as a form of co-optive power.

coordination with In consultation with. The expression means that government agencies "coordinated with" shall participate actively; that their concurrence shall be sought; and that if concurrence is not obtained, the disputed matter shall be referred to the next higher authority.

corollary An addition to an existing doctrine or policy. The meaning comes from mathematics and logic where it refers to a proposition that needs little or no proof because it so closely follows something already proven.

coroner The county official responsible for determining the causes of deaths occurring under violent, unusual, or suspicious circumstances. Ideally, a coroner (whose title comes from the days when such officers represented the Crown) should be a medical examiner (who performs autopsies) and a trained criminal investigator. Unfortunately, many jurisdictions impose no particular qualifications for the office, and it is often a political plum. Coroners usually have the power to hold a formal hearing or inquest into suspicious deaths. If evidence of wrongdoing is discovered, the case is then turned over to an appropriate prosecutor or grand jury.

corporation An organization formed under state or federal law that exists, for legal purposes, as a separate being or an artificial person. It may be public (set up by the government) or private (set up by individuals), and it may be set up to carry on a business or to perform almost any function. It may be owned by the government or by a few persons, or it may be a "publicly owned corporation"; that is, owned by members of the general public who buy its shares on an open stock market.

corporation counsel An attorney for a municipal corporation (a city).

corporatism 1. The designation for a form of social organization in which corporations, nongovernment bodies with great authority over the lives and professional activities of their members, play an intermediary role between public and state. The practice goes back to medieval times when trade guilds controlled the activities of craftsmen and traders; at the height of their power the guilds represented a third force in society along with the Church and the nobility. 2. A theoretical concept developed by the French sociologist Emile Durkheim (1858–1917) that found political expression in the fascist institutions of the 1930s and 1940s. Fascist corporatism suggested that people engaged in a particular trade—employers as well as workers—had more in common with one another than with people of the same class or status in other trades. Thus, in Spain and Italy, legislative assemblies and councils of state were organized around such trade corporations rather than around geographic constituencies. Corporatist theory appealed to the fascists because it bypassed class-conflict and democratic elections. 3. The increasing tendency for states to work closely with major business corporations and trade unions to enhance international competitiveness; sometimes called *neo-corporatism.*

corruption, political The unauthorized use of public office for private gain. Common forms of corruption include bribery, extortion, and the misuse of inside information. Recurrent scandals and instances of official mischief in government, no matter how much they threaten to cost, pose a great threat to the democratic notions of the rule of law. When public office is misused for self-gain, the rule of law no longer obtains and, there ensues, in effect, a return to tyranny. By engaging in such self-aggrandizement, corrupt representatives of the people illegally put themselves above the law. Moreover, a public official's act of wrongdoing is destructive of the claim that in a democracy all individuals are equal. Along with the pig in George Orwell's *Animal Farm* who cannot accept the idea that "all animals are equal," these self-interested officials, like Orwell's pig, are in effect saying that "some of us are more equal than others." The porcine imagery continues when you think of them not only feeding at the public trough but also "hogging" more than their share. *Compare to* HONEST GRAFT/DISHONEST GRAFT.

cost overrun A situation in the procurement of big-ticket items (usually defense) such as ships and planes when the cost to the government is greater than originally planned. Cost overruns are usually caused by a change in contract specifications requested by the government or to the need to respond to the latest technology.

cost-benefit approach A process that seeks to determine the effectiveness of spending in relation to costs.

cost-effectiveness analysis An analytical technique used to choose the most efficient method for achieving a program or policy goal. The costs of alternatives are measured by their requisite estimated dollar expenditures. Effectiveness is defined by the degree of goal attainment, and may also (but not necessarily) be measured in dollars. Either the net effectiveness (effectiveness minus costs) or the cost-effectiveness ratios of alternatives are compared. The most cost-effective method chosen may involve one or more alternatives. The limited view of costs and effectiveness distinguishes this technique from cost-benefit analysis, which encompasses society-wide impacts of alternatives.

cost-of-living adjustment (COLA) An increase in compensation in response to increasing inflation. Some labor union contracts and some entitlement programs (such as social security) provide for automatic COLAs if inflation reaches predetermined levels.

cost-of-living index *See* CONSUMER PRICE INDEX.

costing-out In the context of labor relations, costing-out determines the cost of a contract proposal (wages and fringe benefits).

Council of Economic Advisers (CEA) The U.S. president's primary source of economic advice. It assists the president in preparing various economic reports, including the annual *Economic Report of the President.* Established in the Executive Office of the President by the Employment Act of 1946, the CEA consists of three economists (one designated chair) appointed by the president (with the advice and consent of the U.S. Senate), who formulate proposals to "maintain employment, production, and purchasing power."

council of government (COG) An organization of cooperating local governments that seeks a regional approach to planning, development, transportation, environment, and other issues; multijurisdictional cooperative arrangements to permit a regional approach to planning, development, transportation, environment, and other problems that affect a region as a whole. The COGs are substate regional planning agencies established by states and are responsible for the area-wide review of projects applying for federal funds and for the development of regional plans and other special-purpose arrangements. COGs are composed of designated policymaking representatives from each participating government within the region. Some COGs assumed a more enterprising role in the 1980s by acting as their local governments' contractors and service providers.

council ward A legislative district from which a person is elected to a city council.

councillor A member of a council. This is in contrast to a COUNSELOR (one who gives advice, such as a lawyer).

council-manager plan/county-manager system A form of municipal government in which an elected city council appoints a professional city manager to administer the city government. A county-manager system offers the same essential structure at the county level. *Compare to* CITY MANAGER.

counselor/counsellor 1. A lawyer. 2. A formal advisor. Some of the top staff members at the White House are titled "Counsellor to the President."

countercyclical Descriptive of government actions aimed at smoothing out swings in economic activity. Countercyclical actions may take the form of MONETARY and FISCAL POLICY (such as countercyclical revenue sharing or jobs programs). Automatic (built-in) stabilizers have a countercyclical effect without necessitating changes in government policy.

countervailing theory BALANCE OF POWER thinking applied domestically; when one group grows too powerful in a pluralist society, another group or coalition springs up to counter or oppose the first group's power.

county The basic unit for the administrative decentralization of state government. Although a county is typically governed by an elected board or commission, there is a movement at present toward a county administrator or executive (sometimes elected). In Louisiana, the comparable unit is called a *parish;* in Alaska, a *borough.* In 2002, the United States had 3,042 county governments. Each state determines for itself how many counties it will have. Two states, Connecticut and Rhode Island, have no counties at all. The elected officials of county government have a bewildering array of titles. According to Commissioner Harvey Ruvin of Dade County, Florida, county officials "are supervisors in California, judges in Texas, jurors in Louisiana, freeholders in New Jersey, county legislators in New York, commissioners in Dade. If I tell somebody from New York I'm a commissioner, they think I'm the dog catcher. No wonder the public and the media focus on governors and mayors" (*Governing,* May 1989).

county agent A field officer of the Department of Agriculture and one of over 3,000 county government officials who are responsible for disseminating information about new agricultural techniques developed through research funded by the Department of Agriculture and state land-grant universities. The county agent is the grassroots officer of the Cooperative Extension Service, a partnership of all three levels of government authorized by the Smith-Lever Act of 1914.

county board The generic term for the governing board of a county.

county clerk The secretary to a county board and an elected office in more than half the states. A county clerk's job ranges from maintaining county records to a bewildering variety of other duties.

county commissioner An elected member of the governing body of a county government, often called a *county board* or *board of supervisors.* In some Southern states, the elected county commissioners are formally called *judges,* even though their judicial duties are minimal.

county committee A political party's governing apparatus at the county level; typically composed of people elected at the precinct level.

county seat The capital of a county; the city or town that is home to the courts and administrative offices. In much of the United States, the county seat was so located in the geographical center of the county that it would not be more than one day's ride on horseback from the farthest part of the county.

county single-executive plan A county government structure that calls for the election of one individual to administer all county programs and services. This county equivalent to a strong mayoral form of municipal government is particularly popular in urban areas.

county supremacy movement Legal and symbolic efforts by county governments, mostly in the West, to gain control of the public (meaning "federal") lands within their borders.

county-manager system *See* COUNCIL-MANAGER PLAN/COUNTY-MANAGER SYSTEM.

cozy triangles/iron triangles The mutually supportive relations among government agencies, interest groups, and the legislative committee or subcommittee with jurisdiction over their areas of common concern. Such coalitions constantly exchange information, services, and money (in the form of campaign contributions from the interest groups to the members of the legislative committee, and budget approval from the committee to the agency). As a whole, they tend to dominate policymaking in their areas of concern. The triangles are considered to be as strong as iron, because the supportive relations are so strong that others elected or appointed to control administrative policy as representatives of the public's interest are effectively prohibited from interfering on behalf of the public. *Compare to* ISSUE NETWORKS.

cradle to the grave/womb to tomb Slang phrases that refer to the total security offered citizens in the fully realized welfare state. "Cradle to the grave" may have first been used in Edward Bellamy's novel *Looking Backward* (1888), in which he predicts: "The nation guarantees the nurture, education, and comfortable maintenance of every citizen from cradle to the grave."

craft unions A labor organization that restricts membership to skilled workers (such as plumbers, carpenters, and electricians) as opposed to an industrial union, which seeks to organize all the workers in an industry.

credibility 1. In diplomacy, the belief in the mind of the opposition that a threat or a promise will be fulfilled if specific contingencies arise. One side in a negotiation can be said to have credibility if the other side believes its adversary is not bluffing—even if it is. 2. A military posture that would allow one side to do unacceptable damage to an aggressor even after absorbing a first strike. Thus credibility functions as a DETERRENT.

credibility gap The difference between an official description of events and the public's understanding of those events from other sources, chiefly the news media and political critics. A credibility gap engenders public mistrust of elected officials.

crisis 1. An unstable situation ripe for decisive change. As then Senator John F. Kennedy said in a speech on April 12, 1959, "When written in Chinese, the word *crisis* is composed of two characters—one represents danger and the other represents opportunity." 2. A foreign policy problem involving a threat to the security of the state and dealt with by the highest level of a government forced to make crucial decisions within a short time.

crisis intervention A private company or government program that provides support for individuals undergoing a crisis in their lives. Crisis intervention takes many forms, such as help after a sudden death in a family and counseling after an attempted suicide.

critical-incident method Identifying, classifying, and recording significant examples—critical incidents—of an employee's behavior for purposes of performance evaluation. The theory behind the critical-incident approach holds that certain key acts of behavior make the difference between success and failure. After the incidents are collected, they can be ranked in order of frequency and importance and assigned numerical weights. Once scored, they can be equally as useful for employee development and counseling as for formal appraisals.

critical path method (CPM) Network analysis technique for planning and scheduling. The "critical path" is a sequence of activities connecting the beginning and end of events or program accomplishments.

crowding out The displacement of private investment expenditures by increases in public expenditures financed by the sale of government securities. It is often suggested that, as the federal deficit increases, the money borrowed from the public to pay for it is unavailable for private investment. Such crowding out could thus lead to a recession or worse.

current dollar The dollar value of a good or service in terms of prices current at the time the good or service was sold. This is in contrast to the value of the good or service in constant dollars.

customs The authorities designated to collect duties levied by a country on imports and exports. The term also applies to the procedures involved in such collection.

customs union A group of nations that has eliminated trade barriers among themselves and imposed a common tariff on all goods imported from all other countries. The European Union is a customs union, as are the United States in themselves. A customs union can also be described as a free-trade bloc. The United States agreements with Canada and Mexico have led to a North American customs union or free-trade bloc.

cybernetic Descriptive of self-regulating biological, social, or technological systems that can identify problems, correct them, and receive feedback that enables them to adjust themselves automatically. *See* SYSTEMS ANALYSIS.

cycles of American history The concept popularized by Arthur Schlesinger, Jr., in his 1986 book of the same title. According to Schlesinger, U.S. politics operate in thirty-year cycles that alternate between conservative and liberal periods of politics.

czar 1. A former Russian absolute monarch; also anglicized as "tzar." 2. A nickname for a high-ranking administrator who is given great authority over something; for example, an energy czar, a housing czar.

D

damage control 1. In naval usage, measures necessary aboard ship after it has sustained damage from enemy action or accident to keep the ship afloat and maintain its ability to fight. 2. Applied to politics, efforts to contain the effects of a mistake or scandal so that the political actors involved will once again find themselves in a stable situation with an ability to continue fighting the political wars.

Davis-Bacon Act of 1931 The federal prevailing wage law, which requires federal contractors on construction projects to pay the rates of pay and fringe benefits that prevail in the geographic area. In recent years, the law has been heavily criticized for unnecessarily raising the cost of federal construction.

de facto 1. A Latin phrase meaning "in fact"; "actual." For example, de facto segregation has occurred without the formal assistance of government; it evolved from social and economic conditions. In contrast, de jure (by law) segregation in schools was once a legal requirement in many states. Although segregation practices are no longer sanctioned by government (are no longer de jure), they often remain de facto. 2. Diplomatic recognition that implies acceptance but falls short of formal, legal (de jure) recognition.

de jure A Latin phrase meaning "by right"; "by law." *See* DE FACTO.

debriefing 1. Interrogating someone (a spy, a soldier, a diplomat, etc.) when that person returns from a mission. 2. Formally instructing individuals about their responsibilities in dealing with government secrets as they leave positions dealing with classified information.

debt financing Paying for government programs or capital improvements by borrowing. The ability to incur debt is in many respects a hallmark of governments. They usually exist, in part, to undertake projects the value of which will last for many generations. This is why Alexander Hamilton wrote in an April 30, 1781, letter to Robert Morris that "A national debt, if it is not excessive, will be to us a national blessing." Debt is a way of matching costs with those who benefit from the borrowing; for example, of seeing that future generations pay their share of the costs of roads or buildings we put in place now; of ensuring "intergenerational equity." In the United States, governments ranging from the federal government to the tiniest local government can issue bonds and incur debt. *See* DEFICIT FINANCING.

debt-for-equity swap A financial arrangement whereby a THIRD WORLD state pays off a substantial portion of its debt to a foreign bank(s) with the proviso that the funds are to be reinvested in the local economy—thereby generating economic development.

debt-for-nature swap A financial arrangement whereby a conservation group buys a deeply discounted THIRD WORLD state's debt, then donates the debt obligation to that state in return for specific conservation measures—such as preserving a specific portion of a tropical rain forest.

debt, general obligation A long-term FULL-FAITH-AND-CREDIT obligation other than one payable initially from nontax revenue. It includes a debt payable in the first instance from earmarked taxes, such as motor fuel sales taxes or property taxes.

debt limit The official ceiling established by the U.S. Congress on the total amount of money the federal government can borrow. Because the debt limit must be raised every few years to accommodate the growing national debt, many members of Congress use the needed legislation as an opportunity to make speeches about the evils of the budget deficit and to attach unrelated riders. Without the new legislation raising the debt limit, the federal government can literally come to a standstill because no funds can be legally spent for anything. Consequently, a president is under great pressure to sign such legislation even if it has unappealing riders.

debt, national The national debt is the total outstanding debt of a central government. The national debt is often confused with the nation's budget deficit in a given year. The debt is, in effect, the total of all the yearly deficits (borrowing), and their accumulated interest, that have not been repaid.

debt, nonguaranteed Long-term debt payable solely from pledged specific sources; for example, from earnings of revenue-producing activities (such as university and college dormitories, toll highways and bridges, electric power projects, and public-building authorities) or from specific nonproperty taxes. It includes only debt that does not constitute an obligation against other resources if the pledged sources are insufficient.

debt relief In the context of international affairs, a means of releasing developing countries from the obligations to repay loans from the commercial banks of the developed world and international institutions such as the World Bank.

debt restructuring The rescheduling of the international debts of a state so that the carrying charges (interest and principal) are easier to bear. Debt restructuring may or may not include provisions for forgoing past-due interest or for gratuitously reducing principal.

debt service The regular payment of principal, interest, and other costs (such as insurance) to pay off a financial obligation.

debtor nation 1. A nation that borrows more from other nations than it loans them. 2. A nation that receives more investments from foreign sources than from its own internal sources.

decisionmaking The process of selecting the most desirable course of action from among alternatives. In a larger sense, decisionmaking is the total process by which managers act to achieve organizational goals.

decision rule A directive established to make decisions in the face of uncertainty. For example, a payroll office might be given a decision rule to deduct one hour's pay from an employee's wages for each lateness that exceeds ten minutes but is less than one hour.

decision theory A body of knowledge concerned with the nature and process of decisionmaking. Decision theory abstracts given situations into a structured problem that calls for the decisionmaker to make an objective judgment. Because decision theory is usually dependent upon quantitative analysis, it is also called *statistical decision theory* and *Bayesian decision theory*. *Bayesian* refers to Thomas Bayes (1702–1761), who provided a mathematical basis for probability inference.

decision tree A graphic method of presenting various decisional alternatives so that the various risks, information needs, and courses of action are visually available to the decisionmaker.

declaratory policy 1. The formally promulgated FOREIGN POLICY positions of a nation. 2. The publicly announced doctrine about when, and how, a country will use its nuclear forces. Declaratory policy does not tell what tactics and strategy a nation might use in a nuclear war; it basically serves to highlight the political conditions under which nuclear weapons will be used and offers a justification for such use.

default Failure to pay a debt when due. Unlike the private sector, where a corporate default can result in the end of the corporation and the division of all remaining assets, governmental organizations inevitably live on. There is life after default; but often it becomes a hell of litigation.

deference principle The administrative law doctrine by which courts accept or defer to the judgment of expert agency administrators.

deficiency payments Government payments to compensate farmers for all or part of the difference between domestic market price levels for a commodity and a higher target price.

deficit The amount by which a government's expenditures exceed its revenues. With the federal government, this is not a straightforward exercise in arithmetic because all sorts of budgetary gimmicks are used to make the deficit look smaller than it really is. For example, a ROSY SCENARIO typically overestimates tax revenues so that the deficit will appear smaller than it really is.

deficit financing A situation in which a government's excess of outlays over receipts for a given period is financed primarily by borrowing from the public. Depending on the economist you listen to, a large deficit is either considered a major drag on the economy (*see* CROWDING OUT) or a significant stimulus (*see* JOHN MAYNARD KEYNES). The national debt is the sum total of all federal deficits and interest currently owed to holders of federal government securities, such as Treasury bills and savings bonds.

definition of the situation The way policymakers perceive the situation facing them. This phrase, coined by Richard Snyder and others in *Foreign Policy Decision-Making* (1962), also implies that the perceptions of policymakers are dynamic rather than static, recognized in their notions of successive, overlapping definitions of a situation.

deinstitutionalization Allowing incarcerated people (such as convicted prisoners, the mentally ill, the mentally retarded) to leave large homogenous institutional environments for halfway houses or as out-patients in community mental facilities.

delegated power Specific or IMPLIED POWERS that the U.S. Constitution grants to the national government; also called *enumerated powers.* These are often contrasted with the RESERVED POWERS granted to state governments.

delegation 1. A group sent to represent a larger group. For example, a state-level political party would send a delegation to its party's national convention. 2. The official party sent to an international conference. 3. The specific powers granted to an agency or individual; for example, a diplomat's authority in a given situation is his "delegation."

delegation of power The empowering of one to act for another. The delegation of power from one part of government to another and from one official to another is fundamental to U.S. government. Article I, Section 8, of the U.S. Constitution enumerates the powers of the U.S. Congress and then grants to the Congress the power "to make all laws which shall be necessary and proper for carrying into execution the foregoing powers, and all other powers vested by this Constitution in the government of the United States, or in any department or officer thereof." But how explicit must such laws be? If the Congress should attempt to legislate in such a fashion as to give complete direction to administrative officials, an unworkable government would result. Every contingency would have to be anticipated in advance;

the legislature would have to be expert in all phases of all policy areas. Moreover, changes in the nature of carrying out statutes would have to be accomplished by new laws; the congressional workload would be crushing. Consequently, the Congress typically avoids writing highly detailed legislation, preferring to state broad policy objectives and allow administrators to choose the means of attaining them. Although administrative discretion is clearly necessary, it can raise important constitutional questions. If the delegation is so broad as to allow administrators to exercise legislative power without congressional guidance or standards, the requirements of the separation of powers may be breached. *See also* NECESSARY AND PROPER CLAUSE; REGULATION; *UNITED STATES V. CURTISS-WRIGHT EXPORT CORPORATION.*

deliberate speed The pace of school integration. In *Brown v. Board of Education of Topeka, Kansas* (1954), the U.S. Supreme Court held that school integration should proceed "with all deliberate speed." This is a good example of the Court's use of a vague phrase to avoid dealing head on with a difficult policy problem. Although this phrase is most associated with the *Brown* decision, it has a long history. For example, Justice Oliver Wendell Holmes, Jr., in *Virginia v. West Virginia* (1911), said, "A question like the present should be disposed of without undue delay. But a State cannot be expected to move with the celerity of a private business man; it is enough it if proceeds . . . with all deliberate speed."

Delphi Method A procedure for forecasting specific technological and social events. Delphi was the hometown of the most famous fortune-teller in ancient Greece. Experts are asked to give their best judgment as to the probable occurrence of a specific event. The results are collated and then returned to the original experts for their perusal along with an opportunity to revise their own predictions. Revised estimates with supporting arguments are then recorded and recirculated again and again; in theory, the feedback always narrows the range of answers. In the end, a group prophecy will have been arrived at without the possibility of distortion from face-to-face contact, leadership influences, or the pressures of group dynamics.

democracy The Greek word for *rule by the ordinary populace,* the plebian public, whose well-being was necessary for the stability of the state but whose judgment could not necessarily be trusted in the management of the state. The growth of democracy as an ideal thus depended upon the slow evolution of classes of educated and experienced citizens, whose capacity to govern themselves and others depended upon the transformation of ways of understanding and interpreting the will of the people—although not necessarily giving the people the power to exercise that will for themselves. The term *democracy* is often used by totalitarian regimes and their people's democracies. So one person's democratic regime is another's totalitarian despotism. By becoming a term that could be used to describe so broad a range of institutional possibilities, democracy has thus tended to lose its meaning in political debate—but not its vitality. It continues to serve as an ideal over which political debate can take place. The founders of the United States were rightly suspicious of the pure democracy available to the free male citizens of ancient Athens. As Aristotle had warned, time and again throughout history pure democracies have degenerated into dictatorial tyrannies. On April 15, 1814, John Adams wrote in a letter to John Taylor, "Remember, democracy never lasts long. It soon wastes, exhausts, and murders itself. There never was a democracy yet that did not commit suicide." This well-justified fear of the mob led the founders to create a REPUBLIC, a form of government one step removed from democracy, that presumably protects the people from their own passions. The frustration of coming to grips with the concept and the reality of democracy is illustrated by Winston Churchill's remark in the House of Commons on November 11, 1947, that "no one pretends that democracy is perfect or all wise. Indeed, it has been said that democracy is the worst form of government except all those other forms that have been tried from time to time."

democracy, digital The use of the Internet for greater participation in the democratic process. The speed of the Internet allows policymakers and citizens to survey massive amounts of information about almost any policy. Citizens do not need their own staffs to research issues and can make advocacy decisions that are as informed as those made by legislators with substantial staff support. The Web has become, in effect, the people's staff.

democracy, direct A governing system in which decisions are made directly by the people, as opposed to being made by elected representatives. Examples of direct democracy include the political meetings of male citizens in the ancient Greek city-states and the New England town meeting. More modern forms of direct democracy include such processes as the initiative, the referendum, and the recall, which allow citizens to enact laws directly or to remove officials by voting.

democracy, industrial A variety of efforts designed to encourage employees to participate in an organization's decisionmaking processes by identifying problems and suggesting solutions to them in a formal manner. Although the terms *industrial democracy* and *participative management* tend to be used almost interchangeably, there is a distinction. *Industrial democracy* was used as far back as 1897 by the English economists Beatrice Webb (1858–1943) and Sidney Webb (1859–1947) to describe democratic practices within the

British trade union movement. The term's modern usage to cover innumerable types of joint or cooperative management programs dates from World War I, when it connoted a scheme to avoid labor-management disputes that might adversely affect war production. Today, industrial democracy connotes joint action by management and workers' representatives. *Participative management,* in contrast, connotes cooperative programs that are unilaterally carried out from on high. Nevertheless, both terms seem rapidly to be losing their distinctive connotations.

democracy, participatory The direct involvement of individuals and groups in the decisionmaking processes of government. This involvement is often made manifest by citizen participation in the planning and implementation activities of the various government agencies. Many laws have built-in features of participatory democracy, such as hearings (where the public may testify) preliminary to changes, such as in rules, regulations, and tax rates. The "new left" picked up on this theme when, in the 1960s, it called for citizen control of local public services. The main problem with participatory democracy is that self-appointed spokespersons for the people often have a disproportionate impact on public policy; so the situation may all too quickly turn oligarchic, rather than democratic.

democracy, representative A form of governance in which the citizens rule through representatives who are periodically elected and thus kept accountable. The United States, as a republic, is a representative democracy.

democratic accountability The principle that in a democracy the government should be responsible to the people (through elections) and to its representative institutions (through oversight).

deniability The prearranged insulation of a political executive from a decision that he or she actually made, but later is plausibly able to deny because a paper or other trail that would lead to the top is absent. Arrangements for deniability are important parts of covert actions and diplomacy.

department 1. A CABINET-level agency of the U.S. government. 2. One of the three branches of government: executive, legislative, or judicial. 3. A general term for an administrative subdivision. 4. Usually the largest and most important administrative agencies at all levels of government.

dependency theory A radical critique of the relations that Western capitalist nations have with the THIRD WORLD. The basic notion is that major capitalist powers have not really given up their colonial powers, but in fact exercise enormous political control over Latin American, African, and Asian countries. However, they do this now by the use of economic pressure and by exploiting their superior market position to extract unfair advantages in international trade.

deregulation The lifting of restrictions on business, industry, and other professional activities for which government rules were established and bureaucracies created to administer. The modern movement toward deregulation, which really began during the Jimmy Carter administration under the leadership of Alfred Kahn at the Civil Aeronautics Board, was supported by both parties, but for different reasons. Republicans tended to support it because they were inclined to be philosophically hostile toward government interference with business in the first place. Democrats tended to support it because they felt that greater market competition would bring down prices for the consumer. *See also* REGULATION.

detail The temporary assignment of an employee to a different position for a specified period with the assumption that the employee will return to "normal" duties at the end of the detail. Technically, a position cannot be "filled" by a detail because the employee continues to be the incumbent of the position from which he was detailed.

deterrence 1. The doctrine that known punishment will inhibit certain actions, mainly crime, by fear of the consequences. 2. A state of mind brought about by a credible threat of unacceptable counteraction. This is the essence of U.S. defense policy. The basic argument is that, as long as a potential enemy believes that the United States is capable of responding to an attack with a devastating counterattack, there will be no war. Therefore, a massive defense establishment is essential to maintain the peace. In some ways, deterrence has always been the role of all military forces except those specifically intended for wars of conquest. In its broadest use, deterrence means a strategy, force position, or policy that is intended to persuade a potential enemy not to attack.

devaluation 1. The lowering of the value of a nation's currency in relation to gold, or to the currency of other countries, when this value is set by government intervention in the exchange market. Devaluation normally refers to fixed exchange rates. In a system of flexible rates, the falling value of the currency is referred to as depreciation; if rising, the value of the currency is referred to as appreciation. 2. A diplomatic stratagem whereby something once considered of great value in negotiations is deliberately, as a matter of policy, considered of less value than it was before. For example, after the Iran-Contra scandal broke, the Ronald Reagan administration "devalued" the U.S. hostages held in Lebanon.

developed countries Industrialized countries with high per capita incomes and high standards of living in comparison to the nonindustrialized world. Whether a country is termed *developed* or *developing* is decided by such fac-

tors as GROSS NATIONAL PRODUCT, education, level of industrial development and production, health and welfare, and agricultural productivity.

developing countries Used interchangeably with THIRD WORLD, less-developed
countries, and underdeveloped countries to refer to countries with low per
capita incomes and comparatively low standards of living. Very low-income
developing countries are often referred to as the FOURTH WORLD.

development 1. The gradual process of increasing economic growth so that
the benefits of increased production and a more equitable distribution of income improve social and political conditions. The word is usually used in
the context of the Third World, but the differences are a matter only of degree. After all, the comparatively rich industrialized states are still developing, too. 2. Fund-raising by nonprofit organizations.

development administration The management of THIRD WORLD political and
economic assistance programs. This is usually a joint effort between donor
and recipient states often with the additional involvement of international
organizations.

devolution The transfer of a power or function of government from a central
to a local jurisdiction.

devolution, second order What happens when a state accepts the devolution
of programmatic responsibility from the federal government and, in turn,
devolves that responsibility to a local government or nonprofit organization.

diffusion theory of taxation The assertion that the real burden of an increase
in taxes of any kind is eventually distributed throughout the population because of price changes.

digital divide 1. The difference between groups that have the best information
via Internet access and those that do not enjoy the same access. 2. The disparities in technological skills and access across international borders, socioeconomic background, educational background, and/or geographic
location.

Dillon's rule The criteria developed by state courts to determine the nature
and extent of powers granted to municipal corporations. It is a very strict
and limiting rule, stating that municipal corporations have only those powers (1) expressly granted in the city charter, (2) necessarily or fairly implied
by or incidental to formally expressed powers, and (3) essential to the declared purposes of the corporation. "Any fair, reasonable, substantial doubt"
about a power is to result in denying that power to the corporation. The rule
was formulated by John F. Dillon (1831–1941) in his *Commentaries on the
Law of Municipal Corporations,* 5th ed. (1911). In some states, the rule has
been relaxed, especially in dealing with HOME RULE cities. The essence of

Dillon's rule was upheld by the U.S. Supreme Court in *City of Trenton v. State of New Jersey* (1913).

diminishing marginal utility of income The principle that the marginal value of an additional dollar of income to a rich person is less than to a poor person. This concept underlies progressive taxation: proportionally larger tax payments by those enjoying higher incomes recognizes the diminishing marginal utility of income. *Compare to* ABILITY TO PAY.

diplomacy 1. A state's foreign policy; although this is the most popular usage of the term, a policy in itself is not diplomacy. Foreign policies, made by governments or heads of state, represent the ends or goals of a nation's diplomacy. The word comes from the Greek *diploma,* which means "a document that has been folded twice," a reference to the format of state papers and letters historically carried by diplomats. 2. The formal relations that independent nations maintain with each other; in effect, all the normal and idiosyncratic intentional communications that nations have with each other short of war. Indeed, it is often said that diplomacy has failed when war begins. On the other hand, many nations throughout history have taken Clausewitz's attitude that war is only the continuation of diplomacy "by other means." 3. The art of maintaining and conducting international relations and negotiations. 4. Skillful negotiations in all areas.

diplomatic privileges and immunities The special rights that formally accredited diplomatic officials have, to be immune from the civil and criminal laws of the nation to which they are assigned. This immunity also applies to the physical grounds of an embassy, which is technically considered the soil of the foreign government. Abuses of diplomatic immunity often receive widespread publicity. They range from excessive parking tickets received by United Nations diplomats in New York City to using diplomatic offices as centers for terrorism against the host country. The most outrageous abuse of diplomatic immunity by a host government in recent times was the IRANIAN HOSTAGE CRISIS.

diplomatic recognition The establishment of formal diplomatic relations with a regime. The granting or withholding of such recognition is a powerful tool of foreign policy. The entire history of the United States might have been different if the United Kingdom had recognized the Confederacy during the American Civil War. The new state of Israel achieved immediate international legitimacy because of recognition from the United States. Whether to recognize Communist China was a major issue of U.S. politics from the late 1940s to the Richard M. Nixon administration's rapprochement in the 1970s. Winston Churchill, in a November 17, 1949, speech in the House of Commons on this very issue of recognizing Communist China, said, "Recognizing a person is not necessarily an act of approval. . . . One has to recognize lots of things and people in this world of sin and woe that one does not like. The reason for having diplomatic relations is not to confer a compliment, but to secure a convenience."

direct legislation The use of direct democratic techniques, such as the INITIATIVE, the REFERENDUM, or the RECALL.

directive 1. An order, whether oral or written, issued by one civilian government official commanding action from lower-ranking officials. **2.** An order from an international agency that is binding on member states.

dirty hands dilemma A graphic phrase for the tendency of public officials to commit an act generally considered to be a wrong to further the common good. This is a dilemma in the sense that doing bad seems to lead to something good.

discomfort index The MISERY INDEX.

discount rate The interest rate paid by a commercial bank when it borrows from a Federal Reserve Bank. The discount rate is one of the tools of monetary policy used by the Federal Reserve System. The Federal Reserve customarily raises or lowers the discount rate to signal a shift toward restraining or easing its money and credit policy.

discrimination 1. Bigotry in practice; intolerance toward those who have different beliefs or different religions. **2.** In employment, the failure to treat equals equally. Whether deliberate or unintentional, an action that has the effect of limiting employment and advancement opportunities because of an individual's sex, race, color, age, national origin, religion, physical handicap, or other irrelevant criteria, is discrimination. Because of the EEO and civil rights legislation of recent years, people aggrieved by unlawful discrimination now enjoy a variety of administrative and judicial remedies. Employment discrimination has its origins in the less-genteel concept of bigotry. **3.** The inequity of trade treatment accorded one or more exporting nations by an importing nation. This inequity may take two forms: preferential tariff rates for imports from particular countries or trade restrictions that apply to the exports of certain countries but not to similar goods from other countries. *See also* CIVIL RIGHTS ACT OF 1964; EQUAL EMPLOYMENT OPPORTUNITY; SEX DISCRIMINATION.

discrimination, age Discrimination against those who are considered old. The Age Discrimination in Employment Act (ADEA), first passed in 1967 and often amended, prohibits employment discrimination on the basis of age and (with certain exceptions, such as airline pilots) prohibits mandatory retirement. The ADEA prohibits help-wanted advertisements that indicate preference, limitation, specification, or discrimination based on age. For example, terms such as *girl* and *35–55* may not be used because they indicate the exclusion of qualified applicants based on age. Many states also include age discrimination laws or provisions in their fair employment practices laws. Some of these laws parallel the federal law and have no upper limit in protections against age discrimination in employment; others protect workers until they reach sixty, sixty-five, or seventy years of age. In 1983, the U.S. Supreme Court in *Equal Employment Opportunity Commission v. Wyoming* upheld the federal government's 1974 extension of the Age Discrimination in Employment Act to cover state and local government workers.

discrimination, disabilities Discrimination against those who are considered disabled. The federal government has a long history of legislative efforts to provide employment for the disabled. Disabled veterans were first formally given employment preference toward the end of the American Civil War. In 1919, just after World War I, employment preferences were extended to the wives of disabled veterans. It was not until the Vocational Rehabilitation Act of 1973, however, that federal contractors were required to take affirmative action to seek out qualified handicapped individuals for employment. But it was not until the passage of the Americans with Disabilities Act (ADA) of 1990 that there was a comprehensive federal law to ban discrimination against physically and mentally handicapped individuals in employment, transportation, telecommunications, and public accommodations. All employers with more than fifteen workers are required to accommodate disabled employees—not just federal contractors as before. Although the U.S. Supreme Court has not ruled that AIDS is a covered disability under the ADA, with its decision in *School Board of Nassau County v. Arline* (1987), it has signaled the possibility that it might be. Here the Court held that a public school teacher suffering the contagious disease of tuberculosis was "a handicapped individual" within the meaning of the Rehabilitation Act. This case has been the basis for some lower court rulings that the Rehabilitation Act protects persons with AIDS from employment discrimination. In 1988, the Court offered its first substantive review of the ADA in *Bragdon v. Abbott.* Here it held that people with the HIV infection that leads to AIDS—people showing no AIDS symptons as yet—were protected by the ADA. The Equal Employment Opportunity Commission, which enforces the provisions of the ADA, stipulates that an employer may not ask about the existence, nature, or severity of a disability and may not conduct medical examinations until after it makes a conditional job offer to the applicant. This prohibition ensures that a disability not obviously apparent is not considered before the applicant's nonmedical qualifications are evaluated.

discrimination, sexual orientation Discrimination against homosexuals—gays and lesbians. Although sexual orientation is not protected by the federal civil rights laws, many federal agencies have internal regulations prohibiting discrimination on the basis of sexual orientation. In addition, at least fifteen states and more than 140 local jurisdictions have laws or executive orders that forbid sexual orientation discrimination in employment. The core problem of dealing with the civil rights of gays and lesbians is the activity that defines them (consensual sodomy) has been considered a crime in many states. But no longer. In 2003, the U.S. Supreme Court in *Lawrence v. Texas* declared unconstitutional the Texas ban on consensual sodomy and in effect asserted a broad constitutional right to sexual privacy. This case overruled a 1986 decision in which the Court upheld Georgia's sodomy law *(Bowers v. Hardwick)*. The 2003 decision effectively nullified sodomy laws in the thirteen other states besides Texas that still had such laws. The 2003 *Lawrence* decision on homosexual rights has its origins in the 1965 case of GRISWOLD V. CONNECTICUT, which first asserted that there was a constitutional right to bedroom privacy even when the word *privacy* does not appear in the U.S. Constitution.

dissent 1. Political disagreement. President Dwight D. Eisenhower in a May 31, 1954 speech said: "Here in America we are descended in blood and in spirit from revolutionaries and rebels — men and women who dared to dissent from accepted doctrine. As their heirs, may we never confuse honest dissent with disloyal subversion." 2. A minority opinion of a court.

district attorney The county official, usually elected, who initiates prosecutions against criminals. Variously called the *county attorney* or *county prosecutor.* Federal government prosecutions in federal courts, in contrast, are undertaken by U.S. Attorneys. Prosecuting attorneys, whether county or federal, offer great visibility to ambitious lawyers. Many a national political career started in the district attorney's office.

district council A level of labor organization below the national union but above the locals. The district council is composed of local unions in a particular industry within a limited geographic area. The district councils of local government employee unions are often major influences in municipal affairs.

diversity 1. Variety. 2. The goal of equal employment opportunity and the legal rationale for affirmative action programs. 3. A compelling state interest. In *Grutter v. Bollinger* (2003), the U.S. Supreme Court agreed that the University of Michigan Law School could continue to give advantages to minority applicants for admission. But the justification for such preferences was not to remedy past practices of discrimination but to further diversify for its own sake. The majority opinion, written by Justice Sandra Day O'Connor, held that the U.S. Constitution "does not prohibit the law school's narrowly tailored use of race in admissions decisions to further a compelling interest in obtaining the educational benefits that flow from a diverse student body." In this 5-to-4 decision, the Court asserted that "effective participation by members of all racial and ethnic groups in the civic life of our nation is essential if the dream of one nation, indivisible, is to be realized." Justice Lewis F. Powell had initially advocated the diversity rationale in the 1978 *Bakke* decision. In this 2003 case, the Court endorsed Justice Powell's "view that student body diversity is a compelling state interest that can justify the use of race in university admissions." But even in accepting that diversity is a "compelling state interest," the Court has asserted that this interest, no matter how "compelling," must be temporary because such compellance flies in the face of the Fourteenth Amendment's requirement for equal treatment. In an unusually blatant appeal to a future Supreme Court, Justice O'Connor stated that "race-conscious admissions policies must be limited in time. This requirement reflects that racial classifications, however compelling their goals, are potentially so dangerous that they may be employed no more broadly than the interest demands. Enshrining a permanent justification for racial preferences would offend this fundamental equal protection principle." She concluded that "all governmental use of race must have a logical end point." Then she quite literally provided the end point: "We expect that twenty-five years from now, the use of racial preferences will no longer be necessary to further the interest approved today."

diversity management 1. Directing the work of a heterogeneous workforce. 2. Different strokes for different folks; the highly contentious contention that women and minorities should be managed in ways suitable to their special sensitivities.

diversity of citizenship The situation that exists when the parties in a lawsuit come from different states. Article III, Section 2, of the U.S. Constitution gives jurisdiction in such cases to the federal courts. But the U.S. Congress has since given exclusive jurisdiction for these cases to state courts if no federal question is involved and the amount in question is less than $10,000. For higher amounts, CONCURRENT JURISDICTION applies.

divestiture 1. The removing of something from one's possession; to be legally deprived of an asset; a stripping off. 2. A court's order to a corporation that it get rid of something (another company, stock, property) because of ANTITRUST LAWS. Also, the carrying out of the court's order. 3. A policy calling for companies or for the administrators of pension and endowment funds to sell off all assets of, or stock in, companies holding assets in specified states in an effort to encourage those states to change their policies. *Compare to* BOYCOTT.

division of labor A production process that has individual workers specializing in the varying aspects of a larger task. Adam Smith's 1776 *The Wealth of Nations* devotes its first chapter, "Of the Division of Labour," to a discussion of the optimum organization of a pin factory. Why? Because the specialization of labor was one of the pillars of Smith's "invisible hand" market mechanism in which the greatest rewards would go to those who were the most efficient in the competitive marketplace. Traditional pin makers could produce only a few dozen pins a day; but when pin factory workers were organized so that each one performed a limited operation, they could produce tens of thousands a day. Smith's chapter, coming as it did at the dawn of the Industrial Revolution, is the most famous and influential statement on the economic rationale of the factory system, even though factory systems had existed since ancient times.

do gooders A derisive term for social and political reformers. Do gooders are often joined by goo-goos, who stand for good government.

draconian Very harsh or severe regulations or laws; from an ancient Greek (Athenian) legislator, Draco (seventh century B.C.), who drafted a harsh code of laws in which death was the penalty for most offenses.

draft *See* CONSCRIPTION.

dramaturgy The manner in which a person acts out or theatrically stages an organizational or political role. Political candidates who make an effort to look or sound senatorial or presidential are engaging in dramaturgy. Of course, if they have to make an effort to look it or sound it, they may not have it. One is reminded of the traditional advice to actors: "Always be sincere. If you can fake that, you've got it made."

duck test An empirical aid to the clarity of political discourse: "If it looks like a duck, quacks like a duck, and walks like a duck, then it must be a duck." This was a fashionable way of divining communists in the 1950s and taxes in the 1980s.

due process of law A right guaranteed by the Fifth, Sixth, and Fourteenth amendments and generally understood to mean that legal proceedings will follow rules and forms established for the protection of private rights. The Fourteenth Amendment's provision that "no person shall be deprived of life, liberty, or property without due process of law" is considered a powerful restraint on government interference in the rights or property interests of citizens.

due process, procedural The legal process and machinery that ensures due process. Daniel Webster (1782–1852) gave the classic description of due process as that "which hears before it condemns, which proceeds upon inquiry, and renders judgment only after trial." Procedural due process thus requires that the legal system follow the rules.

due process, substantive The formal legal requirement that due process requirements be observed by government or its agents. Thomas M. Cooley's *Constitutional Limitations* (1868) is considered the doctrinal foundation of substantive due process in the United States. According to Bernard Schwartz in *The Law in America: A History* (1974), "Cooley identified due process with the doctrine of vested rights drawn from natural law, which had been developed to protect property rights. This meant that due process itself was the great substantive safeguard of property." It was "Cooley's analysis which prepared the way for the virtual takeover of American public law by the Due Process Clause of the Fourteenth Amendment." Thus, the threads of Cooley's analysis can be found whenever a U.S. court strikes down an executive or legislative act for being arbitrary or unreasonable and thus lacking in substantive due process.

duty 1. A tax imposed on imported products. A duty is the actual tax imposed or collected; not to be confused with a tariff, which is technically the schedule of duties. In practice, however, the words are used interchangeably. 2. A legal obligation to do something because of an office one holds or a profession one practices. But as George Bernard Shaw warns in *Caesar and Cleopatra,* Act III (1899), "When a stupid man is doing something he is ashamed of, he always declares that it is his duty." 3. A moral obligation that, if left unfulfilled, would cause only a bruised conscience. 4. The obligation of a person in military service to die for his country if circumstances warrant. According to Richard A. Gabriel and Paul L. Savage, *Crisis in Command* (1978): "Military life . . . is unique in that it clearly levels upon the officer . . . responsibilities which transcend his career or material self-interest. . . . at some point an officer may be called upon to do his duty and 'be faithful unto death.'"

duty officer An administrative officer detailed to be constantly available for call in emergencies during a specific period. In the military this is often equivalent to "officer of the day," or "officer of the deck."

E

easement *See* RIGHT-OF-WAY.

economic indicators Measurements of various economic and business movements and activities in a community, such as employment, unemployment, hours worked, income, savings, volume of building permits, and volume of sales, the fluctuations of which affect and may be used to determine overall economic trends. The various economic time series can be segregated into leaders, laggers, and coinciders in relation to movements in aggregate economic activity. *Compare to* LEADING INDICATORS.

economic liberalism *See* LIBERALISM.

economic loss Wages foregone because one is unjustly fired, disciplined (suspended for a time), or not promoted.

economic man The concept that finds humans motivated *solely* by economic factors—always seeking the greatest reward at the least possible cost. A management philosophy that assumes workers are motivated by money and can be further motivated only by more money is premised on the "economic man" concept.

economic mobilization The organizing of a domestic economy in response to a wartime emergency.

economic policy The processes by which a government manages its economy. Economic policy generally consists of three dimensions—FISCAL POLICY, MONETARY POLICY, and facets of public policy having economic implications, such as energy policy, farm policy, and labor union policy. The interaction of these dimensions of economic policy is crucial because none operate in a vacuum. Although monetary policy basically exercises control over the quantity and cost (interest rates) of money and credit in the economy, fiscal policy deals with the sizes of budgets, deficits, and taxes. Other policy areas, such as housing policy (also dependent upon interest rates) and programs dependent upon deficit spending, involve aspects of both monetary and fiscal policy. However, their interrelationship does not exist with regard to implementation. Monetary policy, although receiving major inputs from the president and other executive agencies, is the responsibility of the Federal Reserve Board, an independent agency. Fiscal policy, although receiving similar inputs from the Federal Reserve Board, is primarily the responsibility of the president and the U.S. Congress. The degree of equality and subsequent share of responsibility varies within a stable range. A president may wish to spend this or that amount, but only the Congress has the constitutional ability to levy taxes (although tax laws, like all others, must be signed or vetoed by the president). A president's discretion over economic policy is further limited by previous decisions to fund, for example, welfare, entitlement, and pension programs, which are not easily changed.

economics 1. The study of how people or states use their limited resources to satisfy their unlimited wants; how scarce resources are allocated to competing needs. 2. The science that deals with how goods and services are produced, distributed, and consumed. 3. The "dismal science" according to Thomas Carlyle (1795–1881) in his *Latter Day Pamphlets* (1850).

economies of scale Cost savings realized by doing things in larger rather than smaller units. This decreases the overall average cost.

economy 1. EFFICIENCY. 2. The prosperity of a state relative to previous levels of individual income or GROSS NATIONAL PRODUCT. Thus, an economy is healthy and growing if such economic indicators are rising; unhealthy or declining if such indicators are descending.

economy, underground *See* UNDERGROUND ECONOMY.

EEO *See* EQUAL EMPLOYMENT OPPORTUNITY.

effectiveness Traditionally, the extent to which an organization accomplishes some predetermined goal or objective; more recently, the overall performance of an organization from the viewpoint of some strategic constituency. Effectiveness is not entirely dependent upon the efficiency of a program because program outputs may increase without necessarily increasing effectiveness.

efficiency Competence as well as speed in performance. Americans have historically been suspicious of a too-efficient government because a truly efficient administration of public affairs could eventually eat into political liberties. Chief Justice Warren Burger, writing for the U.S. Supreme Court in *Immigration and Naturalization Service v. Chadha* (1983) said, "It is crystal clear from the records of the [Constitutional] Convention, contemporaneous writings and debates, that the Framers ranked other values higher than efficiency. . . . The choices we discern as having been made in the Constitutional Convention impose burdens on governmental processes that often seem clumsy, inefficient, and even unworkable, but those hard choices were consciously made by men who had lived under a form of government that permitted arbitrary governmental acts to go unchecked. There is no support in the Constitution or decisions of this Court for the proposition that the cumbersomeness and delays often encountered in complying with explicit Constitutional standards may be avoided."

e-government 1. Electronic government; the use of information technology to support government operations and expand citizen participation. 2. Conducting government business operations over the Internet, from providing information by government to paying bills to government. The current reality of e-government is visible in most jurisdictions at all levels of government. In North Carolina, citizens can use their credit cards to pay for their automobile registration renewals. In Miami, those unfortunate enough to have earned parking tickets can now pay for them online twenty-four hours a day, seven days a week. In Riverside County, California, you can pay your property taxes online. You can even download the Internal Revenue Service's income tax forms and then file your federal income tax return online. The whole point is to allow citizens to conduct their government business, as the e-government battle cry says, "online rather than in line." The question is not whether e-government is here. It clearly is. How big it will become is the question to be asked now. E-government has two faces: internal and external. The internal face refers to the operations of government itself; for example, using the Internet for electronic procurement, electronic forms, and Web-based management information systems. The external face refers to the online services offered to citizens and businesses; for example, community calendars, bill payment portals, and application forms for employment. E-government is in essence the overarching term for all uses of the Internet in simplifying governmental activities for the public and the public's employees. *See also* DIGITAL DIVIDE.

elastic clause *See* NECESSARY AND PROPER CLAUSE.

elite theory 1. The belief that only those with special talents or belonging to a particular group should govern society. This theory has been widely criticized for being undemocratic and ultimately oppressive. All monarchical and fascist regimes are founded on this meaning of elite theory. 2. Empirical political analyses that see the real controlling power in democratic societies encompassed in the small groups that come to dominate various interests, such as the military, business, politics, religion, and labor. *See* C. WRIGHT MILLS; PLURALISM.

emergency management Actions taken to prepare for, prevent, or lessen the effects of natural (such as floods and tornadoes) and human (terrorism) disasters. Since 2001, emergency management has taken on a new sense of urgency and has been given significant new resources with the advent of the war on terrorism.

emergency powers 1. Special powers granted to a government or executive agency that allow normal legislative procedures and/or judicial remedies to be suspended. In Western democracies, such emergency powers are usually strictly controlled by the legislature and permitted only for a limited period. 2. The enlarged authority that the president of the United States is deeded to have, either by statute, from the U.S. Constitution (Article II, Sections 2 and 3), or because of the nature of the emergency, to deal with the problem at hand. An exercise of emergency powers may or may not be later upheld by the U.S. Supreme Court. In the case of *Korematsu v. United States* (1944), the Court affirmed President Franklin D. Roosevelt's World War II decision to relocate by force U.S. citizens of Japanese origin. Yet, in the case of *Youngstown Sheet and Tube v. Sawyer* (1952), the Court denied President Harry S. Truman's assertion that he enjoyed inherent emergency powers to seize civilian steel mills so that wartime production could be maintained. The president can pretty much do what he wants under the rubric of emergency powers until he is checked by one of the other branches of government. The existence of such checks goes a long way in keeping a president's emergency powers "in the closet" until there is substantial agreement that they are needed.

eminence grise A French term meaning "gray eminence," or the power behind the throne. Staff officers are sometimes accused of exercising such power.

eminent domain 1. A government's right to take private property for the public's use. The Fifth Amendment requires that, whenever a government takes an individual's property, the property acquired must be taken for public use, and the full value thereof paid to the owner. Thus a government cannot take property from one person simply to give it to another. However, it is permissible to take private property for such purposes as urban renewal, even though ultimately the property taken will be returned to private ownership because the taking is for the benefit of the community as a whole. Property does not have to be physically taken from the owner to acquire Fifth Amendment protection. If government action leads to a lower value of private property, that may also constitute a "taking" and therefore require payment of compensation. 2. In the context of international law, eminent domain can mean EXPROPRIATION.

empirical Findings or conclusions derived from direct and repeated observations of a phenomenon under study.

employee assistance program (EAP) A formal program designed to assist employees with personal problems through (1) internal counseling and aid, and (2) a referral service to outside counseling resources. The thrust of such programs is to increase productivity by correcting distracting outside personal problems.

Employment Act of 1946 *See* FISCAL POLICY.

employment-at-will The common law concept that an employment having no specific term may be terminated by either party with or without notice or cause. In recent years, discharged employees have increasingly challenged what they consider to be wrongful discharges. They have based their court suits on claims of violation of public policy, the existence of an implied contract, and the covenant of good faith and fair dealing. In general, only employees protected by collective bargaining, antidiscrimination laws, civil service, and teacher tenure laws are not subject to "at-will" discharges.

empowerment 1. Giving a person or organization the formal authority to do something. It is relatively easy for managers to gain the traditional authoritarian powers of domination that allow them to control and punish subordinates; what is far more difficult is the obtaining of the power needed for positive accomplishment. This kind of power is less formally given than informally earned—often by empowering others. Thus the paradox that managers can often make themselves more powerful by giving power away. By empowering others, leaders actually acquire more "productive power"—the power truly needed to accomplish organizational goals. Managers who cannot delegate, who will not trust or empower subordinates, become less and less powerful, and correspondingly more and more incompetent, as they increasingly seek to hoard power. Remember power, much as with money—a variant of power—is like manure: You have to spread it around for it to do any good. 2. In the context of antipoverty programs, for example, by giving the poor more power over their lives by allowing public housing tenants to manage or buy their homes.

end game 1. In chess, the play when only a few pieces are left on the board. 2. The last part (the last events) of a policy line that is coming to a conclusion, coming to a natural finish. For example, once the U. S. decided to pull all Americans out of Vietnam as the South Vietnamese government began to collapse in 1975, the "end game" began.

enterprise zone/urban enterprise zone Originally an area of high unemployment and poverty that is granted business tax reductions by a state to lure industry and concomitant prosperity. More than thirty-seven states have enterprise zones of one kind or another; however, the trend has been to use them less as a means to help poor neighborhoods and more as part of overall regional economic development programs geared equally to retaining old businesses and attracting new ones.

entitlement A government program that pays benefits to individuals, organizations, or other governments that meet eligibility requirements set by law. Social Security is the largest federal entitlement program for individuals. Others include farm price supports, Medicare, Medicaid, unemployment insurance, and food stamps. Entitlement programs have great budgetary significance in that they lock in such a great percentage of the total federal budget each year that changes in the budget can be made only at the margin.

entrepreneurialism 1. The traditional efforts of a business leader who combines the factors of production (capital, land, and labor) to create a new enterprise. 2. As applied to the modern public sector, a call for managers to be transformational leaders who strive to change organizational culture. Managers must develop a new vision for the organization—then convert that vision into reality. Entrepreneurial vision cannot and should not be limited to the top; at every organizational level, managers need vision and dreams, need the ability to assess the situation and plan for a better future. Those who cannot do this, who cannot visualize and plan for change, are by definition incompetent. After all, organizations that do not change must eventually die—even in the public sector. Besides, if you don't have a dream—if you don't have a vision—how will you ever know whether it comes true? *See also* PUBLIC POLICY ENTREPRENEUR.

enumerated powers Powers of the U.S. government specifically provided for and listed in the U.S. Constitution. *Compare to* IMPLIED POWER; RESERVED POWERS.

environmental impact statement A document assessing the impact of a new program upon the environment.

environmental justice A concern for the disparities in distribution of the harmful effects of environmental hazards; particularly why the poor are often forced by circumstances into environments that put their health at risk.

environmental movement The grassroots mobilization of citizens that grew out of the earlier CONSERVATION movement and that is concerned with the quality of natural and human environment. The movement receives its organizational expression through interest groups that engage in lobbying, court litigation, and public-information activities.

equal employment opportunity (EEO) A concept fraught with political, cultural, and emotional overtones. Generally, it applies to a set of employment procedures and practices that effectively prevent an individual from being adversely excluded from employment opportunities on the basis of race, color, sex, religion, age, national origin, and/or other factors that cannot lawfully be used in employing people. Although the ideal of EEO is an employment system devoid of intentional and unintentional discrimination, achieving this ideal may be a political impossibility because of the problem of definition. One man's equal opportunity may be another's institutional racism or a woman's institutional sexism. Because of this problem of definition, only the courts have been able to say whether, when, and where EEO exists. *See also* AFFIRMATIVE ACTION; CHILLING; DISCRIMINATION; MAKE WHOLE; REPRESENTATIVE BUREAUCRACY; REVERSE DISCRIMINATION.

Equal Employment Opportunity Act of 1972 An amendment to Title VII of the 1964 Civil Rights Act strengthening the authority of the Equal Employment Opportunity Commission and extending antidiscrimination provisions to state and local governments, labor organizations, and employment agencies.

Equal Employment Opportunity Commission (EEOC) A five-member commission created by Title VII of the CIVIL RIGHTS ACT OF 1964. The EEOC members (one designated chair) are appointed for five-year terms by the president, subject to the advice and consent of the U.S. Senate. The EEOC's mission is to end discrimination based on race, color, religion, sex, and/or national origin in hiring, promotion, firing, wages, testing, training, apprenticeship, and all other conditions of employment, and to promote voluntary action programs by employers, unions, and community organizations to make EQUAL EMPLOYMENT OPPORTUNITY an actuality.

equal employment opportunity plan An organization's written plan to remedy past discrimination against, or the underutilization of, women and minorities. The plan itself usually consists of a statement of goals, timetables for achieving them, and specific program efforts.

Equal Pay Act of 1963 An amendment to the Fair Labor Standards Act of 1938 prohibiting pay discrimination because of sex and providing that men and women working in the same establishment under similar conditions must receive the same pay if their jobs require equal (similar) skill, effort, and responsibility.

equal pay for equal work The principle that salary rates should not be dependent upon factors unrelated to the quantity or quality of work.

equal protection of laws The constitutional requirement that a government will not treat people unequally, nor set up illegal categories to justify treating people unequally, nor give unfair or unequal treatment to a person based on that person's race and/or religion. The Fourteenth Amendment prohibits states from denying their residents the equal protection of the law. The due process clause of the Fifth Amendment has also been held, in *Bolling v. Sharpe* (1954), to include a requirement of equal protection. *Compare to* REVERSE DISCRIMINATION. Although equal protection has been the law since the ratification of the Fourteenth Amendment in 1868, it was largely a dormant concept until awakened by the Warren Court in the

1950s. Landmark decisions, such as *BROWN V. BOARD OF EDUCATION,* used the equal protection clauses to revolutionize U.S. society.

Equal Rights Amendment (ERA) A proposed amendment to the U.S. Constitution passed by the U.S. Congress in 1972 that never became law because too few states ratified it.

equalization The adjustment of assessments and taxes on real estate to make sure that properties are properly valued and are fairly taxed according to value.

establishment 1. Those who hold the real power in society; a basically conservative and secretive ruling class. The term first surfaced in England during the 1950s and is often traced to an article written by Henry Fairlie in the *Spectator* (September 1955). But it soon crossed the Atlantic and by the 1960s there was much talk of an "Eastern Establishment" and a "Protestant Establishment." Now the word has become so trite and overused that "establishments" are to be found all over; or not found because secretiveness is part of their essence. 2. The collective holders of power in a segment of society: political, military, social, academic, religious, or literary. It is always the establishment that revolutionaries — whether political, intellectual, organizational, or others — wish to overthrow, so they can become the new establishment. 3. A government installation, together with its personnel and equipment, organized as an operating entity.

ethics A set of moral principles or values that can be applied to societies or social groups as a whole but that may also involve standards of behavior constituting implied responsibilities for professional activity. There are many ethical people in government, as there are in each of the professions. However, their ethical standards tend to reflect their personal backgrounds rather than some abstract standard of professional conduct. Analyses of the ethical issues in public life range from the always-plead-innocent school of venality to the philosophic concerns of providing equitable public services to each member of the community. *See also* CODE OF ETHICS; WHISTLE-BLOWER.

ethics, citizenship Viewing the ethical obligations of public employees as not being limited to their bureaucratic roles, but being expanded because of their moral obligations as citizens.

Ethics in Government Act of 1978 The federal statute that seeks to deal with possible conflicts of interest by former federal executive branch employees by imposing postemployment prohibitions on their activities. The restrictions in the law are concerned with former government employees' representation or attempts to influence federal agencies, not with their employment by others. What is prohibited depends on how involved a former employee was with a matter while with the government and whether that person was one of a specified group of senior employees.

evaluation 1. An attempt to assess specific policy options by conducting experiments, assessing their outcomes, and recommending whether the new concept should be broadly applied. In 1967, Edward Suchman of Columbia University published the first major work on evaluation theory, *Evaluative Research.* Suchman's work argued that evaluation was essentially a field of study; that evaluative research and practice can and must be studied in a general context outside of evaluation applications in the various fields of specialization; that evaluation was generic. Generic? Yes. But in whatever context it surfaced, it was also intensely political. 2. In intelligence usage, appraisal of an item of information for credibility, pertinency, and accuracy. Appraisal is accomplished at several stages within the intelligence cycle with progressively different contexts. Initial evaluations, made by case officers and report officers, are focused upon the reliability of the source and the accuracy of the information as judged by data available at or close to their operational levels. Later evaluations, by intelligence analysts, are primarily concerned with verifying accuracy of information and may, in effect, convert information into intelligence. 3. The appraisal of a government employee's job performance.

evaluation, policy The analysis of policy alternatives in advance of a decision.

evaluation, program 1. The systematic examination of an activity or a group of activities undertaken by government to make a determination about the short- and long-range effects. Program evaluation is distinguished from management evaluation (also called *organization evaluation*), because the latter is limited to a program's internal administrative procedures. Although program evaluations use management and organizational data, the main thrust is necessarily on overall program objectives and impact. A formal program evaluation effort normally implies that a relationship of "arm's length" independence has been established between the program and those evaluating it. In-house evaluations, however well conducted, are likely to be suspected of special pleading on behalf of the agency concerned. 2. An assessment of the effectiveness of a program or grant project after it has been completed. It is undertaken by the granting agency to determine whether its funds were spent effectively, legally, and according to the original grant application.

ex officio A Latin phrase meaning "by virtue of the office." Many people hold positions on boards, commissions, and councils because of another office they occupy. For example, the mayor of a city may be an ex officio member of the board of trustees of a university in that city.

ex parte A Latin phrase meaning "with only one side present." *Ex parte* usually refers to a hearing or trial in which only one side is present because the other side failed to show up or was not given notice.

ex post facto law A law that makes something retroactively illegal—makes unlawful an act that was not a crime when it was committed. The U.S. Constitution prohibits ex post facto laws by the federal government (Article I, Section 9) and by the states (Article I, Section 10). These prohibitions have been interpreted to prevent the imposition of a greater penalty for a crime than that in effect when the crime was committed. However, laws that retroactively determine how a person is to be tried for a crime may be changed as long as no important rights are lost. Laws are not considered ex post facto if they make the punishment less severe than it was when the crime was committed.

excepted positions/exempted positions U.S. civil service positions that have been excepted or exempted from merit system requirements. Most of these positions are excluded by statute and are under merit systems administered by agencies, such as the Tennessee Valley Authority, the Federal Bureau of Investigation, the U.S. Foreign Service, and the U.S. Postal Service. They are in the same category as unclassified positions, positions excepted by law, positions excepted by executive order, positions excepted by civil service rule, and positions outside the competitive service.

exclusive power Powers that constitutionally belong to one level of government only. For example, the federal government has exclusive power over currency, postal service, and foreign policy. This is in contrast to a concurrent (or shared) power, such as taxation.

executive 1. The highest manager(s) in an organization. 2. That branch of government concerned with carrying out the policies and laws created by a legislature.

executive agreement A device that permits the president to enter into open or secret arrangements with foreign governments without obtaining the approval of the U.S. Congress. The vast majority of executive agreements are entered into in pursuit of specific congressional authority. Because there is often a thin line between what constitutes an executive agreement a president can make on his own and a treaty that must be ratified by the U.S. Senate, considerable concern can arise that a president might be using executive agreements to avoid the Senate's advice and consent role. The U.S. Supreme Court in *United States v. Belmont* (1937) unanimously held an executive agreement to be a valid international compact, state policy notwithstanding. The Court said, in part, "In respect of all international negotiations and compacts, and in respect of our foreign relations generally, state lines disappear." The Court has ruled, however, that the president is not free to enter into executive agreements that violate constitutional provisions. See *United States v. Guy W. Capps, Inc.* (1955); and *Reid v. Covert* (1957). By the Case Act of 1972, Congress required that the secretary of state transmit to the Congress all executive agreements to which the United States is a party no later than sixty days after such agreement has entered into force. The president need report secret agreements only to the Foreign Relations committees of the two houses. The act did not give the Congress the authority to disapprove an executive agreement.

executive branch In a government with SEPARATION OF POWERS, that part responsible for applying or administering the law. Thus a president, a governor, and a mayor, and their respective supporting bureaucracies, are the executive branches of their respective jurisdictions. But not all the federal bureaucracy is part of the executive branch. Some agencies, such as the General Accounting Office, are directly responsible to the U.S. Congress. Others, such as the Federal Trade Commission (and other regulatory agencies), have been held by the U.S. Supreme Court not to be part of the executive branch. *See HUMPHREY'S EXECUTOR V. UNITED STATES.*

executive department A cabinet-level agency in the federal government.

executive director 1. The head of a public agency. 2. The highest-ranking staff member of a private nonprofit organization.

Executive Office of the President (EOP) The umbrella office consisting of the top presidential staff agencies that provide the president help and advice in carrying out his major responsibilities. The EOP was created by President Franklin D. Roosevelt under the authority of the Reorganization Act of 1939. Since then, presidents have used executive orders, reorganization plans, and legislative initiatives to reorganize, expand, and/or contract the EOP. *See also* BROWNLOW COMMITTEE; PRESIDENTIAL POWER.

executive officer A military term, now commonly if informally used in government offices, for the person who is just under the boss and runs the day-to-day operations of the agency.

executive order 1. A rule or regulation issued by a chief administrative authority that, because of precedent and existing legislative authorization, has the effect of law. 2. The principal mode of administrative action on the part of the president of the United States. The power of a president to issue executive orders emanates from the constitutional provision requiring him to "take care that the laws be faithfully executed," the commander-in-chief clause, and express powers vested in him by congressional statutes.

Executive Order 8802 The presidential executive order of June 25, 1941. It required (1) that defense contractors not discriminate against workers because of race, creed, and/or national origin, and (2) established a Committee on Fair Employment Practice to investigate and remedy violations.

Executive Order 9981 The presidential executive order of July 26, 1948, by which President Harry S. Truman mandated the racial integration of the military and naval forces of the United States and called for an end to racial discrimination in all federal employment.

Executive Order 10925 The presidential executive order of March 6, 1961. This order required for the first time that "affirmative action" be used to implement the policy of nondiscrimination in employment by the federal government and its contractors.

Executive Order 10988 The presidential executive order of January 17, 1962, establishing the right of federal employees to bargain with management over certain limited issues. Considered the "Magna Carta" of labor relations in the federal government, it was superseded by Executive Order 11491.

Executive Order 11246 The presidential executive order of September 24, 1965, requiring federal government contractors to have affirmative action programs.

Executive Order 11491 The presidential executive order of October 29, 1969. The order granted each federal employee the right to join or not to join a labor organization, created the Federal Labor Relations Council (which was superseded by the Federal Labor Relations Authority), and generally expanded the scope of bargaining for federal employees.

executive oversight The total process by which executives attempt to control their organization and to hold individual managers responsible for carrying out their programs.

executive power The authority guaranteed to a political executive by a governing constitution or subsequent legislation. In the U.S. republic, the legislature is supreme. After all, it has the greatest number of enumerated powers and the executive and judicial branches must enforce its laws. As James Madison wrote in *Federalist* No. 51: "In republican government, the legislative authority necessarily predominates." President Franklin D. Roosevelt in a press conference on July 23, 1937, put it another way: "It is the duty of the President to propose and it is the privilege of the Congress to dispose." However, many political executives, whether mayors, governors, or presidents, have tried—often for sound cause relating to the public good—to give themselves more policymaking power than may be constitutionally warranted. Just how far can an executive deviate from the legislative will or the letter of the constitution in a republican government? The amount of deviation is usually a function of the political strength of the executive as evidenced by a large electoral mandate, control by the executive's party in the legislature, and/or public-opinion poll ratings. Strong executives are able to put into place more of the policies they espouse.

executive privilege The presidential claim that the executive branch may withhold information from the U.S. Congress or its committees and the courts to preserve confidential communications within the executive branch or to secure the national interest. Although the U.S. Constitution does not explicitly grant the executive a privilege to withhold information from the Congress, presidents have from the beginning of the Republic claimed it. President George Washington withheld from the U.S. House of Representatives papers and documents connected with the Jay Treaty (1794) because, he argued, the House had no constitutional role in making treaties. The presidential claim of executive privilege was not seriously challenged until President Richard M. Nixon sought to use executive privilege to sustain immunity from the judicial process. *See UNITED STATES V. NIXON.*

executive session 1. A secret meeting. **2.** The confidential meeting of a governing body. **3.** The meeting of a U.S. Senate or U.S. House of Representatives committee (or, occasionally, of the entire membership) that only the group's members are privileged to attend. Witnesses usually appear before committees meeting in executive session, and other members of the U.S. Congress may be invited, but the public and press are not allowed to attend. As a result of SUNSHINE LAWS, most committee meetings in the Congress are now open to the public. **4.** A meeting of the U.S. Senate when it is dealing with executive functions, such as the confirmation of presidential nominations and the ratification of treaties. In this context, an executive session is distinguished from a legislative session.

executive summary A brief description (usually a few pages) of a much larger report (usually a few hundred pages).

executive, chief 1. The highest elected office in a jurisdiction, whether it be the mayor of a city, the governor of a state, or the president of the United States. **2.** The highest-level manager of an organization no matter what the formal title might be. **3.** The President of the United States. All chief executives, because they occupy a highly visible office, have significant public relations responsibilities. As President Calvin Coolidge wrote in his *Autobiography* (1929): "It has become the custom in our country to expect all Chief Executives, from the President down, to conduct activities analogous to an entertainment bureau. No occasion is too trivial for its promoters to invite them to attend and deliver an address."

executive, plural *See* PLURAL EXECUTIVE.

exempt 1. Tax-exempt; referring to nonprofit organizations not usually subject to taxation. **2.** Employees who, because of their administrative, professional, and/or executive status, are not covered by the overtime provisions of the Fair Labor Standards Act. In consequence, their employers are not legally required to pay them for overtime work. *Compare to* EXCEPTED POSITIONS/EXEMPTED POSITIONS.

exemption A deduction from gross income for income tax purposes allowed for the support of one's self and dependents.

exit interview A tool that monitors employee terminations and seeks information about why the employee is leaving and what that person liked or disliked about the job, working conditions, and/or company policy. Exit interviews are usually, and most desirably, conducted by the personnel department and not by the supervisor of the exiting employee.

expectancy theory The theory that individuals have cognitive "expectancies" regarding outcomes that are likely to occur as a result of what they do, and that individuals have preferences among these various outcomes. Consequently, motivation occurs according to an individual's expectations and choices. An "expectancy" in this context refers to an employee's perceived probability that a given level of effort will result in a given outcome, such as a promotion or raise in salary. The value that an employee places on this outcome, the strength of the employee's preference for it, has been termed *valence* by Victor H. Vroom, *Work and Motivation* (1964). Valence can be positive or negative, depending on whether an individual is attracted to a possible outcome or repelled by it.

expenditures The actual spending of money as distinguished from its appropriation. Expenditures are made by the disbursing officers of a government; appropriations are made by a legislature. The two are rarely identical: In a given fiscal year, expenditures may represent money appropriated one, two, or more years previously.

expressed powers Powers specifically stated, or expressed in a constitution. *See also* NECESSARY AND PROPER CLAUSE.

expropriation The confiscation of private property by a government, which may or may not pay a portion of its value in return. *Compare to* NATIONALIZATION.

F

Fabian strategy 1. Avoiding a decisive battle with a superior force but constantly seeking to delay and harass it; named after the Roman general, Fabius, who eventually defeated Hannibal with this technique during the Second Punic War (218–201 B.C.E.) 2. By analogy a political strategy that seeks to gradually wear down the opposition with a series of small victories. Many socialists early in the twentieth century called for a Fabian strategy to gradually create the modern WELFARE STATE. The strategy worked.

face time The time that a bureaucrat spends making an impression on someone that can help his or her career, such as an immediate boss or an influential member of Congress.

fact finding An impartial review of the issues in a labor dispute by a specially appointed third party, whether it be an individual, a panel, or a board. The fact finder holds formal or informal hearings and submits a report to the administrative agency and/or the parties involved. The fact finder's report, usually considered advisory, may contain specific recommendations.

faction 1. In English political history, any group whose motives for supporting a given action were inherently suspect because of the assumption of selfish interest, as opposed to the welfare of the community as a whole. 2. The term used by James Madison in *Federalist No.* 10 to describe "a number of citizens, whether amounting to a majority or minority of the whole, who are united and actuated by some common impulse of passion or of interest, adverse to the rights of other citizens, or to the permanent and aggregate interests of the community." 3. Any subgroup within a larger organization; for example, the moderate faction of the Republican party, the conservative faction of the Democratic party.

Fair Labor Standards Act of 1938 (FLSA) The federal statute, also called Wages and Hours Act, that, as amended, established standards for minimum wages, overtime pay, equal pay, record keeping, and child labor. The U.S. Supreme Court upheld the FLSA in *United States v. Darby Lumber* (1941), and in *Garcia v. San Antonio Metropolitan Transit Authority* (1985) extended coverage to state and local government employees.

Faith-Based Initiative The George W. Bush administration's efforts to use nonprofit agencies—especially religious organizations—to provide social services. Bush has even created an Office of Faith-Based and Community Initiatives to further this agenda. And five departments—Health and Human Services, Housing and Urban Development, Justice, Education, and Labor—have created centers to further faith-based efforts.

Family and Medical Leave Act of 1993 The federal law that requires employers in the public and private sectors with at least fifty workers to allow up to twelve weeks of unpaid leave (for childbirth, care of spouse or parent, new adoption of a child, and so on) during a twelve-month period for all employees (whether male or female) employed for at least a year.

family policy A vague term for the totality of current or future legislation (or corporate policies) aimed at reconciling the roles of women as mothers and members of the workforce. Family policies seek to help working mothers better cope with their family responsibilities through paid maternity leave, subsidized or free day-care programs for children, and so on. A main difference in attitudes toward family policy is that liberals, as opposed to conservatives, seek policies that call for additional government spending; conservatives, as opposed to liberals, seek policies that emphasize traditional religious values and the enforcement of their standards of morality (for example, in regard to abortion and pornography) for the entire society.

fatigue curve A graphic representation of productivity increases and decreases influenced by fatigue. As workers "warm up" or practice their tasks, productivity increases; thereafter, fatigue sets in and productivity decreases. After lunch or coffee breaks, productivity should rise again slightly, but thereafter continuously declines until the end of the day. This pattern varies with type of work. Fatigue curve measurements are essential in establishing realistic work standards.

Fayol, Henri (1841–1925) French executive engineer who developed the first comprehensive theory of management. While Frederick W. Taylor was tinkering with the technology employed by the individual worker, Fayol was theorizing about the elements necessary to organize and manage a major corporation. Fayol's major work, *Administration Industrielle et Generale* (published in France in 1916), was almost ignored in the United States until Constance Storr's English translation, *General and Industrial Management*, appeared in 1949. Since that time, Fayol's theoretical contributions have been widely recognized and his work is considered fully as significant as that of Taylor. Fayol believed that his concept of management was universally applicable to every type of organization. He espoused six principles: (1) technical (production of goods), (2) commercial (buying, selling, and exchange activities), (3) financial (raising and using capital), (4) security (protection of property and people), (5) accounting, and (6) managerial (coordination, control, organization, planning, and command of people). Fayol's primary interest and emphasis was on his final principle, managerial, which addressed such variables as the division of work, the unity of command, the unity of direction, the subordination of individual interest to general interest, the remuneration of personnel, the stability of personnel tenure, authority and responsibility, discipline, centralization, scalar chains, order, equity, initiative, and esprit de corps. Fayol was the first to explain why principles beyond the golden rule and other moral precepts were needed.

Federal Labor Relations Authority (FLRA) The agency created by the Civil Service Reform Act of 1978 to oversee the creation of bargaining units, to supervise elections, and otherwise to deal with labor-management issues in federal agencies. A general counsel investigates alleged unfair labor practices and prosecutes them before the FLRA. Also within the FLRA and acting as a separate body, the Federal Service Impasses Panel (FSIP) acts to resolve negotiation impasses.

Federal Reserve System Colloquially known as "the Fed," this is in effect the central bank of the United States, created by the Federal Reserve Act of 1913 and charged with administering and making policy for the nation's credit and monetary affairs. Run by a seven-member board of governors appointed by the president (who also appoints their chairman), the system includes twelve Federal Reserve banks, twenty-four branches, all national banks, and many state banking institutions. Three major monetary tools are available to the Federal Reserve System to control the economy's supply of money and credit: (1) open-market operations, which, through the purchase or sale of government bonds, increase or decrease the availability of dollars to member banks; (2) discount-rate adjustments, which increase or decrease the interest rate charged to member banks for the money they borrow; and (3) reserve requirements, which, through changes in levels of reserve, increase or decrease the number of dollars a bank may make available for loan. Two less significant tools, moral suasion and selective controls over stock purchase margin requirements, are also used to help manage the economy. *See* FISCAL POLICY; MONETARY POLICY.

Federal Service Impasses Panel *See* FEDERAL LABOR RELATIONS AUTHORITY.

Federal Trade Commission (FTC) The independent regulatory agency, created by the Federal Trade Commission Act of 1914, the objective of which is to prevent the free enterprise system from being stifled, substantially lessened, fettered by monopoly or restraints on trade, or corrupted by unfair or deceptive trade practices. It has no authority to punish; its function is to prevent, through cease-and-desist orders and other means, those practices condemned by the law of federal trade regulation. *See HUMPHREY'S EXECUTOR V. UNITED STATES.*

federalese *See* GOBBLEDYGOOK.

federalism 1. A system of governance in which a national, overarching government shares power with subnational or state governments. History indicates clearly that the principal factor in the formation of federal systems of government has been a common external threat. Tribes, cities, colonies, and states have joined together in voluntary unions to defend themselves. Not all systems so formed have been federal. A federal system has (1) a written constitution that divides government powers between the central government and constituent governments, giving substantial powers and sovereignty to each; (2) levels of government, through their own instrumentalities, exercising power directly over citizens (unlike a confederation, in which only subnational units act directly on citizens and the central government acts only on the subnational governments); and (3) a constitutional distribution of powers that cannot be changed unilaterally by any level of government or by the ordinary process of legislation. 2. An approach to integration that attempts to link states still acknowledged as separate entities through the establishment of some form of power sharing at the center of the federation.

federalism, cooperative 1. The notion that the national, state, and local governments are cooperating, interacting agents, jointly working to solve common problems, rather than conflicting, sometimes hostile competitors, pursuing similar or, more likely, conflicting ends. Although some cooperation has always been evident in spite of the conflict, competition, and complexity of intergovernmental relations, it was most prominent between the 1930s and the 1950s. The emergency funding arrangements of the Depression years known collectively as the New Deal and the cooperation among federal, state, and local authorities during World War II to administer civilian defense, rationing, and other wartime programs are noteworthy examples of cooperative federalism in the United States. 2. The fiscal arrangements whereby the federal government offers states and localities grants to encourage them to pursue national goals.

federalism, creative The Lyndon B. Johnson administration's term for its approach to intergovernmental relations, which was characterized by joint planning and decisionmaking at all levels of government (as well as in the private sector) in the management of intergovernmental programs. Many new programs of this period had an urban-metropolitan focus, and much attention was given to antipoverty issues. Creative federalism sought to foster the development of a singular Great Society by integrating the poor into the U.S. mainstream; its expansive efforts were marked by the rapid development of categorical grant programs to state and local governments and by direct federal grants to cities that frequently bypassed state governments entirely.

federalism, dual The nineteenth-century concept that the functions and responsibilities of the federal and state governments were theoretically distinguished and functionally separate from each other. Nevertheless, as recently as 1997, the U.S. Supreme Court in *Printz v. United States* reasserted the "dual sovereignty" of dual federalism. Some analysts suggest that this kind of federalism, which largely went out when the New Deal of 1933 came in, is what the Ronald Reagan and all subsequent Republican administrations sought, at least rhetorically, to return to. The basic idea of dual federalism was expressed succinctly in *The American Commonwealth* (1891) by James Bryce, a British scholar who visited the United States in the 1880s to observe its political system: "The characteristic feature and special interest of the American Union is that it shows us two governments covering the same ground yet distinct and separate in their action. It is like a great factory wherein two sets of machinery are at work, their revolving wheels apparently intermixed, their bands crossing one another, yet each doing its own work without touching or hampering the other."

federalism, fiscal The fiscal relations between and among units of government in a federal system. The theory of fiscal federalism, or multiunit government finance, addresses the question of the optimal design of governments in a multilevel (or federal) governmental system. The public sector has three principal economic problems to solve: (1) the attainment of the most equitable distribution of income; (2) the maintenance of high employment with stable prices; and (3) the establishment of an efficient pattern of resource allocation. The theory of fiscal federalism postulates that a federal form of government can be especially effective in solving these problems because of the flexibility it has in dealing with some problems at the national or central level and some at the local or regional levels. It argues that, for a variety of reasons, the first two problems, equitable distribution of income and the maintenance of high employment with stable prices, are problems that the national level of government is best equipped to handle. However, according to the theory, the decentralized regional or local units of government can more efficiently deal with the third problem, allocation of resources, because such units of government are more familiar than the central or national government with local needs and the desires of citizens for public services. Even so, grants-in-aid from the national level of government to local levels may be needed to stimulate local government spending for national purposes, to provide for uniform or minimum service levels (as in education), or to compensate citizens of one area for benefits from services they finance that spill over to residents of another area. Spillover benefits are especially common in programs such as clean water and air pollution control, health, and education.

federalism, horizontal State-to-state interactions and relations. Interstate relations take many forms, including compacts and commissions established for specific purposes: river basin management, transportation, the extradition of criminals, the conservation of forests and wildlife, and the administration of parks and recreation. Horizontal relations between local governments also are numerous. Cities frequently contract for services from various neighboring local governments (and even from private providers).

federalism, marble-cake The concept that the cooperative relations among the varying levels of government result in an intermingling of activities; in contrast to the more traditional view of layer-cake federalism, which holds that the three levels of government are totally or almost totally separate. Marble-cake federalism is usually associated with Morton Grodzins (1917–1964), who pointed to rural county health officials called *sanitarians:* Sanitarians are appointed by the state government under merit standards established by the federal government, and although their base salaries come from state and federal funds, the county provides them with offices and office amenities and pays a portion of their expenses. See Morton Grodzins, *The American System* (1966).

federalism, new 1. The reconceptualization of federalism as INTERGOVERNMENTAL RELATIONS. 2. The actual relations between the levels of government as they shared in the performance of expanding government functions in the early 1970s. The term *new federalism* has its origins in the liberal Republican effort to find an alternative to the centralized state perceived as having been set up by the New Deal, but an alternative that nonetheless recognized the need for effective national government. During the Richard M. Nixon administration, the term referred to the style of decentralized management at the federal level symbolized by General Revenue Sharing and the decentralization of federal regional management to ten administrative regions. New federalism as developed by the Ronald Reagan administration disregarded the Nixon approach of decentralized federal regional management and turned to the development of direct relations between the federal government and the states. The intent was to return power and responsibility to the states and to reduce dramatically the federal government's role in domestic programs, reminiscent of the DUAL FEDERALISM that prevailed in the United States in the nineteenth century. Reagan's new federalism included the use of new block grant programs to give states greater flexibility in using federal monies. This form of new federalism has now evolved into DEVOLUTION.

federalism, picket fence The concept implying that bureaucratic specialists at the various levels of government (along with clientele groups) exercise considerable power over the nature of intergovernmental programs. Bureaucratic or program specialists at national, state, and local government levels for such fields as public housing, vocational education, health and hospitals, and higher education represent the pickets in the picket fence. They communicate with each other in daily work, belong to the same professional organizations, and have similar professional training. They are likely to be in conflict with general-purpose government officials (mayors, governors, the president), who attempt to coordinate the vertical power structures, or pickets. The general-purpose officials are the cross pieces of the fence. The metaphor is credited to Terry Sanford, coined when he was the governor of North Carolina. See his *Storm Over the States* (1967).

federalism, vertical State-national government interactions. These interactions are not limited to the executive branches of the national and state governments; close coordination also exists between the federal and state court systems. Crisscrossing vertical relations also have become more common. For example, the executive branch of the national government embarked upon several programs for assistance to state courts and state legislatures in the 1970s.

federalism, world An overarching government encompassing all states. It implies that a worldwide organization, such as the United Nations, would someday have enough authority to cope with the inherent anarchy of the international system. World federalism is an idealist concept that has no hope of realization until all states are willing to give up elements of traditional sovereignty for the general good.

***Federalist* No. 35** The *Federalist* paper in which James Madison discusses the nature and advantages of a legislature representing all classes of society, something he considered "altogether visionary." Madison concluded that, as long as the votes of the people are free, "the representative body . . . will be composed of landholders, merchants, and men of the learned professions," who out of their own self-interest would look after the interests of those not directly represented.

***Federalist* No. 51** The *Federalist* paper in which James Madison explains how the federal Constitution provides for a SEPARATION OF POWERS whereby "those who administer each department [have] the necessary constitutional means and personal motives to resist encroachments of the others." This ideal is achieved by "contriving the interior structure of the government as that its several constituent parts may, by their mutual relations, be the means of keeping each other in their proper places." *Compare to* CHECKS AND BALANCES.

Federalist No. 78 *See* JUDICIAL REVIEW; LEAST DANGEROUS BRANCH.

Federalist No. 10 The *Federalist* paper in which James Madison discusses the problem of FACTIONS and the danger they pose to a political system. Madison feared that the interests of parties and pressure groups could destabilize a government; but he believed that an overarching representative government, one with a functional as well as territorial separation of powers, could prevent this. Madison's brief essay, a defense of a pluralistic society, is the best known of the *Federalist Papers*. In the federal union he advocated, Madison envisioned "a republican remedy for the diseases most incident to republican government." The essay is one of the first attempts by an American to explain the political nature of man. Madison found the causes of political differences and the creation of factions to be "sown in the nature of man." The essay is the classic explanation of why it is not easy to achieve change in the U.S. political system. The constitutional structure is purposely designed to protect minorities from the possible tyranny of 50 percent plus 1. The essay was more or less rediscovered by political analysts early in the twentieth century when they sought to build a historical justification for modern interest group theory.

Federalist Papers The commentary on the U.S. Constitution and the theories behind it, published in 1787–1788, and considered by many political scientists to be the most important work of political theory written in the United States—the one product of the American mind counted among the classics of political philosophy. The papers were originally newspaper articles written by Alexander Hamilton, James Madison, and John Jay (under the name Publius) to encourage New York to ratify the new U.S. Constitution. The papers reflect the genius of the balance achieved in the U.S. system between the views of Madison, an exponent of limited government, and Hamilton, an admirer of an energetic national government.

federated governments *See* METROPOLITAN GOVERNMENT.

federation 1. A union of states in which power is shared with a central authority handling issues such as foreign, security, and overall economic policies, and the separate units having authority over other issues. The union is the federation. *Compare to* FEDERALISM. **2.** What efforts at regional integration attempt to achieve through constitutional or power sharing arrangements as opposed to a functionalist approach.

feedback A concept derived from communication theory and systems theory that refers to the process whereby information about the effect of action on the environment returns to the organism, thereby allowing a modification of behavior to take place if necessary. This process is more likely when negative feedback suggests that a policy or action is not having the desired effect. If the feedback is positive, the action or policy is more likely to be continued without modification. Feedback is effective to the extent that it is noisy. The people who set the goals and make the decisions must hear it. Sometimes feedback is heard as a complaint about slow service or poor-quality products. Sometimes it is the silent noise of the citizens voting to throw the rascals out. And sometimes it is an exploding rocket ship, as in the space shuttle disasters.

fiduciary 1. A relationship where one person acts for another in a formal and legally binding position of trust usually in overseeing the property or affairs of another. 2. A concept in the theory of representation. A "fiduciary" is a representative who votes as the voters he or she represents would vote if they were present to vote for themselves; that is, the representative acts as a fiduciary for constituents. *Compare to* TRUSTEE.

field theory Visualizing and understanding an administrator's environment by using a force field analysis of the pressures that bear upon an agency. Field theory originated in physics. It was borrowed by the psychologist KURT LEWIN to explain how an individual's behavior at any given time is the result of that person's personality interacting with the psychological forces in the environment. Organizational analysts refocused field theory from the individual to the group, the group that made up an organization. By systematically examining all the forces—all the powers—in the organization's field (meaning environment)—thus a force field analysis—they were better able to understand why the organization acted the way it did. Those wishing to understand why a government or an agency does seemingly irrational or contradictory things use a force field analysis to arrive at an explanation.

filibuster 1. A pirate who waged irregular warfare for private gain. 2. A time-delaying tactic used by a legislative minority in an effort to prevent a vote on a bill. The most common method is unlimited debate, but other forms of parliamentary maneuvering may be used. True filibusters are not possible in the House, because no member is permitted to speak for longer than one hour without unanimous consent. Moreover, a majority can call for the "previous question" and bring a bill to an immediate vote. In the Senate a member can filibuster without speaking continuously; he or she may yield to a colleague for a question or call for a quorum without losing the floor. In the event a recess is called, he or she is entitled to regain the floor when the Senate reassembles. A filibuster is a kind of guerrilla warfare on the part of a minority to prevent a majority from exercising its will. In this sense, it is antidemocratic, especially as it was once notoriously used by U.S. senators from the South to delay or defeat civil rights bills. In 1917, the Senate adopted the first cloture rule. As amended in 1975, it provides that the Senate may end debate—may end a filibuster—on a pending bill by a three-fifths vote of the entire Senate membership. In the modern Senate, filibusters—and cloture—are more common than ever.

financial disclosure Requirements under various federal laws that top federal officials and candidates for federal office disclose the sources of their personal income as well as sources of campaign contributions.

financial report A written statement—also called an *accountant's certificate, accountant's opinion,* or *audit report*—prepared by an independent accountant or auditor after an audit. It is addressed to the owners, directors, and stockholders of the audited enterprise. The auditor states briefly the nature and the scope of the examination and expresses a professional opinion as to the fairness of the appended financial statement in presenting the firm's financial position and operating results for the specified period. The opinion may be unqualified, or it may contain exceptions, qualifications, or other comments regarding the treatment of particular items, the limitations of the auditing procedures followed, and changes of accounting methods from those used in previous years.

financial statement A summary of the results of operations; a statement of what a company or other organization owns and what it owes. It may be in the form of a balance sheet, a profit and loss statement, or an annual report. Sometimes the word is used broadly to include all reports concerning money, even operating reports; but more strictly, it shows the financial status of an organization at a given time.

finding 1. A decision (by a judge or jury) on a question of fact or law. 2. A formal, written, signed-off-on, presidential determination that a covert operation conducted by the CIA is legal, important to national security, and (according to law) will be reported to the appropriate congressional committee in a timely fashion. Title XXII of the Intelligence Oversight Act of 1980 mandates "a report to the Congress concerning any finding or determination under any section of this chapter. That finding shall be reduced to writing and signed by the president."

Finer, Herman *See* ACCOUNTABILITY, ADMINISTRATIVE.

First World Rich, industrialized democracies such as the United States, Canada, Western Europe, Australia, New Zealand, and Japan. *See* SECOND WORLD; THIRD WORLD; FOURTH WORLD.

fiscal Having to do with taxation, public revenues, and public debt.

fiscal federalism *See* FEDERALISM, FISCAL.

fiscal integrity 1. A characteristic of a government budget that spends no more than anticipated revenues. A balanced budget has fiscal integrity; a budget showing a significant deficit does not. 2. Agreement on fiscal matters. You will be deemed to have fiscal integrity when the person so deeming agrees with your fiscal policies. If that same person disagrees with your policies, you may be deemed so lacking in fiscal responsibility as to be considered fiscally irresponsible.

fiscal policy The manipulation of government finances by raising or lowering taxes or levels of spending to promote economic stability and growth. Stability and growth must be combined, because stability without growth is stagnation. The use of fiscal policy for economic objectives is a decidedly recent phenomenon. For the greater part of the two-hundred-year history of the United States, fiscal policy was not a factor; the national budgetary policy was premised upon expenditures equaling revenues (a balanced BUDGET). With the exception of war years, budgeting before the 1900s was primarily an exercise in deciding how to get rid of excess revenues, generated mostly by tariffs. Certainly modern fiscal policies might have saved the nation considerable distress from assorted recessions and depressions, but the nineteenth century held that the economy followed a natural order. The first major tampering with the natural order of things came in 1913, with the advent of the federal income tax and the establishment of the FEDERAL RESERVE SYSTEM. In 1921, the Budget and Accounting Act provided for a unified federal executive budget. The Great Depression of the 1930s, along with the initiation of Social Security and unemployment compensation programs, provided the first recognitions of the need for a national economic policy. However, legitimization of the goal of a national economic policy came with the passage of the Full Employment Act of 1946. The act not only created a Council of Economic Advisers (CEA) for the president but also prescribed objectives for economic prosperity and charged the president with insuring their achievement. Basically, fiscal policy offers two courses of action, discretionary and built-in. The first involves changing policy decisions. Discretionary fiscal policy has two major facets—the level of receipts and the level of expenditures. The major fiscal policy actions of recent years are replete with tax cuts and temporary reductions. Given the time lags involved in legislating tax changes, it is easy to see why presidents have preferred to wage fiscal policy battles in terms of government spending. The second dimension involves built-in fiscal stabilizers; that is, preset or automatic policy. These are the transfer payments, the progressive tax rates, and the changing federal budget deficits and surpluses that move automatically to counter economic downturns or to control excessive periods of demand and business activity. For example, as people are laid off from work in a recessionary period, payments for unemployment compensation mount automatically. This outgo increases the federal budget deficit, which in turn stimulates the economy and moves to offset the economic downswing. If the economy heats up, regular and overtime wages increase, fueling demand for goods and services and creating inflation. As personal income increases, however, more and more people move into higher tax brackets; the tax structure thus functions as an automatic stabilizer by absorbing more personal income and thus restraining demand for goods and services. *See also* ECONOMIC POLICY; MONETARY POLICY; POLITICAL ECONOMY.

fiscal year A yearly accounting period without regard to a calendar year. The fiscal year for the federal government through fiscal year 1976 began on July 1 and ended on June 30. Since fiscal year 1977, fiscal years for the federal government begin on October 1 and end on September 30. The fiscal year is designated by the calendar year in which it ends (e.g., fiscal year 2004 was the fiscal year ending September 30, 2004).

fog of war KARL VON CLAUSEWITZ's assertion from *On War* (1832), that "war is the province of uncertainty; three-fourths of the things on which action in war is based lie hidden in the fog." The fog of war is the descriptive phrase for the confusion inherent in combat. It is as if a literal fog were to descend upon the battlefield and blind the combatants to what the enemy and even other elements of their own forces are doing. Today, wherever far-flung or large-scale operations are coordinated, whether military or managerial, fog or uncertainty is always a possibility. The field of management information systems has grown up in recent decades to reduce the inevitable fog to manageable proportions. But the reduction mechanisms themselves—computer data and memorandums in a seemingly endless stream—often create more problems than the fog they were designed to dispel.

foggy bottom An irreverent phrase for the U.S. Department of State, because its present building is located on a site that was once considered a swamp (now drained). The term continues in use because it aptly describes the pronouncements so often necessitated by diplomacy.

Follett, Mary Parker (1868–1933) An early social psychologist who anticipated, in the 1920s, many of the conclusions of the Hawthorne experiments of the 1930s and the post–World War II behavioral movement. In calling for "power with," as opposed to "power over," she anticipated the movement toward more participatory management. Her "law of the situation" is contingency management in its humble origins. Major works include *The New State* (1918), and *Creative Experience* (1924). For her collected papers, see Henry C. Metcalf and

Lyndall Urwick, eds., *Dynamic Administration: The Collected Papers of Mary Parker Follett* (1940).

food stamps A welfare program designed to improve the nutrition of the poor. Administered by the Department of Agriculture and state and local welfare organizations, the program provides coupons (stamps) that can be exchanged for food at many grocery stores. This is the nation's largest welfare program; more than 20 million people are food stamp recipients. It is a good example of an ENTITLEMENT PROGRAM. The idea of food stamps originated in the late New Deal as a way of providing food to the poor from surpluses held by the government.

foreign policy The totality of a state's relations with and policies toward other states. George F. Kennan, in *Realities of American Foreign Policy* (1954), stated that "a political society does not live to conduct foreign policy; it would be more correct to say that it conducts foreign policy in order to live." A nation's foreign policy, even though it may be largely the prerogative of an executive branch, is always grounded in its domestic policy and must be carried out in the NATIONAL INTEREST.

foreign service A corps of professional diplomats. The Rogers Act of 1924 combined the U.S. diplomatic and consular services into the present U.S. Foreign Service, the diplomatic corps, its members (known as "Foreign Service Officers [FSOs]") being responsible for administering U.S. foreign policies. Although most U.S. ambassadors gain their positions through a long career in the Foreign Service, historically a significant number of them are patronage appointees whose only outward qualification for the job is a demonstrated ability to make large campaign contributions to the party in power. Although many distinguished outsiders have been appointed to ambassadorships, the de facto selling of these offices is a continuous, if quiet, bipartisan national scandal.

forward funding The practice of obligating funds in one fiscal year for programs that are to operate in a subsequent year.

fourth branch of government 1. The press; the mass media in general. 2. The bureaucracy. Although technically under the control of the executive branch, it sometimes seems to function as if it had a will, power, and legal authority all its own. 3. The independent regulatory agencies.

fourth estate The press; the media in general; the journalistic profession. The term is usually credited to EDMUND BURKE, who observed that in the reporters' gallery in the British Parliament "there sat a Fourth Estate more important by far than them all." The word *estate* is used here to mean "class"—the other three estates being the nobility, the commons, and the clergy.

Fourth World Developing countries with very low per capita annual incomes, no financial reserves, little expectation of economic growth, and few natural resources—in effect, the poorest of the poor. Fourth World countries are also considered the least-developed countries. *Compare to* FIRST WORLD; SECOND WORLD; THIRD WORLD.

fraud *See* ABUSE.

free rider One who does not belong to an organized group, such as a union or a political party, but who nevertheless benefits from its activities. For example, a worker in a given organization who does not belong to a union, when most of the other workers do, may receive all the wage increases and fringe benefits bargained for by the union without paying dues to the union. *See* AGENCY SHOP.

free trade A theoretical concept that refers to international trade unhampered by government restrictions or tariffs. Since World War II, U.S. policy has been in favor of free trade—with a variety of politically expedient limitations. The argument for free trade is that it leads to greater competition and specialization as nations concentrate on efficient production. The rationale is that all nations will benefit by being able to obtain better products at lower prices. Free trade, however, also means that inefficient industries are vulnerable to competition from overseas—as the United States automobile industry has discovered in relation to Japan. The English historian Lord Macaulay (1800–1859) wrote that "free trade, one of the greatest blessings which a government can confer on a people, is in almost every country unpopular." This observation is still true today. *Compare to* PROTECTIONISM.

free trade protectionist A member of the U.S. Congress who believes in free trade "in principle" but seeks "temporary" protectionist legislation for industries in the member's district that are adversely affected by foreign imports.

freedom of choice A phrase used in the context of abortion to mean a woman's right to make personal decisions on abortion without government interference; usually shortened to PRO CHOICE.

Freedom of Information Act of 1966 The law that provides for making information held by federal agencies available to the public unless the information falls within one of the specific categories exempt from public disclosure. Exempt records are those whose disclosure would impair rights of privacy or national security.

freeze To maintain at present levels. For example, a "job freeze" ordered by an executive prohibits an organization from hiring new employees; a "budget freeze" means no additional funds; a "flexible freeze" means a freeze on jobs or money unless an agency has enough political influence for some thawing. All freezes are inherently temporary.

friction KARL VON CLAUSEWITZ's concept from *On War* (1832): No matter how well planned a military operation is, the reality of delays and misunderstandings will make its inevitable execution less than ideal. Although military in origin, friction has become a generally recognized phenomenon in other aspects of public administration. The term *friction* is related to von Clausewitz's idea of the FOG OF WAR.

Friedman, Milton (1912-) A conservative economist of the Chicago school, generally considered the leading proponent of a return to laissez-faire economics. A 1976 Nobel Prize winner, he has been a major influence on thinking about monetary policy, consumption, and government regulation. Friedman is generally considered to be the intellectual godfather to the movement toward government deregulation. His most important work, *A Monetary History of the United States, 1867–1960* (1963), with Anna Schwartz, is a major reconstruction of the history of money and banking. In it, he argues that the Great Depression was caused not by a failure of free markets but by a sharp and continuous decline in the money supply for which the government was responsible. Consequently, Friedman is the leading advocate for a monetary policy that calls for a constant and predictable money growth. Friedman's other works include *A Theory of the Consumption Function* (1957); *Capitalism and Freedom* (1962); *Essays in Positive Economics* (1966); and *Free to Choose: A Personal Statement,* with Rose Friedman (1980).

Friedrich, Carl J. *See* ACCOUNTABILITY, ADMINISTRATIVE.

frontage assessment A tax to pay for improvements (such as sidewalks or sewer lines) charged in proportion to the frontage (number of feet bordering the road) of each property.

fudge factory 1. The Department of State. 2. The Pentagon. 3. The bureaucracy in general. Here the term refers not to the candy so called but to its usage as a verb meaning "to cheat" or "to talk nonsense." *See* MERIT SYSTEM.

full faith and credit 1. The clause in Article IV, Section 1, of the U.S. Constitution that requires states to give legal recognition (i.e., full faith and credit) to the official acts of other states. Although the clause ensures that property rights, wills, deeds, and so on, will be honored for all citizens in all states, it is limited to civil judicial proceedings. 2. The descriptive term for debt obligations, such as certain bonds, that have first claim upon the resources of the state.

full power Diplomatic representatives who enjoy full authority to act for the governments they represent subject only to constitutional restrictions (such as a requirement for treaty ratification by a legislature) that cannot be waived.

full responsibility In administrative theory, the principle that an executive bears responsibility for the actions of subordinates whether or not the executive had actual knowledge of the actions. Full responsibility is based, again in principle, on the belief that the selection of subordinates and the monitoring of their behavior is an executive responsibility.

functus officio A Latin phrase for one who has fulfilled the duties of an office that has expired and who, in consequence, has no further formal authority. Arbitrators and judges are said to be functus officio concerning a particular case after they have made their decisions about it.

fund An accounting device established to control receipt and disbursement of income from sources set aside to support specific activities or attain certain objectives.

fungible Interchangeable; a description for things that are easily substituted for one another. For example, bushels of wheat and barrels of oil are fungible; a GRANT may be fungible when the recipient is able to use the grant funds for purposes other than those specified in the grant authorization. Thus, fungibility is an important aspect of budgeting. Power is fungible when it can be transferred from one function to another. The term is sometimes used in relation to particular types of military capabilities. Cruise missiles, for example, are fungible weapons because they can be adapted to a variety of platforms and can be launched from land, sea, or air.

future shock Alvin Toffler's term, from his book *Future Shock* (1970), for the "distress, both physical and psychological, that arises from an overload of the human organism's physical adaptive systems and its decisionmaking processes. Put more simply, future shock is the human response to overstimulation."

G

game theory A mathematical approach to decisions related to problems of conflict and collaboration between rational actors in an uncertain world. Game theory is based on the essential logical features of competitive games. Given assumptions about preferences, psychological tendency to risk, and sets of rules defining actions and the possible gains and losses from these actions, it is possible to determine how people will most likely react to the actions of others. Game theory was first approached in the 1920s by John von Neumann (1903–1957) and developed during the 1940s by him and Oskar Morgenstern (1902–1977). The theory is excellent for classes of games where winners take all by optimizing strategy, but it can go awry for games in which parties gain by collaboration. Game theory is often illustrated by the "Prisoner's Dilemma" paradigm, which supposes that two men have been arrested on a suspicion of committing a crime together and are being held in separate cells. There is not enough evidence to prosecute unless one confesses and implicates the other. Both of them know this, but cannot talk to each other. The dilemma is that the best outcome, that of not being convicted, is available only if the prisoners trust each other. So if X decides to trust Y, but Y fears X may not be trustworthy, Y may confess to get a lesser sentence; X then gets a worse one. The dilemma calls for both to cooperate, to minimize the worst that can happen, rather than to try for the maximum outcome. This action is called the *"Minimax" strategy;* game theorists consider it to be the most probable outcome. Prisoner's dilemma and, indeed, other game structures such as zero sum and chicken are sometimes used to describe or explain relations among states. Particularly noteworthy is Robert Axelrod's *Evolution of Cooperation* (1984), which demonstrates that when games are iterative and tit-for-tat strategies are followed in prisoner's dilemma, the long-term benefits of cooperative strategies become clear. Cooperative strategies can be illustrated in relation to the arms race or to highlight the dangers of escalation. When both states strive to achieve superiority in armaments, especially at the nuclear level, the most likely outcome is that they will simply achieve stalemate at a higher level of arms and at great cost. If they have a degree of trust and neither tries to maximize gains at the expense of the adversary, then they can find less-costly solutions. Similarly, escalatory strategies can simply make both sides in a crisis much worse off than if they had cooperated to keep things under control. Although game theory is useful for highlighting some of the dilemmas in public policy decisionmaking and for illuminating the outcomes in situations of strategic interdependence, it also has its limitations: it is excessively formal and the assumptions about rational choice are, in many respects, artificial.

gaming simulation A model of reality with dynamic parts that can be manipulated to teach the manipulator(s) how better to cope with the represented processes in real life.

Gantt Chart The chart developed during World War I by Henry L. Gantt (1861–1919). The Gant Chart's distinguishing feature is that work planned and work done are shown in the same space in their relation to each other and in their relation to time. Today, charts that use straight lines to compare planned and actual progress over time could be called *Gantt Charts.*

GAO *See* GENERAL ACCOUNTING OFFICE.

garden city An urban residential area that includes gardens and is surrounded by a greenbelt. At the beginning of the twentieth century, the general belief in the efficacy of science and the growing awareness of the consequences of urbanization led to a series of movements based on ideal cities: residential areas that fulfilled citizens' needs through technology combined with the physical, social, and healthful amenities of rural life.

gatekeeper 1. A critical decisionmaker in a political system. Such a person or institution decides who shall and who shall not receive political rewards and can effectively veto a person's advance in a political or social system. For example, a local political leader may be the gatekeeper for nominations for city council membership; a legislative committee chair may be a gatekeeper for certain kinds of bills. 2. A mass media decisionmaker who decides which stories will be printed or broadcast; in effect, what will become news. 3. A staff member of an executive or legislator who screens problems and issues and decides which ones will be reviewed by the boss. *Compare to* AGENDA SETTING.

gay rights movement The total efforts to achieve full civil rights for homosexuals, to repeal laws that hold that homosexual acts are illegal, and to create a more positive image of homosexuals. A landmark in the gay rights movement was the 1975 decision of the American Psychiatric Association to remove homosexuality from its list of mental disorders. Some jurisdictions, such as San Francisco and New York City, have enacted laws making it illegal to discriminate against someone because of sexual orientation. The increasing demands for acceptance of homosexual lifestyles is a direct result of the civil rights movement, which made it possible for all minorities to insist upon their full rights as citizens. *See also* DISCRIMINATION, SEXUAL ORIENTATION.

gender balance 1. A situation that will exist only when women hold half of all positions of political power. 2. A reference to laws in some states (such as Iowa, North Dakota, and Delaware) that require the governor's appointments to state boards and commissions to be divided between the sexes.

General Accounting Office (GAO) A support agency created by the Budget and Accounting Act of 1921 to AUDIT federal government expenditures and to assist the U.S. Congress with its legislative oversight responsibilities. The GAO is directed by the comptroller general of the United States, who is appointed by the president with the advice and consent of the U.S. Senate for a term of fifteen years. Although the GAO originally confined itself to auditing financial records to see that funds were properly spent, since the 1960s it has redefined its mission to include overall program EVALUATION.

general manager/city administrator/chief administrative officer The administrative official appointed in a council-mayor system of government who is typically appointed by the mayor and shares powers with that office. *Compare to* CITY MANAGER.

general revenue All the taxes that are paid to a government whose use is unrestricted. Excluded from general revenue are funds that can be used for specified purposes only, such as earmarked taxes or categorical grants.

general welfare clause That part of Article I, Section 8, of the U.S. Constitution that authorizes the U.S. Congress to "provide for the common Defense and general Welfare of the United States." It has long been argued whether this is an unlimited grant of power to spend or whether its power is limited to spending on those activities specifically mentioned in other parts of the Constitution. A liberal interpretation has prevailed, and the spending power of the Congress has never been successfully challenged in the courts.

gentlemen's agreement An oral agreement that is not legally binding. It is traditionally defined by lawyers as "an agreement which is not an agreement, made between two persons, neither of whom is a gentleman, whereby each expects the other to be strictly bound without himself being bound at all." Informal international agreements have been called *gentlemen's agreements.* In a larger sense, all international agreements are gentlemen's agreements because, short of war, they are not enforceable. Nevertheless, they are very useful in international relations when formal treaties are inappropriate or when governments want essentially secret agreements that are not binding on successive governments.

gentrification The gradual replacement of the poor of a neighborhood by people with middle and high incomes; the upgrading of inner-city neighborhoods when well-to-do families refurbish vacant or abandoned properties. Gentrification can have many social and political implications. The most intractable problem is that, once gentrification starts, poorer residents are forced out because they cannot pay increased rents or property taxes.

Gilbreth, Frank Bunker (1868–1924) and **Lillian Moller** (1878–1972) The husband and wife team who were the pioneers of time-and-motion study. Frank and Lillian Gilbreth's influence on the scientific management movement was rivaled only by that of Frederick W. Taylor. Frank Gilbreth became the archtypical "efficiency expert." Two of their twelve children illustrated his mania for efficiency in their memoir, *Cheaper By the Dozen,* Frank B. Gilbreth, Jr., and Ernestine Gilbreth Carey (1948).

giveback Management's demand that a union negotiate a new contract with lower salaries and/or benefits, usually to preserve jobs.

glass ceiling The unseen barrier through which an organization's highest-level positions can be seen but not reached. Women and minorities often perceive that a "glass ceiling" prevents their advancement to the top.

global village The notion that because of modern electronic communications the people of the whole world have become as closely linked as the people in a premodern archetypal village. The Canadian communications theorist Marshall McLuhan (1911–1980) first wrote that "the new electronic interdependence re-creates the world in the image of a global village," *The Gutenberg Galaxy* (1962).

global warming The gradual change in the Earth's climate brought about by the consequences of burning fossil fuels, clearing rain forests, and using chemicals not found widely in nature. Global warming is one of the most important issues for environmental policy and protection. It is contended that if global warming is not halted, many coastal regions and port cities will be in danger of flooding as the polar ice cap gradually melts and raises the level of the oceans; additional changes will occur in agricultural growing regions. However, not all scientists believe that there is a real danger or that a real change exists. Some analysts assert that what is perceived as global warming is merely a normal cyclical change that will eventually and naturally reverse. *Compare to* GREENHOUSE EFFECT.

globalism A term describing a U.S. foreign policy of active political and military involvement in all parts of the world; the opposite of ISOLATIONISM.

GNP *See* GROSS NATIONAL PRODUCT.

goals 1. The achievements sought by individuals and organizations. 2. Realistic objectives that an organization endeavors to achieve through affirmative action. Quotas, in contrast, restrict employment or development opportunities to members of particular groups by establishing a required number or proportionate representation, which managers are obligated to attain, without regard to equal employment opportunity. To be meaningful, a program of goals or quotas must be associated with a specific timetable—a schedule of when the goals or quotas are to be achieved. Quotas tend to be mandated by courts to remedy patterns of past discrimination.

gobbledygook/officialese/federalese/bafflegab Slang terms for the obtuse language so frequently used by bureaucrats. Gobbledygook was coined by the World War II administrator Maury Maverick (1896–1954). Maverick, a former representative from Texas (1934–1938) was so angered by the convoluted language he found in so many government documents that he invented the special word for it. As he told the *New York Times* (May 21, 1944): "People ask me where I got gobbledygook. I do not know. It must have come in a vision. Perhaps I was thinking of the old bearded turkey gobbler back in Texas who was always gobbledy-gobbling and strutting with ludicrous pomposity. At the end of this gobble there was a sort of gook." The terms *officialese* and *federalese* are obvious derivatives of *legalese;* thus, a term referring to language that only a lawyer can understand is applied to language that only an official or a member of the federal government can understand. The term has since been extended to *Pentagonese. Bafflegab* surfaced in the 1950s to mean almost unintelligible jargon.

goldbricking *Goldbrick* was a slang term for something that had only a surface appearance of value well before it was adopted by the military to mean shirking or giving the appearance of working. The word has now come to imply industrial work slowdowns, whether they be individual initiatives (or the lack of individual initiative) or group efforts (organized or otherwise).

golden handcuffs The term refers to the feeling of being bound to remain in a job because financial benefits would be forfeited upon resignation.

golden handshake Providing a dismissed employee with a large cash bonus.

golden parachute The substantial financial benefit given to an employee who leaves an organization.

gold-plating A critical term for military procurement policies that use all the bells and whistles available for a weapons system instead of less-expensive, more basic equipment.

good faith Honesty in the context of equal employment opportunity, good faith is the absence of discriminating intent. Good-faith bargaining is a requirement of the National Labor Relations Act, which makes it illegal for an employer to refuse to bargain in good faith about wages, hours, and other conditions of employment with the representative selected by a majority of the employees in a unit appropriate for COLLECTIVE BARGAINING.

good offices The disinterested use of one's official position, one's office, to help others settle their differences; an offer to mediate a dispute.

Goodnow, Frank J. (1859–1939) A leader of the progressive reform movement and one of the founders and first president (in 1903) of the American Political Science Association. Goodnow is now best known as one of the principal exponents, along with President Woodrow Wilson, of public administration's POLITICS-ADMINISTRATION DICHOTOMY. Goodnow's most enduring work is *Politics and Administration* (1900).

governance 1. The process of government; the exercise of government power; government action. 2. PUBLIC ADMINISTRATION. 3. A system or method of government; for example, democracy or fascism. 4. The state of being under the control of a higher legal or political authority. Thus, citizens are under the governance of their national government, agencies are under the governance of their jurisdictions, and police officers are under the governance of their department. 5. The collective actions of a board of directors, board of trustees, or a board of governors in providing policy guidance to the organization the board was established to manage.

governance, new Interpersonal and interorganizational efforts to cope with public or cross-boundary problems by using networks of people and organizations.

governing class 1. A vague term for those citizens both in and out of office who take an active and effective interest in public affairs. 2. A pejorative term for the rich special interests who manipulate republican institutions for their own ends. According to President Theodore Roosevelt, speaking at Harvard University on February 23, 1907: "In a republic like ours the governing class is composed of the strong men who take the trouble to do the work of government; and if you are too timid or too fastidious or too careless to do your part in this work, then you forfeit your right to be considered one of the governing and you become one of the governed instead — one of the driven cattle of the political arena."

government 1. The formal institutions and processes through which binding decisions are made for a society. A government can be as small as a tribal council or as vast and complex as the U.S. government. It can be democratic and responsive to its people, or it can consist of a despot and his henchmen. It is still a government so long as it rules a defined land area and group of people. Henry David Thoreau (1817–1862) wrote in *Civil Disobedience* (1849) that "that government is best which governs least." This statement is often attributed to Thomas Jefferson; but although it certainly reflects his philosophic sentiments, it has never been found in Jefferson's writings. 2. The apparatus of a state, consisting of executive, legislative, and judicial branches. 3. A political entity that has taxing authority and jurisdiction over a defined geographic area for some specified purpose, such as fire protection or schools. 4. The individuals who temporarily control the institutions of a state or subnational jurisdiction. 5. The U.S. government, especially as in "the government."

government corporation A government-owned corporation or an agency of government that administers a self-supporting enterprise. Such a structure is used (1) when an agency's business is essentially commercial, (2) when an agency can generate its own revenue, and (3) when the agency's mission requires greater flexibility than government agencies normally have. Examples of federal government corporations include the Saint Lawrence Seaway Development Corporation, the Federal Deposit Insurance Corporation, the National Railroad Passenger Corporation (AMTRAK), and the Tennessee Valley Authority. At the state and municipal levels, corporations (often bearing different names, such as authorities) operate such enterprises as turnpikes, airports, and harbors.

government of laws A governing system in which the highest authority is a body of law that applies equally to all (as opposed to the rule of men, in which the personal whim of those in power can decide issues). The idea of the desirability of a "government of laws, and not of men" can be traced back to ARISTOTLE. The earliest U.S. reference is in the 1779 Massachusetts Constitution. Chief Justice John Marshall also used a succinct legal description in *Marbury v. Madison* (1803): "The government of the United States has been emphatically termed a government of laws, and not of men. It will certainly cease to deserve this high appellation, if the laws furnish no remedy for the violation of a vested legal right."

Government Performance and Results Act of 1993 The most comprehensive adoption of performance management by the U.S. government to date, this legislation is a typical performance management system. The act seeks to link resource allocations and results, to improve program performance, to provide better information for congressional policymaking, to force agencies to specify their missions, objectives, and strategies, and to require them to advise the U.S. Congress just how they've gone about the consultation process. The General Accounting Office has been given a special role in monitoring the implementation of the Results Act.

government relations 1. Corporate public relations toward government. 2. A euphemism for the LOBBYING of government by corporations.

government, divided A government in which different political parties control the legislative and executive branches.

government, unitary A system of governance in which all authority is derived from a central authority, such as a parliament, an absolute monarch, or a dictator. The United States is not a unitary government. *Compare to* FEDERALISM.

governor The elected chief executive of a state government. A governor's responsibilities sometimes parallel those of a U.S. president, on a smaller scale, but each governor enjoys only the powers granted to the office by the state constitution. Some states severely limit executive powers; others give their governors such powers as the item veto (*see* VETO, ITEM), which are greater than those possessed by the president of the United States. The term of office for a governor is four years, except in four states (Arkansas, New Hampshire, Rhode Island, and Vermont), where it is two. In one sense, it is a misnomer to call a governor the chief executive of a state. The reality is that most state constitutions provide for what amounts to a plural executive, because governors, in marked contrast to the U.S. president, typically must share powers with a variety of other independently elected executive branch officers, such as a secretary of state, an attorney general, a treasurer, and an auditor (or controller). Consequently, a governor's informal powers as a lobbyist for initiatives and as head of the party may often be far more useful than the formal authority that comes with the office. Nevertheless, the management job of a governor compares favorably in responsibility to those of the highest-paid corporate executives. For example, in revenues, twenty-five states rank among the top one hundred corporations in the United States. Thirty-eight states are among the top two hundred. *Compare to* GUBERNATORIAL.

governor, lieutenant The elected state official who would replace the governor should he or she be unable to complete a term of office. The lieutenant governor in a state government parallels the position of the vice president in the national government but differs in that in many states the lieutenant governor is separately elected and thus may be of a different party from the governor. This situation can sometimes cause considerable friction when the two officeholders are political rivals—and especially when, as in California, the lieutenant governor has some of the governor's powers to act whenever the governor is out of the state. Seven states have felt no need for a lieutenant governor: Arizona, Maine, New Hampshire, New Jersey, Oregon, West Virginia, and Wyoming. In four of these states, the president of the state senate would succeed to the governorship; in the other three, the secretary of state succeeds. The story is often told of Calvin Coolidge, then the lieutenant governor of Massachusetts, who met a woman at a dinner party. She asked, "What do you do?" He replied, "I'm the lieutenant governor." "How interesting, you must tell me all about it." Coolidge then said, "I just did."

graft *See* HONEST GRAFT/DISHONEST GRAFT.

grandfather clause Originally, a device used by some states of the Old South to disenfranchise black voters. Grandfather clauses, written into seven state constitutions during the Reconstruction Era, granted the right to vote only to persons whose ancestors—"grandfathers"—had voted before 1867. The U.S. Supreme Court ruled in *Guinn v. United States* (1915), that all grandfather clauses were unconstitutional because of the Fifteenth Amendment. Today, the term *grandfather clause* is a colloquial expression for a provision or policy that exempts a category of individuals from meeting new standards. For example, if a jurisdiction were to establish a policy that all managers had to have earned a master's degree in public administration as of a certain date, it would probably exempt managers without such degrees who were hired before that date. This statement of exemption would be a grandfather clause.

grant 1. A form of gift that entails certain obligations on the part of the grantee and expectations on the part of the grantor; for example, grants from a king or a tax-exempt charitable foundation. 2. An intergovernmental transfer of funds (or other assets). Since the New Deal, state and local governments have become increasingly dependent upon federal grants for an almost infinite variety of programs; these grants made up 17 percent of all federal outlays in 2001. From the era of land grant colleges to the present, a grant by the federal government has been a continuing means of providing states, localities, public (and private) educational or research institutions, and individuals with funds to support projects the national government considered useful for a wide range of purposes. In recent decades, grants have supported the arts as well as the sciences. All such grants are capable of generating debate over what the public as a whole, acting through the grant-making agencies of the federal government, considers useful and in the national interest. *Compare to* REVENUE SHARING.

grant, block A grant distributed in accordance with a statutory formula for use in a variety of activities within a broad functional area, largely at the recipient's discretion.

grant, categorical A grant that can be used only for specific, narrowly defined activities, such as for the construction of interstate highways. The authorizing legislation usually details the parameters of the program and specifies the types of eligible activities, but sometimes these may be determined by administrators.

grant, conditional A grant awarded with limitations (conditions) attached to the use of the funds. Categorical and block grants are conditional, although the categorical grant generally imposes more conditions and of greater severity.

grant, discretionary A grant awarded at the discretion of a federal administrator and subject to conditions specified by legislation; the term is interchangeable with *project grant.*

grant, formula project categorical A project categorical grant for which a formula specified in statutes and regulations is used to determine the amount available for a state. Funds are then distributed at the discretion of the administrator in response to project applications submitted by substate entities.

grant, formula-based categorical A categorical grant under which funds are allocated among recipients according to factors specified in legislation or in administrative regulations.

grant, open-end reimbursement A grant often regarded as a formula grant but characterized by an arrangement wherein the federal government commits itself to reimbursing a specified portion of state and local program expenditures with no limit on the amount of such expenditures. Examples are FOOD STAMPS and MEDICAID.

grant, project categorical Nonformula categorical grants awarded competitively to recipients who submit specific, individual applications in the form, and at the times, indicated by the grantor agency.

grant, target A grant that packages and coordinates funds for wide-ranging public services directed at a specific clientele group or geographic area.

grant-in-aid Federal payments to states; federal or state payments to local governments for specified purposes and usually subject to supervision and review by the granting government or agency in accordance with prescribed standards and requirements. One function of a federal grant-in-aid is to direct state and local funding to a purpose considered nationally useful by providing federal money, but on the condition that the jurisdiction receiving it match a certain percentage of it. The federal government actively monitors the grantee's spending of the funds to insure compliance with the spirit and letter of federal intent. Grants-in-aid also have other public policy implications because a jurisdiction that accepts federal money must also accept the federal "strings," or guidelines, that come with it. All federal grantees must comply with federal standards on equal employment opportunity in the selection of personnel and contractors, for example.

grants-in-kind Donations of surplus property and commodities.

grantsmanship The art, science, and practice of obtaining grant money from private or public sources. Grantsmanship implies a skill in writing grant proposals (requests for grants) and negotiating with granting agencies.

grapevine The informal means by which organizational members give or receive messages. The word is derived from the practice of stringing early telegraph wires from tree to tree in a vine-like fashion.

grass roots 1. The rank and file of a political party or of a large bureaucracy. 2. The voters in general. 3. Decentralized political or administrative power. 4. A patronizing way of referring to the origin of political power.

grassroots lobbying Influencing government decisionmakers through pressure (usually in the form of letters, e-mail, and phone calls) from large numbers of constituents; also called *indirect lobbying*.

gravitas Intellectual weight. A politician or administrator must exhibit a certain degree of gravitas if he or she is to be taken seriously for high office.

gray power A general phrase for the political efforts of "older" Americans to achieve better government benefits and services for people in their age group.

Great Society The label for the 1960s domestic policies of the Lyndon B. Johnson administration, which were premised on the belief that social and economic problems could be solved by new federal programs. This was Johnson's effort to revive the federal reform presence in social change represented in the progressive movement and the New Deal. In a May 23, 1964, speech, President Johnson said that "we have the opportunity to move not only toward the rich society and the powerful society, but upward to the Great Society. The Great Society rests on abundance and liberty for all; it demands an end to poverty and racial injustice." Richard Goodwin (1931–), then a Johnson speechwriter, is generally credited with coining the phrase, but earlier authors had also used it.

green 1. Unripe or inexperienced; someone who has much to learn. 2. Having to do with the environment. Thus "green politics" are environmental politics. A "green party" is mainly concerned with environmental issues; it does not necessarily have to have the word "green" in its name. "Green taxes" tax things that are environmentally undesirable. "Green building" uses energy-efficient materials.

green card A small document identifying an alien as a permanent resident of the United States and legally entitled to find employment.

greenhouse effect The assertion that Earth is getting ever warmer because gases produced by the firing of fossil fuels (oil and coal) in the atmosphere, notably carbon dioxide, trap infrared radiation. The greenhouse effect is thought to affect weather patterns. *See* GLOBAL WARMING.

gridlock 1. Traffic so bad that virtually no vehicles can move. 2. A government so divided over issues that no substantial changes can be made in either direction.

grievance A dispute over the meaning, application, and/or enforcement of a labor contract.

grievance machinery The totality of the methods, usually enumerated in a collective bargaining agreement, used to resolve the problems of interpretation arising during the life of an agreement. Grievance machinery is usually designed so that those closest to the dispute have the first opportunity to reach a settlement.

Griggs et al. v. Duke Power Company (1971) The most significant U.S. Supreme Court decision concerning the validity of employment examinations. The Court unanimously ruled that Title VII of the Civil Rights Act of 1964 "proscribes not only overt discrimination but also practices that are discriminatory in operation." Thus, if employment practices operating to exclude minorities "cannot be shown to be related to job performance, the practice is prohibited." The ruling dealt a blow to restrictive credentialism, stating that, although diplomas and tests are useful, the "Congress has mandated the commonsense proposition that they are not to become masters of reality." In essence, the Court held that the law requires that tests used for employment purposes "must measure the person for the job and not the person in the abstract." The *Griggs* decision applied only to the private sector until the Equal Employment Opportunity Act of 1972 extended the provisions of Title VII to cover public employees.

Griswold v. Connecticut (1965) The U.S. Supreme Court case that, in holding the state regulation of birth control devices was an impermissible invasion of privacy, helped to establish privacy as a constitutionally protected right under the Ninth and Fourteenth amendments. Justice William O. Douglas wrote, in the majority opinion, that "the First Amendment has a penumbra where privacy is protected from governmental intrusion." He asked, "Would we allow the police to search the sacred precincts of marital bedrooms for telltale signs of the use of contraceptives? The very idea is repulsive to the notions of privacy surrounding the marriage relationship."

gross national product (GNP) The monetary value of all the goods and services produced in a nation in a given year, one of the most important tools for measuring the health of a nation's economy. The Department of Commerce is responsible for gathering GNP data. All GNP figures must be adjusted for inflation or deflation if they are to be accurate reflections of the economy's growth or nongrowth.

group cohesion The shared beliefs, values, and assumptions of a group that allow it to function as a team.

group dynamics The subfield of organizational behavior concerned about the nature of groups, how they develop, and how they interrelate with individuals and other groups. Usually, the term *group* refers to what is more technically known as a "primary group"—a group small enough to permit face-to-face interaction among its members and that remains in existence long enough for personal relations, sentiments, and feelings of identification or belonging to develop.

group psychotherapy A form of psychological treatment involving more than one subject. Organization development efforts can be considered a form of group psychotherapy.

group theory *See* INTEREST GROUP THEORY.

groups, formal Groups officially created by a larger organization usually for the purpose of accomplishing tasks. Employees are assigned to formal groups based upon their positions in the organization. There are two basic types of formal groups: command groups and task groups. Command groups are specified in a formal organization chart; these include supervisors and the people who report directly to them. Groups of this type are the essential building blocks of organizational structure. They vary from a mail-room staff to the employees of a small branch office to an entire headquarters staff. Task groups are formally sanctioned job-oriented units with short lives in which employees work together to complete a particular project or task and then disband. An ad hoc TASK FORCE or temporary committee is an example.

groups, informal Groups resulting from spontaneously developed relation-ships and patterns of interactions in work situations. Included are employees who associate voluntarily, primarily to satisfy social needs. Although infor-mal groups at work may have goals and tasks (for example, ethnic support groups, bowling clubs, and luncheon speaker groups), their primary reasons for existence are friendship, affiliation, and shared interests. Although infor-mal groups are seldom formally sanctioned, they are important to the work-ing of organizations because their norms, values, beliefs, and expectations have significant impacts on work-related behavior and attitudes. Chester I. Barnard in *The Functions of the Executive* (1938) has provided the classic statement on the vital significance of informal groups: "Informal organiza-tion, although comprising the processes of society which are unconscious as contrasted with those of formal organization which are conscious, has two important classes of effects: (a) it establishes certain attitudes, understand-ings, customs, habits, institutions; and (b) it creates the condition under which formal organization may arise."

groupthink The psychological drive for consensus, which tends to suppress both dissent and the appraisal of alternatives in small decisionmaking groups. Groupthink tends to occur when individuals value membership in the group and identify strongly with their colleagues. It may also occur be-cause the group leader does not encourage dissent or because stressful situa-tions make the group more cohesive. The essence for it, though, is that the members suppress doubts and criticisms about proposed action, with the re-sult that the group chooses riskier and more ill-advised policies than it would have chosen otherwise. The word *groupthink,* because it implies a deterioration of mental efficiency and moral judgment due to in-group pressures, has an invidious connotation. The term derives from Irving L. Janis, *Victims of Groupthink: A Psychological Study of Foreign Policy Decisions and Fiascoes* (1972; 1982).

gubernatorial Things pertaining to the office of governor. This strange word comes from the Greek *kybernan,* meaning "to direct a ship." The Romans borrowed the word from the Greeks as *guberno.* Then the French took it and sent it across the English Channel as *governor.* When the word is used as an adjective, it goes back to its Latin roots; thus *gubernatorial.*

Gulick, Luther (1892–1993) Perhaps the most highly honored reformer, researcher, and practitioner of public administration in the United States. Often called the *dean of U.S. public administration,* Gulick was intimately involved with the pioneering development and installation of new budget, personnel, and management systems at all levels of government. He was a member of the BROWNLOW COMMITTEE and a close advisor to President Franklin D. Roosevelt. Gulick was also a founder of the Institute of Public Administration, the American Society for Public Administration, and the National Academy of Public Administration. For an appreciation of Gulick's career, see Stephen K. Blumberg, "Seven Decades of Public Administration: A Tribute to Luther Gulick," *Public Administration Review* (March/April 1981).

gun control A government effort to regulate the use of firearms by the civilian population. Although minor laws deal with the registration of guns and the prohibition of their sale to criminals, there is no effective gun control in the United States. Proponents of free access to all kinds of weapons point to the Second Amendment of the U.S. Constitution: "A well-regulated militia, being necessary to the security of a free state, the right of the people to keep and bear arms, shall not be infringed." Opponents of easy access to guns point out that the "right" referred to in the amendment belongs only to members of the militia; not to all citizens. Right or wrong about the "right," gun control advocates have been consistently overwhelmed by the political strength of those who advocate free access.

guns and butter A phrase that since the 1930s has succinctly summarized a government's policy option between military expenditures (the guns) and domestic spending (the butter).

H

hard cases Cases in which fairness may require judges to be loose with legal principles. "Hard cases make bad law," because the specific complexity of the issues may force judges to take positions that, while appropriate to the circumstances presented to them, may suggest future legal applications that are likely to be considered unjust.

hard line Any policy that is unyielding to compromise.

hardball A serious game as opposed to softball, which is less serious or for children. According to Christopher Matthews in *Hardball* (1988), hardball "is clean, aggressive Machiavellian politics. It is the discipline of gaining and holding power, useful to any profession or undertaking, but practiced most openly and unashamedly in the world of public affairs."

harmonization 1. Cutting tariffs in a way that will tend to make tariffs on most items more nearly uniform within each country's tariff schedule. 2. Creating common laws and standards for member states in an economic union.

Hatch Act The collective, popular name for two federal statutes restricting the political activities of federal employees. The 1939 act restricted almost all federal employees, whether or not they were in the competitive service. The impetus for this legislation came primarily from a decrease in the proportion of federal employees in the competitive service, a result of the creation of several score New Deal agencies outside the merit system. Senator Carl Hatch (1889–1963), a Democrat from New Mexico, had worked for several years to have legislation enacted that would prevent federal employees from being active at political conventions. He feared that their involvement and direction by politicians could develop into a giant national political machine. A second Hatch Act, in 1940, extended these restrictions to federally financed positions in state employment.

Hatch Acts, little State laws that parallel the federal government's prohibition on partisan political activities by public employees.

haves and have-nots 1. The rich and the poor. 2. The industrialized states and the third world. The phrase dates back at least to Miguel de Cervantes

(1547–1616) who wrote in his novel *Don Quixote*, "There are in the world two families only, the Haves and the Have-Nots."

Hawthorne effect The discovery made during the HAWTHORNE EXPERIMENTS that production increases as a result of the known presence of benign observers. The attentiveness and concern of the researchers toward the workers, who naturally wanted to be reciprocally nice, led them to increase production. This "effect" caused great confusion at first because the changing physical conditions (lighting, rest breaks, etc.) seemed to make no difference. Output just kept going up. Once the researchers realized that the workers' perception of participation was the true "variable," the effects of the "effect" were understood.

Hawthorne experiments The late 1920s and early 1930s management studies undertaken at the Hawthorne Works of the Western Electric Company near Chicago. Conducted by Elton Mayo (1890–1949) and his associates from the Harvard Business School, they became the most famous management experiments ever reported. The decade-long series of experiments started out as traditional scientific management examinations of the relationship between work environment and productivity. But the experimenters, because they were initially unable to explain the results of their findings, literally stumbled upon a finding that today seems so obvious: Factories and other work places are first of all social situations. The Hawthorne studies are generally considered the genesis of the human relations school of management thought; they made the first major empirical challenge to the scientific management notion that the worker was primarily an economic animal who would work solely for money.

Hayek, Friedrich August von (1899–1992) The Austrian-born 1974 Nobel Prize winner in economics who advocated laissez-faire capitalism and advanced the theory of business cycles. His *Road to Serfdom* (1944) warned of the dangers of central planning and big government. Hayek argued that "the unforeseen but inevitable consequences of socialist planning create a state of affairs in which, if the policy is to be pursued, totalitarian forces will get the upper hand." To Hayek, state intervention in the economy in Great Britain and the United States differed only in degree, not in kind, from the fascism of Hitler and the communism of Stalin. The evil to be resisted was collectivism whether or not it wore a swastika. By asserting that Allied economic policies were headed in the direction of Nazi policies, Hayek was being deliberately provocative. Hayek's book, which can be condensed into five words—government planning leads to dictatorship— was an immediate sensation on both sides of the Atlantic. But it made Hayek decidedly unpopular in a postwar Britain that was implementing the socialist agenda of the Labour Party. After a messy divorce that alienated him from even more friends and colleagues, Hayek moved across the pond to the University of Chicago. In a world moving increasingly toward centralized planning, Hayek seemed more like a crank than a prophet during the next two decades. Nevertheless, his work became the foundation of the modern conservative movement. And he inspired important disciples, among them Margaret Thatcher and Ronald Reagan.

hearing 1. A legal or quasi-legal proceeding in which arguments, witnesses, and evidence are heard by a judicial officer or administrative body. 2. A legislative committee session for hearing witnesses. At hearings on legislation, witnesses usually include specialists, government officials, and representatives of those affected by the bills under study. Subpoena power may be used to summon reluctant witnesses. The public and press may attend open hearings but not closed (executive) hearings.

hearing examiner *See* ADMINISTRATIVE LAW JUDGE.

Heart of Atlanta Motel v. United States (1964) The U.S. Supreme Court case that upheld the constitutionality of Title II of the Civil Rights Act of 1964, which prohibited discrimination because of race, color, sex, religion, or national origin in restaurants, hotels, and other places of public accommodation engaged in interstate commerce.

heir apparent 1. The next in line for an hereditary office such as king. 2. By analogy an administrative or political figure who, it is assumed, will achieve the office or power of a current leader upon that leader's death or retirement. Many an heir apparent has turned out to be less apparent than was apparent.

hidden agenda The unannounced or unconscious goals, personal needs, expectations, and strategies held by each individual or group. Parallel to a group's open agenda are the private or hidden agendas of each of its members.

hierarchy An ordering of persons, things, or ideas by rank or level. The administrative structures are typically hierarchical in that each level has authority over levels below and must take orders from levels above. Elliot Jaques in "In Praise of Hierarchy," *Harvard Business Review* (1990) contends that those who argue against hierarchy are "simply wrong, and all their proposals are based on an inadequate understanding of not only hierarchy but also human nature." Hierarchical layers add value to organizations by separating tasks into a manageable series of steps: "What we need is not some new kind of organization. What we need is managerial hierarchy that understands its own nature and purpose." According to Jaques, hierarchy is the best alternative for large organizations: "We need to stop casting about fruitlessly for organizational Holy Grails and settle down to the hard work of putting our managerial hierarchies in order." *See also* BUREAUCRACY.

high politics The traditional focus of statecraft; the issues of power and national security. Foreign policy analysis was initially concerned almost exclusively with high politics—the major decisions of peace and war. Increasingly, though, this exclusive preoccupation has given way to a recognition that the study of high politics must be accompanied by a focus on low politics; that is, issues relating to mundane but important matters, such as economic well-being.

higher law The notion that no matter what the laws of a state are, people have an even greater obligation to a higher law. A higher law is often appealed to by those who wish to attack an existing law or practice that courts and legislators are unlikely or unwilling to change. In a famous speech in the U.S. Senate on March 11, 1850, William Henry Seward of New York argued against slavery by asserting that "there is a higher law than the Constitution which regulates our authority." Martyrs throughout the ages have asserted a higher law in defiance of the state, thus earning their martyrdom. The classic presentation of this concept is in Sophocles's (496–406 B.C.E.) play *Antigone*, in which the heroine defies the king, asserts a higher law as her justification, and forces the king to have her killed. Because the courts will enforce only the law of the land, appealing to a higher law is always chancy business. Examples of Americans who have appealed to a higher law and wound up in jail as a result are Henry David Thoreau (*see* CIVIL DISOBEDIENCE), Martin Luther King, Jr., and Vietnam War resisters.

hill, the The U.S. Congress, because it is literally situated on a hill; it is eighty-eight feet above sea level; the White House is fifty-five feet above sea level. Now there can be no doubt about which is the higher branch of government.

hired gun 1. A mercenary. 2. A political consultant who works only for the money and not because of a commitment to the cause of candidate. 3. A "neutral gun for hire"; a longstanding description of apolitical career bureaucrats.

home rule The ability, the power, of a municipal corporation to develop and implement its own charter. At the beginning of the twentieth century, home rule resulted from the urban reform movement, which hoped to remove urban politics from the harmful influence of state politics. Home rule can be either a statutory or a constitutional system and varies in its details from state to state.

honest broker A disinterested third party who helps others negotiate an agreement. The term is often used in diplomacy when one country seeks to help two others reach agreement on a contentious issue.

honest graft/dishonest graft 1. The classic distinction between the two genres of graft, made by George Washington Plunkitt, a politico associated with New York's Tammany Hall early in the twentieth century. Dishonest graft, as the name implies, involves bribery, blackmailing, extortion, and other illegal activities. As for honest graft, let Plunkitt speak: "Just let me explain by examples. My party's in power in the city, and it's goin' to undertake a lot of public improvements. Well, I'm tipped off, say, that they're goin' to lay out a new park at a certain place. I see my opportunity and I take it, I go to that place and I buy up all the land I can in the neighborhood. Then the board of this or that makes its plan public, and there is a rush to get my land, which nobody cared particular for before. Ain't it perfectly honest to charge a good price and make a profit on my investment and foresight? Of course, it is. Well, that's honest graft." For more of Plunkitt's wisdom, see William Riordon, *Plunkitt of Tammany Hall* (1963). **2.** The new style of honest graft involves legal "campaign contributions" from individuals and groups. According to Amitai Etzioni, "The law forbids only explicit deals. A lobbyist may visit a member of Congress shortly before a vote. He'll express the position the lobby favors, will make a campaign contribution sometime before the vote, and—if the vote is satisfactory—another after it is cast. So long as no direct link is forged between the contribution and vote, giver and receiver are home free." *New York Times* (November 23, 1982). *Compare to* HONORARIUM.

honeymoon period The relatively short time after taking office that an elected executive may have harmonious relations with the press, the legislature, and the public. Honeymoons, which may last from a few hours to a few months, tend to end once the executive (whether a president, governor, or mayor) starts to make the hard decisions that alienate one constituency or another. As political terms go, *honeymoon* is quite old. In a December 27, 1796, letter to Edward Rutledge, Thomas Jefferson uses it in an analysis of the presidency: "I know well that no man will ever bring out of that office the reputation which carries him into it. The honeymoon would be as short in that case as in any other, and its moments of ecstasy would be ransomed by years of torment and hatred." The word is still actively used. As President Gerald R. Ford told a joint session of the U.S. Congress on August 12, 1974: "I do not want a honeymoon with you. I want a good marriage."

honorable A form of address used for various public officials, such as judges, mayors, and members of the U.S. Congress. Honorable does not necessarily imply personal honor or integrity; it merely signifies current (or past) incumbency.

honorarium **1.** A symbolic sum paid to a speaker. Traditionally an honorarium was a modest amount given to a visiting academic or other dignitary who gave a speech or otherwise contributed services. Propriety forbade "haggling" over fees. As politicians and other public figures (in or out of office) began to command substantial speaking fees, the term *honorarium* continued to be used long after the sums involved ceased to be symbolic. 2. A legal bribe paid to a government official for a specific act or, more likely, for a continuing sympathetic view toward the interests of those who give honorariums. *Compare to* HONEST GRAFT.

human capital A concept that views employees as assets in the same sense as financial capital. It presupposes that an investment in human potential will yield significant returns for the organization. Human capital theory holds that people make human capital investments in themselves (such as higher education) to increase their earning potential. Similarly, organizations make capital investments in their employees through training and development.

human relations The discipline concerned with the application of the behavioral sciences to the analysis and understanding of human behavior in organizations.

human resources administration An increasingly popular euphemism for the management of social welfare programs. Many jurisdictions that had departments of public or social welfare have replaced them with departments of human resources.

human resources management (HRM) A term used synonymously with *personnel management.* HRM transcends traditional personnel concerns by taking the most expansive view of the personnel department's mandate. Instead of viewing the personnel function as simply that collective of disparate duties necessary to recruit, pay, and discharge employees, the HRM approach assumes that personnel's appropriate mission is the maximum use of its organization's human resources.

human services The general term for organizations that seek to improve the quality of their clients' lives by providing such services as counseling, rehabilitation, and help with nutrition.

Humphrey's Executor v. United States (1935) The U.S. Supreme Court case prohibiting the dismissal of commissioners of the Federal Trade Commission by the president for reasons of disagreement over policy. The Court reasoned that an FTC commissioner "occupies no place in the executive department and . . . exercises no part of the executive power."

I

idealism The use of high moral principles as a guide to foreign policy. This is in contrast to REALISM, which is more pragmatic and concerned with immediate NATIONAL INTEREST. However, proponents of idealism maintain that moral force is ultimately more effective and more enduring than physical power. President Woodrow Wilson's futile advocacy that the United States join the League of Nations after World War I is considered one of the twentieth century's great examples of idealism in INTERNATIONAL RELATIONS.

immunity 1. An exemption from a duty or obligation. For example, foreigners with diplomatic immunity cannot be prosecuted for breaking the laws of their host countries; they can only be expelled. 2. An exemption from prosecution granted to persons to force them to testify in a criminal matter without violating their Fifth Amendment protections against self-incrimination. Those who refuse to testify to a grand jury or a court after being granted immunity can be held in contempt and sent to jail to reconsider. (Jail time may be limited to the end of a grand jury's term or a court's session.) 3. The freedom of governments in the U.S. federal system from being taxed by other governments. 4. An exemption from ordinary legal culpability while holding public office. Government officials generally need protection against lawsuits, whether frivolous or not, that might be brought against them by people dissatisfied with their actions or adversely affected by them. Otherwise, government could be brought to a standstill by such suits, or be crippled by their threat. In general, judges and legislators are well protected by judicial doctrines concerning immunities, whereas police officers, sheriffs, and most public administrators are not.

immunity, congressional The immunity of members of the U.S. House of Representatives and the U.S. Senate from lawsuits derived from what they say on the floors of the Congress. This limited immunity is established by the "speech and debate" portion of the U.S. Constitution, Article I, Section 6, which also holds that legislators may not be arrested except for "treason, felony and breach of the peace." So they are clearly subject to criminal prosecution; furthermore, what they say in newsletters and press releases is also prosecutable.

immunity, presidential The immunity of the president of the United States from judicial action. There are many reasons for this: case law (*Kendall v. U.S.* [1838]); the futility of prosecuting a person who has the power of pardon; the separation of powers, which asserts that one branch of government is not answerable to another; and the need for the undisturbed exercise of the office of the president. Consequently, impeachment was traditionally the only way to bring a president to account. Then in 1998 the U.S. Supreme Court in *WILLIAM JEFFERSON CLINTON V. PAULA CORBIN JONES* put limits on presidential immunity in the context of a civil suit.

immunity, transactional The immunity that prevents a witness from being prosecuted only for the crime about which he or she is specifically being questioned.

immunity, use The immunity that prevents a witness from being prosecuted for crimes revealed through compelled testimony or leads derived from the testimony. This is the most common form of immunity.

impasse A condition that exists during labor-management negotiations when either party feels that no further progress can be made toward a settlement —unless the process of negotiating changes. The most common techniques used to break an impasse are mediation, fact finding, and arbitration.

impeachment A quasi-judicial process for removing public officials from office. Impeachment is the beginning of the process by which the president, vice president, federal judges, and some high-level civil officials may be removed from office if convicted of the charges brought against them. Officials may be impeached for treason, bribery, and other high crimes and misdemeanors. The U.S. House of Representatives has the sole authority to bring charges of impeachment (by a simple majority vote), and the U.S. Senate has the sole authority to try impeachment charges. An official may be removed from office only upon conviction, which requires a two-thirds vote of the Senate. The U.S. Constitution provides that the chief justice shall preside when the president is being tried for impeachment. *See WILLIAM JEFFERSON CLINTON V. PAULA CORBIN JONES.*

implementation The process of putting a government program into effect; it is the total process of translating a legal mandate, whether an executive order or an enacted statute, into appropriate program directives and structures that provide services or create goods. Implementation, the doing part of public administration, is an inherently political process. Architects often say that "God is in the details." So is implementation. Its essence is in the details. A law is passed, but the process of putting it into effect requires countless small decisions that necessarily alter it but seldom intentionally distort it. However, substantial FRICTION can occur. Implementation is political in a very fundamental sense in that the resulting activities shape who gets what, when, and how from government.

implied power That authority not explicitly granted by the U.S. Constitution but inferred, based on a broad interpretation of other expressed or enumerated powers. The notion of implied power was first given voice in the case of *McCulloch v. Maryland* (1819), when Chief Justice John Marshall wrote, "Let the end be legitimate, let it be within the scope of the Constitution, and all means which are appropriate, which are plainly adapted to that end, which are not prohibited, but consist with the letter and the spirit of the Constitution are constitutional."

impoundment A tactic available to fiscal strategists—the withholding by the executive branch of funds authorized and appropriated by law. There are several types of impoundment decisions. The earliest example traces back to Thomas Jefferson, who impounded funds designed to finance gunboats for the Mississippi River. A primary and accepted mode of impoundment is for emergencies, as in war. President Franklin D. Roosevelt impounded funds slated for numerous programs that were "superseded" by the events of late 1941. Another mode of impoundment is to confiscate funds when the program objective has been accomplished. Presidents Dwight D. Eisenhower and Harry S. Truman used impoundment to redeem "extra" funds from programs that had met their objectives or did not need funds. Another mode of impoundment is for legal compliance. President Lyndon B. Johnson impounded funds and threatened to impound other funds for local governments and school districts in violation of the Civil Rights Act or federal court orders. The case for fiscal impoundment was made by the Richard M. Nixon administration as being necessary for economic stabilization and to enable the president to accomplish his legal responsibilities under the Employment Act of 1946. Fiscal impoundment really amounts to a form of line-item VETO. Several state governments empower their governors with the right to specify a budgetary figure for each program in the budget; if the legislature exceeds the recommended sum, the governor may veto the legislatively added sum above the original recommendation. Of course, cuts made by the legislature are binding. However, the line-item veto is not an executive power granted by either the U.S. Constitution or by subsequent legislation. The arguments in favor of impoundment made by the Nixon administration focused on the difficulties that the executive had in planning a budget (based on the revenue estimates) and then having the Congress essentially tack on from $20 to $30 billion for "favorite programs." As a direct result of the impoundment controversy, the Congress set up its own parallel budget machinery in 1974 under the Congressional Budget and Impoundment Control Act. Significant for fiscal policy is the fact that the act established a new congressional budget process requiring the U.S. Congress to set a maximum limit (recognizing the fiscal implications) and to make the various subcommittees keep the total final budget under that ceiling. Of course, this doesn't prevent the Congress from establishing a high ceiling, but it does force it to face the total fiscal issue directly. The ad hoc impoundments of the Nixon administration were repeatedly rejected by the federal courts when they were challenged. Now Title X of the Congressional Budget and Impoundment Control Act provides for two kinds of legal impoundment: (1) deferrals that are presidential decisions not to spend funds until a later date, and (2) rescissions that are presidential decisions not to spend funds at all. Deferrals and rescissions must also be approved by the Congress.

impoundment resolution A resolution by either the U.S. House of Representatives or the U.S. Senate that expresses disapproval of a proposed rescission or deferral of budget authority. Whenever all or part of a budget authority provided by the U.S. Congress is deferred, the president is required to transmit a special message to the Congress describing the deferrals. Either house may, at any time, pass a resolution disapproving this deferral of budget authority, thus requiring that the funds be made available for obligation. When no congressional action is taken, deferrals may remain in effect until, but not beyond, the end of the fiscal year.

income support A government program designed to provide cash benefits for persons whose incomes and other resources are limited.

incomes policy 1. A general phrase for the totality of a national government's influence upon wages, prices, and profits. 2. Direct government control on prices and wages.

incorporation 1. The creation of a government corporation by a legislature. 2. The creation of a private corporate entity by following procedures called for in applicable state law. The corporation then created becomes a legal entity, an artificial person, subject to legal action. 3. The selective application of protections provided by the federal Bill of Rights to the states, also called *absorption*. This nationalization was accomplished mostly through the due process clause of the Fourteenth Amendment. The incorporation doctrine overcame the U.S. Supreme Court's ruling in *Barron v. Baltimore* (1833) that the Bill of Rights limited only the actions of the federal government, not those of individual state governments.

incrementalism 1. The view associated with CHARLES E. LINDBLOM that most public policy decisions are not made by rational (total information) processes but are dependent upon small incremental decisions that tend to be made in response to short-term political conditions. Incrementalism can be either an intellectual response to uncertainty or a political response to pressures against bolder moves or more fundamental initiatives. The danger with incremental decisionmaking is that the policymakers rarely stand back and ask whether the overall direction is appropriate. By its very nature, incrementalism militates against a fundamental reappraisal of policy and can therefore lead to creeping commitments or creeping escalation. Incrementalism is an especially important aspect of budgeting. **2.** A normative theory of government that views policymaking as a process of bargaining and competition involving the participation of people holding conflicting points of view. *See* PUBLIC POLICYMAKING.

independent agency/regulatory commission A federal executive agency not included in an executive department or within the Executive Office of the President. Some, such as the Smithsonian Institution, are of long standing. Many others were created in the twentieth century as the responsibilities of government increased. A regulatory commission is an independent agency established by the U.S. Congress to regulate some aspect of U.S. economic life. Among these are the Securities and Exchange Commission and the Federal Trade Commission. These agencies are, of course, not independent of the U.S. government. They are subject to the laws under which they operate as these laws are enacted and amended by the Congress. Independent agencies and regulatory commissions can be divided into units under the direct supervision and guidance of the president, and therefore responsible to him, and units not under that supervision and guidance, and therefore not responsible to the president. The units in the first group can be categorized as independent executive agencies; those in the second group can be subdivided into independent regulatory commissions and government-sponsored enterprises. Independent executive agencies, with rare exceptions, are headed by single administrators appointed by the president and confirmed by the U.S. Senate. These administrators serve at the pleasure of the president and can be removed by him at any time. In addition, they must submit their budget requests to the Office of Management and Budget (OMB), which is located within the Executive Office of the President, for review and clearance. Examples of independent executive agencies include the Environmental Protection Agency, the General Services Administration, and the Small Business Administration. Independent regulatory commissions (such as the Federal Trade Commission) and government-sponsored enterprises (such as the Tennessee Valley Authority) are bodies headed by several commissioners, directors, or governors, also appointed by the president and confirmed by the Senate. Unlike administrators of independent executive agencies, they serve for fixed terms and cannot be removed at the pleasure of the president. Although all the independent regulatory commissions and most of the government-sponsored enterprises submit their budget requests to the OMB for review and clearance, the degree of dependence on these budgets varies considerably. Nearly all the government-sponsored enterprises generate a considerable part of their financial resources from outside sources, but the independent regulatory commissions rely on the government for their funding. Units subject to periodic authorization and appropriations hearings (all the independent executive agencies and independent regulatory commissions and most of the government-sponsored enterprises) must undergo a review of their activities at those congressional hearings. Note that many regulatory functions are also performed by regular cabinet departments. For example, the Food and Drug Administration is located within the Department of Health and Human Services, and the Food Safety and Inspection Service is under the auspices of the Department of Agriculture. Independent agents and regulatory commissions have long been considered patronage dumping grounds. What Esther Peterson said in 1976 is still valid today: "Past Administrations with notable though limited exceptions, have peopled regulatory agencies with cast-off party functionaries, well-connected lawyers whose prior careers were marked with single-minded devotion to the interests of oil companies and other regulated industries, ideological zealots bent upon the destruction of the very laws they were appointed to uphold, cronies of favored Senators and Congressmen surmounting the selection system by affability and contacts; and perhaps worst of all 'inoffensive' mediocrities," *New York Times* (February 1, 1976). *Compare to* REGULATION.

indexing A system by which salaries, pensions, welfare payments, and other kinds of income (as well as income tax brackets) are automatically adjusted to account for inflation.

industrial policy Government regulation of industrial planning and production through law, tax incentives, and subsidies. The United States does not have a comprehensive industrial policy as other nations do (especially Japan, where the government exercises considerable control over industrial planning and decisionmaking) because of a traditional abhorrence of central planning, which is associated with communism and considered the antithesis of the free enterprise system.

industrial psychology The study of those aspects of human behavior related to work organizations; its focus has been on the basic relations in organizations between (1) employees and their coworkers, (2) employees and machines, and (3) employees and the organization. Because the term *industrial psychology* holds a restrictive connotation, the field is increasingly referred to as industrial and organizational psychology, or I/O Psychology.

infrastructure 1. A general term for a jurisdiction's fixed assets, such as bridges, highways, tunnels, and water treatment plants. 2. A political party's or a government's administrative structure, the people and processes that make it work. 3. The institutional framework of a society that supports the educational, religious, and social ideology, which in turn supports the political order. 4. The permanent installations and facilities for the support, maintenance, and control of naval, land, and air forces.

inherent power An authority that is an integral part of sovereignty and that, although not expressly stated, is implied by the nature of government and is necessary for a government to function.

initiative A procedure that allows citizens, as opposed to legislators, to propose the enactment of state and local laws. An initiative, the proposed new law, is placed on the ballot (often as a proposition) only after the proper filing of a petition containing signatures from 5 to 15 percent of the voters. Fewer than half the states provide for the initiative. Initiatives are not possible under federal legislation because Article I of the U.S. Constitution prevents the U.S. Congress from delegating its legislative responsibilities. *Compare to* REFERENDUM.

initiative, indirect A citizen-initiated proposal that must first be submitted to the legislature. It is submitted to the voters only if the legislature rejects it or proposes a substitute measure.

injunction A court order forbidding specific individuals or groups to perform acts the court considers injurious to the property or other rights of a person or community. There are two basic types of injunctions: (1) a temporary restraining order, which is issued for a limited time prior to a formal hearing; and (2) a permanent injunction, which is issued after a full formal hearing. Once an injunction is in effect, the court has contempt power to enforce its ruling through fines or imprisonment, or both.

in-kind transfers Welfare benefits other than cash, such as clothing, food, and food stamps.

ins versus outs The descriptive reference to the continuing political conflict between members of a political party "in" power and their opponents who are "out" of power; in a legislative context, this parallels majority versus minority.

inspector general The job title (of military origin) for the administrative head of an inspection or investigative unit of a larger agency.

institutional discrimination Practices contrary to equal employment opportunity policies, without intent to discriminate. Institutional discrimination (also known as "institutional racism") exists whenever a practice or procedure has the effect of treating one group of employees differently from another.

institutional memory The collective memory of government organizations; this can be achieved through the continuity of personnel and through written records.

integration 1. A policy that encourages interaction between members of different races. 2. In education, the purposeful policy of having children of different races attend the same public schools. Integration was mandated by the U.S. Supreme Court in BROWN V. BOARD OF EDUCATION and has often resulted in WHITE FLIGHT. 3. A stage in the intelligence cycle in which a pattern is formed through the selection and combination of evaluated information. 4. The process of making differing military units or services more compatible so that they may better operate as an integrated force in time of war. 5. A voluntary process of joining together to create a new political community—one that is generally regarded as larger than the traditional nation-state.

intelligence 1. The ability to cope with one's environment and to deal with mental abstractions. 2. Information. The military, as well as other organizations concerned with national security, use the word thus in its original Latin sense. In this context, *intelligence* also implies secret or protected information even though some of the best sources are open rather than covert. 3. The product of organizations engaged in such intelligence-gathering activities.

intelligence community 1. All the spies in the world; the totality of the employees of the world's civilian and military intelligence agencies. 2. The military and civilian intelligence-gathering agencies of one nation. More than forty federal agencies perform intelligence work of one kind or another. The leading members of the U.S. intelligence community include the Central Intelligence Agency, the National Security Agency, the Defense Intelligence Agency, the Department of State, and the Federal Bureau of Investigation.

intelligence estimate The appraisal of available intelligence relating to a specific situation or condition with a view to determining the actions open to the enemy or potential enemy and the order of probability for their adoption.

intelligence oversight The review of the policies and activities of intelligence agencies, such as the Central Intelligence Agency and the Federal Bureau of Investigation, by the appropriate congressional committees. This was not formally done by the U.S. Congress until the 1970s, when reports that the FBI and CIA were abusing their operating mandates encouraged the Congress to watch over them carefully, systematically, and formally.

intelligence, domestic Intelligence relating to activities or conditions within a state that threaten internal security and that might require the employment of troops. The Federal Bureau of Investigation is the U.S. domestic intelligence agency. The Central Intelligence Agency had no legal mandate to engage in domestic intelligence-gathering activities. However, the war on terror that began in 2001 is forcing these agencies to cooperate as never before.

intelligence, strategic 1. Information gathered by intelligence agencies that can be used for formulating a nation's diplomatic and military policies; it is long range and widely focused, as opposed to tactical intelligence, which is short range and narrowly focused. 2. Information relating to an adversary's strategic forces.

interest 1. A benefit or advantage that one seeks to gain through the political process. 2. The extra money a person or institution receives in return for lending money to another person; money paid for the use of money. 3. Engagement in an occupation or profession that influences one's attitudes toward other social, economic, and/or political actions. 4. A right to something, whether an intangible, such as freedom, or concrete, such as half ownership in a cement factory. 5. A group of persons who share a common cause that puts them into political competition with other groups or interests. Thus, the oil interests want better tax breaks for the oil industry; and the consumer interests want new laws protecting consumer rights vis-à-vis the business interests, who want fewer laws protecting consumer rights.

interest group pluralism *See* THEODORE J. LOWI.

interest group theory A theory based on the premise that individuals function primarily through groups and that these groups act as appropriate and necessary to further group goals (based on common interests). The group process, including the formulation of group objectives and the development of specific group actions and response, is seen as a fundamental characteristic of the political process. The significance of groups in the political process has been recognized for over 2,000 years: Aristotle noted that political associations were significant and commonplace because of the "general advantages" members obtained. One of the first specific references to groups in the U.S. political process was James Madison's famous discussion of factions in *Federalist No. 10*. In Madison's view, the group was inherent in the nature of people, and its causes were unremovable. The only choice then was to control the effects of group pressure and power. A more elaborate discussion of group theory can be traced to John C. Calhoun's treatise on governance, *A Disquisition on Government* (1853). Although essentially an argument for the protection of minority interests, the treatise suggested that ideal governance must deal with all interest groups because they represent the legitimate interests of the citizens. If all groups participated on some level of parity within the policymaking process, then all individual interests would be recognized by the policymakers. Although the work of Calhoun represents the development of early group theory, modern political science group theory has taken greater impetus from the work of ARTHUR F. BENTLEY. But it remained for David B. Truman (1913–2003) and Earl Latham (1907–1977) to conceptualize the theoretical implications of group action and to begin assembling a theory of the group process. Truman's principal work, *The Governmental Process* (1951), viewed group interaction as the real determinant of public policy, the primary focal point of study, in his view. Earl Latham's *The Group Basis of Politics* (1952) was particularly significant because of his conceptualization that government itself is a group just like the various private groups attempting to access policy. Latham viewed the legislature as the referee of the group struggle, responsible for "ratifying the victories of the successful coalitions and recording the terms of the surrenders, compromises, and conquests in the form of statutes." The function of bureaucrats is quite different, however; they are like "armies of occupation left in the field to police the rule won by the victorious coalition." Although Latham's description was aimed primarily at regulatory agencies, he saw the bureaucrat being deluged by the losing coalitions of groups for more favorable actions despite the general rules established. The result is that "regulatory agencies are constantly besought and importuned to interpret their authorities in favor of the very groups for the regulation of which they were originally granted." Latham distinguished three types of groups, which he based on their phases of development: incipient, conscious, and organized. An incipient group is one "where the interest exists but is not recognized" by the potential members; a conscious group is one "in which the community sense exists but which has not become organized"; and an organized group is "a conscious group which has established an objective and formal apparatus to promote the common interest." Latham's incipient and conscious groups are essentially the same as David B. Truman's potential groups, which always exist but don't come together until there is a felt need for action on an issue. The concept of potential groups keeps the bureaucratic policymaking process honest (or perhaps balanced), given the possibility that new groups might surface or that some issues could influence decisionmaking. The potential groups concept also serves as a counterargument to the claim that group theory is undemocratic. Once the concept of potential group is married to the active role of organized groups, the claim can be made, in Truman's words, that "all interests of society by definition are taken into account in one form or another by the institutions of government." *See also* PRESSURE GROUP; LOBBY.

interface 1. A common boundary between things; for example, in tailoring the term refers to a fabric that is placed between two other fabrics to give them body and shape. 2. The point of contact, or the boundary between organizations, people, jobs, or systems. Nowadays, verbose politicians do not mix with or visit their constituents; they have the pleasure of interfacing with them. During the Jimmy Carter administration, Vice President Walter Mondale observed that "in the Senate, you have friends; in the executive, you interface."

intergovernmental expenditure An amount paid to other governments as political, fiscal, or programmatic aid in the form of shared revenues and grants-in-aid, as reimbursements for the performance of general government activities, and for specific services for the paying government (e.g., the care of prisoners and contractual research), or in lieu of taxes. *See also* FEDERALISM; FISCAL.

intergovernmental management Efforts to cope with intergovernmental problems (crime, education, welfare) through governmental as well as nongovernmental means. *Intergovernmental management* is a vague term without a consensus definition; nonetheless, the political dialogue in U.S. politics is always full of intergovernmental management issues. Politicians running for president or Congress love nothing better than telling the voters what they are going to do about crime and education once elected. But these are only marginal concerns of the federal government. State and local police are responsible for law enforcement. The Federal Bureau of Investigation, although highly visible in the public's crime-fighting imagery, is minuscule in comparison. State and local governments employ more than 0.5 million uniformed police officers. The FBI has only about 12,000 special agents. Education is the province of local school boards. The bottom line is that, aside from minor funding for special programs, there is practically nothing the federal government can do about these issues—nothing but talk. And federal officials, as well as would-be federal officials, spend so much time talking about such hot-button issues that the public often thinks the federal government can do something simple, such as mandating more homework for third graders or telling teenagers not to become sexually active before marriage, to make a real difference. But although politicians may think the public naive, the complex questions of intergovernmental management have no simple answers.

intergovernmental organizations International organizations through which nations cooperate on a government-to-government level. Examples include the International Monetary Fund and the Organization of American States.

intergovernmental relations (IGR) The complex network of interrelationships among governments; political, fiscal, programmatic, and administrative processes by which higher units of government share revenues and other resources with lower units of government, generally accompanied by special conditions that the lower units must satisfy as prerequisites to receiving the assistance. There are eternal questions concerning the structure of intergovernmental relations: Which level of government will have overall responsibility for what functions? When functions are shared between levels of government, how will each function be divided among national, state, and local governments? Should the taxes needed to finance local government be raised by the government that is to spend them, or by the higher level of government most successful at tax raising? Should a national government have the objective of redistributing revenues to reduce the differential between the richest and poorest regions of a nation? Some of these questions are answered by the very nature of a federal system; for example, only a national legislature can establish policies of redistribution. Others are answered by the structure of intergovernmental relations created over time by a multitude of laws, court precedents, and traditional political expediency. *See also* FEDERALISM.

intergovernmental revenue Amounts received from other governments as fiscal aid in the form of shared revenues and grants-in-aid, as reimbursements for the performance of general government functions, and specific services for the paying government (e.g., care of prisoners and contractual research), or in lieu of taxes.

international 1. Relating to the relationship of two or more nations. The word was first coined by JEREMY BENTHAM in *Principles of Morals and Legislation* (1780) to differentiate internal or domestic law from that which came into play in relations among nations. He said it was "calculated to express, in a more significant way, the branch of law which goes under the name of the law of nations." 2. An attitude, approach, or orientation that goes beyond the domestic matters of a particular nation.

international affairs A loose term that is used as a synonym for international politics. It can include almost anything that is not exclusively domestic in nature.

international civil service A term that refers not to a particular government entity but to a bureaucratic organization that is by legal mandate composed of differing citizenships and nationalities. Examples include the United Nations Secretariat, the International Labor Organization, and the European Union. Sometimes the term is used collectively to refer to the employees of all international bureaucracies.

international law The totality of treaties, customs, and agreements among states. When the international concerns that are at issue apply to individuals, it becomes a matter of CONFLICT OF LAWS.

international organizations 1. Organizations with nation-states for members. They can be universal in scope, such as the United Nations, or regional, such as NATO (North Atlantic Treaty Organization), the Organization of American States, and the Organization of African Unity. The essential point is that they have a formalized structure and procedure, as well as rights and obligations that accompany membership. These organizations can be used by state governments as an instrument of policy when it is expedient to do so. 2. A term that includes functional organizations given the task of regulating a particular specialized activity that crosses national boundaries, such as telecommunications. 3. Nongovernmental organizations (NGOs) that deal with particular international issues such as humanitarian assistance or human rights. Amnesty International is an example.

international politics 1. The totality of the principles, personalities, and processes that determine who gets what, when, and how at the international level. 2. The study of the relations among states. *International politics* is a narrower term than *international relations* because it generally focuses upon government-to-government interactions and upon relations among states rather than among peoples. It is often distinguished from the study of domestic politics by the lack of a central overriding authority that is able to provide the kind of law and order that characterizes domestic politics—at least in stable states.

international relations 1. All interactions among states and other international actors. It includes international economic relations and international law as well as international politics. This is the academic field of study that examines the political, military, and economic interactions among nation-states and other nongovernmental actors. It is a broader term than *international politics* because it includes nongovernmental relations and can encompass the actions of private individuals and groups as well as activities that are not necessarily political in character, such as cultural exchanges. 2. A term that is sometimes used instead of *international politics* by those who want to emphasize new developments, such as growing interdependence among states. 3. Loosely—and technically incorrectly—used as a synonym for *world politics* or *international politics*. *International politics* is more exclusive than *international relations,* even though the terms are often used interchangeably. Some scholars believe that as the focus of attention has changed from high politics involving such issues as war, peace, and security to low politics of international trade and regulation, economic interdependence, and integration, so the term *international relations* is a much more appropriate one to describe the discipline. 4. The totality of private interactions among citizens of differing countries. 5. The practice of diplomacy. As an academic discipline, international relations focuses upon the relations among states and other actors in the international system. International relations did not really develop as an academic discipline until the twentieth century—partly because political philosophy focused on the principles and practices of governance within political units rather than on the relations between them.

international studies 1. A loosely used term to describe the study of international politics or international relations. 2. A broad focus of study that encompasses everything outside a given state, including the studies of a particular foreign region even if it focuses upon the domestic politics, economics, culture, society, and history of that state, rather than its interactions with others. This is an all-embracing use of the term *international.*

interstate compacts Formal arrangements entered into by two or more states, generally with the approval of the U.S. Congress, to operate joint programs. Although Article I, Section 10, of the U.S. Constitution requires that interstate compacts be approved by the Congress, as a practical matter many agreements on minor matters ignore this requirement. The initial intent was to prevent states from forming regional alliances that might threaten national unity.

investment grade Refers to bonds that fall into the top four categories, from AAA to BBB or from Aaa to Baa, for Standard & Poors' and Moody's ratings, respectively. Some institutions are required by law to buy only investment-grade issues.

invisible government 1. A powerful organization, whether public or private, that wields secret, extensive, unwarranted, and unaccountable power. The Central Intelligence Agency has often been called an *invisible government.* 2. Rule by political party bosses (*see* BOSSISM), the real, although unseen, powers behind the elected representatives of the people.

invisible hand *See* CAPITALISM.

Iranian hostage crisis The wholesale violation of diplomatic privileges and immunities that occurred when the Iranian government-backed "students" captured the American Embassy complex of buildings in Teheran on November 4, 1979, and held fifty-three Americans hostage for 444 days, until January 20, 1981. The crisis so dominated the last year of the Jimmy Carter administration that it badly damaged Carter's reelection prospects, especially after an unsuccessful rescue effort on April 24, 1980. The Iranians agreed to free the hostages only after the Carter administration agreed to some of the Iranian demands "in principle." As one last insult to the Carter administration, the hostages were freed on the day Ronald Reagan succeeded Jimmy Carter as president.

iron law of oligarchy "Who says organization says oligarchy." This is Robert Michels's theory, stated in *Political Parties* (1915, 1949), that organizations are by their nature oligarchic because majorities within an organization are not capable of ruling themselves: "Organization implies the tendency to oligarchy. In every organization, whether it be a political party, a professional union, or any other association of the kind, the aristocratic tendency manifests itself very clearly. The mechanism of the organization, while conferring a solidity of structure, induces serious changes in the organized mass, completely inverting the respective position of the leaders and the led. As a result of organization, every party or professional union becomes divided into a minority of directors and a majority of the directed."

iron triangles *See* COZY TRIANGLES/IRON TRIANGLES.

isolationism The policy of curtailing as much as possible a nation's international relations so that one's country can exist in peace and harmony by itself in the world. Isolationism was the dominant U.S. foreign policy for many periods in its history, particularly during most of the nineteenth century and the two decades between the world wars—although during the 1920s and 1930s the United States was involved economically and legally in international politics. President George Washington, in his Farewell Address, September 17, 1796, advocated a policy of isolationism: "Why quit our own to stand upon foreign ground? Why, by interweaving our destiny with that of any part of Europe, entangle our peace and prosperity in the toils of European ambition, rivalship, interest, humor or caprice?" Washington's comment is revealing because isolationism has always been directed far more against possible involvement in Europe than against involvement in Asia. But modern trade, communications, and military weapons make isolationism virtually impossible for all nations today, even though such wishful thinking will continue to be a significant factor in domestic politics. Since 1945, the U.S. has abandoned isolationism, replacing it with a clear international commitment made evident by policies such as the TRUMAN DOCTRINE and formal alliances such as NATO. *Compare to* GLOBALISM.

issue A matter of political contention; a point in question. *The* issues are what politicians always say are important in a political campaign. However, it is these same issues that critics say they ignore.

issue group A politically active organization created in response to a specific issue. For example, the Right to Life Association was created as a response to the U.S. Supreme Court's 1973 *Roe v. Wade* decision legalizing abortion.

issue networks 1. The totality of public and private actors who interact and combine either to put forth public policy initiatives or to oppose them. This inherently chaotic process has little neatness or definition. The concept is mainly used after the fact by policy analysts to explain how a policy or issue came into being. 2. The bureaucratic experts, professional associations, and private-sector practitioners of a technical specialty that formally and informally define standards of practice and development consensus on public policy issues affecting their profession. *Compare to* COZY TRIANGLES/IRON TRIANGLES.

issue-attention cycle A model developed by Anthony Downs that attempts to explain how many policy problems evolve onto the political agenda. The cycle is premised on the proposition that the public's attention rarely remains focused on any one issue for very long, regardless of the objective nature of the problem. The cycle consists of five steps: (1) the pre-problem stage (an undesirable social condition exists, but has not captured public attention); (2) alarmed discovery and euphoric enthusiasm (a dramatic event catalyzes the public attention, accompanied by an enthusiasm to solve the problem); (3) the recognition of the cost of change (the public gradually realizes the difficulty of implementing meaningful change); (4) the decline of public interest (people become discouraged or bored or a new issue claims attention); and (5) the postproblem stage (although the issue has not been solved, it has been dropped from the nation's agenda). See Anthony Downs, "Up and Down with Ecology: The 'Issue-Attention Cycle,'" *Public Interest* 28 (Summer 1972).

J

job 1. A colloquial term for one's position or occupation. 2. A group of positions that are identical with respect to their major duties and responsibilities. 3. A discrete unit of work within an occupational specialty. Historically, jobs were restricted to manual labor. Samuel Johnson's *English Dictionary* (1755) defines a job as "petty, piddling work; a piece of chance work." Anyone not dwelling in the lowest strata of employment had a position, a profession, a calling, or (at the very least) an occupation. However, our language strives ever toward egalitarianism and now even an executive at the highest level would quite properly refer to his position as a *job*.

job action A strike or work slowdown, usually by public employees.

job analysis The determination of a position's specific tasks and of the knowledge, skills, and abilities that an incumbent should possess. This information can then be used in making recruitment and selection decisions, creating selection devices, developing compensation systems, and approving training needs.

job ceiling The maximum number of employees authorized at a given time.

job cycle The amount of time required for an employee to perform a discrete unit of work.

job description A summary of the duties and responsibilities of a job.

job design A general term for increasing job satisfaction and productivity by making jobs more interesting and efficient.

job dilution Dividing a relatively sophisticated job into parts that can be performed by less-skilled labor.

job enlargement Adding additional but similar duties to a job.

job enrichment Diversifying duties so that the work is performed at a higher level and is more personally satisfying.

job evaluation The process that seeks to determine the relative worth of a position; a formal comparison of the duties and responsibilities of various positions that ascertains the worth, rank, and/or classification of one position relative to all others in an organization. Although job content is obviously the primary factor in evaluation, market conditions must also be considered.

job family A group or series of jobs in the same general occupational area, such as accounting or engineering.

job freeze A formal halt, inherently temporary, to an organization's discretionary hiring and promoting.

job mobility A measure of the degree to which individuals can move from job to job within one organization; or the degree to which individuals can market their skills to other organizations.

job rotation The transfer of a worker from one assignment to another and thus minimize boredom and/or enhance skills.

job satisfaction The totality of employees' feelings about the various aspects of their work; the emotional appraisal of whether a job lives up to an employee's values.

judge-made Descriptive of laws created by judicial PRECEDENTS as opposed to statutory laws.

judicial activism The making of new public policies through the decisions of judges. This may be the reversal or modification of a prior court decision, the nullification of a law passed by the legislature, or the overturning of an action of the executive branch. The concept of judicial activism is most associated with the U.S. Supreme Court, which from time to time has found new interpretations to old provisions of the law. However, judges at any level can be said to engage in judicial activism when their judicial positions are used to promote what they consider to be desirable social goals. The main argument against judicial activism is that it tends to usurp the power of the legislature. The counterargument holds that, because laws—being products of compromise—tend to be vague on "hot" issues, the courts are in effect forced by the nature of the cases they receive to sort things out in a manner that seems "activist" to critics. In a larger historical sense, John Marshall's introduction of JUDICIAL REVIEW began judicial activism by claiming a special constitutional authority for the Supreme Court over the actions of other branches of government. Compare to JUDICIAL SELF-RESTRAINT.

judicial review 1. The power of the U.S. Supreme Court to declare actions of the president, the U.S. Congress, or other agencies of government at all levels to be invalid or unconstitutional. Although it was first asserted by the Supreme Court in *Marbury v. Madison* (1803), it was used sparingly in the nineteenth century; however, its use became more common in the twentieth, especially after 1933. 2. A court's power to review executive actions, legislative acts, and the decisions of lower courts (or quasi-judicial entities, such as regulatory agencies) either to confirm them or to overturn them. As long ago as 1835, in *Democracy in America,* Alexis de Tocqueville observed: "The power vested in the American courts of justice of pronouncing a statute to be unconstitutional forms one of the most powerful barriers that have ever been devised against the tyranny of political assemblies." *See also* LEAST DANGEROUS BRANCH.

judicial self-restraint A self-imposed limitation on judicial decisionmaking; the tendency on the part of judges to favor a narrow interpretation of the laws and to defer to the policy judgment of the legislative and executive branches. Justice Harlan Fiske Stone wrote in *United States v. Butler* (1936), that "while unconstitutional exercise by the executive and legislative branches is subject to judicial restraint, the only check on our own exercise of power is our own sense of self-restraint." *Compare to* JUDICIAL ACTIVISM; POLITICAL QUESTION.

juridical democracy An alternative to interest group liberalism offered by THEODORE J. LOWI in *The End of Liberalism* (1969), which calls for the federal courts to take a stronger role in achieving democratic ideals by forcing the U.S. Congress into a greater "rule of law" posture. Such force would come about by increasingly declaring statutes unconstitutional if they continue to be so vague that significant policy powers are delegated to government agencies who use this discretion to play the interest group game. Lowi views the competition of interest groups for influence over program implementation as inherently undemocratic and believes these decisions should be made in great detail in the legislation itself. And only the courts can force the Congress to do this.

jurisdiction 1. A territory, subject matter, or person over which lawful authority may be exercised. 2. A union's exclusive right to represent particular workers within specified industrial, occupational, or geographical boundaries. 3. The power of a court to act on a case. 4. A legislative committee's area of responsibility.

jurisdiction, original The power of a court to hear a case first. This is in contrast to appellate jurisdiction, which means that the court reviews cases only after they have been tried elsewhere.

jurisdictional dispute 1. A disagreement between two government entities over which should provide services to a disputed area; which has the authority to tax a disputed source; and which has the prior right to initiate prosecution in a criminal or noncompliance case. 2. A disagreement between two unions over which should control a particular job or activity.

jurisdictional strike A strike that results when two unions are in dispute about which one's members should perform a particular task, and one or the other strikes to get its way. For example, electricians and carpenters both may claim the right to perform the same tasks at a construction site. Because the employer is caught in the middle, the Labor-Management Relations (Taft-Hartley) Act of 1947 makes jurisdictional strikes illegal.

justice 1. The title of a judge; for example, an associate justice of the U.S. Supreme Court. 2. An elusive quality of treatment by one's nation that is perceived by the overwhelming majority of the citizens to be fair and appropriate. 3. The philosophic search for perfection in governance. Thucydides cynically observed in *The Peloponnesian Wars* (fifth century B.C.E.) that: "Into the discussion of human affairs the question of justice only enters where there is equal power to enforce it, and that the powerful exact what they can, and the weak grant what they must." Many would suggest that things haven't changed much since ancient time. Nevertheless James Madison wrote in Federalist No. 51 that "justice is the end of government. It is the end of civil society." 4. The ideal that each nation's laws seek to achieve for each of its citizens. According to Alexis de Tocqueville in *Democracy in America* (1835): "There is one universal law that has been formed or at least adopted ... by the majority of mankind. That law is justice. Justice forms the cornerstone of each nation's law." 5. A cynical justification for tyranny. Plato in the *Republic* (370 B.C.E.) wrote that "justice is but the interest of the stronger." 6. The name of a law enforcement agency.

just war doctrine The teachings dealing with the questions about when it is morally acceptable to go to war and what forms of warlike activities are permissible. According to St. Thomas Aquinas in *Summa Theologica* (1267–1273): "For a war to be just, three conditions are necessary—public authority, just cause, right motive." A major tenet of just war theory is the doctrine of proportionality; that the damage from a military action had to be justified in its proportionality to the original justification for going to war. A distinction is usually made between *jus ad bellum* (justification for going to war) and *jus in bello* (justification for acts in war). Just war theory sets two main restrictions on the use of force that pose acute difficulties in modern warfare. The requirement that discrimination should be maintained between those who are actively and willingly engaged in the combat and those who are innocent noncombatants is particularly difficult to observe in an age of total war and weapons of mass destruction. The second requirement, that of proportionality, which teaches that to be just means "ought to be appropriate to the ends which they hope to achieve," seems equally difficult to maintain in a world in which the dominant security regime is based on the threat to annihilate the population of the adversary.

K

Kafkaesque A reference to Franz Kafka's (1883–1924) novels and short stories, most particularly *The Trial* (posthumously published in 1937), which detailed the experiences of characters accused of crimes that are never explained to them and punished by agents whose authority they cannot understand for actions they have no clear sense of having committed. Kafka's name has come to stand for bureaucratic behavior that is threatening to the individual without being intelligible, behavior not based on rules the individual can be expected to know, or behavior not subject to any redress to which the individual has access.

Kerner Commission The National Advisory Commission on Civil Disorders, chaired by Governor Otto Kerner (1908–1976) of Illinois, which reported in 1968 that the "nation is rapidly moving toward two increasingly separate Americas; one black and one white."

Key, V. O., Jr. (1908–1963) The political scientist who did pioneering work in developing empirical methods to explore political and administrative behavior. His article "The Lack of a Budgetary Theory," *American Political Science Review* 34 (December 1940), posed what was soon acknowledged as the central question of budgeting — "on what basis shall it be decided to allocate X dollars to activity *A* instead of activity *B?*" His *Politics, Parties and Pressure Groups* 5th ed., (1964) was the pioneering text in the functional analysis of the various elements in the political process. His *Southern Politics in State and Nation* (1949) was the classic study of why the Democratic party dominated the South for so long after the Civil War.

Keynes, John Maynard (1883–1946) The English economist who wrote the most influential book on economics of the twentieth century, *The General Theory of Employment, Interest and Money* (1936). Keynes founded a school of thought known as "Keynesian economics," which called for using a government's fiscal and monetary policies to exert a positive influence on a capitalistic economy. Keynesian economics also developed the framework of modern macroeconomic theory. All U.S. presidents since Franklin D. Roosevelt have, whether admittedly or unadmittedly, used Keynes's theories to justify deficit spending as a way of stimulating the economy. Even Republican President Richard M. Nixon admitted that "we're all Keynesians now." Keynes observed in his *General Theory* that "practical men, who believe themselves to be quite exempt from any intellectual influences, are usually the slaves of some defunct economist." He provided the definitive economic forecast when he asserted that "in the long run we are all dead."

kick upstairs A slang term used when an individual is removed from a position for unsatisfactory performance and then promoted to a higher position in the organization.

King, Martin Luther, Jr. (1929–1968) The black southern Baptist minister who became the preeminent leader of the civil rights movement. His tactics of nonviolent confrontation with southern segregational policies aroused enough sympathy and support in the rest of the nation that they led to landmark civil rights legislation. King was assassinated in Memphis, Tennessee, on April 4, 1968. His influence as the "saint" of civil rights was so strong that his birthday was made a national holiday in 1983.

KISS "Keep It Simple, Stupid"; a major principle of strategy, tactics, and administration implying that complicated plans have a tendency to fail when a simplistic approach might succeed.

L

labor movement 1. An inclusive phrase for the progressive history of union-ism in the United States. Sometimes the term is used in a broader sense to encompass the fate of workers. The political influence of unions in the United States has been declining precipitously in recent decades. In 1955, close to 40 percent of all non-farm workers belonged to unions. By 2003, that number had dropped to less than 13 percent. **2.** The political organization of working-class interests.

labor union A group of employees who create a formal organization (the union) to represent their interests before management. Labor relations is the term for all the interactions between the union leaders (representing the employees) and management (representing the corporation or jurisdiction). *See also* COLLECTIVE BARGAINING.

laboratories of democracy A phrase first coined by Justice Louis S. Brandeis to refer to state governments that develop innovative policies to deal with social and economic problems. The implication is that if the policies succeed they will be adopted by other states and/or the federal government. As Brandeis wrote in a dissenting opinion to *New State Ice Co. v. Liebmann* (1932): "It is one of the happy incidents of the federal system that a single courageous State may, if its citizens choose, serve as a laboratory; and try novel social and economic experiments without risk to the rest of the country."

Labor-Management Relations Act of 1947/Taft-Hartley Act The federal statute that modified what the U.S. Congress thought was a pro-union bias in the National Labor Relations (Wagner) Act of 1935. Essentially a series of amendments to the National Labor Relations Act, Taft-Hartley (1) allowed national emergency strikes to be put off for an eighty-day cooling-off period, during which the president might make recommendations to the Congress for legislation; (2) delineated unfair labor practices by unions to balance the unfair labor practices by employers delineated in the Wagner Act; (3) made the closed shop illegal, allowing states to pass right-to-work laws; (4) excluded supervisory employees from coverage under the act; (5) allowed suits against unions for contract violations (judgments enforceable only against union assets); (6) required a party seeking to cancel an existing collective bargaining agreement to give sixty days' notice; (7) gave employers the right to seek a representation election if a union claimed recognition as a bargaining agent; (8) allowed the National Labor Relations Board to be reorganized and enlarged, from three to five members; and (9) provided for the creation of the Federal Mediation and Conciliation Service to mediate labor disputes. The act was passed even though President Harry S. Truman vetoed it.

Labor-Management Reporting and Disclosure Act of 1959/Landrum-Griffin Act The federal statute enacted in response to findings of corruption in the management of some unions. The act provided for the reporting and disclosure of certain financial transactions and administrative practices of labor organizations and employers and created standards for electing the officers of labor organizations. The U.S. Congress determined that certain basic rights should be assured to members of labor unions, and these are listed in Title I of the act—as a "bill of rights." Executive Order 11491 applied these rights to members of unions representing employees of the executive branch of the federal government.

Laffer curve The purported relation between tax rates and government revenues publicized by economist Arthur B. Laffer (1940–). According to Laffer, higher taxes reduce government revenues because high tax rates discourage taxable activity. Following this logic, a government can raise its total revenues by cutting taxes. This strategy should stimulate new taxable activity, and the revenue should more than offset the loss from lower tax rates. Although Laffer may have been the first to draw his curve, many others had earlier expressed the ideas behind it. For example, as JOHN MAYNARD KEYNES wrote, "Taxation may be so high as to defeat its object. . . . Given sufficient time to gather the fruits, a reduction of taxation will run a better chance, than an increasing, of balancing the budget." Even President John F. Kennedy observed in a speech of December 14, 1962, that "it is a paradoxical truth that tax rates are too high today and tax revenues are too low—and the soundest way to raise revenues in the long run is to cut tax rates now." *Compare to* SUPPLY-SIDE ECONOMICS.

laissez-faire 1. A hands-off style of governance that emphasizes economic freedom so the capitalist invisible hand can work its will. The concept is most associated with ADAM SMITH and his *Wealth of Nations* (1776). Although laissez-faire is still used to express a philosophic attitude toward government, it has long been rejected by the mainstream of U.S. politics. Even President William Howard Taft, a conservative Republican, said in a September 17, 1909, speech that "we have passed beyond the time of . . . the laissez-faire school which believes that the government ought to do nothing but run a police force." 2. A presidential style of decisionmaking that can mean the president either is above the battle or is remote from the details.

Lakewood plan *See* SERVICE CONTRACT.

lame duck 1. An officeholder who is serving out the remainder of a fixed term after declining to run again, suffering defeat, or is ineligible for reelection. The authority of such an officeholder is considered impaired, or lame. The phrase originated in the early days of the London stock market (known as Exchange Alley until 1773). A broker who went bankrupt would "waddle out of the Alley" like a lame duck. By the time of the American Civil War, the phrase had crossed the Atlantic to refer to a bankrupt politician. 2. Anyone in an organization whose leaving has been announced, whether for retirement, promotion, or transfer.

lame duck appointment A political appointment made by a lame duck or outgoing executive. A lame duck appointment was one of the major questions at issue in *Marbury v. Madison.*

Landrum-Griffin Act *See* LABOR-MANAGEMENT REPORTING AND DISCLOSURE ACT OF 1959/LANDRUM-GRIFFIN ACT.

Lasswell, Harold D. (1902–1978) One of the most influential and prolific of social scientists. Although he made major contributions to communications, psychology (he pioneered the application of Freudian theory to politics), political science (as a major voice in the CHICAGO SCHOOL), sociology, and law, his most lasting legacy is probably his pioneering work in developing the concept and methodology of the POLICY SCIENCES. Lasswell's major works include *Propaganda Technique in World War I* (1927); *Psychopathology and Politics* (1930); *Politics: Who Gets What, When, How* (1936); *Power and Society,* with Abraham Kaplan (1950); *The Policy Sciences,* edited with David Lerner (1951); *Pre-View of Policy Sciences* (1971).

law 1. A generalization about nature that posits an order of behavior that will be the same in every instance involving the same factors. 2. Enforceable rules that apply to every member of society. Thus when politicians such as Mayor Frank Hague of Jersey City, N.J., say, "I am the law," *New York Times* (November 11, 1937), or when President Richard M. Nixon (in a television interview of May 20, 1977) said, "When the President does it, that means that it is not illegal," they are expressing contempt for the entire concept of law. There is no true law if someone can get away with being above the law. 3. A statute passed by a legislature and signed by an executive or passed over a veto. 4. The totality of the rules and principles promulgated by a government. 5. A codified reflection of the POLITICAL CULTURE of a community. According to Ralph Waldo Emerson, "Politics,"

Essays: Second Series (1903), "The form of government which prevails is the expression of what cultivation exists in the population which permits it. The law is only a memorandum." **6.** The ultimate source of binding authority in a political community. Thus even despotic governments have law; they are just not a government of laws. *Compare to* ACT; ORDINANCE; STATUTE.

law and order 1. The suppression of crime and the maintenance of public order. **2.** A powerful CODE WORD for controlling domestic violence by curtailing the civil rights of minorities.

law of the land 1. The U.S. Constitution. Article VI states that "this Constitution . . . shall be the supreme law of the land." **2.** Laws enforced throughout a geographical area. **3.** A nation's customs, which over time are incorporated into the common law.

law of the situation A notion developed by the social psychologist MARY PARKER FOLLETT that one person should not give orders to another person, but both should agree to take their orders from the situation. If orders are simply part of the situation, the question of whether someone gives and someone receives does not come up.

law of triviality C. Northcote Parkinson's discovery, from his *Parkinson's Law* (1957), that "the time spent on any item of the agenda will be in inverse proportion to the sum involved."

law reviews The scholarly journals of the legal profession. The better law schools publish law reviews that are edited by their best students. According to the Harvard University law professor Morton J. Horwitz, law is "an odd profession that presents its greatest scholarship in student-run publications," *Newsweek* (September 15, 1975).

law, good samaritan A statute that gives malpractice protection to medical specialists when they use their skills to help people in an emergency, a situation in which they might not be covered by regular malpractice insurance.

law, labor All laws that apply to employment, wages, conditions of work, unions, and labor-management relations.

law, natural The rules that would govern human kind in a state of nature, before governments or positive law existed. Correspondingly, natural rights are the rights that all people enjoy no matter which governing system they live under. The tenets of natural law were a great influence on the American Revolution. For example, James Otis wrote in *The Rights of the British Colonies Asserted and Proved* (1764): "There can be no prescription old enough to supersede the Law of Nature and the grant of God Almighty, who has given to all men a natural right to be free, and they have it ordinarily in their power to make themselves so, if they please."

law, organic The fundamental or underlying law of a state; the U.S. Constitution is the organic law of the United States.

law, Parkinson's *See* PARKINSON'S LAW.

law, positive Law that has been created by a recognized authority, such as a legislature, as opposed to natural or common law.

law, private *See* PRIVATE LAW.

law, public *See* PUBLIC LAW.

law, statutory All laws that are based upon STATUTES enacted by a legislature.

laws, right-to-work *See* RIGHT-TO-WORK LAWS.

leadership 1. The exercise of authority, whether formal or informal, in directing and coordinating the work of others. The best leaders are those who can simultaneously exercise both kinds of leadership: the formal, based on the authority of rank or office; and the informal, based on the willingness of others to give service to a person whose special qualities of authority they admire. It has long been known that leaders who must rely only upon formal authority are at a disadvantage when compared to those who can also mobilize the informal strength of an organization or nation. The job of an organization's leader is to persuade people to do things they have never done before, to do things that are not routine, and to take risks—and sometimes even to die—for the common good. Once the organization accepts the credo of Alexander Dumas's three musketeers—"one for all and all for one"—then they have been led, and only then have they been molded into an organization. In essence, the most basic task of a leader is to create organization out of disorder and to make people more capable as a cohesive group than they are as unorganized individuals. 2. Those who hold formal positions of power in a legislature such as a speaker, a majority leader, or a whip; usually referred to as "the leadership." *See also* CHARISMA; FULL RESPONSIBILITY; POWER.

leadership, contingency theory of *See* CONTINGENCY THEORY.

leadership, functional Leadership that emerges from the dynamics associated with the particular circumstances under which groups integrate and organize their activities rather than from the personal characteristics or behavior of an individual.

leadership, moral Leading people in new directions of action and thought because it is the right and decent thing to do. Governor Franklin D. Roosevelt, during the presidential campaign of 1932 said, "The Presidency is not merely an administrative office. That's the least of it. It is more than an engineering job, efficient or inefficient. It is pre-eminently a place of moral leadership," *New York Times* (September 11, 1932). But those other than presidents can offer moral leadership. For example, Louis W. Sullivan, secretary of Health and Human Services, was considered one of the most ineffectual members of the George H. W. Bush administration until, in 1990, he started attacking cigarette companies for targeting the marketing of cigarettes to minorities and women. His popularity and stature immediately soared.

leadership, trait theory of An approach to leadership that assumes leaders possess traits that are fundamentally different from followers. Advocates of trait theory believe that some people have unique leadership characteristics and qualities that enable them to assume responsibilities that not everyone can execute. Therefore, they are "born" leaders. The most damaging criticism of trait theory, however, has been its lack of ability to identify which traits make an effective leader. Even among the traits that have been most commonly cited—intelligence, energy, achievement, dependability, and socioeconomic status—there is a lack of consensus across studies. The most obvious proof that leadership involves more than possessing certain traits is the reality that a leader may be effective in one setting and ineffective in another. It is no longer fashionable to contend that people will be effective leaders because they possess certain traits—without also considering other variables that influence leadership effectiveness. The arguments against trait theory are persuasive and come from various points of view. First, trait theory has largely fallen out of favor because reality never matched the theory. Instead, beginning in the late 1950s, standard practice has been to view leadership as a relationship, an interaction between individuals. The interaction was called a *transaction*, so that the term *transactional leadership* has become the umbrella label encompassing many theories of leadership. Second, the situation strongly influences leadership.

leadership, transformational Leadership that strives to change organizational culture and directions, rather than continuing along traditional paths. It reflects the ability of a leader to develop a values-based vision for the organization, to convert the vision into reality, and to maintain it over time.

leading indicators Statistics that generally precede a change in a situation. For example, an increase in economic activity is typically preceded by a rise in the prices of stocks. Each month, the Bureau of Economic Analysis in the Department of Commerce publishes data on hundreds of economic indicators. Several dozen of these are classified as "leading." The bureau's composite index of twelve leading indicators is a popular means of assessing the general state of the economy. Typical leading indicators include average workweek of production workers in manufacturing, average weekly claims for state unemployment insurance, new factory orders for consumer goods, and new building permits issued. Although the leading indicators of the Department of Commerce are relatively new, the concept is old. William Shakespeare in the first act of *Troilus and Cressida* (1601), noted their usefulness: "And in such indexes, although small pricks / to their subsequent volumes, there is seen / The baby figure of the giant mass / Of things to come at large."

leak 1. The deliberate disclosure of confidential or classified information by someone in government who wants to advance the public interest, embarrass a bureaucratic rival, or help a reporter disclose incompetence or skulduggery to the public. As James Reston (1909–1995) wrote, "The government is the only known vessel that leaks from the top." One way to trace leaks is to salt a memo: Give ever so slightly altered versions of the same memo to members of a group and see whose version is leaked. 2. The inadvertent disclosure of secret information.

learning curve The time it takes to achieve optimal efficiency in performing a task. When workers repeatedly perform a new task, the amount of labor per unit of output initially decreases according to a pattern that can be plotted as a curve on a graph.

learning organization Peter Senge's term, from his *Fifth Discipline* (1994), for organizations in which new patterns of thinking are nurtured, and in which people are continuously learning together to improve not only the organization but also their personal lives.

least dangerous branch The federal judiciary; the U.S. Supreme Court; the judicial branch in general. This is Alexander Hamilton's description of the judicial department of government in *Federalist* No. 78: "Whoever attentively considers the different departments of power must perceive that, in a government in which they are separated from each other, the judiciary, from the nature of its functions, will always be the least dangerous to the political rights of the Constitution; because it will be least in a capacity to annoy or injure them. The Executive not only dispenses the honours, but holds the sword of the community. The legislature not only commands the purse, but prescribes the rules by which the duties and rights of every citizen are to be regulated. The judiciary, on the contrary, has no influence over either the sword or the purse; no direction either of the strength or of the wealth of the society; and can take no active resolution whatever. It may truly be said to have neither force nor will, but merely judgment; and must ultimately depend upon the aid of the executive arm even for the efficacy of its judgments."

least-developed countries Countries without significant economic growth, with very low per capita incomes, and with low literacy rates; also called *Fourth World countries*.

legislation The end product of legislative action: laws, statutes, and ordinances. There may not always be an end product. Depending on one's attitude toward a bill, the best legislation may be no legislation. President Woodrow Wilson poetically wrote in *Congressional Government* (1885), his landmark study, that "once begin the dance of legislation, and you must struggle through its mazes as best you can to its breathless end—if any end there be." The legislative process is inherently messy. It is so full of compromise, hypocrisy, and self-interest that its end product, legislation, is sometimes compared to sausage, in that a wise person will avoid watching them being made.

legislation, direct Laws enacted by a jurisdiction's population via an INITIATIVE, a REFERENDUM, or a TOWN MEETING, in contrast to laws enacted by an elected legislature.

legislative history The written record of the writing of an act. It may be used in writing rules, or by courts in interpreting the law, to ascertain the intent of the legislature if the act is ambiguous or lacking in detail.

legislative intent The supposed real meaning of a statute as interpreted from its legislative history. Sometimes, during the legislative debate on a bill, a member will specifically talk about what is intended or not intended by the bill so that the ensuing legislative history will be a better guide to future interpretations. *Compare to* ORIGINAL INTENT.

legislative liaison The coordination of executive branch communications to the legislature. Liaison is a critical activity if an executive, whether president, governor, mayor, or executive agency, is to see legislative proposals enacted into law. In effect, the legislative liaison is a chief executive's or an agency's lobbyist.

Legislative Reorganization Act The 1946 law that dramatically reduced the number of standing committees in the U.S. Senate and U.S. House of Representatives, provided for a major expansion of the Legislative Reference Service (now known as the Congressional Research Service), and promoted the creation of a professional, nonpartisan staff for committees, as well as increased staff for individual members. This was the first effort of the U.S. Congress to establish an effective staff system and so decrease its dependence on executive agencies for information.

legislative supremacy The notion that although there are three "co-equal" branches of government, the legislature is nevertheless supreme. After all, it has the greatest number of enumerated powers and the executive and judicial branches must enforce its laws. As James Madison wrote in *Federalist* No. 51: "In republican government, the legislative authority necessarily predominates." President Franklin D. Roosevelt in a press conference on July 23, 1937, put it another way: "It is the duty of the President to propose and it is the privilege of the Congress to dispose."

legislature 1. The lawmaking branch of a representative government. It is not necessary for a legislature to have the word *legislature* in its formal title because it could be an assembly or a city council. 2. The lawmaking branch of the government of the United States. Article I, Section 1, of the U.S. Constitution states that all legislative power shall be vested in the U.S. Congress. This means that the president is specifically denied the power to make laws. All his authority must be based either on expressed or implicit powers granted by the Constitution or on statutes enacted by the Congress.

legitimacy 1. The characteristic of a social institution, such as a government or a family, whereby it enjoys a legal as well as a perceived right to make binding decisions for its members. Legitimacy is granted to an institution by its public—by that public conforming to established practices. In the federal government, the separation of powers allows each branch to judge the legitimacy of, and if necessary to take action to check, the acts of the others. Legitimacy is a specific legal concept, meaning that something is lawful, and at the same time an amorphous psychosociological concept referring to an important element in the social glue holding our societal institutions together. MAX WEBER, the most famous analyst of the legitimacy of governing structures, asserted that there are three pure types of domination: charismatic (in which the personal qualities of a leader command obedience); traditional (in which custom and culture yield acquiescence); and legal (in which people obey laws enacted by what they perceive to be appropriate authorities). 2. The quality of an administration that has come to power through free elections or established constitutional procedures. Thus, a government imposed by military force may lack legitimacy.

level of analysis One of the classic issues in the study of politics. It poses the eternal question: Should the focus of political analysis be the individual political actor, a local government, a national government, or the international political system as a whole?

levy 1. The assessment or collection of taxes. 2. The conscription of men for military service.

Lewin, Kurt (1870–1947) The psychologist popularly noted for his assertion that "there is nothing so practical as a good theory." He was the most influential experimental psychologist of the twentieth century. His research originated the modern concepts of group dynamics, action research, field theory, and sensitivity training.

liaison 1. The function of maintaining contact or communication between differing organizations. 2. An administrative officer who performs this function. Many federal agencies have liaison offices to facilitate smooth relations with the U.S. Congress.

liberalism 1. Originally, a political doctrine that espoused freedom of the individual from interference by the state, toleration by the state in matters of morality and religion, laissez-faire economic policies, and a belief in natural rights that exist independently of government. This is sometimes referred to as "classical liberalism." Although liberal concepts can be traced back to the Magna Carta of 1215 and through the writings of the major political theorists of the eighteenth-century European Enlightenment, by the nineteenth century, liberalism had come to stand for a kind of limited governance, its policies most favoring individual liberty and political equality. In this sense, the Founding Fathers were all liberals. 2. The use of resources by a government to achieve social change. In the twentieth century, liberalism had come to stand for the advocacy of government programs for the welfare of individuals; without such welfare state advantages, the masses had little chance to enjoy the traditional freedoms long espoused by the political theorists. So a term that meant "small government" and "low taxation" in one century had in the next century come to mean "big government" and "high taxation." By the beginning of the twenty-first century the Republican Party positioned itself as the party of classical liberalism while it sought to demonize the Democratic Party as "tax and spend" advocates of intrusive big government. Consequently, liberal as a political label has taken on such a bad odor that many genuine liberals hesitate to refer to themselves by the "L word." 3. Economic liberalism that places the emphasis on market operation rather than on government intervention and control. 4. A tradition in international affairs that places the emphasis on international institutions and the rule of law rather than on power and force.

liberalization Reductions in tariff and other measures that restrict world trade, unilaterally or multilaterally.

libertarianism A pure form of classical LIBERALISM, which asserts that a government should do little more than provide police and military protection; other than that, it should not interfere—either for good or ill—in the lives of its citizens.

license A permission granted to an individual or organization by competent authority, usually public, to engage in a practice, occupation, or activity that would be otherwise unlawful. It is usually granted on the basis of examination and/or proof of education rather than on measures of performance. License when given is usually permanent but may be conditioned on an annual fee, proof of continuing education, or proof of competence. Common grounds for revoking a license include incompetence, the commission of a crime (whether or not related to the licenses practice), and moral turpitude.

lifeboat ethics A framework for NORTH-SOUTH issues put forth by Garrett Hardin and holding that "each rich nation can be seen as a lifeboat full of comparatively rich people. In the ocean outside each lifeboat swim the poor of the world, who would like to get in, or at least share some of the wealth." *Psychology Today* (September 1974).

Lindblom, Charles E. (1917–) The leading proponent of the incremental approach to policy decisionmaking. In his most famous work, "The Science of Muddling Through," *Public Administration Review* (Spring 1959), Lindblom took a hard look at the rational models of the decisional processes of government. He rejected the notion that most decisions are made by rational (total information) processes. Instead, he saw such decisions—indeed, the entire policymaking process—as dependent upon small incremental decisions that tend to be made in response to short-term political conditions. Lindblom's thesis, essentially, held that decisionmaking was controlled infinitely more by events and circumstances than by the will of those in policymaking positions. His thesis encouraged considerable work in the discipline on the boundary between political science and public administration—public policy. Lindblom restated his muddling thesis in "Still Muddling, Not Yet Through," *Public Administration Review* (January/February 1980). Lindblom's other major works include *Unions and Capitalism* (1949); *Politics, Economics and Welfare,* with Robert A. Dahl (1953); *A Strategy of Decision,* with David Braybrooke (1963); *The Intelligence of Democracy: Decision-Making Through Mutual Adjustment* (1965); *Politics and Markets* (1978); *The Policymaking Process,* 2d ed. (1980).

line managers Those who are responsible for the primary purposes of an organization. In a civilian context, they supervise the provision of goods or services. In the military, they lead the actual fighting.

line organizations Segments of a larger organization that perform the major functions of the organization and have the most direct responsibilities for achieving organizational goals. *Compare to* STAFF.

linkage institution An institution that is the means for the will of the people to get onto a government's agenda. Political parties, because they are the links between ordinary citizens and elected policymakers, are considered linkage institutions.

linking pin Someone who belongs to two groups within the same overall organization, usually as a superior in one and as a subordinate in the other.

litmus test The test that determines the alkaline or basic nature of a chemical solution and that has been applied to politics as an indicator of a politician's true ideological nature. Thus a stand or vote on a given issue may be considered a litmus test for whether the person in question is a real conservative or a true liberal.

Lloyd-LaFollette Act of 1912 The federal statute that guarantees civilian employees of the federal government the right to petition the U.S. Congress, either individually or through their organizations. The act was the only statutory basis for the organization of federal employees until the Civil Service Reform Act of 1978. In addition, it provided the first statutory procedural safeguards for federal employees facing removal. It states that "no person in the classified civil service of the United States shall be removed or suspended without pay therefrom except for such cause as will promote the efficiency of such service and for reasons given in writing."

loan guarantee An agreement by which a government pledges to pay part or all of the loan principal and interest to a lender or holder of a security in the event of default by a third-party borrower. The purpose of a guaranteed loan is to reduce the risk borne by a private lender by shifting all or part of the risk to the government. If it becomes necessary for the government to pay part or all of the loan's principal or interest, the payment is a direct outlay; otherwise, the guarantee does not directly affect budget outlays.

lobby An individual, group, or organization that seeks to influence legislation or administrative action. Lobbies can be trade associations, individual corporations, good-government public interest groups, or other levels of government. The term arose from the use of the lobbies, or corridors, of legislative halls as places to meet with and persuade legislators to vote a certain way. The right to attempt to influence legislation is based on the First Amendment to the U.S. Constitution, which holds that the U.S. Congress shall make no law abridging the right of the people "to petition the government for a redress of grievances." Lobbying in general is not an evil; many lobbies provide legislatures with reliable first-hand information of considerable value. However, some lobbies have given the practice an undesirable connotation because they often contribute money to political campaigns and offer special favors to elected and appointed officials. All such contributions and favors are given, of course, in the expectation of favorable treatment on some issue in the future. In effect, they are often thinly but effectively disguised BRIBERY. Common forms of lobbying include testifying before a legislative hearing, formal and informal discussions with elected and appointed government officials, sending research results or technical information to appropriate officials, seeking publicity on an issue, drafting potential legislation, and organizing letter-writing campaigns.

Lobbying Act of 1946 The Federal Regulation of Lobbying Act of 1946, which requires that persons who solicit or accept contributions for lobbying purposes keep accounts, present receipts and statements to the clerk of the U.S. House of Representatives, and register with the clerk of the House and the secretary of the U.S. Senate. The information received is published quarterly in the *Congressional Record*. The purpose of this registration is to disclose the sponsorship and source of funds of lobbyists but not to curtail the right of persons to act as lobbyists. The constitutionality of the Lobbying Act was upheld in *United States v. Harris* (1954).

local affairs, department of The generic name of a state agency with oversight responsibilities for local government. Sometimes local governments are required to submit audit and budget reports to such an agency, the exact requirements varying from state to state.

local government A government entity that is not clearly state or federal. This could include general local governments, such as counties, municipalities, and towns, as well as special-purpose local governments, such as school districts, port authorities, and fire districts.

local option The authority given by a state to its localities to determine by a local referendum election a specific policy for that locality; for example, liquor sales on Sunday.

local union A regional organization of union members chartered by the national union with which it is affiliated. For example, the National Education Association charters local unions in thousands of school districts.

logical-positivism An approach to scientific explanation that emphasizes empirical methods and uses quantitative analysis wherever appropriate to create logical and formal explanations for the phenomena under study.

logistics Traditionally the art and science of moving military forces and keeping them supplied; those inventory, production, and traffic-management activities that seek the timely placement of materiel and personnel at the proper time and in the appropriate quantities.

loop 1. An informal term for a communications network for policy or bureaucratic purposes. Thus, those "in the loop" regularly receive information not usually available to others. Those "out of the loop" don't really know what is going on regarding a particular issue. 2. An inner circle of high-level advisors to a chief executive.

loophole 1. A small opening in a wall. 2. A TAX LOOPHOLE. 3. The provision of a law that allows someone to be exempted from its overall provisions.

loose cannon Someone who is uncontrollable and liable to cause great damage to someone else. The term comes from the obvious danger of having a loose cannon rolling about the deck of a ship. A political loose cannon may be a politician's relative or an overzealous staffer.

loose constructionist *See* STRICT CONSTRUCTIONIST.

lottery 1. A form of decisionmaking in which a choice is made by randomly selecting one entry from all entries submitted; the selection of one lot from among the entirety placed in a container; for example, draft selections in World Wars I and II were made from jars of numbers, each number having been assigned to a potential draftee. The intention of a lottery is to assure the absence of favoritism or special influence; it is a form of gambling in which the luck of the draw controls the selection of a winner. 2. State-sponsored and state-administered gambling undertaken as an alternative to raising taxes. Government lotteries have a long tradition in the United States. Many of the colonies were subsidized by lotteries. Even the Continental Congress authorized a lottery in 1776 to raise funds for the War of Independence. After a spate of scandals in the nineteenth century, the lottery fell into disfavor and disuse. The first of the modern state lotteries began in 1964 in New Hampshire. Most of the U.S. population now lives in states that run lotteries. The lottery is praised by those who see it as a popular alternative to higher taxes and condemned by those who say it takes advantage of the poor, who play it disproportionately, overwhelmingly lose, and thus subsidize the middle class and rich, who would have to pay higher taxes if there were no lottery.

low politics Politics and policies concerned with economic and social issues rather than the traditional themes of statecraft, war, peace, and security. Some analysts argue that foreign policy in advanced industrialized states has become much more concerned with low politics than with HIGH POLITICS. In fact, it is not a matter of either/or; foreign policy is concerned with both.

Lowi, Theodore J. (1931–) The leading critic of interest group pluralism, who is also noted for his classification of all public policies as either distributive, regulatory, or redistributive. His *The End of Liberalism: Ideology, Policy, and the Crisis of Public Authority* (1969; 2d ed., 1979) provided a provocative critique of modern democratic government and a condemnation of the paralyzing effects of interest group pluralism. Lowi asserted that when public authority is parceled out to private interest groups, the result is a weak, decentralized government incapable of long-range planning. These powerful interest groups operate to promote private goals; they do not compete to promote the public interest. Government then becomes not an institution capable of making hard choices among conflicting values but a holding company for interests. The various interests are promoted by alliances of interest groups, relevant government agencies, and the appropriate legislative committees. Lowi denied the very virtues that other group theorists saw in their promotion of interest group pluralism. Lowi's analysis is a scathing indictment of a governing process in which agencies charged with regulation are seen as protectors of those being regulated. *See also* INTEREST GROUP THEORY; JURIDICAL DEMOCRACY; PUBLIC POLICYMAKING. Lowi's other works include *At the Pleasure of the Mayor: Patronage and Power in New York City, 1898–1958* (1964); "American Business, Public Policy, Case-Studies, and Political Theory," *World Politics* (July 1964); *Private Life and Public Order* (1968); *The Politics of Disorder* (1971); *The Personal President: Power Invested, Promise Unfulfilled* (1985).

M

machinery of government All the structural arrangements (the various offices, bureaus, and departments) adopted by governments to deliver their legally mandated programs and services. This of necessity includes the central management arrangements of government. In all jurisdictions, the organization and eventual reorganization of executive branch agencies is the everlasting machinery of government issue. The machinery that a government creates to work its will must be judged by the quality of public administration that it yields. Most of the debate over reinventing government and the best public management practices is not about fundamentally changing the nature of governing institutions; it's about fine-tuning the machinery. To use a mobile metaphor, it's not about reinventing the automobile; it's about getting more miles per gallon of fuel and using fewer and less expensive parts.

madman theory President Richard M. Nixon's theory that if the president of the United States seemed to be a little bit crazy and irrational, the other side would be more responsive and pliable in international dealings.

make or buy analysis A method of determining whether it is cheaper to make or to buy certain parts or components. On the surface, it may seem a very simple decision to choose to buy for $20 those components that cost an organization $22.50 each to make. But realistic planning involves much more than consideration of unit costs alone. A production manager must also consider the various costs involved, including facilities use, labor, and transportation.

make whole A legal remedy that provides for an injured party to be placed, as near as may be possible, in the situation he or she would have occupied if the wrong had not been committed. The concept was first put forth by the U.S. Supreme Court in the 1867 case of *Wicker v. Hoppock*. In 1975, the Court held in *Albermarle Paper Company v. Moody* that Title VII of the Civil Rights Act of 1964 intended a make whole remedy for unlawful discrimination.

malfeasance The performance of a consciously unlawful act on the part of a public official. *Compare to* MISFEASANCE.

management A word that refers not only to the people responsible for running an organization but also to the running process itself—the use of numerous resources (such as employees and machines) to accomplish an organizational goal. We need to distinguish between leadership and management. The two functions and roles overlap substantially. Management involves power (usually formal authority) bestowed on the occupant of a position by a higher organizational authority. With the power of management comes responsibility and accountability for organizational resources. In contrast, leadership cannot be bestowed upon a person by a higher authority. Effective managers may also be leaders, and many leaders become managers, but the two sets of roles and functions differ.

management by exception A management control process that permits a subordinate to report to an organizational superior only exceptional or unusual events that might call for decisionmaking on the part of the superior. In this way, a manager may avoid unnecessary detail that confirms only that all is going according to plan. Although this concept is credited to Frederick W. Taylor, its antecedents can be found in the Bible (Exodus 18:22–26).

management by objectives (MBO) A technique of performance appraisal the hallmark of which is a mutual—by organizational subordinate and superior—setting of measurable goals to be accomplished by an individual or team over a set period. This concept was first popularized by Peter Drucker in *The Practice of Management* (1954).

management, contingency A management style recognizing that the application of theory to practice must necessarily take into consideration, and be contingent upon, the given situation.

management control That aspect of management concerned with the comparison of actual versus planned performance as well as the development and implementation of procedures to correct substandard performance. Control, which is inherent to all levels of management, is a feedback process that ideally should report only unexpected situations. *See* MANAGEMENT BY EXCEPTION.

management, cross boundary Programmatic efforts that cut across the boundaries of discipline, organizations, and jurisdictions. For example, many homeland security programs involve the combined efforts of the public, private, and nonprofit sectors.

management, cutback A phrase that describes the decline of public organizations in times of fiscal stress.

management development A conscious effort on the part of an organization to provide a manager with the skills needed for future duties, such as rotational assignments and/or formal educational experiences. The semantic difference between training workers and developing managers is significant.

Workers are trained so that they can better perform their present duties; managers are developed so that they can be of greater organizational value in present and future assignments. In such a context, the development investment made by the organization in a junior manager may pay off only when and if that individual grows into a bureau chief. One common method of developing managers is to provide them with the kinds of assignments and experiences that will allow them to grow professionally.

management, generic Management practices that are equally applicable in the public, private, and nonprofit sectors. The underlying doctrine holds that a properly trained manager will be effective in any type of organization, whether public or private, whether in service or manufacturing.

management information systems Computer-based operations that produce necessary information in proper form and at appropriate intervals for the management of a program or other activity. Such systems should measure program progress toward objectives and report costs and problems needing attention.

management, principles of *See* PRINCIPLES OF MANAGEMENT.

management, project The management of an organizational unit created to achieve a specific goal. Although a project may last from a few months to a few years, it has no further future; indeed, a primary measure of its success is its dissolution. The project staff necessarily consists of a mix of skills from the larger organization. The success of project management is most dependent upon the unambiguous nature of the project's goal and the larger organization's willingness to delegate sufficient authority and resources to the project manager.

management, public *See* PUBLIC MANAGEMENT.

management rights *See* RESERVED RIGHTS.

management rights clause That portion of a collective bargaining agreement that defines the scope of management rights, functions, and responsibilities, essentially all those activities that management can undertake without the consent of the union.

management scorecards Tally sheets for performance, not of individuals, but of the individual units or functions of a large organization. This allows the managers at the top to get an overview of how well their tactical managers are playing the "game." The whole point of the scorecard approach was to allow executives to instantly scan, by looking at the scores, the status of their organization units. In the early 1990s "balanced scorecards" first became fashionable in the private sector as a means to evaluate a company's performances from several perspectives simultaneously. Traditionally, the emphasis had been on financial performance (the bottom line) but a balanced scorecard complemented financial performance with data on customer satisfaction, internal processes, and ability to learn among other measures. Although report cards of this nature are as old as school, the scorecard approach suddenly became "hot" in government once they were introduced in 2002 as part of the Bush administration's President's Management Agenda. Scorecards are mainly a way of artificially creating the competitive forces inherent in the private sector. To a large degree this is management by shame—no agency wants to be ashamed of its rankings. Not surprisingly, the scores have been going up. But the question remains: Will federal managers, like students, work mainly for the grade at the expense of real learning or real reform? Only two things are certain: (1) nothing will be "reinvented" as that was the goal of the previous administration, and (2) the next administration will have a new set of strategic management tools.

managerialism An entrepreneurial approach to public management that emphasizes management rights and a reinvigorated scientific management. *Managerialism* as a term has long been used by sociologists as a reference to the economic and bureaucratic elites that run an industrial society. In the 1980s, this well-established sociological "ism" took on new connotations. The concept of managerialism romantically assumes that a managerial elite can radically change and control the direction, culture, and purpose of organizations. The romance of managerialism would not be possible if there were not heroes to romanticize. Who are these new-style heroes? Why, the managers themselves, who have come to revitalize the public service by slaying the dragons of self-serving unions and inefficient bureaucrats. The core theme of managerialism is management rights: giving managers enough room to maneuver so that they can accomplish their goals. This additional managerial room is necessarily taken from the rank and file. Thus, managerialism is quite comfortable with authoritarian management styles and a new version of scientific management—except the search for the "one best way" has been updated to the constant installation of the latest in behavioral and mechanistic technologies. To gain maximum control of personnel costs and see minimal problems with introducing labor-saving technologies, managerialism contracts out to the private sector as much of the public's business as it can. The techniques of administrative improvement advocated by managerialism, such as management audits and program evaluations, are comparatively old. What's new is that these same old techniques are being reinvigorated by a new doctrine or guiding philosophy.

managerial revolution James Burham's concept from *The Managerial Revolution* (1941) that as control of large businesses moved from the original owners to professional managers, society's new governing class would be not the traditional possessors of wealth but those who have the professional expertise to manage and lead large organizations.

mandamus/writ of mandamus A court order that compels the performance of an act.

mandate 1. The perceived popular or electoral support for a public program, political party, or a particular politician. U.S. presidents who win elections by overwhelming majorities may rightly feel the vote was a mandate to carry out their proposed policies, but presidents who win by narrow margins may perceive no mandate to implement their programs. Thus, a president's mandate or electoral margin can often have a significant effect on legislative proposals. The greater the mandate, the more deferential the U.S. Congress is likely to be. **2.** One level of government requiring another to offer—or pay for—a program as a matter of law or as a prerequisite to partial or full funding either for the program in question or for other programs. The only way to comprehend the full scope of the mandate problem is to look at their different categories. First, are they direct orders (which imply civil or criminal penalties for disobeying) or merely a condition for receiving aid? If they are the latter, they may not be considered a mandate at all, for they have no effect unless you want the aid. Then you must also take the strings, the mandates, that come with it. Second, are they programmatic or procedural? Programmatic mandates state the type and quality of program to be implemented; for example, a school lunch program must meet specified national standards for nutrition. A procedural mandate requires jurisdictions to do what they were going to do anyway but according to new requirements: Personnel have to be hired according to equal opportunity provisions; formal meetings and records have to be open to the public. Although programmatic mandates may cost a great deal, many procedural mandates may cost little or nothing—or have a one-time-only cost.

marginal analysis A technique that seeks to determine the point at which the cost of something (for example, an additional employee or machine) will be worthwhile or pay for itself.

marginal employees Members of an organization who contribute least to the organization's mission because of their personal sloth or the inherent nature of their duties.

marginal tax rate The tax rate or percentage applied on the last increment of income for purposes of computing federal or other income taxes.

marker 1. An IOU (I owe you); the statement of a debt (usually gambling). **2.** A boundary indicator. In this sense, the word is used in the phrase "lay down a marker" to send a signal not to cross a line, whether figurative or literal. **3.** A political obligation to someone.

marketplace failure The inability of a society's free markets to provide a needed service. This situation allows the nonprofit sector to show that it is a uniquely democratic phenomenon. In some respects, nonprofits are the most capitalistic of our economic responses, reacting to marketplace failure by filling economic voids with volunteers and charitable contributions. In contrast, more socialistic economies tend to meet similar types of community needs through tax-supported government programs and services. Nonprofits provide a flexible alternative to tax-supported government action.

market testing *See* PUBLIC ADMINISTRATION, COMPETITIVE.

marketplace of ideas The public forum in which political beliefs and policy innovations compete for attention and support. In this market people buy, meaning support, the ideas they like best.

Marshall Plan The economic aid program for post–World War II Europe. The plan worked so well and became so well known that the term entered the language and means the massive use of federal funds to solve a major social problem. George Marshall was the head of the U.S. Army during the war. As secretary of state on June 5, 1947, Marshall proposed the European Recovery Program, the massive U.S. aid program that became known as the "Marshall Plan," in a speech at Harvard University: "Our policy is directed not against any country or doctrine but against hunger, poverty, desperation and chaos. Its purpose should be the revival of a working economy in the world so as to permit the emergence of political and social conditions in which free institutions can exist."

Marxism The doctrine of revolution based on the writings of Karl Marx (1818–1883) and Friedrich Engels (1820–1895). Marxism maintains that human history is a struggle between the exploiting and exploited classes. Marx and Engels's *Communist Manifesto* (1848) avows that the proletariat will suffer so from alienation that it will overthrow capitalism. Marx's *Das Kapital* (1867) is frequently referred to as the bible of socialism. With the collapse of the Soviet Union, Marxism as a political, social, and economic force has suffered an irreversible blow.

mass production Generally, a high volume of output; but more specifically, mass production also assumes product simplification, the standardization of parts, continuous production lines, and the maximum possible use of automatic equipment

master plan *See* COMPREHENSIVE PLAN/MASTER PLAN.

matching funds 1. Funds provided for a specific purpose by one level of government as a condition for receiving additional funds for this same purpose from another level of government. Thus, a state government may agree to pay 50 percent of the cost of a local capital improvement program if the local government provides the other 50 percent. 2. Funds provided by private foundations and government agencies that are contingent upon the raising of equivalent funds from other sources by the recipient organization. 3. Funding for presidential elections optionally available to candidates who agree to abide by contribution and expenditure limits.

matrix organization An organization using a multiple command system whereby an employee might be accountable to one superior for overall performance as well as to one or more leaders of particular projects.

mayor The elected chief executive officer of a municipal corporation; the chief ceremonial officer of a city. In most modest-sized and small cities, the office of mayor is a part-time job. Depending on whether the job of mayor is administratively strong or weak, the mayor may simply be the first among equals on a city council. Although many big-city mayors have become national figures, no mayor has ever made the leap from city hall to the White House.

mayor-council system A system of urban government with a separately elected executive (the mayor) and an urban legislature (the council) usually elected in partisan ward elections. If the office of mayor is filled by separate citywide elections and enjoys such powers as veto, appointment, and removal, it is a strong mayor system; if it does not enjoy these powers, it is a weak mayor system. This designation does not take into account the informal powers possessed by the incumbent mayor, only the formal powers of the office. Hence Richard J. Daley (1902–1976) of Chicago was a strong mayor in a weak mayor system.

McCulloch v. Maryland (1819) The U.S. Supreme Court decision that upheld the implied powers granted to the U.S. Congress by the NECESSARY AND PROPER CLAUSE of the U.S. Constitution, upheld the supremacy of the national government in carrying out functions assigned to it by the Constitution, and established the doctrine of intergovernmental tax immunity. In stating that "the power to tax is the power to destroy," the Court held that the Bank of the United States was not subject to taxation by the State of Maryland. *Compare to* STRICT CONSTRUCTIONIST.

means test An income criterion used to determine whether someone is eligible for government welfare or other benefits. For example, a family might be allowed certain welfare benefits only if its annual cash income is less than $18,392 in the federal government's 2002 definition of poverty for a family of four. Means-tested entitlement programs are often compared to non-means-tested programs, such as social security, which citizens are entitled to regardless of their private means. It has even been suggested that one way of reducing the nation's social security liability is to subject future benefits to a means test; that is, people otherwise eligible for social security benefits would receive them only if their incomes were below a specified level.

med-arb A combination of mediation and arbitration that engages a third party neutral in mediation and arbitration. The main idea is to mediate in an effort to resolve the impasse, or at least to reduce the number of issues going to arbitration.

media event An activity undertaken as a means of generating publicity from the news media. The defining criterion for a media event is that it would not take place if cameras and reporters were not present. Examples include protest demonstrations scheduled for the convenience of the early evening television news programs or a walk through a poor or ethnic neighborhood by a candidate for public office to demonstrate meaningful (photogenic) concern. *Compare to* PSEUDOEVENT.

mediation Attempts by an impartial third party to settle disputes. A mediator has no power but that of persuasion. The mediator's suggestions are advisory and may be rejected by both parties. *Mediation* and *conciliation* tend to be used interchangeably to denote the entrance of an impartial third party into a dispute. There is a distinction, however. *Conciliation* is the less active term; technically, it refers to efforts to bring the parties together so that they may resolve their problems themselves. *Mediation* is a more active term; it implies that an active effort will be made to help the parties reach agreement by clarifying issues, asking questions, and making specific proposals. However, usage has been so blurred that only in a dictionary is it absolutely necessary to distinguish between the two terms.

Medicaid The federally aided, state-operated, and state-administered program that provides medical benefits for certain low-income people in need of health and medical care. Authorized by 1965 amendments to the Social Security Act, it covers only members of one of the categories of people who can be covered under the welfare cash payment programs—the aged, the blind, the disabled, and members of families with dependent children where one parent is absent, incapacitated, or unemployed. Subject to broad federal guidelines, states determine coverage, eligibility, payment to health care providers, and the methods of administering the program.

Medicare The national health insurance program for the elderly and the disabled authorized by a 1965 amendment to the Social Security Act. The two parts of Medicare—hospital insurance and medical insurance—help protect people of sixty-five and older from the high costs of health care. Also eligible for Medicare are disabled people younger than sixty-five who have been entitled to social security disability benefits for twenty-four or more consecutive months (including adults who are receiving benefits because they have been disabled since childhood). Insured workers and their dependents in need of dialysis and/or a kidney transplant because of permanent kidney failure also receive Medicare protection.

meet-and-confer discussions A technique used mostly in the public sector for determining conditions of employment whereby the representatives of the employer and the employee organization hold periodic discussions to seek agreement on matters typically covered by collective bargaining. A written agreement is in the form of a nonbinding memorandum of understanding. This technique is often used where formal collective bargaining is not authorized.

mentor A trusted counselor. The term has become increasingly important in the context of organizational and political careers because empirical evidence has shown that an influential mentor is critically important to an individual's career advancement. The word comes from Homer's *Odyssey*. When Odysseus set off for the war at Troy, he left his house and wife in the care of his friend, Mentor. When things got rough at home for Odysseus's family, Athena, the goddess of wisdom, assumed the shape of Mentor and provided Telemachus, the son of Odysseus, with some very helpful advice about how to deal with the problems of his most unusual adolescence.

merit system A public-sector concept of staffing. The term implies that no test of party membership is involved in the selection, promotion, and/or retention of government employees and that a constant effort is made to select the best-qualified individuals available for appointment and advancement. The vast majority of civil service employees within the merit system enter, perform, and advance according to their own talents and the design of the system. At the same time and within the same system, however, there are two groups of employees who enter the system and advance according to criteria other than those provided for by merit system regulations. The first group consists of employees who were appointed for considerations other than personal fitness. Here are hidden the political appointees in excess of those policymaking and confidential positions that are legally the chief executive's prerogative. These appointments are made only after candidates have spent months of diligent effort performing political good works such as aiding the mayor's, the governor's, or the president's election campaign or playing up to some other influential political actor. It is a time-honored practice for a limited number of such politicos to be fudged into presumably merit system positions. *Fudge,* meaning "to cheat" or "to exaggerate grossly," is one of the most important words in personnel management. Indeed, it can be said that the entire public personnel netherworld only exists because of the ability of personnel administrators to produce a seemingly endless supply of fudge. The extent of such placements depends upon such factors as the strength and longevity of the merit system, the political culture of the community, and the personal integrity of a chief executive who, having taken an oath to uphold all the laws of the jurisdiction, can make such appointments only in violation of the spirit, if not the letter, of that oath. Although the merit system is frequently perverted for traditional political purposes, it is similarly abused for more scrupulous purposes. The excessively rigid procedures for entering and advancing in most merit systems have long been recognized as being hindrances to effective management practices. To compensate for the lack of management discretion caused by these rigidities, career civil servants, as well as other highly qualified individuals from outside the system, have been advanced or installed through a fudging of the civil service regulations that is similar to the processes by which politicos are foisted on the merit system. Consequently, what frequently exists, although nowhere is it officially recognized, is a first-class and second-class civil service. This duality does not define the quality of the individual or the productive value of each class; it merely shows how people are treated by the merit system. Although the politically uninfluential who comprise the civil service proletariat must be content with careers bounded by the full force of the frequently unreasonable and always constraining regulations, others—fortunate enough to be recognized for their talents or in spite of their talents—benefit markedly by having these same regulations waived, fraudulently complied with, or simply ignored.

Merit Systems Protection Board (MSPB) The independent federal government agency, created by the Civil Service Reform Act of 1978, designed to safeguard the merit system as well as individual employees against abuses and unfair personnel actions. The MSPB consists of three members, their appointments bipartisan, who serve seven-year nonrenewable terms. The MSPB hears and decides employee appeals and orders corrective and disciplinary actions against an employee or agency when appropriate. Within the MSPB is an independent special counsel, appointed by the president for a five-year term. The special counsel has the power to investigate charges of prohibited personnel practices (including reprisals against whistle-blowers), to ask MSPB to stop personnel actions in cases involving prohibited personnel practices, and to bring disciplinary charges before the MSPB against those who violate merit system law.

meritocracy 1. A word coined by Michael Young in *The Rise of Meritocracy, 1870–2033* (1958). The book is about a governing class, intelligent and energetic, that sows the seeds of its own destruction through its obsession with test scores and paper qualifications. Eventually, those deemed to have lesser IQs revolt. The slogan of the revolutionaries is "beauty is achievable by all." Today, *meritocracy* often refers to an elitist system of government or education, the grisly connotation of its original meaning effectively forgotten. 2. A bureaucracy wherein members rise on their merits as opposed to one in which race, creed, gender, national origin, and/or political influence is a factor.

metropolitan government A central government for a metropolitan area. It is a consolidated government if all the existing local governments at the time of its formation are abolished. In contrast, under a pure federated government, each local unit retains its identity and some of its functions; other functions are transferred to the metropolitan government. However, there are so many variants and exceptions to this formula that it is impossible to generalize accurately about the structure of metropolitan governing arrangements. The adoption of the appropriate machinery of government for a metropolis depends on values. Often, rich and predominantly white residents prefer to withdraw to the suburbs and live under a fragmented local government system; the costs of aging urban infrastructure and the social costs of policing and schooling in poorer areas are thus avoided. But fragmented local government lacks the muscle to put investment into social capital that benefits everybody—such as extensive transit systems, art galleries, and libraries.

Mickey Mouse The pejorative term for many aspects of government administration. When Walt Disney's famous mouse made it big in the 1930s, he appeared in a variety of cartoon shorts that had him building something that would later fall apart (such as a house or boat), or generally going to a great deal of trouble for little result. So Mickey Mouse gradually gave his name to anything requiring considerable effort for slight results, including many of the Mickey Mouse requirements of bureaucracy.

micromanagement 1. Leading too much. *Micromanage* is the pejorative term for supervising too closely. A manager may be guilty of micromanagement for refusing to allow subordinates any real authority or responsibility, thereby ensuring that subordinates will never become effective managers. Further, the managers are kept so busy micromanaging that they never have time to do what managers are supposed to do—such as develop long-term strategy and overall vision. 2. Too close supervision by policymakers in the implementation of programs. The U.S. Congress has been accused of micromanagement when it writes detailed rules governing programs into legislation, thus denying line managers any real administrative discretion. 3. A form of PATRONAGE that occurs when influential members of Congress insist that government programs, especially in the area of military procurement, contain elements that benefit their districts. For example, the U.S. Army may be forced into buying more of a weapon than it needs simply because the factory that makes it is in an influential member's congressional district.

Miles' Law "Where you stand depends upon where you sit." Rufus E. Miles, Jr., wrote the history of his law in a 1978 *Public Administration Review* article after it had been folk wisdom among federal bureaucrats for many years. Although admitting that his "concept was as old as Plato," the "phraseology" evolved from a specific sequence of events that occurred when Miles was supervising a group of budget examiners. One of the examiners was offered a higher-paying new job as a budget analyst at one of the agencies he had been reviewing. Because he had been particularly critical of this agency in his capacity as a reviewing budget examiner, he told Miles (his boss) that he would prefer to stay in his present job if his salary could be raised. When Miles, ever concerned about federal expenditure levels, refused to support the raise, the subordinate resigned and accepted the job with the agency he felt was not very efficient. Miles then remarked to the workers still under his supervision that soon the former employee would be defending the new budget policies that he had so vociferously criticized. His fellow budget examiners were skeptical; after all, the exiting analyst was a man of strongly felt judgments and integrity. But Miles insisted, and was proved correct by events. Now that the former employee was sitting elsewhere, his views would naturally evolve to reflect his new position.

military-industrial complex A nation's armed forces and their industrial suppliers. During his January 17, 1961, farewell address, President Dwight D. Eisenhower warned that "in the councils of government we must guard against the acquisition of unwarranted influence, whether sought or unsought, by the military-industrial complex. The potential for the disastrous rise of misplaced power exists and will persist." Malcolm C. Moos (1916–1982), Eisenhower's chief speechwriter during the second term, is usually credited with coining what has become Eisenhower's most memorable warning: to "guard against . . . the military-industrial complex." It was President Ronald Reagan who, in his February 6, 1985, State of the Union Address, observed, "You know, we only have a military-industrial complex until a time of danger: then it becomes 'the arsenal of democracy.'"

Mills, C. Wright (1916–1962) The radical sociologist whose most famous book, *The Power Elite* (1956), asserted that the United States was ruled by a political, military, and business elite whose decisional powers essentially preempted the democratic process. Mills wrote, "The leading men in each of the three domains of power—the warlords, the corporation chieftains, the political directorate—tend to come together to form the power elite of America." Most contemporary analyses of elitism in U.S. governance have their intellectual foundations in Mills's work, even if Mills himself is not acknowledged.

minimum wage The smallest hourly rate that may be paid to a worker. Although many minimum wages are established by union contracts, state and local laws, and organizational pay policies, minimum wage usually refers to the federal minimum wage law—the FAIR LABOR STANDARDS ACT (FLSA)— established by the U.S. Congress via FLSA amendments. The minimum wage started at $0.25 an hour in 1938; in 2003 it was $5.15 an hour. The secretary of labor regulates exceptions (lower rates) based on age or physical disabilities. Raising the minimum wage has generally been favored by Democrats and opposed by Republicans.

ministerial function Required action. In determining the liability of government agents for the consequences of their actions, courts have created a distinction between ministerial and discretionary functions. Though often blurred in specific cases, the distinction attempted to limit liability to acts done by the agents' volition (discretionary), in comparison to actions compelled by the U.S. Constitution, a statue, a charter, or other law (ministerial).

minority set-asides *See* SET-ASIDES.

misery index The total of the rates of inflation and unemployment; first used by the economist Arthur Okun (1928–1980) in the 1970s.

misfeasance The improper or illegal performance of an otherwise lawful act that causes harm to someone. Nonfeasance is a failure to perform at all. *Compare to* MALFEASANCE.

mission statement/objectives statement The first phase of a STRATEGIC MANAGEMENT process. A mission or objective statement answers the question, What do we do? The answer is normally a static description, timeless and without directionality. A statement of objectives (often called a *mission statement*), however, answers the question, What are we trying to achieve? The statement should be (1) succinct, and limited to the organization's sphere of influence; (2) directional, with mention of specific future states to be achieved; (3) time limited, with indications when each objective is to be achieved; and (4) measurable, so that achievement or progress can be evaluated.

mixed economy An economic system that lies somewhere between socialism and laissez-faire capitalism. All the industrialized countries of the free world have mixed economies in that aspects of socialism lie side by side with free market capitalism. For example, the United Kingdom has a comprehensive system of socialized medicine within a basically capitalistic economy. In France, the telephone system is owned and operated by the government; in the United States, the telephone system is in private hands but regulated by various levels of government.

mixed scanning A decisionmaking model put forth by Amitai Etzioni in *Public Administration Review* (December 1967) that calls for seeking short-term solutions to problems by using incrementalism and comprehensive approaches to problemsolving.

model A simplification of reality for analytical purposes; a reduction in time and space that allows for a better understanding of reality. The representation may be expressed in words, numbers, or diagrams. For example, a book may describe how something works. That is a model. Then it may have diagrams representing how the thing works. That, too, is a model. Models are simplified representations of more complex phenomena intended to further understanding. We all use models. It's how we think of the world. When you think of the government, what do you see? If you see a diagram of the three equal branches (executive, legislative, and judicial), that's a model. If you think of driving to Washington, D.C., and imagine all the links on the interstate highway system you will take to get there, that's a model. It is not a question of whether to model or not to model but of which models are most useful.

model, normative A model that offers specific recommendations. It identifies fixed (always the same) and variable (usually changing) components in a system, assigns them numerical or economic values, and relates them to each other in a logical fashion. Now you can derive optimal solutions to operational problems by manipulating the components of the model. This is the essence of benefit-cost analysis, or of make or buy analysis.

model, procedural A model that will use line drawings to represent options among variables; for example, a DECISION TREE.

modus vivendi A Latin phrase meaning "a temporary understanding pending a final agreement." It is the acceptance of a continuing working relationship, fundamental disagreements ignored or held in abeyance.

monetarism The economic theory suggesting that changes in the supply of money are the main determinants of economic activity; it holds that if government just keeps the money supply growing at the same rate as the growth of overall productivity, the free market will work efficiently.

monetary policy A government's formal efforts to manage the money in its economy to realize specific economic goals. Three basic kinds of monetary policy decisions can be made: (1) decisions about the amount of money in circulation; (2) decisions about the level of interest rates; (3) decisions about the functioning of credit markets and the banking system. Controlling the amount of money is, of course, the key variable. In 1913, the United States passed into law the Federal Reserve Act, which created a strong central bank, the Federal Reserve. Like most central banks, the Federal Reserve is empowered to control the amount of money in circulation by either creating or canceling dollars. The implementation of money control is achieved through putting up for sale or buying government securities, usually called *open-market operations,* which means that the Federal Reserve competes with other bidders in the purchasing and selling of securities. The difference is that when the Federal Reserve buys securities, it pays in the form of new currency in circulation. If it sells some of its securities, it decreases money available, because in effect it absorbs currency held by others. This does not mean, however, that the money stock fluctuates greatly. It steadily increases. It is in the margin of the increase that money supply has its impact. Through the use of the two other tools, the

Federal Reserve can attempt to affect investments and loans. First, it can change its discount rate—the interest rate it charges other banks for loans of money that these banks can use in turn to make loans. Second, it can change the reserve requirement—the amount of money a bank must have on hand in comparison with the amount of money it has out on loan.

morale 1. The level of psychological and emotional functioning of an individual or group with respect to purpose, confidence, loyalty, and the ability to accomplish tasks. 2. The collective attitude of the workforce toward their work environment and a crude measure of the organizational climate.

more-developed countries A euphemism for the comparatively rich states of the West that is preferred by many in the THIRD WORLD; it suggests a sense of cultural equality and avoids opposites, as implied by the terms *rich* and *poor, advanced* and *backward.*

most-favored nation An international trade policy whereby countries agree to give each other the most favorable of the trade concessions they give to foreign countries.

motivation An amalgam of all of the factors in one's working environment that foster (positively or negatively) productive efforts. Theatrical lore has it that as a famous actor struggled to find just the right characterization for a scene, he turned to his director and asked, "What's my motivation?" The director sarcastically replied, "To keep your job!" And so it is with most work done off the stage as well. "Keeping the job" has been the primary goal of industrial workers ever since they abandoned their farms to find work in the factories of the city. The perennial problem for managers is to motivate workers to do more than is minimally necessary to keep their jobs. Although there always has been consensus about the need for motivated employees, the same cannot be said for beliefs about how to induce higher levels of motivation—and concomitant productivity. Not only have prevailing views (or theories) of motivation changed radically over time but also incompatible theories have usually competed with each other at the same points in time. Some theories assume that employees act rationally: Managers simply need to manipulate rewards and punishments logically, fairly, and consistently. Other theories start from the position that managerial assumptions about employees—which undergird systems of rewards and punishments—actually stifle employee motivation.

motivation-hygiene theory One of the first extensive empirical demonstrations of the primacy of internal worker motivation put forth by Frederick Herzberg, Bernard Mausner, and Barbara Snyderman, in a landmark 1959 study titled *The Motivation to Work.* Five factors were isolated as determiners of job satisfaction: (1) achievement, (2) recognition, (3) the work itself, (4) responsibility, and (5) advancement. Five factors associated with job dissatisfaction were similarly realized: (1) company policy and administration, (2) supervision, (3) salary, (4) interpersonal relations, and (5) working conditions. The satisfying factors were all related to job content, the dissatisfying factors to the environmental context of the job. The factors that were associated with job satisfaction were quite separate from those associated with job dissatisfaction. Because the environmental context of jobs, such as working conditions, interpersonal relations, and salary, served primarily as preventatives, they were termed *hygiene factors*, an analogy to the medical use of hygiene that means "preventative" and "environmental." The job-content factors such as achievement, advancement, and responsibility were termed *motivators* because these are the things that motivate people to superior performance.

movers and shakers Those members of a community who lead public opinion and are active enough in politics or business that they can make things happen. The term is often used as an informal reference to a community's power structure.

muckrakers President Theodore Roosevelt's term, taken from John Bunyan's (1628–1688) *Pilgrim's Progress* (1678), for a journalist who wrote exposés of business and government corruption. Some of the most famous muckrakers were Lincoln Steffens (1866–1935), Ida M. Tarbell (1857–1944), and Upton Sinclair (1878–1968). Today, anyone who writes an exposé of governmental corruption or incompetence might be called a *muckraker*.

muddling through *See* CHARLES E. LINDBLOM.

municipal 1. Of local government concern—such as municipal bonds or municipal parks. 2. Of internal concern to a nation (as opposed to international). 3. Of concern to only one government, whether state or local. In Latin, *municipium* referred to a self-governing body within the Roman Empire.

municipal commercial paper Short-term promissory notes issued by local jurisdictions.

municipal corporation 1. The political entity created pursuant to state law by the people of a city or town for the purposes of local government. 2. A formally created subnational government.

municipal court A local government court with exclusive jurisdiction over violations of municipal ordinances. State law may also grant limited jurisdiction in criminal and civil cases arising within the jurisdiction.

municipal law 1. Local legislation. 2. National law, as opposed to international law.

municipal ordinance A local law.

municipality 1. A municipal corporation. 2. The officials who manage a municipal corporation.

N

national 1. Pertaining to an independent political unit. 2. Pertaining to a central as opposed to lower levels of government. 3. A citizen of a particular state. 4. A resident who, though not a citizen of a state, still owes permanent allegiance to that state. 5. Nationwide in scope.

national debt The total outstanding debt of a central government. The national debt is often confused with the nation's budget deficit in a given year. The debt is, in effect, the total of all the yearly deficits (borrowing) that have not been repaid, plus accumulated interest.

national interest 1. Policy aims identified as the special concerns of a given nation; their violation, either in the setting of domestic policy or in international negotiations, would be perceived as damaging to the nation's future in domestic development and international competition. The classic statement on this was made by Lord Palmerston in a House of Commons speech, March 1, 1848: "We have no eternal allies, and we have no perpetual enemies. Our interests are eternal, and those interests it is our duty to follow." 2. In the context of foreign policy, the security of the state. Theorizing about the national interest is often traced back to Niccolo Machiavelli, who held that national advantage ought to be the goal of foreign policy. *See also* REAL-ISM. 3. Whatever the policymakers say it is. In practice, national interest is an elusive concept. Policymakers use it to justify their actions, but critics may argue that these same actions are inimical to the national interest. Unequivocal criteria for determining whether action is in the national interest are often difficult to find.

National Labor Relations Act of 1935 (NLRA) Popularly known as the Wagner Act, this is the nation's principal labor relations law applying to all private-sector interstate commerce, except railroad and airline operations (which are governed by the Railway Labor Act). The NLRA seeks to protect the rights of employees and employers, to encourage collective bargaining, and to eliminate certain practices on the part of labor and management that are harmful to the general welfare. It states and defines the rights of employees to organize and to bargain collectively with their employers through representatives of their own choosing. To ensure this, the act establishes a procedure by which workers can exercise their choices at a secret ballot election conducted by the National Labor Relations Board. Further, to protect the rights of employees and employers and to prevent labor disputes that would adversely affect the rights of the public, the U.S. Congress has defined certain practices of employers and unions as unfair labor practices. The NLRA is administered and enforced principally by the National Labor Relations Board, which was created by the act. In common usage, the National Labor Relations Act refers not to the act of 1935 but to the act as amended by the Labor-Management Relations (Taft-Hartley) Act of 1947 and the Labor-Management Reporting and Disclosure (Landrum-Griffin) Act of 1959.

national planning 1. Comprehensive, national, societal planning, as opposed to local or regional planning. 2. Centralized, government-conducted or co-ordinated economic planning and development. The concept has been highly controversial because of its identification with socialistic and communistic approaches to the governmental management of national economies. *Compare to* INDUSTRIAL POLICY.

national policy An action or a statement of guidance adopted by a national government in pursuit of its objectives in a specific area. Thus, there is often said to be a national policy for health, and a national policy for education. All national policies are inherently vague and seldom fully achieved, or even achievable. For example, the Employment Act of 1946 states that the federal government must promote full employment; and the Housing Act of 1949 states that all Americans should, as soon as possible, have the opportunity to own a decent home.

national security 1. A reference for the need to protect the physical integrity and value system of a state against threats from other states. Threats to security are endemic in an international system that remains anarchic in character. Consequently, governments take prudent precautions. But one nation's defensive actions may appear threatening to others, thereby provoking hostility and confirming the original sense of feeling threatened. Because states can never be sure that the precautionary measures of others are simply that, the result may be a spiral of fear and mistrust known as the SECURITY DILEMMA. 2. A phrase used as justification to hide embarrassing or illegal activities on the part of a national government. *Compare to* CREDIBILITY GAP. 3. A defense posture capable of successfully resisting hostile or destructive action from within or without, overt or covert. *Compare to* SECURITY.

National Security Act The 1947 law that combined the U.S. Army, Navy, and Air Force into the National Military Establishment. It also created the

National Security Council and the Central Intelligence Agency. Amendments to the act in 1949 replaced the National Military Establishment with the present Department of Defense and placed the National Security Council in the Executive Office of the President.

National Security Council (NSC) The organization within the Executive Office of the President the statutory function of which is to advise the president about the integration of domestic, foreign, and military policies relating to national security. The council's members are the president, the vice president, and the secretaries of state and defense. The council's staff is directed by the assistant to the president for national security affairs. As a source of intelligence evaluation, as well as representing the president's own thinktank for developing policy in all military, strategic, and foreign affairs matters, the NSC is a natural rival to the departments of State and Defense.

national service 1. The concept that a nation's youth should serve the state for a set period in a military or civilian capacity before completing higher education and starting a career **2.** A euphemism for CONSCRIPTION.

national supremacy The doctrine that national laws are superior to state laws and therefore take precedence over them.

nationalism The development of a national consciousness; a feeling of belonging; the totality of the cultural, historical, linguistic, psychological, and social forces that pull a people together with a sense of belonging and shared values. This development tends to lead to the political belief that a national community of people and interests should have their own independent political order that is equal to all other political communities in the world. The modern nation-state was forged from such nationalistic sentiment.

nationalization The taking over by government of a significant segment of a country's private-sector industry, land, and transport. Compensation is usually paid to the former owners. Socialist governments tend to favor extensive nationalization. Indeed, the level of nationalization is an accurate measure of the degree of a nation's socialism.

nation-building Conscious efforts to create a sense of common belonging and cohesiveness among a disparate group of people within a common state. This was one of the goals of the political, social, and economic development efforts of the United States in South Vietnam and other THIRD WORLD states during the 1950s and 1960s. Since the failure of the U.S. effort in Vietnam, the term has been used sparingly in the United States. Even so, for many Third World states emerging from decolonization in the aftermath of World War II, building a sense of national identity among disparate groups has been a matter not simply of importance but of survival; for this reason, nation-building is sometimes regarded as a key element in the security policies of Third World states.

nation-state 1. A country with defined and recognized boundaries. The citizens of nation-states share common characteristics, such as race, religion, customs, and language. 2. A country (such as the United States) with defined and recognized boundaries and a diverse ethnic population. Citizens share political ideals and practices to such an extent that unity and internal peace prevail.

necessary and proper clause That portion of Article I, Section 8, of the U.S. Constitution (sometimes called *the elastic clause*) that makes it possible for the U.S. Congress to carry out its responsibilities by enacting all "necessary and proper" laws. Chief Justice John Marshall, in *McCulloch v. Maryland* (1819), gave this clause broad effect when he wrote that "in the desire to remove all doubts respecting the right to legislate on that vast mass of incidental powers which must be involved in the Constitution if that instrument be not a splendid bauble," the Founding Fathers included the necessary and proper or elastic clause.

need to know A criterion used in security arrangements requiring those who receive classified materials to establish that they must have access to such information to perform their official duties. The system often fails because the bureaucratic movement of secret items is so often done by those who have no need to know at all; thus, many espionage successes come from corrupting the messengers and clerks who have access to information that would be denied to senior officers in other departments on a "need to know" basis.

needs hierarchy Abraham H. Maslow's (1908–1970) overview of human motivation in his 1943 *Psychological Review* article, "A Theory of Human Motivation." Maslow asserted that humans had five sets of goals or basic needs arranged in a hierarchy of prepotency: (1) physiological needs (food, water, shelter, etc.), (2) safety needs, (3) love or affiliation needs, (4) esteem needs, and (5) self-actualization needs—when people theoretically reach self-fulfillment and become all they are capable of becoming. Once the lower needs are satisfied, they cease to motivate behavior. Conversely, higher needs cannot motivate until lower needs are satisfied. Simply put, a person will risk being eaten by a hungry lion if that risk is the only way to get food and water. Only after the body is sustained can thoughts turn to safety and the other higher needs. According to Maslow, "It is quite true that man lives by bread alone—when there is no bread. But what happens to man's desires when there is plenty of bread and when his belly is chronically filled? At once other (and higher) needs emerge and these, rather than physiological hungers, dominate the organism." When these needs in turn are satisfied, new and even higher needs will emerge. Maslow's psychological analysis of motivation proved to be the foundation for much subsequent research.

neighborhood 1. A specific geographic area. 2. An informally designated subsection of a city having distinctive characteristics. 3. A community. Although the terms *neighborhood* and *community* tend to be used interchangeably, *neighborhood* has more of a geographic focus because a neighborhood's residents share a common area. *Community*, in contrast, implies that the population consciously identifies with the community and works together for common ends.

neighborhood association An organization of residents of a neighborhood. In many U.S. cities, neighbors in a particular area have formally organized into associations. These associations often play important political roles; for example, they lobby local government to protect neighborhood interests. They often reflect a movement calling for a decentralization of local government. At the extreme are advocates for neighborhood self-sufficiency, who see economic and political power possible for poorer neighborhoods only to the extent that they become independent of the dominant urban government. *See also* BUSINESS IMPROVEMENT DISTRICT.

neighborhood watch A crime prevention program where community groups aid police by making a neighborhood "crime conscience" and by reporting suspicious activities to police.

nepotism A practice by which officeholders award positions to members of their immediate families. The term is derived from the Latin *nepos,* meaning "nephew" or "grandson." Rulers of the medieval Church were often thought to give special preference to their "nephews" in distributing churchly offices; at that time, *nephew* was a euphemism for an illegitimate son.

neutral competence The concept that envisions a continuous, politically uncommitted cadre of bureaucrats at the disposal of elected or appointed political executives. It is no longer sufficient for public managers to be "neutral guns for hire" passively performing the tasks set by political masters. Charles G. Dawes, the first modern budget director of the U. S. government (and later vice president from 1925 to 1929), explained the traditional concept of neutral competence this way: "If Congress . . . passed a law that garbage should be put on the White House steps, it would be our regrettable duty, as a bureau, in an impartial, nonpolitical and nonpartisan way to advise the Executive and Congress as to how the largest amount of garbage could be spread in the most expeditious and economical manner" (*The First Year of the Budget of the United States,* 1923). *See also* HIRED GUN.

new industrial state John Kenneth Galbraith's concept (from his 1967 book of the same name) holding that modern organizations have become so complex that traditional leaders are no longer able to make major decisions. They can only ratify the decisions made for them by a technostructure composed of specialists who may be more interested in maintaining themselves than in achieving goals.

new town A large-scale integrated housing, industrial, and cultural development created as a self-contained community. Examples of new towns in the United States include Reston, Virginia; and Columbia, Maryland.

news management 1. The informal efforts of an administration to direct and control the reporting of its activities by the news media. 2. The use of professional public relations staffs by political and administrative leaders who seek extensive media coverage and a specific media image. News management includes scheduling press conferences in time to make the evening news broadcasts, denying (or granting) access to unfavorable (or favorable) reporters, allowing (or not allowing) reporters to cover military stories, planting stories with favored reporters, and anything else that makes it easier or harder for honest and fair news coverage to proceed. Although they usually deny they are doing so, all administrations at all jurisdictional levels attempt to manage news to one extent or another.

Nixon in China Syndrome The ability of someone who seemingly has a great stake in something to change or reform it more effectively than someone else who might have been for the reform all along. Because it was President Richard M. Nixon, the vehement anticommunist, who fought all his political life to deny recognition of "Red" China, who initiated the rapprochement with China, there was far less criticism than if the initiative had been taken by almost anyone else.

noblesse oblige A French term meaning "nobility obliges"; the notion that the nobility has a special obligation to serve society. It has often been suggested that wealthy Americans enter politics out of noblesse oblige in an effort to serve their fellow citizens. Don't believe such nonsense. Although wealthy American families once took noblesse oblige seriously (the Roosevelts are a good example), today the children of the very wealthy tend to enter politics for the same reasons other people do—because it's fun, it offers ego gratification, and, most important, because it satisfies their desire for power.

nongovernmental organization (NGO) 1. A private organization. 2. Transnational organizations of private citizens that are actively concerned with the United Nations or other aspects of foreign relations; they can be professional organizations, multinational businesses, or groups that lobby for a particular policy. 3. An international organization that has not been created by an intergovernmental agreement. Many NGOs have consultative status at the United Nations.

nonpartisan 1. Not affiliated with a political party. 2. A local election in which a candidate runs for office without formally indicating political party affiliation. Judges and members of school boards, for example, are often elected in nonpartisan elections. The rationale for nonpartisan local elections has often been attributed to New York City Mayor Fiorello La Guardia (1882–1947): "There is no Democratic or Republican way of cleaning the streets."

nonprofit organization An organization created and operated for public or societal purposes (such as the alleviation of poverty) rather than private benefit purposes (such as returns on shareholders' investments). Governments at all levels are increasingly using nonprofit organizations. Services previously performed by government are increasingly being turned over to them—or "privatized" because they are private organizations—so that government can save money and eliminate direct responsibility for perennially troublesome social programs that seek to assuage the lot of the poor and unfortunate. The nonprofit sector is a uniquely democratic phenomenon. In some respects, it is the most capitalistic of our economic responses, reacting to marketplace failure by filling economic voids with volunteers and charitable contributions. In contrast, more socialistic economies tend to meet similar types of community needs through tax-supported government programs and services. Nonprofits provide a flexible alternative to tax-supported government action. Despite common misconceptions to the contrary—and within well-defined limitations—nonprofit organizations can realize profits from their activities and programs, and they can engage in commercial-type enterprises. However, profits must be returned to the operations of the agency. Nonprofit organizations range from large international religious denominations and seminational hospital chains to small, local, nonincorporated associations of people having common interests. From a relatively narrow, legalistic point of view, we can argue that a nonprofit organization is, in effect, an organization prescribed by the laws, rules, and codes of tax exemption. From a tax-exemption viewpoint, there are two basic types of nonprofit organization: (1) publicly supported charitable organizations that engage directly in religious, education, and social welfare programs; and (2) private foundations, which tend to support other tax-exempt organizations' programs.

nontariff barriers Government restrictions, other than tariffs, that distort the flow of international trade. All countries impose nontariff barriers. Among them are restrictions on the quality of goods that may enter a country; sanitary and health requirements; methods of classifying and placing values on imports; antidumping regulations; border taxes; and domestic subsidies. Nontariff barriers tend to gain importance as import duties are lowered.

normative Findings or conclusions that are premised upon morally established norms of right or wrong.

norms 1. The average or standard behavior for members of a group. The "norm" is what is normal. 2. The socially enforced requirements and expectations about basic responsibilities, behavior, and thought patterns of members in their organizational roles. *Compare to* RECIPROCITY. 3. In psychological testing, tables of scores from a large number of people who have taken a particular test.

North American Free Trade Agreement The 1992 treaty between the United States, Canada, and Mexico that eliminates trade barriers by creating a common market.

North-South dialogue Economic discussions between the North (the rich industrialized and developed countries generally located in the Northern Hemisphere) and the South (the poor developing countries located mainly in the Southern Hemisphere).

no-show jobs Government positions for which the incumbent collects a salary but is not required to report to work. No-show jobs are illegal, but are not uncommon.

notary public A semipublic official who can administer oaths, certify the validity of documents, and perform a variety of formal witnessing duties. A *notarius* was a person who took notes during legal actions in ancient Rome. Since then, notarization, a notary's certification of documents, has been a required part of legal proceedings in all Western European–oriented countries. Almost 4 million citizens are notaries in the United States. State requirements to be a notary vary greatly. Some states require examinations; others demand only the endorsement of a few local citizens. Many judges and state legislators are EX OFFICIO notaries. Three states (Florida, Maine, and North Carolina) allow notaries to perform marriages.

Nuremberg defense The now traditional excuse of those caught performing illegal acts for their political or military superiors: "I was only following orders." The term and the tactic comes from war crimes trials in Nuremberg, Germany, of top Nazi leaders in the aftermath of World War II. The fallacy of this defense is that no soldier (or civilian employee) can be required to obey manifestly illegal orders.

O

Office of Management and Budget (OMB) The office that supplanted the Bureau of the Budget in the Executive Office of the President on July 1, 1970. The OMB is the tool by which the president exercises power over every facet of the executive branch. The OMB (1) assists the president in the preparation of the budget and the formulation of fiscal policy; (2) assists in developing coordinating mechanisms to expand interagency cooperation; (3) assists the president by reviewing the organizational structure and management procedures of the executive branch to ensure that they are capable of producing the intended results; (4) supervises and controls the budget; (5) clears and coordinates departmental advice on proposed legislation and makes recommendations about presidential action on legislative enactments; (6) assists in developing regulatory reform proposals; and (7) assists in the consideration, clearance, and preparation of proposed executive orders and proclamations.

Office of Personnel Management (OPM) The central personnel agency of the federal government, created by the Civil Service Reform Act of 1978. The OPM took over many of the responsibilities of the U.S. Civil Service Commission. As the central personnel agency, the OPM develops policies governing civilian employment in executive branch agencies and delegates certain personnel powers to agency heads, subject to OPM standards and review.

officialese *See* GOBBLEDYGOOK.

oligarchy 1. Rule by political elites who govern mainly for the benefit of themselves and their class. 2. Rule by self-appointed elites, who wield informal but effective power because of wealth or position. 3. Minority rule. *Compare to* IRON LAW OF OLIGARCHY.

OMB *See* OFFICE OF MANAGEMENT AND BUDGET.

ombudsman/ombudswoman An official whose job it is to investigate the complaints of the citizenry concerning public services and to ensure that these complaints will reach the attention of officials at levels above the original providers of service. The word is Swedish and means "a representative of the king." Ombudsmen and ombudswomen are now found in many countries at a variety of jurisdictional levels. Many of the functions of ombudsmen in U.S. local, state, and national governments are performed by members of their respective legislatures as casework. An organization ombudsman is a high-level staff officer who receives complaints and grievances about his organization directly from the employees; this officer serves mainly as an open channel of communication between employees and top management.

open shop A nonunion work organization. The term also applies to work organizations with unions but that do not make union membership a condition of employment. Historically, a so-called open shop was one that tended to discriminate against unions.

open-end program An ENTITLEMENT PROGRAM for which eligibility requirements are determined by law (e.g., Medicaid). Fiscal obligations and the resultant outlays are limited only by the number of eligible persons who apply for benefits, and by the benefits paid to them.

operating statement The detailed financial information that supplements a BALANCE SHEET.

operational environment The existing environment as opposed to the psychological environment perceived by decisionmakers.

operational level Organizational elements that decide how the big ideas from the top will be implemented at the bottom. Although the military calls this level *operations,* meaning "a command" or "a planning center," in the civilian sector this is known as "middle management."

OPM *See* OFFICE OF PERSONNEL MANAGEMENT.

opposite number One who has an equal status and rank in another organization. Diplomatic and military officers often deal with their opposite numbers in other governments.

opportunity cost The value that resources, used in a particular way, would have if used in the best possible or another specified alternative way. When opportunity costs exceed the value the resources have in the way they are being used, they represent lost opportunities to acquire value from the resources. *Opportunity cost* is sometimes more narrowly defined as the rate of profit earned by investing money rather than putting it into a particular project.

order A communication, written, oral, or by signal, that conveys instructions from a superior to a subordinate. In a broad sense, the terms "order" and "command" are synonymous. However, an order implies discretion as to the details of execution whereas a command does not. It is critical that orders be clear and unambiguous. Helmuth von Moltke (1800–1891), the founder of the German General Staff in the nineteenth century was fond of saying: "Remember, gentlemen, an order than can be misunderstood will be misunderstood."

ordinances Regulations enacted by a local government that have the force of law but must comply with state and national laws. They are issued under the authority derived from a grant of power (such as a city charter) from a sovereign entity (such as a state).

organization A group of people who jointly work to achieve a common goal.

organization chart The visual representation of the structure of an organization, usually in the form of a diagram.

organization development (O.D.) Planned organizational change. Organizations exist in internal and external dynamic environments to which they must respond to avoid becoming ineffectual. The responsibility of O.D. advisors, specialists on applied behavioral science, is to use their knowledge of the behavioral sciences to improve the organization. These advisors can be either external independent consultants or internal employees of the organization. A beneficent managerial philosophy is one frequently desired change. More modest goals might include creating an atmosphere of trust to ensure better communications or developing participatory mechanisms that would stimulate productivity. An organization that wishes to survive, or simply to remain healthy, must periodically eliminate factors that contribute to its malaise. O.D. itself is not a philosophy; it is an approach or strategy for increasing organizational effectiveness. As a process, it has no value biases, but it is usually associated with the idea that effectiveness is found by integrating the individual's desire for growth with organizational goals. There is no universal O.D. model that can easily be plugged into a troubled organization. The basic task of the O.D. advisor is to adapt appropriate portions of the generally available O.D. technology to the exigencies of the organizational problem; for this reason, the O.D. advisor must be thoroughly conversant with the findings of modern management's behavioral technology. Because no textbook will provide a case study of the exact organizational problem to be remedied, these advisors must be prepared to draw upon their backgrounds to improvise. O.D. advising, like much of the rest of public administration, contains a large element of art.

organization, flat An organization structured on comparatively few levels.

organization man A generic term to describe an individual within an organization who accepts the values of the organization and finds harmony in conforming to its policies. The term was popularized by William H. Whyte, Jr., in his best-selling book, *The Organization Man* (1956).

organization theory A set of propositions that seeks to explain or predict how groups and individuals behave in differing organizational arrangements. The newest thing about organization theory is the study of it. Not until the twentieth century was intellectual substance and tradition given to a field that was the instinctual artistic domain of adventuresome entrepreneurs and cunning politicos. It was artistic in the sense that it was done naturally; that is, without formal learning. Leaders in every field during every age used organization theory as naturally as they used their oratorical powers. Organization theory was always there in the military's authoritarian model. Although many of its premises were understood by the ancients, it did not coalesce as a self-conscious field of knowledge until society found a practical use for it: to help manage the ever-burgeoning industries and institutions brought about by the Industrial Revolution.

organization theory, classical The first theory of its kind that continues to be the base upon which other schools of organization theory have been built. Its basic tenets and assumptions, however, which were rooted in the Industrial Revolution of the 1700s, as well as in the professions of mechanical engineering, industrial engineering, and economics, have never changed. They were only expanded upon, refined, and made more sophisticated. Thus, an understanding of classical organization theory is essential not only because of its historical interest but also, more important, because subsequent analyses and theories presume a knowledge of it. The fundamental tenets of classical organization theory state, in summary, that (1) organizations exist to accomplish production-related and economic goals; (2) there is one best way to organize for production, and that way can be found through systematic, scientific inquiry; (3) production is maximized through specialization and division of labor; and (4) people and organizations act in accordance with rational economic principles.

organization theory, feminist approaches to The general recognition that the long-standing male control of organizations has been accompanied and maintained by male perspectives of organization theory. Thus it has been mainly through male lenses that we see and analyze organizations. As women increasingly climb the organizational ladders, they leave their mark—they gradually change the culture. Substantial research has already shown that women tend to have differing management styles than men. Organizations will gradually but surely change their operating styles to reflect ever-increasing female management styles and influences. The alternative hypothesis is that instead of making their organizations more hospitable to feminine management culture, the female managers—subject to the same stimuli for increased production as men have traditionally been—will become more like the men, will adapt more masculine attitudes because that is the way to thrive in the competitive environment of organizational life.

organization theory, neoclassical Theoretical perspective that revises and/or is critical of classical organization theory—particularly for minimizing issues related to the humanness of organizational members, coordination needs among administrative units, internal-external organizational relations, and organizational decision processes. The major writers of the classical school did their most significant work before World War II. The neoclassical writers gained their reputations as organization theorists by attacking the classical writers after the end of the war. They sought to "save" classical theory by introducing modifications based upon research findings in the behavioral sciences. The neoclassical school was important because it nudged the theoretical movement away from the oversimplistic mechanistic views of the classical school. The neoclassicists challenged some of the basic tenets of the classical school head on—and they did so at a time when the classical school was the only school.

organization theory, structural The study of vertical differentiations, that is, hierarchical levels of organizational authority and coordination, and horizontal differentiations between organizational units; for example, between product or service lines, geographical areas, or skills. The organizational chart is the ever-present "tool" of a structural organizational theorist.

organizational behavior The academic field consisting of those aspects of the behavioral sciences that focus on the understanding of human behavior in organizations. Using traditional authoritarian attitudes toward organizations, Hugo Münsterberg (1863–1916) pioneered the application of psychological findings from laboratory experiments to practical matters. He sought to match the abilities of new hires with a company's work demands, to create a positive influence on employees' attitudes toward their work and their companies, and to understand the impact of psychological conditions on employees' productivity. Münsterberg's pre–World War I approach was typical of how the behavioral sciences tended to be applied in organizations well into the 1950s. In contrast to Münsterberg's traditional perspective on organizational behavior, a new style of applied behavioral science emerged in the 1960s. It focused attention on seeking to answer questions such as how organizations could encourage their workers to grow and develop. The belief was that an organization's creativity, flexibility, and prosperity would flow naturally from its employees' growth and development. The essence of the relationship between an organization and its people was redefined from dependence to codependence.

organizational culture The patterns of fundamental beliefs and attitudes that determine members' behaviors in and around the organization, persist for extended periods, and pervade all elements of the organization (albeit to different extents and with varying intensity); a parallel but smaller version of a societal culture. It is made up of intangible things such as values, beliefs, assumptions, and perceptions. An organizational culture is transmitted to new members through socialization (or enculturation); it is maintained and transmitted through a network of rituals and interactions; it is enforced and reinforced by group norms and the organization's system of rewards and controls. It is the unseen and unobservable force that is always present in organizational activities.

organizational iceberg The concept that the formal or overt aspects of an organization are just the proverbial tip of the iceberg. The greater part of the organization—the feelings, attitudes, and values of its members, for example—remain covert or hidden from obvious view. In short, the formal organization is visible, but the informal is hidden and waiting to sink the ship that ignores it.

organizational politics The use of influence and power to affect the allocation of organization resources, typically through the informal organization.

organizers Employees of a national union who work to encourage nonunionized workers to join the union that the organizer represents or to sign authorization cards that could force an election on unionization.

original intent What the 1787 framers of the U.S. Constitution really meant; what they really intended, by their words, phrases, and sentences used in the document. The original intent of the framers is often a debatable issue, often espoused by STRICT CONSTRUCTIONISTS, and often a CODE WORD (or phrase) for conservative attempts to reverse U.S. Supreme Court decisions on social policy and individual rights. *Compare to* LEGISLATIVE INTENT.

outlays What a government spends over a given time; outlays include checks issued, interest accrued on debts and on other payments minus refunds and reimbursements.

overhead agency An AUXILIARY AGENCY.

oversight The means by which the legislators monitor the activities of executive branch agencies to determine if the laws are being faithfully executed. Oversight takes many forms. The most obvious are the annual hearings on agency budget requests, in which agency activities have to be justified to the satisfaction of the legislators. Members of the U.S. Congress can instigate an investigation as part of their oversight responsibilities. Most of these investigations are small matters properly falling under the rubric of CASEWORK. But if something more significant turns up worthy of a larger inquiry, an appropriate committee or subcommittee always has the right to initiate a further examination. The entire Congress is in effect a permanently sitting grand jury always waiting to hear of improper acts by executive branch agencies so that hearings can be launched and witnesses called.

oversight, executive *See* EXECUTIVE OVERSIGHT.

P

paradigm A conceptual model for a situation or a condition. Thomas S. Kuhn (1922–1996) used it to explain how theoretical knowledge in all intellectual fields evolves and is ultimately supplanted. In his landmark 1970 book, *The Structure of Scientific Revolutions,* Kuhn explained that as the natural sciences progressed, they amassed a body of ever-changing theory. Scientific advances were not based on the accumulation of knowledge and facts; but rather on a dominant paradigm (or model) used during a specific period to explain the phenomena under study. Rather than refuting previous theories, each paradigm would build upon the body of relevant knowledge and theories. Once a paradigm was accepted by consensus among current scholars, it would last as long as it remained useful. Ultimately, it would be displaced by a more relevant and useful paradigm. This process of replacement was Kuhn's "scientific revolution."

parish 1. The term for a county in Louisiana. 2. An ecclesiastical district; a local church and its members. 3. An administrative district (in some countries).

parity Equality; essential equivalence.

parity, employment The long-term goal of affirmative action, achieved when all categories of an organization's employees are proportionately representative of the population in the organization's geographic region.

parity, farm A price, guaranteed by the government, designed to allow a farmer to maintain a purchasing power equal to a previous base period. In theory, the parity price that the government is willing to pay gives a farmer a fair return on investment when contrasted with cost. Since the 1930s, the federal government has been using price supports (accompanied by production controls) to stabilize the prices of agricultural commodities. In this context, a price support is a guarantee to buy farm products at set prices.

parity, potty The informal name given to state laws requiring all new restrooms in theaters, restaurants, and other public facilities to have as many stalls in women's restrooms as there are stalls and urinals in men's restrooms. California in 1987 became the first state (New York has followed) to take legal action to reduce the long lines that tend to form outside of women's restrooms.

parity, racial A situation in which the economic status of all racial groups in a community is essentially equivalent.

parity, wage The requirement that the salary level of one occupational classification be the same as for another. The most common example of wage parity is the link between the salaries of police and firefighters.

Parkinson's law C. Northcote Parkinson's (1909–1993) law that "work expands so as to fill the time available for its completion." It first appeared in his *Parkinson's Law and Other Studies in Administration* (1957). With mathematical precision, Parkinson "discovered" that a given public administrative department will invariably increase its staff an average of 5.75 percent per year. In anticipation of suggestions that he advise what might be done about this problem, he asserted that "it is not the business of the botanist to eradicate the weeds. Enough for him if he can tell us just how fast they grow."

parliamentary system A means of governance whereby power is concentrated in a legislature that selects the prime minister and the cabinet officers from among its members. The government—that is, the prime minister and the cabinet—stays in power so long as it commands a majority of the parliament. In a parliamentary system, the legislative and the executive branch are one. *Compare to* CABINET GOVERNMENT.

patronage The power of elected and appointed officials to make partisan appointments to office and to confer contracts, honors, and other benefits on their political supporters. Although subject to frequent attack from reformers, patronage has traditionally been the method by which political leaders assure themselves a loyal support system of people who will carry out their policies and organize voters for their continued political control. Patronage has always been one of the major tools by which executives at all levels in all sectors consolidate their power and attempt to control a bureaucracy. In the 1990 case of *Rutan v. Republican Party*, the U.S. Supreme Court ruled that traditional patronage in public employment is unconstitutional. Writing the majority opinion, Justice William J. Brennan, Jr., said: "To the victor belong only those spoils that may be constitutionally obtained." In earlier cases, *Elrod v. Burns* (1976) and *Branti v. Finkel* (1980), the Court held that the First Amendment forbids government officials to discharge or threaten to discharge public employees solely for not being supporters of the political party in power unless party affiliation is an appropriate requirement for the position involved. In the *Rutan* case, the Court was asked to decide the constitutionality of several related political patronage practices—"whether promotion, transfer, recall and hiring decisions involving low-level public employees may be constitutionally based on party affiliation and support. We hold that they may not."

patronage, direct Benefits that a legislator can provide constituents, such as PORK BARREL projects, intervening with the bureaucracy, and traditional jobs.

patronage, social The ability of chief executives to use their political prestige to wine and dine and otherwise personally impress critical political actors whose support is desired. Because this depends as much upon force of personality as anything else, some executives, such as President Ronald Reagan, have been far more successful at getting political mileage out of social patronage than others.

pay as you go 1. The automatic withholding of income tax liabilities by means of a payroll deduction. 2. A FISCAL POLICY calling for a BALANCED BUDGET. 3. A pension plan in which employers pay pension benefits to retired employees out of current income.

paying your dues The experiences that one must have before being ready for advancement. In effect, you have to pay your dues before you can be perceived as a legitimate occupant of a higher position.

pay plan A listing of rates of pay for each job category in an organization. A pay range, also known as "salary" or "wage range," indicates the minimum through maximum rates of pay for a job. The various increments that make up the pay range are known as the "pay steps." The pay grade or pay level is the range of pay or a standard rate of pay for a specific job. The totality of the pay grades make up the pay structure.

Pendleton Act of 1883 The Act to Regulate and Improve the Civil Service of the United States that introduced the merit concept into federal employment and created the U.S. Civil Service Commission. Although it was termed a *commission,* it was by no means independent. It was an executive agency that for all practical purposes was subject to the administrative discretion of the president. The act gave legislative legitimacy to many of the procedures developed by the earlier, unsuccessful, Civil Service Commission during the Ulysses S. Grant administration. *See also* CIVIL SERVICE REFORM ACT OF 1978.

pensions Periodic payments to an individual who retires from employment (or simply from a particular organization) because of age, disability, or the completion of service. Such payments usually continue for the rest of the recipient's life and sometimes extend to legal survivors. Although pensions have a long history as royal beneficences, the first formal pension plan in the United States was the 1875 program of the American Express Company. In the public sector, the first civilian pension plans appeared just before World War I for some of the larger municipal police and fire departments. Federal civilian employees had to wait for the Retirement Act of 1920 before they were eligible for retirement benefits.

performance appraisal The formal methods by which an organization documents the work performance of its employees. An employee evaluation process is essential for managerial decisions on retention, advancement, and separation. Lamentably, most performance evaluation systems have not been very successful. The main reason may be because supervisors find it difficult to write useful and objective performance reports. They submit appraisals that tend to be subjective, impressionistic, and noncomparable with the reports of other raters. Performance appraisals are designed to serve a variety of functions; among them are (1) changing or modifying dysfunctional work behavior; (2) communicating to employees managerial perceptions of the quality and quantity of their work; (3) assessing the potential of an employee to recommend appropriate training and/or developmental assignments; (4) assessing whether the present duties of an employee's position are appropriately compensated; and (5) providing a documented record for disciplinary and separation actions.

performance pay A formal system of one-time bonuses or permanent salary increases for above-average on-the-job efforts.

personnel 1. A collective term for all the employees of an organization. The word is of military origin—the two basic components of a traditional army being materiel and personnel. 2. The personnel management function. The organizational unit responsible for administering personnel programs. The function of a personnel staff, or even an entire personnel agency, is to serve line management. Typical services include recruiting, selecting, training, evaluating, compensating, disciplining, and terminating. Although the terms *personnel administration* and *personnel management* tend to be used interchangeably, there is a distinction. The former is mainly concerned with the technical aspects of maintaining a full complement of employees within an organization; the latter concerns itself as well with the larger problems of an organization's human resources such as how motivated and productive they are.

Peter principle The principle promulgated by Laurence J. Peter (1919–1990) in *The Peter Principle: Why Things Always Go Wrong,* with Raymond Hull (1969), that "in a hierarchy every employee tends to rise to his level of incompetence." Corollaries of the Peter principle hold that "in time, every post tends to be occupied by an employee who is incompetent to carry out its duties." In answer to the logical question of who, then, does the work that has to be done, Peter asserts that "work is accomplished by those employees who have not yet reached their level of incompetence."

phenomenology A frame of reference with which to view organizational phenomena. To a phenomenologist, an organization exists on two planes: in reality and in the mind of the person perceiving its actions.

picketing 1. A political demonstration in which demonstrators walk a symbolic area (e.g., in front of the White House) while carrying signs that express political messages. Picketing of this kind is often done to gain media attention for an issue. 2. An act that occurs when one or more persons are present at an employer's business (1) to publicize a labor dispute, (2) to influence others (employees as well as customers) to withhold their services or business, or (3) to demonstrate a union's desire to represent the employees of the business being picketed. The U.S. Supreme Court held, in the case of *Thornhill v. Alabama* (1940), that the dissemination of information concerning the facts of a labor dispute was within the rights guaranteed by the First Amendment. However, picketing may be lawfully enjoined if it is not peaceful, is for an unlawful purpose, or is in violation of a state or federal law.

planned unit development (PUD) A generic name for local governments' requirements that developers include in their development plans such public facilities as streets, schools, and parks. It is a legal designation and requires a set process if the developer or subsequent owners desire to change the original plan.

planning The formal process of making decisions for the future of individuals and organizations. Planning never occurs in a vacuum; it is an inherently political process. Consequently, the success of a plan of any kind is often a function of the political astuteness of the planner. Things are still the same as when Alexander Hamilton advised in *Federalist* No. 70 (1788) that "men often oppose a thing merely because they have had no agency in planning it, or because it may have been planned by those whom they dislike."

planning horizon The time frame during which the objectives of a strategic plan are to be achieved.

planning, operational Arranging for (1) the implementation of the larger goals and strategies that have been determined by strategic planning, (2) improving current operations, and (3) the allocation of resources through the operating budget.

planning programming budgeting system (PPBS) A budgeting system that requires agency directors to identify program objectives, to develop methods of measuring program output, to calculate total program costs over the long run, to prepare detailed multiyear program and financial plans, and to analyze the costs and benefits of alternative program designs. The system was developed in the Department of Defense during the late 1950s. In the 1960s, the PPBS took the budgeting world by storm. It began by insisting that it could interrelate and coordinate the three management processes constituting its title. Planning would be related to programs that would be keyed to budgeting. To further emphasize the planning dimension, the system pushed the time horizon out to half a decade, requiring five-year forecasts for program plans and cost estimates. It placed a new emphasis on program objectives, outputs, and alternatives, and it stressed the new watchword of evaluation: the effectiveness criterion. Finally, the PPBS required the use of new analytical techniques from strategic planning, systems analysis, and cost-benefit analysis to make government decisionmaking more systematic and rational. President Lyndon B. Johnson made PPBS mandatory for all federal agencies in 1965. By 1970, the PPBS, as a formal system, was expanding in some jurisdictions, contracting in others. Opposition to the system came from various quarters, especially from bedeviled agency administrators and staff who experienced one difficulty after another in complying with the PPBS's submission requirements. The system was formally abandoned by the Richard M. Nixon administration in 1971. State and local governments, in the meantime, were rapidly modifying their PPBS programs and installing hybrid versions. Whatever happened to the PPBS? The answer, in short, is that jurisdictions all over the nation modified it to fit their needs.

planning, strategic *See* STRATEGIC PLANNING.

plural executive 1. The de facto arrangement of most state governments because most GOVERNORS share executive authority with other independently elected officers, such as a secretary of state, treasurer, attorney general, or auditor. **2.** A formal arrangement whereby more than one individual or office shares executive power; county commissioners, for example.

pluralism 1. Cultural diversity in a society stratified along racial lines. **2.** A political system in which there are multiple centers of legitimate power and authority. **3.** A theory of government that attempts to reaffirm the democratic character of society by emphasizing the role of competitive groups. Pluralism assumes that power will shift from group to group as elements in the mass public transfer their allegiance in response to their perceptions of their individual interests. However, power-elite theory argues that, if democracy is defined as popular participation in public affairs, then pluralist theory is inadequate as an explanation of modern U.S. government. Pluralism, according to this view, offers little direct participation because the elite structure is closed, pyramidal, consensual, and unresponsive. Society is divided into two classes: the few who govern and the many who are governed; that is, pluralism is covert elitism instead of a practical solution to preserve democracy in a mass society.

pluralism, cultural 1. The belief that a nation's overall welfare is best served by preserving ethnic cultures rather than by encouraging the integration and blending of cultures. This is in contrast to the assimilationist belief that all immigrants should take their turn in a national melting pot and come out homogenized. **2.** A social and political condition in which diverse ethnic groups live in relative peace and harmony.

point of no return 1. That point in a voyage when it is just as far to proceed to the destination as it is to return to the place of origin. **2.** In policy analysis, the point at which it is just as costly in money, prestige, and time to proceed with a decision as it is to reverse it. Shakespeare's Macbeth (*Macbeth* 3.4) arrives at a similar policy analysis after he has embarked on his series of murders: "I am in blood / Stepp'd in so far that, should I wade no more, / Returning were as tedious as go o'er."

police Paramilitary state and local government organizations the most basic responsibilities of which include maintaining public order and safety (through the use of force if necessary), investigating and arresting persons accused of crimes, and securing the cooperation of the citizenry. The term *police,* although referring to law enforcement officers in general, is usually a reference to municipal law enforcement officers. County officers are called *sheriffs;* state officers are usually called *the state police, state troopers,* or *highway patrol.* There is no national police force in the United States. The Federal Bureau of Investigation functions as a national police force only in direct response to crimes in violation of federal law. *Compare to* CONSTABLE.

police power The inherent power of a state to use physical force if needed to regulate affairs within its jurisdiction in the interests of the safety and welfare of its citizens. Police power goes far beyond the criminal justice system; it is the legal basis by which governments regulate such areas as public health, safety, and morals.

police review board A panel of ordinary citizens given the formal authority by their municipality to review specific acts of police officers about which citizens have complained and to make recommendations for disciplinary or other administrative actions. The most common issue before police review boards is whether, in a given instance, police have used excessive or unwarranted force.

police state A totalitarian society in which citizens are heavily supervised by police forces, whether open or secret. A police state is an inherent tyranny that rules by explicit or implied terror and that denies its citizens many of the most obvious civil liberties. In a police state, sheer force replaces the legal system and due process of law.

policing, soft A style of law enforcement that deliberately seeks to minimize community conflict in inner-city areas by not rigorously enforcing laws; the more important mission is to maintain public order.

policy A standing decision by an authoritative source such as a government, a corporation, or the head of a family. Thus, for example, citizens must pay sales taxes on purchases, employees will earn one day's vacation for each month worked, and dinner will be served at 6:00 P.M. each evening. More generally, policies can also be goals yet to be achieved. For example, greater prosperity for all, higher corporate profits, and a college education for each child. *Compare to* PUBLIC POLICY.

policy agenda The issues that opinion leaders and the general public consider important enough for political debate and possible government action. *Compare to* AGENDA SETTING.

policy analysis A set of techniques that seeks to answer the question of what the probable effects of a policy will be before they occur. A policy analysis undertaken on a program that is already in effect is more properly called a program EVALUATION. Nevertheless, the term is used by many to refer to both before- and after-the-fact analyses of public policies. All policy analysis involves the application of systematic research techniques (drawn largely from the social sciences and based on measurements of program effectiveness, quality, cost, and impact) to the formulation, execution, and evaluation of public policy to create a more rational or optimal administrative system. To the extent that we make judgments on governmental policies from affirmative action to zoning variances, we all do policy analysis. A judgment on a policy issue requires an analysis, no matter how superficial. Policy analysis can be viewed as a continuum from crude judgments made in a snap ("The mayor is an idiot and all his policies are stupid!") to the most sophisticated analysis using complicated methodologies ("I have just administered an IQ test to the mayor and he really is an idiot."). Policy analysis is like sex: Almost everybody does it; but only a relatively small group does it professionally.

policy analyst An individual, usually trained in economics, law, political science, or public administration, who is employed to study the effects of proposed or actual public policy. Policy analysts should be unbiased when they initially approach a problem. An open mind is essential for the systematic compilation and interpretation of facts. But once the analytical task has been completed, the analyst may be transformed by the conclusions and the attendant circumstances from an analyst to an advocate.

policy paper A formal written argument in favor of (or opposing) a particular public policy. Political candidates typically generate a variety of policy papers on issues of importance to their constituents. Political campaigns often become a "battle" of opposing policy papers. And the modern battlegrounds for these opposing policies are often the Web sites of political candidates. In theory, the voters can read these thoughtful papers on a wide range of policy issues. They may even believe the papers are actually written by the candidate. In reality, the papers are read by few because most voters are content with the minimally informative sound bites that the candidates spit out on TV. Policy papers, although currently written, have an ancient unwritten tradition. When, in the Bible, Moses said to Pharoah (Exodus 5:1): "Let my people go!"; and when Ulysses, in Homer's *Iliad,* told the Greeks besieging Troy to build the Trojan horse, they were presenting policies even before there was paper.

policy sciences A problemsolving orientation that cuts across all disciplines to deal with the most important societal decisions. It is more than applied social science; it is a new science, encompassing all that is involved with policy formulation and execution. It began as a post–World War II effort to distinguish between (1) an objective conception of social science (which rejected public purposes and goals), and (2) the pragmatic approach of policy practitioners (who insisted on the priority of experience and application as the sole basis for education and research). HAROLD D. LASSWELL, a pioneer in the concept, said that these sciences "study the process of deciding or choosing and evaluate the relevance of available knowledge for the solution of particular problems," *Policy Sciences* (Spring 1970). Although the policy sciences are alive and well, policy science as an independent integrating academic discipline has not done well. Its subject matter has been subsumed into policy studies programs that are most often located in political science, public administration, and economics departments. Lasswell's call for a new discipline was simply not heeded. The great contribution of the concept of policy science was to call attention to the inherently interdisciplinary nature of public policy research.

policy studies A broad term that is used to describe a variety of interdisciplinary academic programs that focus on aspects of public policy. Policy studies as a program emphasis or as a specific research effort can be divided into two broad categories: (1) the normative, which critiques public policymaking and makes recommendations on how the process may be made more efficient, more equitable, and more democratic; and (2) the analytic, which uses policy analysis to develop models and explanations for policy outcomes. Policy studies began a significant self-conscious expansion of programs and research in the 1960s. This was the same time that public administration enjoyed explosive growth. But although the growth in public administration leveled off by the early 1980s, policy studies continued to expand. Why? Because it is so much easier to identify with a field that, unlike public administration, is so broad and amorphous that, like a gas, it will fill all space it occupies. Biologists and chemists, who once hid in their laboratories, have now come out as environmental policy experts. Civil engineers and city planners are now urban policy experts. Municipal bond analysts and government accountants are now fiscal policy experts. Social psychologists with interest in how people are motivated to act in the public interest become social policy experts. And it goes on and on. Every discipline has its own policy niche. And in the interdisciplinary field of policy studies, each cries out for a place setting at the table dispensing research grants.

policy wonk A compulsive analyst of public policy processes. *Wonk* is a slang term for a student who is a grind or a nerd. *Policy wonk* came to the fore of

U.S. politics during the 1992 presidential election when it was used to describe Governor (later President) William J. Clinton of Arkansas.

political 1. Having to do with the state and its governing institutions. 2. Having to do with the processes by which people gain and use power in social settings, whether the setting is the city, a factory or office, or the family.

political appointee A person given a job in government mainly because of political connections (or occasionally because of preeminence in a specific field) as opposed to a person who gains a job through the merit system. Although a political appointee is any PATRONAGE appointment, the phrase tends to be reserved for high-level managerial positions, which elected officials use to take over the bureaucracy. *See also* SPOILS SYSTEM.

political clearance The process by which qualified applicants for patronage and merit system appointments are hired only after an appropriate indication of partisan political sponsorship. Although it is illegal to require political clearance for merit system appointments, it remains a common practice.

political commissar 1. In the former Soviet Union, a civilian assigned to a military unit to insure that its commanders followed the policies of the government. 2. By analogy, a representation of a central executive assigned to line agencies to insure that new employees and their policies are politically acceptable. The Richard M. Nixon administration placed political commissars in many federal agencies to assure that new management appointees, patronage and merit system both, had POLITICAL CLEARANCE.

political culture The part of the overall societal culture that determines a community's attitudes toward the quality, style, and vigor of its political processes and government operations. The only way to explain the extreme variations in public bureaucracies is by the cultural context of the host jurisdictions. The quality of bureaucratic operations varies for a variety of reasons, not the least of which is the substantial disagreement on just what constitutes a high-quality operation. But the quality or style of operations is determined only in the lesser part by critics and public officials; the crucial determinant is the political will of the community. It determines the values to be applied to a given public problem; helps establish the obligations of the public role; and establishes the parameters of activities in which an official may participate. Even when corruption is rife, it is the political culture that sets the limits and direction of the corruption.

political economy The conjunction of politics and economics; the study of relations between the economy and the state before either political science or economics became distinct disciplines. Political economy is a public policy concern because of the primacy of economic prosperity to U.S. governments. Not only does the government account for one-third of the gross national product but it also regulates the basic economic conditions of society; for example, it can specify the production of a product, regulate the wages of the production workers, prescribe working conditions, establish production standards, and inspect the quality of the finished product. The recurring policy questions have to do with whether interest rates should be higher or lower, whether government spending on public works should be increased or decreased, and whether inflation should be modestly encouraged or severely discouraged. The perpetual policy problem here is that consensus is seldom reached on how to achieve any of these goals even if the goals themselves could be agreed upon. *See also* ECONOMIC POLICY; FISCAL POLICY.

political executive 1. An individual, such as a president, governor, or mayor, whose institutional position makes that person formally responsible for the governance of a political community. The political executive gains this responsibility through election by the people and can have it rescinded by not being reelected, by being impeached, or by being recalled. 2. A high-level patronage appointee. 3. The institutions of a government responsible for governing; the totality of the departments, agencies, and bureaus of a government.

political machine 1. Historically, an informal organization that controlled the formal processes of a government through corruption, patronage, intimidation, and service to its constituents. A political machine usually centered on one politician—a boss—who commanded loyalty through largesse, fear, or affection. The phrase is usually pejorative, because the machine works to achieve political control through those who run the machine, rather than through the popular will. 2. A grudging compliment to a modern political campaign or organization that is effectively managed with or without some of the elements of the traditional political machine. 3. A government agency used to dispense patronage.

political neutrality The concept that public employees should not actively participate in partisan politics. The Hatch Acts of 1939 and 1940 restricted the political activities of almost all federal employees and those in state employment having federal financing. Many states have "little" Hatch Acts; these further limit the political activities of public employees.

political party An organization that seeks to achieve political power by electing members to public office so that their political philosophies can be reflected in public policies. A viable political party has three elements: (1) the party in the electorate consisting of all those citizens who identify with it, (2) the party organization, which is its formal structure and includes all party officers and workers, and (3) the party in government consisting of all the members the party got elected to public office.

political question 1. An issue that a court chooses not to decide because the court judges the issue inappropriate for a judicial determination; the question is better left to another, more political, branch of government. 2. The doctrine of self-imposed restraint on the part of the U.S. Supreme Court. The Court defers to the judgment of the legislative and executive branches when a political question is at issue. Such questions include decisions to recognize foreign governments, and determinations of when amendments to the Constitution have been ratified. 3. A question that is understood as having no clear-cut, technical answer, and hence, is subject to debate among holders of competing opinions.

politician 1. One who makes a career of seeking or serving in elective or appointive public office; one devoted to the service of a polis, a political community; one engaged in the professional practice of politics. 2. Someone engaged in politics for personal gain; public service is purely incidental.

politico 1. An elected official. 2. A politician who is mainly concerned with re-election, patronage, and personal advancement and enrichment. 3. An unofficial hanger-on and MOVER AND SHAKER of the political process, such as a campaign worker, a wealthy contributor, or a political consultant. 4. A role adopted by legislators that is a pragmatic mix between EDMUND BURKE'S notions of trustee and delegate.

politics 1. The art and science of governance; the means by which the will of the community is arrived at and implemented; the activities of a government, politician, or political party. 2. The pursuit and exercise of the political power necessary to make binding policy decisions for the community and to distribute patronage and other government benefits. 3. The policymaking aspect of government in contrast to its administration. 4. The interpersonal negotiation that leads to consensus within groups and the action they take. 5. A profession engaged in by those who move from one political office to another in an upward spiral toward greater public responsibility and power. As President John F. Kennedy told students in a speech at the University of North Carolina on October 12, 1961: "Those of you who regard my profession of political life with some disdain should remember that it made it possible for me to move from being an obscure lieutenant in the United States Navy to commander in chief in fourteen years with very little technical competence."

politics-administration dichotomy The belief, growing out of the progressive and civil service reform movements, that the spoils system and political interference in administration eroded the opportunity for administrative efficiency. Consequently, the policymaking activities of government ought to be wholly separated from the administrative functions; administrators need an explicit assignment of objectives before they can begin to develop an efficient administrative system. Public administration theorists in the early part of the twentieth century argued that politics and administration could be distinguished, in the words of FRANK J. GOODNOW, as "the expression of the will of the state and the execution of that will." Paul H. Appleby (1891–1963) became the leading critic of this theoretical insistence on apolitical government processes when he asserted that it went against the grain of the U.S. experience. Appleby in *Big Democracy* (1945) held as myth the notion that politics was separate and could somehow be taken out of administration. Political involvement was good—not evil, as many of the progressive reformers had claimed—because political involvement in administration acted as a check on the arbitrary exercise of bureaucratic power. In the future, those who would describe the political ramifications and issues of administration would not begin by contesting the politics-administration dichotomy as incorrect or irrelevant; rather, they would begin from the premise, so succinctly put by Appleby, that "government is different because government is politics." Today, most public administration theorists accept the notion that politics and administration are inherently and inevitably intertwined. The politics-administration dichotomy is traditionally traced to two sources: President Woodrow Wilson, "The Study of Administration," *Political Science Quarterly* 2 (June 1887); and Frank J. Goodnow, *Politics and Administration* (1900).

pork barrel 1. A metaphor for favoritism by a government in the allocation of benefits or resources; legislation that favors the district of a particular legislator by providing for the funding of public works and other projects (such as post offices and defense contracts) that will bring economic advantage to the district and political favor for the legislator. 2. The treasury of a state or national government when it is perceived as a means of providing funds for local interests regardless of their utility to the nation as a whole.

POSDCORB The mnemonic device invented by LUTHER GULICK in 1937 to call attention to the various functional elements of the work of a chief executive. His "Notes on the Theory of Organization" is the best-known statement of this "principles" approach to managing organizations. In 1937, he and Lyndall Urwick edited a collection titled *Papers on the Science of Administration,* originally intended as a staff report for the BROWNLOW COMMITTEE. Overall, these *Papers* were a statement of the "state of the art" of organization theory. It was here that Gulick introduced his famous mnemonic, which stands for the seven major functions of management: (1) planning: working out in broad outline the things that need to be done and the methods for doing them to accomplish the purpose set for the enterprise; (2) organizing: the establishment of the formal structure of authority through which work subdivisions are arranged, defined, and coordinated for the defined objective; (3) staffing: the personnel function of bringing in and training the staff and maintaining favorable work conditions; (4) directing: the continuous task of making decisions and embodying them in specific and general orders and instructions and serving as the leader of the enterprise; (5) coordinating: the all-important duty of interrelating the various parts of the work; (6) reporting: keeping those to whom the executive is responsible informed about what is going on, which thus includes keeping himself and his subordinates informed through records, research, and inspection; (7) budgeting, with all that goes with it in the form of fiscal planning, accounting, and control.

position A group of duties and responsibilities requiring the full- or part-time employment of one individual. A position may, at any given time, be occupied or vacant.

position classification The use of formal job descriptions to organize all jobs in a civil service merit system into classes according to duties and responsibilities for the purposes of delineating authority, establishing chains of command, and providing equitable salary scales. The principles and practices of position classification that are generally used in the public service are throwbacks to the heyday of the scientific-management movement. They were conceived at a time—before 1920—when this school of management thought held sway, and they have never really adapted to modern currents of management thought. Reduced to its essentials, a classification plan is nothing more than a time-and-motion study for the governmental function. To prevent duplication and promote efficiency, the duties of the larger organization are divided into positions. In this schema, a position merely represents a set of duties and responsibilities, not a person. Although position classifications tend to be universally recognized as essential for the administration of a public personnel program, their allegiance to notions of the past often cause them to be denounced not only as unreasonable constraints on top management and sappers of employee morale but also for being little more than polite fictions.

Postal Reorganization Act of 1970 The federal statute that converted the Post Office Department into an independent establishment—within the executive branch of the government—to own and operate the nation's postal system, known as the United States Postal Service. The act also provided for collective bargaining by postal workers, the first instance of true collective bargaining in the federal service.

postbureaucratic organization Constantly changing temporary organizational systems; task forces with diverse skills created in response to a special problem as opposed to continuing need. In a 1952 *American Political Science Review* article, Dwight Waldo prophesied a future society in which "bureaucracy in the Weberian sense would have been replaced by more democratic, more flexible, though more complex, forms of large-scale organization."

Waldo termed such a society *postbureaucratic.* However, it remained for Warren G. Bennis, in the 1960s, to make the term particularly his own with a series of articles and books predicting the "end of bureaucracy." In its place, Bennis wrote in *The Temporary Society* that "there will be adaptive, rapidly changing temporary systems. These will be task forces composed of groups of relative strangers with diverse professional backgrounds and skills organized around problems to be solved." The various task forces would "be arranged in an organic, rather than mechanical, model, meaning that they will evolve in response to a problem rather than to preset, programmed expectations." Thus employees would "be evaluated not vertically according to rank and status, but flexibly according to competence. Organizational charts will consist of project groups rather than stratified functional groups."

postmodernism The belief that constant change is a new fact of life for large organizations that are living on the edge, on the boundary, between order and chaos. In this context, however, *chaos* and *anarchy* are not synonyms. Instead, *postmodernism* refers to a pervasive condition of unpredictability and complexity. Rapidly advancing information technology has accompanied and accelerated the chaos and uncertainty of this approaching postmodern era.

poverty Defined by the United States Bureau of the Census in 2002 as an annual cash income of less than $18,392 for a family of four. This is the subsistence approach. In 2002, 12.1 percent (34.6 million) of Americans lived in poverty. Another way is to regard poverty as a state of relative deprivation in which the poor are those possessing less than most others, even if everyone's economic level is well above subsistence level. Poverty has long been perceived as a natural and normal condition for some members of a society. The New Testament teaches that "ye have the poor always with you" (Matthew 26:11). But in more recent times, poverty has come to be thought of as an essentially unnatural or undemocratic condition that measures the weakness of a society claiming equality for all citizens. As President John F. Kennedy said in his inaugural address of January 20, 1961: "If a free society cannot help the many who are poor, it cannot save the few who are rich."

poverty trap The dilemma that families on means-tested welfare benefits often face. The welfare system is such that they chance losing benefits if their incomes rise; consequently, they are discouraged from seeking employment that pays only marginally better than welfare alone—employment that might have eventually taken them off the welfare rolls.

power The ability or the right to exercise authority over others. Traditionally, according to Chairman Mao, "political power grows out of the barrel of a gun." More recently, power has been residing in the checkbooks of large corporations and powerful lobbyists. Those with traditional power or the power to make large campaign contributions are able to make or heavily influence public policy. Whether they do it with a gun or a check is dependent upon local conditions. The world is organized into an immense hierarchy of power: Political leaders have power over their followers, managers over their workers, and parents over their children. We are all subject to the powers that force us to work and school and constrain us from straying too far from what is expected. Power is clearly visible in this hierarchy of control of stronger over weaker. John R. P. French and Bertram Raven, in "The Bases of Social Power," *Studies in Social Power* (1959), suggest that there are five major bases of power: (1) expert power, based on the perception that the leader possesses special knowledge or expertise; (2) referent power, based on the follower's liking, admiring, or identifying with the leader; (3) reward power, based on the leader's ability to mediate rewards for the follower; (4) legitimate power, based on the follower's perception that the leader has the legitimate right or authority to influence him or her; and (5) coercive power, based on the follower's fear that noncompliance with the leader's wishes will lead to punishment. Subsequent research on these power bases has indicated that the first two (expert and referent power) are more positively related to subordinate performance and satisfaction than the last three (reward, legitimate, and coercive power).

power broker 1. A person who controls a bloc of votes that can be delivered in exchange for a price. The price could be the promise of appointive office, the acceptance of a specific policy, the placement of a favored candidate on the ticket, or plain old-fashioned money. 2. Someone trusted by the contesting sides of an issue to broker an agreement.

power, corridors of The official world, the bureaucracy, the places where leaders make decisions for the rest of us. The phrase comes from the title of a 1964 C. P. Snow novel.

power curve The cutting edge of high-level decisionmaking. Someone who is "behind the power curve" is unaware of the latest decision.

power, inherent 1. An authority that is an integral part of sovereignty and that, although not expressly stated, is implied by the nature of government and necessary for a government to function. 2. A power not expressly granted by the U.S. Constitution but that came about through the NECESSARY AND PROPER CLAUSE.

power of the purse 1. A purse (a money bag) generalized to mean a treasury or other source of funding. The power to control the distribution of funding for public expenditure has been the basis of disputes between executives and legislatures for centuries. 2. The ability of political figures to direct government appropriations to the programs they favor. Under Article I, Section 7, of the U.S. Constitution, the power of the purse belongs to the U.S. House of Representatives because "all bills for raising revenue shall originate" there.

power to persuade The political and bargaining skills used to enhance an executive's constitutional authority. Richard Neustadt wrote the classic book on the fragility and elusiveness of presidential power. Neustadt's *Presidential Power,* published in 1960 on the eve of President John F. Kennedy's taking office, was greeted as a pioneering addition to our understanding of presidential power as if a modern-day Machiavelli had written a new version of *The Prince* just for the U.S. presidency. The exercise of power, Neustadt argued, is more than office-holding, role enactment, or hat wearing; it is the "power to persuade." A president as mere officeholder is so weak that significant numbers of other political actors, especially members of the U.S. Congress, must be persuaded that what the White House wants of them matches their appraisal of what their own responsibilities require them to do in their own interests and on their own authority. Neustadt concluded that a president's capacity to persuade will rest mightily on his bargaining skills, on his professional reputation, and on his popular prestige. The higher a president's ratings are in the public-opinion polls, the greater his reputation and concomitant ability to influence others. And vice versa. As a president's ratings sink, so too, his bargaining strength.

power-elite theory The belief that the United States is ruled by a political, military, and business elite having the decisional powers to preempt the democratic process. *See* C. WRIGHT MILLS; PLURALISM.

powers that be Those who must be obeyed; those who are in control of a state, a company, or other institution. This expression suggests that there are always forces or groups that exercise control, regardless of the legal or constitutional organization that establishes formal power. David Halberstam used the phrase to describe the masters of U.S. communications empires in *The Powers That Be* (1979). But the phrase originates in the Bible (Romans 13:1): "Let every soul be subject unto the higher powers. For there is no power but of God: the powers that be are ordained by God."

Pregnancy Discrimination Act of 1978 An amendment to Title VII of the Civil Rights Act of 1964 that holds that discrimination on the basis of pregnancy, childbirth, or related medical conditions constitutes unlawful sex discrimination. The amendment was enacted in response to the U.S. Supreme Court's ruling in *General Electric Co. v. Gilbert* (1976) that asserted an employer's exclusion of pregnancy-related disabilities from its comprehensive disability plan did not violate Title VII.

presidencies, two Aaron Wildavsky's division of the presidency into two differing spheres of influence: foreign policy and domestic policy. Wildavsky contended that presidential leadership in foreign policy will generally find greater support among the public than leadership in domestic policy. To test his hypothesis, Wildavsky examined congressional action on presidential proposals from 1948 to 1964. For this period, the U.S. Congress approved 58.5 percent of the foreign policy bills; 73.3 percent of the defense policy bills; and 70.8 percent of general foreign relations, the Department of State foreign aid bills, and treaties. During this same period, the Congress approved only 40.2 percent of the president's domestic policy proposals. Thus the two-presidencies thesis was confirmed. Wildavsky's work has spawned a bevy of research articles, none of which has materially diminished his original thesis. For the original presentation, see Aaron Wildavsky, "The Two Presidencies," *Trans-Action* (December 1966).

presidency, imperial A phrase that implies that the president of the United States has grown to be the head of an international empire as well as the head of a domestic political state. It suggests that the presidency has grown too powerful, that it has assumed more authority than is justified by its constitutionally granted powers. The phrase "imperial presidency" is usually credited to the 1973 book of the same title by Arthur Schlesinger, Jr. The book came out just as the Watergate scandal broke and all the excesses of the Richard M. Nixon administration were bared to the world. Although Schlesinger's phrase was a convenient way to summarize Nixon's corrupting of the presidential office, the book, written before the scandal really broke, was not an attack on Nixon but rather an analysis of the gradual enhancement of presidential powers in modern times.

president 1. The head of state in a republic. The powers of such presidents vary enormously. The president of the United States, because he is also the head of the government, enjoys great powers. In contrast, most other presidents (such as those in Israel and Germany) have mainly ceremonial and informal authority. 2. One appointed or elected to preside over a formal assembly. 3. A chief executive officer of a corporation, board of trustees, university, or other institution.

President's Committee on Administrative Management *See* BROWNLOW COMMITTEE.

pressure group 1. An organized group that seeks to influence the policies and practices of government. The difference between a pressure group and a lobby is that a pressure group is a large, often amorphous group that seeks to influence citizens as well as the political system; lobbyists are relatively small groups that seek to influence specific policies of government. Pressure groups are usually composed of committed amateurs. Lobbyists (usually full-time professional entreators) are often hired by pressure groups to help make their pressure more effective. 2. A less-than-kind way of referring to legitimate lobbying organizations. *Compare to* LOBBY.

price support *See* PARITY, FARM.

principles of management Fundamental truths or working hypotheses that serve as guidelines to management thinking and action. Since antiquity, the military has evolved principles about how their authoritarian organizations are best managed. Although many versions of war principles reflect local conditions, they all contain the same basic elements; those having civilian applications have been incorporated into principles of management. Thus concepts once military—such as SPAN OF CONTROL and UNITY OF COMMAND—are now thoroughly civilian as well. When used with common sense and attention to experience, the principles of war can be extremely useful to those public managers who would join the never-ending battle against the evil trinity of waste, fraud, and abuse. This is all the more true for public-sector organizations forced to compete with private-sector competitors. Competition by creating "enemies" clarifies objectives. The difference between a lean, mean fighting machine, as the U.S. Marine Corps aspires to be, and a lean, mean management machine is, in essence, one of objectives. *See* POSDCORB.

prisoner's dilemma *See* GAME THEORY.

private law A statute passed to affect only one person or group, in contrast to a PUBLIC LAW.

privatization The process of returning to the private sector property (such as public lands) or functions (such as trash collection, fire protection) previously owned or performed by government. Conservative Republicans in general tend to be in favor of privatizing government functions that can be performed (in their opinion) less expensively or more efficiently by the private sector. In this context, *privatization* and *reprivatization* tend to be used interchangeably. Some extreme advocates of a wholesale privatization of government functions would even return Social Security, education, and public health to the private sector. There are three basic forms or types of government privatization: (1) the sale of government assets (such as a railroad to a corporation or public housing units to their tenants); (2) the private financing of public facilities (such as toll highways in California or Virginia); (3) the private provision of services (such as trash collection or education). The ultimate statement on privatization comes from Joseph Heller, *Catch–22* (1961): "I'd like to see the government get out of war altogether and leave the whole feud to private industry."

pro bono publico A Latin phrase meaning "for the public good." Often abbreviated to pro bono, it usually stands for work done by lawyers without pay for a charitable or public purpose.

pro choice The policy position of those who are not necessarily in favor of abortion but who are in favor of allowing each woman decide the question for herself. Pro choice political candidates seek to deemphasize the advocacy of abortion and stress the libertarian position that government has no business, indeed no right, to make this decision for a woman. *Compare to* PRO LIFE.

pro death Descriptive of a person or organization in favor of abortion and capital punishment.

pro life The policy position of those opposed to abortion, opposed to the U.S. Supreme Court's decision in *ROE V. WADE,* and opposed to giving a woman the option of abortion. Some pro life proponents believe that abortion should be allowed a woman if she has suffered rape or incest. Others, such as Illinois Congressman Henry Hyde, would not allow this option: "Rape and incest are tragedies, but why visit on the second victim, the unborn child . . . capital punishment?" *Time* (July 9, 1990). *Compare to* PRO CHOICE.

proactive An administrative style that encourages taking risks on behalf of one's clients or one's moral values; the opposite of a reactive style.

procurement Buying items for government from pencils to aircraft carriers. For large items or large amounts of small things, governments often require sealed bids from suppliers. All the bids are theoretically opened at the same time and the low bid gets the order. The process becomes more complicated when research and development is an issue. The *Apollo 15* astronaut David Scott thought about the procurement process while waiting for blast off: "You just sat there thinking that this piece of hardware had 400,000 components, all of them built by the lowest bidder," *Time* (May 19, 1978).

productivity The measured relationship between the quantity (and quality) of results produced and the quantity of resources required for production. Productivity is, in essence, a measure of the work efficiency of an individual, a work unit, or an entire organization. The eternal problem with productivity is that, in some areas, when government produces a service, the labor that goes into it cannot be measured for impact and evaluated for quality as if it were a manufactured product. Thus, it is easy to measure and even improve government productivity when factory-like operations lend themselves to engineered work-measurement standards. But service workers such as police officers, social workers, and grade school guidance counselors create products not always directly measurable, unless by broad social indicators.

program 1. A major organizational, mission-oriented, endeavor that fulfills statutory or executive requirements and is defined according to the principal actions required to achieve a significant objective. A program is an organized set of activities designed to produce a particular result or a set of results that will have a certain impact upon a problem. 2. An announced plan of action that suggests an approach to a problem or that differentiates one policy position from another. *Also see* EVALUATION.

progressive movement A term that has its origins in religious concepts that argued for the infinite improvability of the human condition, rather than ordained class distinctions; by the end of the nineteenth century, the progressive movement had come to mean a responsibility of classes for one another and a willingness to use all government and social institutions to give that responsibility legal effect. The progressives got their name because they believed in the doctrine of progress—that governing institutions could be improved by bringing science to bear on public problems. It was a disparate movement, each reform group targeting a level of government or a particular policy. Common beliefs held that good government was possible and that "the cure for democracy is *more* democracy." To achieve this, they had only to "throw the rascals out." At the national level, they achieved civil service reform; at the state level, they introduced the direct primary, the initiative, the referendum, and the recall; at the local level, they spawned the commission and council-manager forms of government. And it was the progressive influence that initially forged the fledgling discipline of public administration.

Proposition 13/Jarvis-Gann Initiative A state constitutional amendment approved by California voters (it was put on the ballot as an initiative) in 1978 that rolled back and set ceilings on property taxes. Proposition 13 is an important landmark in a national tax-relief movement.

protectionism The use of government policy to determine the prices of foreign manufactured goods on domestic markets; a policy of high tariffs or low import quotas to protect domestic industries. Protectionism is the opposite of a free trade policy. Protectionist legislation is invariably proposed by members of the U.S. Congress from districts where industries are adversely affected by foreign imports. Laid-off factory workers don't want to be told about the theoretical benefits of free trade; they want protectionist legislation that would put import duties on the foreign-made products that have cost them their jobs. *Compare to* FREE TRADE.

proverbs of administration *See* HERBERT SIMON.

pseudoevent The historian Daniel J. Boorstin's (1914–) term from *The Image* (1961) for nonspontaneous, planted, or manufactured "news," the main purpose of which is to gain publicity for the person or cause arranging the "event." An orchestrated news LEAK and the releasing of TRIAL BALLOONS are typical pseudoevents.

psychological ownership Commitment and emotional involvement concerning an intangible something, such as an organizational reform effort.

public 1. The people in general. **2.** The citizens of a jurisdiction. **3.** A subset of a larger public such as a novelist's public (those who read his books) or the reading public (those who regularly read books).

public administration 1. Whatever government does. As an activity, public administration has no values. It merely reflects the cultural norms, beliefs, and power realities of its society. It is simply government doing whatever government does—in whatever political and cultural context it happens to exist. Similar administrative acts can be performed differently in different cultures; thus, a routine customs inspection in one state parallels the solicitation of a bribe by a corrupt customs official in another. The same act that is performed honestly in one state (because of a culture that supports honesty) may be performed corruptly in another (where the culture supports corruption by government officials). Public administration is the totality of the working-day activities of all the world's bureaucrats—whether they are legal or illegal, competent or incompetent, decent or despicable. **2.** The law in action. Public administration is inherently the execution of a public law. Every application of a general law is necessarily an act of administration. Administration cannot exist without this legal foundation. In the United States, the U.S. Constitution of 1789 as amended is the law of the land. All legislation must conform to it—or at the very least not violate it in a manner obvious to the U.S. Supreme Court. The law that creates an agency or program is known as its enabling legislation—the law that legally "enables" a program to exist. In theory, no government administrator can do anything if it is not provided for in the legislation or in the rules and regulations that the legislation allows the agency to promulgate. **3.** Regulation. It is government telling citizens and businesses what they may and may not do. Regulation is one of the oldest functions of government. The Code of Hammurabi in ancient Babylonia provided that "the mason who builds a house which falls down and kills the inmate shall be put to death." Although not exactly a modern building code, this nevertheless proved an effective means of regulating the soundness of housing. **4.** The executive function in government. In democratic states, whether they are republics or constitutional monarchies, it is government agencies putting into practice legislative acts that represent the will of the people. According to Alexander Hamilton writing in *Federalist* No. 72: "The administration of government . . . in its most usual, and perhaps most precise signification . . . is limited to executive details, and falls peculiarly within the province of the executive department." In dictatorial regimes, similar agencies do the bidding of the people who hold power. But the process is far more interactive and dynamic than a separation of powers diagram would suggest. Although the executive, legislative, and judicial branches are separate and distinct in the United States, all sides struggle to influence the others. A president, governor, or mayor is constantly recommending new programs to the U.S. Congress, state legislature, or city council. Modern government executives at all levels do not meekly sit back and merely

public sector, who are ignorant of this perspective are figuratively walking into an unmarked minefield. Reinforcing the importance of this first reason is the simple fact that women in the United States are an ever-increasing majority of public-sector workers. Women constituted 24 percent of all public officials and administrators in 1970. By 1990, they constituted 59 percent. According to Department of Education data published in the *Chronicle of Higher Education* (June 9, 1995), women are earning bachelor's degrees in public administration and related service areas at more than three times the rate as men; master's degrees at twice the rate as men; and doctorates at about the same rate as men. A feminist perspective on public administration is important because the profession is being feminized in the most literal possible sense.

public administration, new A general, mostly undefined movement inspired mainly by younger scholars who challenged several tenets of public administration, primarily the emphasis upon value-neutral administrative research and practice. By the late 1960s, serious questions were being raised concerning the state of the discipline and profession of public administration. DWIGHT WALDO, having noted that public administration was "in a time of revolution," called a conference of young academics in public administration, held in 1968 at Syracuse University's Minnowbrook conference site. The papers that came out of it were edited by Frank Marini and published as *Toward a New Public Administration: The Minnowbrook Perspective* (1971). The goal of the meeting was to identify what was relevant about public administration and how the discipline had to change to meet the challenges of the 1970s. H. George Frederickson, now a professor at the University of Kansas, contributed a paper, "Toward a New Public Administration," which called for social equity in the performance and delivery of public services. Frederickson's new public administration called for a proactive administrator with a burning desire for social equity to replace the traditional impersonal and neutral gun-for-hire bureaucrat. This call was heeded by few but discussed by many. The basic problem with the new public administration's call for social equity was that it was also a call for insubordination—something that is not lightly tolerated in bureaucracies. Victor Thompson immediately attacked the new public administration movement in his aptly titled *Without Sympathy or Enthusiasm* (1975) as an effort by left-wing radicals to "steal the popular sovereignty." Thompson need not have worried. All these "radicals" did was talk—and write. From the 1970s to the present day, and still led by Frederickson, they have produced an endless stream of conference papers and scholarly articles urging public administrators to show a greater sensitivity to the forces of change, the needs of clients, and the problem of social equity in service delivery. This has had a positive effect in that now the ethical and equitable treatment of citizens by administrators is at the forefront of concerns in public agencies.

public administration, postmodern A bundle of theories about perceptions and the social construction of reality offering a means of thinking about social and administrative problems as opposed to a bundle of techniques for resolving them. The major concern is for the semantics of an administrative situation (or the "text" both as written and as perceived). This means that a postmodernist must study both the real facts and the facts as perceived—which may be unreal but real to the observer. This frame of reference whereby a fact exists on two planes at the same time, in realty and in the mind of the person perceiving it, is known as "phenomenology."

public affairs 1. Aspects of corporate public relations that deal with political and social issues. 2. A more genteel-sounding name for a public relations department. 3. The totality of a government agency's public information and community relations activities. 4. An expansive view of the academic field of public administration. Accordingly, a graduate school of public affairs might include, in addition to degree programs in public administration, programs such as police administration and urban studies.

public assistance Local government WELFARE programs. These programs are a right, an entitlement, to those who meet specific criteria for the determination of need. They are often, as are food stamps, heavily subsidized by the federal government. *Compare to* ENTITLEMENT PROGRAM.

public authority A government corporation with powers so similar to that of a business corporation that it is able to complete major government projects such as bridges and tunnels with minimal political interference.

public choice economics That aspect of political economy that deals with public administration based on microeconomic theories that view the citizen as a consumer of government goods and services. It attempts to maximize administrative responsiveness to citizen demand by creating a market system for government activities in which public agencies would compete to provide citizens with goods and services. This might replace a portion of the current system, under which most administrative agencies in effect act as monopolies under the influence of organized pressure groups, which, the public choice economists argue, are institutionally incapable of representing the demands of individual citizens. Philosophically, Republican or conservative governments are much more amenable to public choice approaches than Democratic or liberal governments. Therein lies the constant tension, the constant policy question, over how government services are best delivered—by a government monopoly or by free market competition.

public domain 1. Land owned by the government. 2. A property right held in common by all citizens; for example, the content of U.S. government publications, expired copyrights, and expired patents. 3. The right of government to take property, in exchange for compensation, for a public purpose.

public entrepreneur A nonelected government executive who creates, radically alters, or expands a public organization and then leads it on to significant accomplishment. Admiral Hyman Rickover (1900–1986), the "father" of the atomic submarine, and J. Edgar Hoover (1895–1972) of the Federal Bureau of Investigation are classic examples. *Compare to* PUBLIC POLICY ENTREPRENEUR.

public finance An imprecise term that refers to the totality (1) of the raising and spending of funds by governments, and (2) of the management of government debt. *Compare to* FISCAL POLICY; MONETARY POLICY.

public goods Commodities typically provided by government that cannot, or would not, be separately parceled out to individuals because no one can be excluded from their benefits. Public goods, such as national defense, clean air, and public safety, are neither divisible nor exclusive. This definition applies only to pure public goods. Many goods supplied by governments (public housing, hospitals, and police protection) could be, and often are, supplied privately.

public health The practice and study of promoting and protecting community health. Public health draws from the fields of physical, biological, and social sciences to conduct research, disseminate information, and provide advocacy and education about issues impacting the health of populations. Areas of concern include environmental safety (such as water treatment, waste management), occupational safety (such as accidents, chemical exposure), behavioral health (including diet, physical activity, smoking, drinking), mental health, oral health, maternal and child health, health disparities, and disease prevention.

public hearing A meeting to receive public input—information and opinion—on a designated need, issue, problem, or pending policy or program. Public hearings are held by local, state, and national elected bodies (such as a U.S. Senate subcommittee or a board of county commissioners) and public agencies (e.g., the U.S. Environmental Protection Agency or a state highway department).

public housing Dwelling units paid for or subsidized by government. Public housing, usually available only after a MEANS TEST, has been severely criticized because it tends to concentrate the poor and members of minority groups in high density units that breed crime and other social problems.

public interest The universal label in which political actors wrap the policies and programs that they advocate. Would any lobbyist, public manager, legislator, or chief executive ever propose a program that was not "in the public interest"? Because the public interest is generally taken to mean a commonly accepted good, the phrase is used to further policies that are indeed for the common good and to obscure policies that may not be so commonly accepted as good. In *The Public Philosophy* (1955), Walter Lippmann wrote: "The public interest may be presumed to be what men would choose if they saw clearly, thought rationally, acted disinterestedly and benevolently."

public interest law That portion of a legal practice devoted to broad societal interests rather than to the problems of individual clients. A public interest law firm provides services to advance or to protect important public interests (e.g., the environment or freedom of information issues) in cases that are not economically feasible or desirable for traditional private law firms.

public interest movement A loose phrase for the continuous efforts of public interest groups to gain the passage of legislation that will advance broad societal interests. The movement, the origins of which can be traced back to the progressive era, consistently advances a heterogeneous public policy agenda through a threefold approach: (1) lobbying for legislation, (2) bringing civil suits in the federal courts, and (3) supporting political candidates who support their views.

public law 1. A legislative act that deals with the citizenry as a whole; a statute that applies to all. This is in contrast to a private law, which affects only one person or group. The political victories (and defeats) of all legislative and judicial battles are effectively announced by the new laws that emerge from the fray. Laws passed by a legislature in the form of individual statutes are known collectively as "statutory law." Laws that evolve from court decisions, such as those of the U.S. Supreme Court, are known collectively as "case law." 2. Legal actions initiated by a government agency on behalf of the public, as opposed to private civil actions initiated by a private party for personal benefit. 3. The branch of the law that deals with the relation between a government and its citizens. 4. The codification, the listing, of all the standing public policy decisions made by a state or municipality.

public management A general term referring to a major segment of public administration. Typically, the phrase identifies those functions of public and nonprofit organizations that are internally oriented, such as personnel management, procedures management, and organizational control. Whereas policy management typically focuses on policy formation and the selection of basic strategies, public management focuses on the organizational machinery for achieving policy goals. Planning, organizing, and controlling are the major means by which a public manager shapes government services. These functions constitute the primary knowledge and skills of the public manager and are applied in the form of budgets, performance appraisals, management information systems, program evaluations, organizational charts, cost-benefit analyses, and similar tools.

public management, new MANAGERIALISM applied to the public sector. According to Christopher Pollitt, *Managerialism and the Public Services* (1993), the new public management has four main aspects: (1) a much bolder and larger scale use of market-like mechanisms for those parts of the public sector that could not be transferred directly into private ownership (quasi-markets); (2) intensified organizational and spatial decentralization of the management and production of services; (3) a constant rhetorical emphasis on the need to improve service "quality"; and (4) an equally relentless insistence that greater attention had to be given to the wishes of the individual service user/"consumer."

public office 1. An elected or appointed government job. 2. A public trust; a responsibility to act in the PUBLIC INTEREST. The notion that a "public office is a public trust" goes back to antiquity. President Grover Cleveland used it as his slogan during the 1884 presidential campaign.

public personnel administration *See* PERSONNEL.

public policy 1. A policy made on behalf of a public by means of a public law or regulation that is put into effect by public administration. 2. Decisionmaking by government. Governments are constantly concerned about what they should or should not do. And whatever they do or do not do is public policy. 3. The implementation of a subset of a governing doctrine. The governing doctrine is necessarily an ideology, a comprehensive set of political beliefs about the nature of people and society. It is perhaps best thought of as an organized collection of ideas about the best way for people to live and about the most appropriate institutional arrangements for their societies. In the United States, the governing doctrine is republicanism. Note the lowercase *r*. After all the speeches have been made, after all the negative ads have appeared on TV, after all the soft money has been spent, and after all the votes have been counted, someone is elected. An elected executive (president, governor, mayor) can, upon taking office, make policy within a sphere of constitutional discretion. An elected legislator joins with other members of the assembly to make or obstruct policy. The whole point of the modern democratic process is to designate people to make policy, to make decisions, on behalf of their polity. Without the ritual of selection, of election, public policy cannot be democratic. It is the ritual that gives the ultimately promulgated policies their legitimacy in the eyes of the people.

public policy entrepreneur A political actor who takes a political issue and runs with it. In the ideal capitalistic system of free enterprise, an entrepreneur is the person who organizes the traditional factors of production (land, labor, and capital) to produce goods and services to sell at a profit. Ever optimistic, entrepreneurs hope for riches by using their organizational and managerial skills. In a parallel sense, public policy entrepreneurs hope to enrich society by using their organizational, managerial, and political skills to effect a change in public policy—sometimes for the good of all; but alas, often for just a special-interest group. Thus a senator might make a particular issue his own by sheer force of expertise that, if respected, "forces" colleagues to take cues on the matter from him. Or a staffer might become such an expert on an issue that he or she can heavily influence legislation dealing with it. Thus a public policy entrepreneur can be anyone in the political environment whose expertise and actions can affect an issue.

public policymaking The totality of the decisional processes by which a government decides whether to deal with a particular problem. In seeking an explanation for the mechanisms that produce policy decisions or nondecisions, one is immediately confronted with two early, distinct, and opposite theories. What might be called the rational decisionmaking approach generally has been attributed to Harold Lasswell's *The Future of Political Science* (1963), which posited seven significant phases for every decision: (1) the intelligence phase, involving an influx of information; (2) the promoting or recommending phase, involving activities designed to influence the outcome; (3) the prescribing phase, involving the articulation of norms; (4) the invoking phase, involving establishing correspondence between prescriptions and concrete circumstances; (5) the application phase, in which the prescription is executed; (6) the appraisal phase, assessing intent in relation to effect, and (7) the terminating phase, treating expectations (rights) established while the prescription was in force. The rejection of this approach was urged by Charles E. Lindblom, who, in *Public Administration Review* (Spring 1959), proposed the incremental decisionmaking theory, popularly known as the "science of muddling through." Lindblom saw the rational model as unrealistic. The policymaking process was above all complex and disorderly. Disjointed INCREMENTALISM as a policy course was in reality the only truly feasible route because incrementalism "concentrated the policymaker's analysis on familiar, better-known experiences, sharply reduced the number of different alternative policies to be explored, and sharply reduced the number and complexity of factors to be analyzed." How can one accept that the incremental model is the reality but use the rational model as a conceptual framework for policy analysis? Scholars use the rational model because it affords a dissective capability that can be used to focus on policy specifics and stages, regardless of how well constructed or formulated given decisions may be. Another significant theorist, THEODORE J. LOWI, holds that different models should be constructed for different types of public policies. His now-classic article, "American Business, Public Policy, Case Studies and Political Theory," *World Politics* (July 1964), argued that policy contents should be an independent variable and that there are three major categories of public policies: distribution, regulation, and redistribution. "Each arena tends to develop its own characteristic political structure, political process, elites, and group relations." It seems fair to conclude that no policymaking process by itself produces all policies. Rather, there are numerous policy processes, each capable of producing different policy contents and applicable only in a particular environment.

public policymaking cycle A conceptual model that views the public policy process as moving through the following stages in succession: (1) agenda setting (or the identification of a policy issue); (2) policy or decisionmaking; (3) implementation, program evaluation, or impact analysis; and (4) feedback that leads to revision or termination; thus the process comes full circle—the reason it is called a "cycle."

public-private partnerships Joint efforts on the part of local governments and the business community to plan for, generate public support for, and pay for major social programs or construction projects that will be mutually beneficial. It may be that the partnership is simply one of contracting out or outsourcing; it may be a franchise arrangement in which government sets strict performance requirements for a service; or it may be a fully integrated long-term joint venture in which government and business combine their skills and organizations to deliver a product or service. The partnerships include those under contracting out, or franchising, where government is clearly the principal and the private sector the contractor; but they differ from privatization, where the initiative is passed wholly to the private sector. Under a public-private partnership, government may be only one member of a team of organizations sharing a vision or purpose.

public program All the activities designed to implement a public policy; often this calls for the creation of organizations, public agencies, and bureaus.

public service 1. Participation in public life; voluntary acts for one's community. Jean Jacques Rousseau wrote in *The Social Contract* (1762): "As soon as public service ceases to be the chief business of the citizens, and they would rather serve with their money than with their persons, the state is not far from its fall." 2. Government employment; the totality of a jurisdiction's employees; the totality of a nation's public-sector employees. 3. What a government does for its community; for example, police protection and trash collection. 4. A local public utility. 5 One's DUTY to the STATE.

public service academy A special program in a high school that emphasizes the study of government, public policy, and public administration.

public utilities A legal designation encompassing organizations that produce essential services, usually in a monopolistic fashion; originally, a designation of services—such as water, gas, and electricity— provided by private corporations to large numbers of the public and paid for by community users. The public nature, yet monopolistic character, of such corporations eventually subjected them to public scrutiny and regulation, if not public ownership. They are now all characterized as public, despite differences in ownership, management, and regulation.

public utilities commission A state agency that regulates power companies and railroads. They typically set rates, hold hearings on the quality and level of services, and perform economic analyses on regulated industries.

public welfare 1. Government support of and assistance to needy persons contingent upon their need. *Compare to* WELFARE. **2.** A legal basis for government action; for example, a governor may be bound by a state constitution to protect the public welfare and thus to send National Guard troops to a major disaster site. **3.** The general welfare of the United States. *Compare to* GENERAL WELFARE CLAUSE.

public works A generic term for government-sponsored construction projects. Initially, it was applied to all construction useful to the public, regardless of its potential for private profit. But the use of such projects as a means of providing employment during recession, or as a potential for the distribution of federal resources to states or cities, has given the term a new meaning in economic planning. Since the New Deal, public works projects have sometimes been used in times of economic recession or depression to stimulate the economy. Public works are also major elements in PORK BARREL legislation, designed to benefit an individual congressional district.

pump priming 1. Pouring water into a dry pump to lubricate dry seals and valves and rapidly increase the efficiency of the pump, even though this may waste the initial water. **2.** The concept, originating in the New Deal, of stimulating the economy during a time of economic decline by borrowing money to spend on such projects as public works, defense, and welfare. In theory, the prosperity generated by these expenditures would increase tax revenues, which in turn would pay for the borrowing. *Compare to* JOHN MAYNARD KEYNES.

Q

quality circles Small groups of employees working in the same organizational unit who, with the approval of management, voluntarily meet regularly to identify and solve problems that directly affect their work.

quasi-judicial agency An agency, such as a regulatory commission, that may perform many of the functions ordinarily performed by the courts. Its interpretation and enforcement of rules gives these rules the authority of law. It adjudicates (*see* ADJUDICATION) and may bring charges, hold hearings, and render judgments. *Quasi* is a Latin word meaning "as if," or "almost."

quasi-legislative Descriptive of the rulemaking authority of administrative agencies. The authority of an administrative agency to make rules gives those rules the authority of law; that is, makes them as enforceable as if they had been passed by a legislature.

quid pro quo A Latin phrase meaning "something for something"; initially meaning the substitution of one thing for another. In politics, it suggests actions taken because of some promised action in return.

quorum The number of members who must be in attendance to make valid the votes and other actions of a formal group. In the U.S. Supreme Court, a quorum is six. In the U.S. Senate and the U.S. House of Representatives, it is a majority of the membership.

quotas 1. A quantitative restriction. Quotas are often used in the context of protectionist trade policies. **2.** GOALS.

R

rainy day fund Reserve money put aside by governments to help avoid tax increases during economic declines. More than half the states and many municipalities have these funds, but they are usually limited to 5 percent or less of an annual budget.

rank and file A colloquial expression for the masses. When used in an organizational context, it refers to those members of the organization who are not part of management; those who are the workers and have no status as officers. Rank and file was originally a military term, referring to the enlisted men who had to line up in ranks, side by side, and files, one behind the other. Officers, being gentlemen, were spared such indignities.

rationality 1. The application of reason to decisionmaking. 2. The idea that decisionmaking is based on the calculations of probable gains and losses (or costs and benefits) and that the decisionmaker will generate alternatives, assess them, and choose the one that promises to maximize his values (i.e., give the best ratio of gains to losses). In this sense, rationality is related to the notion of "economic man," who is supposedly always concerned with value maximizing. 3. An abstract and idealized version of what decisionmaking should be, but rarely is; a view of public policymaking that assumes complete information and a systematic, logical, and comprehensive approach to change. Limits on time, intellect, and information mean that policymakers rarely clarify all their values and interests or generate the universe of possible alternatives for achieving their objectives. Instead, they focus on the major values and choose the first alternative that promises to satisfy their requirements, even though it may fall far short of the optimum. This was described by Herbert Simon in *Administrative Behavior* (1947) as "satisficing" as opposed to "maximizing." In practice, therefore, rationality in decisionmaking has many limitations. For the Rational Actor Model *see* GRAHAM T. ALLISON, JR.

Rawls, John (1921–2002) The American philosopher whose *Theory of Justice* (1971) has become one of the most significant works of political theory of the twentieth century. Rawls's theory uses a hypothetical social contract to ascertain the degree of justice of various social arrangements. Rawls's readers are asked to hold information about their own social status behind a "veil of ignorance" and to make rational decisions based upon Rawls's two normative principles: (1) that each person has an equal right to basic liberties compatible with similar liberties for all others; and (2) that sociol-economic inequalities are to be such that basic liberties might benefit even the least advantaged, assuming that offices and positions are open to all. Rawls seeks to reassert a concept of natural rights that holds some values (such as liberty) as absolute and others (such as right to equality) as secondary.

Reagan revolution 1.The resurgence of the Republican Party in the 1980s under the leadership of President Ronald Reagan. **2.** The radical changes in the nation's fiscal and tax policies under the Reagan administration, which redefined domestic priorities and curtailed federal programs designed to solve social problems. As Reagan often said, "Government is not the solution to our problems. Government is the problem." In other words, the national welfare would be better served with general economic prosperity, brought about by tax cuts (*see* SUPPLY-SIDE ECONOMICS/REAGANOMICS), than with expanded welfare programs.

realism The belief that power and self-interest are the main realities of international politics; and that such considerations as ideology, morality, and political rights are inherently secondary. *See also* NATIONAL INTEREST.

realpolitik A German word, now absorbed into English, meaning "realist politics." The term is applied to politics—whether of the organizational or societal variety—premised on material or practical factors rather than on theoretical or ethical considerations. It is the politics of realism: an injunction not to allow wishful thinking or sentimentality to cloud one's judgment.

reasonable accommodation The steps needed to accommodate a handicapped employee's disability (i.e., adequate work space for an employee confined to a wheelchair) required of an employer unless such steps would cause the employer undue hardship.

recall 1. A procedure that allows citizens to vote officeholders out of office between regularly scheduled elections. For a new election to be called, a recall petition must be presented with a prescribed percentage of the jurisdiction's voters' signatures. **2.** The rehiring of employees from a layoff. **3.** The returning of defective products to their manufacturers (often via a retailer) either at the manufacturer's initiative or because of an order from a government regulatory agency enforcing a consumer protection law. *Compare to* REFERENDUM.

recess appointment 1. A presidential appointment to federal office of a person to fill a vacancy (that requires the advice and consent of the U.S. Senate to be filled) while the Senate is not in session. People appointed to office while the

Senate is in recess may begin their duties before their names have been submitted to the Senate. However, the president must submit each such nomination when the Senate reconvenes, and the recess appointment expires at the end of the next session unless the Senate has confirmed each one by a majority vote. Moreover, the recess appointment expires and the office is declared vacant even earlier than the end of the next session if the Senate acts before that time to reject the nominee. 2. A similar appointment by a state governor.

recession A decline in overall business activity that is pervasive, substantial, and of at least several months' duration. Historically, the decline in real gross national product for at least two consecutive quarters of a year has been considered a recession. Although the distinction between a recession and a depression is a matter of usage, recession is generally perceived as a temporary low point in a normal business cycle; a depression suggests more fundamental, underlying shifts in the economy—shifts likely to be permanent and to require basic changes.

recession, growth The economy is growing but at a below-normal rate; not to be confused with euphemisms for *recession* such as "rolling readjustment" or "extended seasonal slump."

reciprocity 1. The giving of privileges to the citizens of one jurisdiction by the government of another, and vice versa. 2. A mutuality in the terms of trade between two nations; this usually refers to the negotiated reduction of a country's import duties or other trade restraints in return for similar concessions from another country. Because of the frequently wide disparity in their economic capacities and potential, the relationship of concessions negotiated between developed and developing countries is generally not one of equivalence. Thus the phrase "relative reciprocity" is used to characterize the practice whereby developed countries seek less than full reciprocity from developing countries in trade negotiations. 3. One of the key norms in a legislature, whereby members exchange favors to further their own, their constituents', and the public's interests. 4. The basis for tacit codes of conduct that help to manage great power rivalry. 5. An approach to the development of international cooperation.

recognition 1. Diplomatic recognition; acknowledgment of the existence of a state with a government that has control over its territory and population. The withholding of recognition, when there is obviously a state that meets these conditions, is generally motivated by political considerations. 2. An employer's acceptance of a union as the bargaining agent for all the employees in a particular bargaining unit.

reconciliation The process used by the U.S. Congress to reconcile amounts for a fiscal year (determined by tax, spending, and debt legislation) with the ceilings enacted in the second required concurrent resolution on the budget for that year. Changes to laws, bills, and resolutions—as required to conform with the binding totals for budget authority, revenues, and the public debt—are incorporated into either a reconciliation resolution or a reconciliation bill.

red tape The ribbon that was once used to bind government documents; the term now stands as the symbol of excessive official formality and overattention to prescribed routines. The ribbon has disappeared, but the practices it represents linger on. Herbert Kaufman, in *Red Tape: Its Origins, Uses and Abuses* (1977), found that the term "is applied to a bewildering variety of organizational practices and features." After all, "one person's 'red tape' may be another's treasured procedural safeguard." Kaufman concluded that "red tape turns out to be at the core of our institutions rather than an excrescence on them."

redistribution Taking from the rich and giving to the poor; domestic policies and programs designed to shift wealth or benefits from one segment of the population to another. The welfare state is founded on the notion of redistribution. The basic mechanism for redistribution is taxation. However, the laws themselves can sometimes redistribute benefits; for example, tax loopholes benefit one group of taxpayers at the expense of others; and the Civil Rights Act, through equal employment opportunity mandates, gave economic benefits to one segment of the population at the theoretical expense of another. *See* THEODORE J. LOWI.

reengineering The fundamental rethinking and redesign of organizational processes to achieve significant improvements in critical measures of performance, such as costs or quality of services. Reengineering takes REORGANIZATION beyond its traditional focus by seeking to rethink and refocus how programs are managed and to take maximum advantage of new technology—especially computers.

referendum A procedure for submitting proposed laws or state constitutional amendments to the voters for ratification. A petition signed by an appropriate percentage of the voters can force a newly passed law onto the ballot; or the legislature could also require that it be put onto the ballot. Although only a minority of the states provide for statutory referenda, practically all states require them for constitutional amendments. Local governments also use the referendum, especially when the law requires that certain issues, such as capital project borrowing, must be submitted to the voters via referenda. *Compare to* RECALL.

reform movement 1. What an out-of-power political party often considers itself. 2. Good, government advocates of changes in governing structures. 3. A loose term for efforts to weed out corruption in public office. **4.** The PRO-GRESSIVE MOVEMENT, which advocated municipal reforms such as the council-manager form of government, civil service reform, the short ballot, and nonpartisan elections.

regime 1. A form of government (republican, totalitarian). **2.** The particular government in power; the group of people constituting the administration. **3.** A system of governance (as opposed to anarchy). **4.** Generally accepted or customary procedures. **5.** A term used in international relations to explain cooperation; for example, the nuclear nonproliferation regime.

regime values John Rohr's term from *Ethics for Bureaucrats* (1986) for the bureaucratic values prevalent in constitutional systems, whether written, as in the United States; or unwritten, as in the United Kingdom. To a person of honor, an oath to "defend the Constitution of the United States against all enemies, foreign and domestic" is a serious matter. Thus, according to Rohr, the U.S. Constitution "is the moral foundation of ethics for bureaucrats."

regulation 1. The totality of government controls on the social and economic activities of its citizens. **2.** The rulemaking process of administrative agencies charged with the official interpretation of laws. These agencies (often independent regulatory commissions), in addition to issuing rules, also tend to administer their implementation and to adjudicate disputes. The Interstate Commerce Commission in 1887 became the prototype of the modern regulatory agency. *See also* DELEGATION OF POWER; DEREGULATION.

regulatory commission An INDEPENDENT AGENCY created by a government to regulate some aspect of economic life.

reign 1. The period of time a government is in power; traditionally the time during which a specific monarch rules. It was Oscar Wilde (1859–1900) who first observed that: "In America the President reigns for four years, and journalism governs for ever and ever," *Fortnightly Review* (1891). **2.** The ultimate source of power, authority, or law in a state. This is what Alexis de Tocqueville meant in *Democracy in America* (1835) when he said: "The people reign over the American political world as God rules over the universe."

reinforcement An inducement to perform in a particular manner. Positive reinforcement occurs when an individual receives a desired reward that is contingent upon some prescribed behavior. Negative reinforcement occurs when an individual works to avoid an undesirable reward.

reinventing government The continuation of the progressive movement's philosophy of continuous improvement. Governments at all levels have been forced by events to change the fundamental ways in which they operate. They must literally rethink, meaning "reinvent," how they operate because they can no longer afford to do what they have been doing—with a reorganization here and a new public relations effort there—to assuage their critics. The simple overriding impetus to reinventing is a lack of money caused by the dual effects of the tax revolt and the Reagan revolution. By 1980, the tax revolt movement had forced thirty-eight states to reduce tax rates, or at least to stabilize them. Then the Reagan revolution made state and local finances even more precarious. The Reagan administration, with its radical changes in the nation's fiscal and tax policies, redefined domestic priorities and curtailed federal programs—especially grants to state and local government—designed to solve social problems. As Reagan often said, "Government is not the solution to our problems. Government is the problem." In other words, the national welfare would be better served with general economic prosperity, brought about by tax cuts rather than with expanded welfare programs. In 1992, David Osborne and Ted Gaebler wrote *Reinventing Government,* a book that essentially categorized many of the things that thousands of governments did throughout the 1980s to cope with this crisis. Bill Clinton, as governor of Arkansas, endorsed the book. As president, he authorized the National Performance Review to seek these same kinds of innovations for the federal government—and for the same reason, money. The federal government was running record deficits. This had to be reduced by reducing (read: reinventing) government. If the federal government was off to the reinventing government races, Vice President Al Gore, put in charge of the National Performance Review, was the jockey riding the reinventing government horse. Gore's defeat in the 2000 presidential race ended reinvention. But by that time, after eight years of the Clinton administration's reform impetus, it badly needed reinventing itself. Its proposals were attacked both by those who felt that its principles didn't fit the traditional values of public administration and by those who felt that its proposals weren't radical enough. During Clinton's second term with a Republican-controlled Congress, reinventing efforts became more rhetoric than reality. The Republican idea of reinventing meant two things: DEVOLUTION and PRIVATIZATION. Thus the Republican Congress (with Clinton's support) devolved the national welfare program and privatization has become the watchword of the subsequent Bush administration. Reinvention has become a Clinton-Gore tainted word. While many reforms will be achieved by the Bush administration, certainly nothing will be "reinvented."

relief Public assistance programs for the poor. "Direct relief" referred to straight welfare payments. "Work relief" referred to any one of the numerous public works projects initiated specifically to provide jobs for the unemployed.

religious test A legal requirement that someone must profess faith in a particular religion to qualify for public office. This practice is expressly forbidden by that portion of Article VI of the U.S. Constitution stating that "no religious test shall ever be required as a qualification to any office or public trust under the United States." Together with the First Amendment, this guarantee expresses the principle that church and government are to remain separate, and that citizens need not fear that their religious convictions will bar them from holding office.

rent control Local laws that regulate the amount by which landlords can raise rents on residential rental properties. The U.S. Supreme Court in *Fisher v. City of Berkeley* (1986) held that municipal rent control laws did not violate federal antitrust statutes. Frustrated by their inability to remove rent controls at the local level, opponents have sought state laws that preempt local ordinances. They have been successful in varying degrees in at least a dozen states. For example, Colorado and Georgia now impose total bans on all forms of rent control, and Minnesota requires a local referendum for the enactment of controls.

rent seeking Efforts to obtain "spoils," "pork," or other advantages through political influence.

reorganization Changes in the administrative structure or formal procedures of government that do not require fundamental constitutional change or the creation of new bodies not previously established by the legislature. Many reorganizations are undertaken (1) for the purposes of departmental consolidation, executive office expansion, budgetary reform, and personnel administration—primarily to promote bureaucratic responsiveness to central executive control; and (2) to simplify or professionalize administrative affairs.

repeal The nullification of a law by the body that made it. Thus a legislature can repeal (meaning to nullify or destroy) a law which it previously enacted. Thomas Paine wrote in *The Rights of Man* (1791): "A law not repealed continues in force, not because it cannot be repealed, but because it is not repealed, and the non-repealing passes for consent." Later President Ulysses S. Grant, would state in his inaugural address of March 4, 1869: "I know no method to secure the repeal of bad or obnoxious laws so effective as their stringent execution."

report *See* FINANCIAL REPORT.

representation, actual A mode of legislative representation in which legislators vote the will of their constituents regardless of their own judgments. *Compare to* TRUSTEE.

representation, agency A situation that exists when the people represented have the power to hire and fire their representatives.

representation, sociological Having elected or appointed representatives with the same racial, ethnic, and/or religious characteristics as the people they serve.

representative bureaucracy The ultimate goal of equal employment opportunity and affirmative action programs. This phrase, originated by J. Donald Kingsley in *Representative Bureaucracy* (1944), asserts that all social groups have a right to participate in and thereby add value to their governing institutions. In recent years, the concept has developed a normative overlay—that all social groups should occupy bureaucratic positions in direct proportion to their numbers in the general population.

representative government A governing system in which a legislature freely chosen by the people exercises substantial power on their behalf. *See* EDMUND BURKE for the distinction between representation and delegation.

republic A Latin word meaning "the public thing"; the state and its institutions; that form of government in which sovereignty resides in the people who elect agents to represent them in political decisionmaking. The United States is a republic. The founders specifically wanted a governing structure that was one step removed from a pure democracy. And they also wanted a governing structure that could function over a large area. As James Madison wrote in *Federalist* No. 14: "In a democracy the people meet and exercise the government in person; in a republic, they assemble and administer it by their representatives and agents. A democracy, consequently, will be confined to a small spot. A republic may be extended over a large region." Yet the Founders all knew that many republics in history, such as the Roman republic, had been replaced by despots. Consequently, when Benjamin Franklin was asked what sort of government had been hatched at the Constitutional Convention, he replied, "A republic, if you can keep it." He knew that "keeping it" was far from certain.

republican One who believes in a government where the people exercise their sovereignty through elected representatives.

rescission A bill or a joint resolution that cancels in whole or in part budget authority previously granted by the U.S. Congress. Rescissions proposed by the president must be transmitted in a special message to the Congress, which must approve such proposed rescissions under procedures in the Budget and Impoundment Control Act of 1974 for them to take effect.

reserve 1. Portion of a body of troops that is deep to the rear, or withheld from action at the beginning of an engagement, and available for a decisive movement. 2. Members of military services who are not in active service but who are subject to call to active duty once war begins. 3. That portion of a budget appropriation or contract authorization held or set aside for future operations or contingencies and in respect to which administrative authorization to incur commitments or obligations has been withheld.

reserved powers The principle of U.S. federalism embodied in the Tenth Amendment of the U.S. Constitution that reserves for the states (or the people) the residue of powers not granted to the federal government or withheld from the states. Chief Justice Harlan F. Stone wrote in *UNITED STATES V. DARBY LUMBER* that the Tenth Amendment is "but a truism that all is retained which has not been surrendered." *Compare to* DELEGATED POWER.

reserved rights Those work-related prerogatives that a labor contract assigns to management; rights that are intrinsic to effective management and thus not subject to collective bargaining.

residency requirement 1. The requirement that a citizen live in a jurisdiction for a specific length of time before being eligible to vote or to hold public office. The U.S. Supreme Court held in *Dunn v. Blumstein* (1972) that a "durational" residency requirement to vote is unconstitutional. However, as a practical matter, the Court recognizes the necessity of closing voter registration rolls thirty to fifty days before an election. **2.** The requirement that a person be (or become) a resident of a jurisdiction to be eligible for employment with the jurisdiction. This was upheld by the Court in *McCarthy v. Philadelphia Civil Service Commission* (1976). **3.** The requirement that a person be a resident of a jurisdiction for a specific period before becoming eligible for welfare benefits. The Court has ruled in *Shapiro v. Thompson* (1969) that jurisdictions cannot discriminate against newer residents in the provision of social benefits. This concept was again upheld by the Court in *Saenz v. Roe* (1999).

restrictive credentialism A general term for selection policies adversely affecting disadvantaged groups because they lack the formal qualifications for positions that, in the opinion of those adversely affected, do not truly need such formal qualifications.

revenue anticipation notes Forms of short-term borrowing used by a jurisdiction to resolve a cash flow problem occasioned by a shortage of necessary revenues or taxes to cover planned or unplanned expenditures.

revenue gainers/revenue enhancement 1. Euphemisms for tax increases. **2.** The manipulation of existing tax laws (or methods) to increase revenues as opposed to the more straightforward approach of raising or creating new taxes.

revenue neutral The characteristic of a tax reform law of which the net effect would be neither to increase nor to decrease the total taxes raised. Instead, it would readjust tax burdens, presumably to make the overall tax system fairer or simpler.

revenue reform 1. A TAX EXTENSION **2.** Taxing things or people not previously taxed; for example, taxing Social Security benefits as regular income.

revenue sharing The sharing of federal tax revenues among subnational levels of government. The argument was made that revenue sharing was economically justified by the federal government's monopolization of the most efficient and progressive tax source—the federal income tax. In 1972, revenue sharing was introduced with the passage of the State and Local Fiscal Assistance Act. With the advent of the Ronald Reagan administration, general revenue sharing was allowed to expire in 1986. The burgeoning of federal budget deficits stands as a major obstacle to renewal.

reverse discrimination A practice generally understood to mean DISCRIMINA-TION against white males in conjunction with preferential treatment for women and minorities. The practice had no legal standing in civil rights laws. Indeed, Section 703(j) of Title VII of the Civil Rights Act of 1964 holds that nothing in the title shall be interpreted in a way that permits an employer to "grant preferential treatment to any individual or group on the basis of race, color, religion, sex or national origin." Yet affirmative action programs necessarily put some white males at a disadvantage. Reverse discrimination is usually most keenly perceived when affirmative action policies conflict with older policies of granting preferments according to seniority and test scores, for example. The practice of reverse discrimination was finally given legal standing when the U.S. Supreme Court in *Johnson v. Santa Clara County* (1987) upheld an affirmative action plan that promoted a woman ahead of an objectively more qualified man. Critics contended that this upset Title VII's requirement that there be no "preferential treatment" because, for the first time, the Court sanctioned and gave legal standing to reverse discrimination. This was not illegal sex discrimination because Paul Johnson was not actually harmed. The Court reasoned that he "had no absolute entitlement to the road dispatcher position. Seven of the applicants were classified as qualified and eligible, and the Agency Director was authorized to promote any of the seven. Thus, the denial of the promotion unsettled no legitimate firmly rooted expectation on the part of [Johnson]." Although Johnson was denied a promotion, he remained employed with the same salary and seniority, and he remained eligible for other promotions. The matter may have been summed up by George Orwell in his 1945 novella *Animal Farm* when he observed that "all animals are equal, but some animals are more equal than others." *See also* DIVERSITY.

right to life The movement to reverse the present legal status of abortion in the United States. *See ROE V. WADE.*

right, natural *See* LAW, NATURAL.

rightful place The judicial doctrine that an individual who has been discriminated against should be restored to the job—to his or her "rightful place"—as if there had been no discrimination—and given the appropriate seniority, merit increases, and promotions. *Compare to* MAKE WHOLE.

right-of-way/easement The legal right to use the land of another, typically for the right of passage to a person, vehicle, underground cables, and so on; for a scenic easement, it is the right to a view.

right-to-work laws State laws that make collective bargaining agreements illegal if they contain maintenance of membership, preferential hiring, union shop, or other clauses calling for compulsory union membership. A typical right-to-work law might state that "no person may be denied employment and employers may not be denied the right to employ any person because of that person's membership or nonmembership in any labor organization." The Labor-Management Relations (Taft-Hartley) Act of 1947 authorized right-to-work laws in Section 14(b): "Nothing in this Act shall be construed as authorizing the execution or application of agreements requiring membership in a labor organization as a condition of employment in any State or Territory in which such execution or application is prohibited by State or Territorial law." The law does not directly prohibit the union or the closed shop; it simply gives each state the option to do so. Twenty states used the option to some degree: Alabama, Arizona, Arkansas, Florida, Georgia, Iowa, Kansas, Louisiana, Mississippi, Nebraska, Nevada, North Carolina, North Dakota, South Carolina, South Dakota, Tennessee, Texas, Utah, Virginia, and Wyoming.

Roe v. Wade (1973) The U.S. Supreme Court case that (by a vote of seven to two) made abortions legal in the United States by ruling that governments lacked the power to prohibit them. Associate Justice Harry Blackmun wrote regarding this case that "freedom of personal choice in matters of marriage and family life is one of the liberties protected by the due process clause of the Fourteenth Amendment. . . . That right necessarily includes the right of a woman to decide whether or not to terminate her pregnancy." This has been one of the most controversial of the Court's decisions, heralded by some groups as a landmark for women's rights and denounced by others as the legalization of murder.

rugged individualism *See* SELF-RELIANCE.

rule-making authority The powers, which have the force of law, exercised by administrative agencies. Agencies begin with some form of legislative mandate and translate their interpretation of that mandate into policy decisions, specifications of regulations, and statements of penalties and enforcement provisions. The process to be followed in formulating regulations is only briefly described in the federal Administrative Procedure Act (APA) of 1946. The APA does distinguish between rule making that requires a hearing and rule making that requires only notice and the opportunity for public comment (notice and comment). Whether the formal or informal procedure is to be used is determined by the enabling statute: the U.S. Supreme Court's decision in *United States v. Florida East Coast Railway* (1973) held that formal rule making need only be followed when the enabling statute expressly requires an agency hearing before a rule is formulated. The APA also requires that rules be published thirty days before their effective dates and that agencies afford interested parties the right to petition for an issuance, an amendment, or a repeal of a rule. In effect, although the APA establishes a process of notice and time for comment, it accords administrative rule makers the same prerogatives that legislatures enjoy in enacting statutes. There is, of course, the additional requirement that the rule enacted be consistent with the enabling statute directing the rule making.

rule of law *See* GOVERNMENT OF LAWS.

rule of three The practice of certifying to an appointing authority the top three names on an eligible list. The rule of three is intended to give the appointing official an opportunity to weigh intangible factors, such as personality, before making a formal offer of appointment. The rule of one certifies only the highest-ranking person on the eligible list. The rule of the list gives the appointing authority the opportunity to choose from the entire list of eligibles.

rules of engagement Military or paramilitary directives that delineate the circumstances and limitations under which force can be used. For example, soldiers might be told to shoot only if they are fired upon first, or police might be told to use deadly force only when lives (as opposed to property) are in immediate danger.

S

safety net The totality of social welfare programs that, in theory, assure at least a subsistence standard of living for all Americans. The first use of the term is often credited to Jack Kemp, who stated in his 1980 book, *An American Renaissance,* that "Americans have two complementary desires. . . . They want an open, promising ladder of opportunity. And they want a safety net of social services to catch and comfort those less fortunate than themselves."

sagebrush rebellion A general term that covers any number of dissatisfactions—hardly a rebellion—that some states of the American West have with the federal government's management and use of the federal lands within their borders. In general, they feel that the states should have more control over the lands and how they are used. The counterargument is that these lands are national trusts and can legitimately be dealt with only by representatives of the national government.

satisficing HERBERT SIMON'S term from *Administrative Behavior* (1947) to explain his concept of "bounded rationality." Simon asserted that it is difficult ever to know all the facts that bear upon a given decision. Because truly rational research on a problem can hardly ever be completed, humans put bounds on their rationality and make decisions based not on optimal information but on satisfactory information; that is by satisficing—choosing a course that meets one's minimum standards for satisfaction.

scalar chain The chain of supervisors from the top of an organization to the bottom.

scapegoating 1. The Old Testament ritual of selecting a goat to be sent into the wilderness symbolically bearing the sins of a whole community. 2. Shifting the blame for a problem or failure to another person, group, or organization — a common bureaucratic and political tactic. Sometimes it is the responsibility of an elected official to be a scapegoat. As President John F. Kennedy told in a press conference on June 15, 1962: "I know when things don't go well, they like to blame the President, and that is one of the things Presidents are paid for." Compare to FULL RESPONSIBILITY.

scenario 1. An outline of a play or movie. 2. An imaginary but usually quite feasible situation that is used for heuristic, planning, and exercise purposes. Scenarios are useful ways to think about options. As a basis for exercises or simulations, scenarios provide an opportunity to become familiar with the procedures used during a crisis.

scenario, rosy An all-too-optimistic estimate of economic growth and interest rate levels made by federal budgeteers so that the estimated federal deficit will seem smaller than realistic estimates would suggest.

school district A SPECIAL DISTRICT for the provision of local public education for all children in its service area. An elected board, the typically governing body, usually hires a professional superintendent to administer the system. School districts, having their own taxing authority, are administratively, financially, and politically independent of other local government units. The number of school districts has been constantly shrinking because the merging of two or more districts is such a common phenomenon. There were more than 108,000 school districts in 1942; today, there are fewer than 14,000.

scientific management A systematic approach to managing that seeks the "one best way" of accomplishing a given task by discovering the fastest, most efficient, and least fatiguing production methods. Frederick Winslow Taylor (1856–1915) became the acknowledged father of the scientific management movement. He pioneered the development of time-and-motion studies, originally under the name "Taylorism" or the "Taylor system." Taylorism, or its successor, scientific management, was not a lone invention but rather a series of methods and organizational arrangements designed by Taylor and his associates to increase the efficiency and speed of machine shop production. Taylor's greatest public-sector popularity came in 1912 after he presented his ideas to the Special Committee of the House of Representatives to Investigate the Taylor and Other Systems of Shop Management. Taylor's comprehensive statement of scientific management principles was focused on what he called the *duties of management:* (1) replacing traditional, rule of thumb methods of work accomplishment with systematic, more scientific methods of measuring and managing individual work elements; (2) the scientific study of the selection and sequential development of workers to ensure their optimal placement into work roles; (3) obtaining the cooperation of workers to ensure the full application of scientific principles; and (4) establishing logical divisions within work roles and responsibilities between workers and management. Taylor's duties seem so obvious today, but they were revolutionary in 1912. Taylor himself even insisted in his *Principles of Scientific Management* (1911) that "scientific management does not necessarily involve any great invention, nor the discovery of new or startling facts."

Nevertheless, it did "involve a certain combination of elements which have not existed in the past, namely, old knowledge so collected, analyzed, grouped and classified into laws and rules that it constitutes a science."

scientific method The procedure for collecting and analyzing data in a systematic and unbiased manner; its four major steps are observation, hypothesis, experimentation, and prediction.

Second World A Cold War–era term for the then-socialist countries of Eastern Europe and the Soviet Union. *See* FIRST WORLD; THIRD WORLD; FOURTH WORLD.

second-class citizen A person who does not enjoy all the civil rights of other citizens. Historically, African Americans were called second-class citizens; and because of segregation and discrimination, that is what they often considered themselves to be. But since the civil rights movement and the new laws that flowed from it, there can be no second-class citizens in the United States. Nevertheless, the phrase is still used in various contexts: by minorities who wish to emphasize economic disparities, by women who feel they have not achieved social equity with men, by prisoners who complain about not being permitted to vote.

security 1. Being safe; a condition that results from protective measures that insure inviolability from hostile acts. 2. A key objective of states in the anarchic international system. A state is relatively secure if its physical survival, territorial integrity, and political independence and values are secure and well protected. 3. The certainty that certain basic needs or requirements will be met; for example, health security and food security. 4. With respect to classified matter, a condition that prevents unauthorized persons from having access to safeguarded information or things. *Compare to* NATIONAL SECURITY.

security classification A category to which national security information and material is assigned to denote the degree of damage that unauthorized disclosure would cause; for example, top secret, secret, and confidential.

security clearance An administrative determination that an individual is eligible for access to classified information.

security dilemma A situation in which one state takes action to enhance its security only to have this action seen as threatening by other states. As a result, the other states engage in countermeasures that intensify the first state's insecurity. The dilemma arises because actions taken to enhance security can end up diminishing it.

security risk 1. A public employee thought to be so susceptible to the influence of foreign agents that he or she cannot be trusted with continued employment or continued access to sensitive information. 2. A disloyal or generally untrustworthy citizen.

security studies 1. Research and teaching on matters relating to domestic and international security; that is, matters involving threats and the actual or potential use of force. 2. A term used almost interchangeably with *strategic studies,* the study of military strategy. Arguably, the term *security studies* has a wider connotation than *strategic studies.* Moreover, it may be further widened as new items on the international agenda, such as narcotics trafficking, terrorism, and environmental problems come under the purview of security studies.

segregation The separation of people by a particular identifying characteristic. Historically, segregation has been practiced in schools, businesses, and public places against racial minorities, women, and persons suffering obvious handicaps. All local laws that called for racial segregation have been invalidated by federal legislation such the Civil Rights Act of 1964, and by U.S. Supreme Court cases such as *BROWN V. BOARD OF EDUCATION. Compare to* INTEGRATION.

select out A bureaucratic phrase for dismissing a government employee.

self-directed work team A work group that will accept responsibility for their processes and products—as well as the behavior of other group members.

self-fulfilling prophecy Actions or statements based on the fear of a particular development that contribute to making the development a reality. For example, if managers believe their employees are not capable, the employees will eventually live up (or down) to expectations. Treating another state as a threat or potential enemy and taking precautions against it may contribute to that state's behaving in a hostile way in response.

self-reliance 1. The title of Ralph Waldo Emerson's (1803–1882) 1841 essay, which urged readers to think for themselves, reminded them that "a foolish consistency is the hobgoblin of little minds," and observed that "an institution is the lengthened shadow of one man." 2. The notion that citizens should take care of their own economic needs and not depend upon the government for the necessities of life. This was President Herbert Hoover's philosophy of "rugged individualism," which called for economic freedom and opposed paternalistic government welfare programs—which he thought undermined character.

senior executive service (SES) The federal government's top management corps, established by the Civil Service Reform Act of 1978. The large majority of the approximately 6,800 SES executives are career managers; there is a 10 percent government-wide ceiling on the number who may be noncareer managers. In addition, about one-third of SES positions are career-reserved; that is, they can be filled only by career executives. *See also* CIVIL SERVICE REFORM ACT OF 1978.

seniority The priority give to the most senior and longest-serving individuals in an organization. Seniority is often used to determine who will be promoted, subjected to layoff, or given/denied other employment advantages. In *Fire Fighters Local Union No. 1784 v. Stotts* (1984) the U.S. Supreme Court held that courts may not interfere with bona fide seniority systems to protect newly hired black employees from layoff. Writing for the majority, Justice Byron R. White said that the law permits remedies only for individuals who can prove they are "actual victims" of job discrimination, rather than for groups of disadvantaged minorities who may not have suffered specific wrongs in a specific job situation.

sensitive position A federal government job requiring access to classified (secret) documents and other information bearing on NATIONAL SECURITY.

separate but equal The doctrine espoused by the U.S. Supreme Court in *Plessy v. Ferguson* (1896), which held that segregated railroad facilities for blacks mandated by Louisiana, facilities that were considered equal in quality to those provided for whites, did not violate the equal protection clause of the Fourteenth Amendment. In a dissenting opinion, Justice John Marshall Harlan wrote, "We boast of the freedom enjoyed by our people. . . . But it is difficult to reconcile that boast with a state of the law which, practically, puts the brand of servitude and degradation upon a large class of our fellow citizens, our equals before the law. The thin disguise of 'equal' accommodations for passengers in the railroad coaches will not mislead anyone, or atone for the wrong this day done." In *BROWN V. BOARD OF EDUCATION,* the Court nullified this doctrine when it asserted that separate was "inherently unequal."

separation of powers The allocation of powers among the three branches of government so that they are a check upon each other. This separation, in theory, makes a tyrannical concentration of power impossible. The U.S. Constitution contains provisions in separate articles for three branches of government: legislative, executive, and judicial. A significant difference exists in the grants of power to these branches: The first article, dealing with legislative power, vests in the Congress "all legislative powers herein granted"; the second vests "the executive power" in the president; and the third states that "the judicial power of the United States shall be vested in one Supreme Court, and in such inferior courts as the Congress may from time to time ordain and establish." The drafters of the Constitution were very familiar with Sir William Blackstone's *Commentaries on the Laws of England* (1783), which asserted that "in all tyrannical governments the supreme magistracy, or the right both of making and of enforcing the laws, is vested in one and the same man, or one and the same body of men; and wherever these two powers are united together, there can be no public liberty." Thus, in *Myers v. United States* (1926), Justice Louis D. Brandeis wrote that "the doctrine of the separation of powers was adopted by the Convention of 1787, not to promote efficiency but to preclude the exercise of arbitrary power. The purpose was, not to avoid friction, but, by means of the inevitable friction incident to the distribution of the governmental powers among three departments, to save the people from autocracy." *Compare to* CHECKS AND BALANCES; *FEDERALIST NO.* 51.

sergeant at arms The officer who, under the direction of the presiding officer, is charged with maintaining order during a formal meeting. *Sergeant* is derived from the French word for "servant." In the early British Parliament, a sergeant at arms enforced laws and arrested people. Although a modern sergeant at arms may no longer be armed, the limited police powers remain.

service contract An agreement between local units of government for one unit (usually larger) to provide a service for another (usually smaller). Because the service contract was first extensively used between the County of Los Angeles and the City of Lakewood, California, it is often called *the Lakewood plan.*

service fee 1. User charges for government services not fully paid for by general taxation. Examples include water fees from municipal governments and admission fees for national parks. 2. The equivalent of union dues that nonunion members of an agency shop pay the union for negotiating and administering the collective bargaining agreement.

set aside A higher court's reversing of a lower court's decision; the decision is literally set aside—made void.

set-asides Government purchasing and contracting provisions that set aside or allocate a certain percentage of business for minority-owned companies. The use of set-asides was upheld by the U.S. Supreme Court in *Fullilove v. Klutznick* (1980) and *Metro Broadcasting v. FCC* (1990), but restricted in *City of Richmond v. J. A. Croson* (1989) and *Adarand Constructors v. Pena* (1995). *Adarand* specifically overruled *Metro.*

sex discrimination A disparate or unfavorable treatment of a person in the workplace because of gender. The Civil Rights Act of 1964 (as amended by the Equal Employment Opportunity Act of 1972) makes sex discrimination illegal in most employment, except where a bona fide occupational qualification is involved. Sex discrimination in employment was by no means a significant concern of the civil rights advocates of the early 1960s. Its prohibition only became part of the Civil Rights Act of 1964 because Representative Howard "Judge" Smith (1883–1976) of Virginia, a leader of the South's fight against civil rights, added one small word—sex—to prohibitions against discrimination based on race, color, religion, and/or national origin.

He felt confident this amendment would make the proposed law ridiculous and cause its defeat. Smith was an "old style" bigot: in his mind, the one thing more ridiculous than equal rights for blacks was equal rights for women. The "sex discrimination" amendment was opposed by most of the leading liberals in the U.S. Congress. They saw it as nothing but a ploy to discourage the passage of the new civil rights law. The major support for adopting the amendment came from the reactionary Southern establishment of the day. Once Smith and his supporters realized the true impact of what they were doing, they sought to withdraw the amendment before the final vote, but the then-few female members of Congress stopped this by insisting that it be done by a recorded vote, as opposed to a voice vote. The male members did not want to be embarrassed by voting against women, so the amendment remained in the bill. There was no discussion of sex discrimination by the U.S. Senate. The momentum for a new civil rights law was so great that Smith's addition not only failed to scuttle the bill but also went largely unnoticed. The legal foundation for the modern women's movement was passed with almost no debate or media attention.

sexual harassment The actions of an individual or a group that lead to a sexually abusive work environment. Typically a supervisor or a coworker in a position to control or influence another's job, career, or grade uses such power to gain sexual favors or punish the refusal of such favors. Sexual harassment on the job varies from inappropriate sexual innuendo to coerced sexual relations. In 1980, after the federal courts had decided that sexual harassment was sex discrimination in a variety of cases, the Equal Employment Opportunity Commission issued legally binding rules clearly stating that an employer has a responsibility to provide a place of work that is free from sexual harassment and intimidation. In 1986, the U.S. Supreme Court reaffirmed this when in *Meritor Savings Bank v. Vinson* it held that sexual harassment creating a hostile or abusive work environment, even without economic loss for the person being harassed, was in violation of Title VIII of the Civil Rights Act of 1964.

sheriff The elected (in all states but Rhode Island) chief officer of a county law enforcement agency, usually responsible for law enforcement in unincorporated areas of the county and for the operation of the county jail. The sheriff— whose title comes from the Middle English *schirreff,* Old English *shire-reeve,* meaning the king's representative in a shire (an English county)— is also the officer of the local court who serves papers and enforces court orders.

shop steward A local union's most immediate representative in a department, usually elected by fellow employees. Typically the steward continues with a regular job and handles union matters part-time.

Simon, Herbert A. (1916–2001) The organization theorist who was awarded the 1978 Nobel Prize for economics for his pioneering work in management decisionmaking. Simon was the most influential of the neoclassical organization theorists. He was the first to challenge seriously the principles approach proposed by Fayol and Gulick. In his 1946 article condescendingly titled "The Proverbs of Administration," he denounced the principles approach to public administration that then dominated administrative thinking. He found the management principles of his era inconsistent, conflicting, and inapplicable to too many of the administrative situations facing managers. He concluded that they were little more than proverbs. Simon also firmly believed that decisionmaking should be the focus of a new "administrative science." He wrote in *Administrative Behavior* (1947) that organization theory is the theory of the bounded rationality of human beings who SATISFICE because they do not have the intellectual capacity to maximize. He was also the first analyst to draw a distinction between "programmed" and "unprogrammed" organizational decisions; he highlighted the importance of the distinction for management information systems. His work on administrative science and decisionmaking went in two major directions: First, he was a pioneer in developing the "science" of improved organizational decisionmaking through quantitative methods (such as operations research) and artificial intelligence. Second, he was a leader in studying the processes by which administrative organizations make decisions.

sinecure A position for which a salary is extracted but little or no work is expected. This was originally an ecclesiastical term for a church office not requiring the care of souls, *sinecure* being Latin for "without care."

sinking fund Money put aside for a special purpose, such as to pay off bonds and other long-term debts as they come due or to replace worn-out and/or outdated machinery and buildings.

slush fund 1. Money collected by the military services in the nineteenth century by selling grease and other refuse (the slush). The resulting funds were used to buy small luxuries for the soldiers and sailors. 2. Discretionary funds appropriated by a legislature for the use of an agency head. 3. Private monies used for campaign expenses. 4. Funds used for bribery. 5. Secret funds. Because of their lack of formal accountability, all slush funds have an unsavory connotation—even when they are perfectly legal.

Smith, Adam (1723–1790) The Scottish economist who provided the first systematic analysis of economic phenomena and the intellectual foundation for laissez-faire capitalism. In *The Wealth of Nations* (1776), Smith discussed an invisible hand that automatically promotes the general welfare as long as individuals are allowed to pursue their self-interest. It has become customary for organization theorists to trace the lineage of present-day theories to Smith's concept of the DIVISION OF LABOR. Greater specialization of labor was one of the pillars of the invisible-hand market mechanism, in which the greatest rewards would go to those who were the most efficient in the competitive marketplace. As Smith's work marks the beginning of economics as an identifiable discipline, he is often referred to as the father of economics. *See also* ABILITY TO PAY.

social Darwinism Charles Darwin's (1809–1882) concept of biological evolution applied to the development of human social organization and economic policy. Although there is a long tradition of government's forcing private organizations to improve the lot of their employees, better treatment was initially inhibited by social Darwinism. Darwin's concepts of natural selection and the survival of the fittest were applied to society in general. Thus, practices such as child labor and the employment of children in a manner detrimental to their health and social development were justified because of the social Darwinist belief that the "fit" children would survive and that this was all part of the normal process of natural selection.

social equity A normative standard holding that equity, rather than efficiency, is the major criterion for evaluating the desirability of a policy or program. Social equity is fairness in the delivery of public services; it is egalitarianism in action—the principle that each citizen regardless of economic resources or personal traits deserves and has a right to be given equal treatment by the political system. Even though the United States has not lived up to this ideal, has not provided equality to all men and women throughout its history, it has nevertheless been constantly moving in that direction. The political theorist Jean Jacques Rousseau warned in *The Social Contract* (1762) that "it is precisely because the force of circumstances tends always to destroy equality that the force of legislation must always tend to maintain it." The United States has a long tradition of using legislation to mitigate the "force of circumstances" that so often inhibits equality. For example, in the early nineteenth century, public schools made education free of charge gradually available to all classes. In 1862, the Homestead Act provided for a citizen to own 160 acres of public land; in return, the homesteader would live on the land for five years. The American Civil War (1861–1865) can be viewed alternatively as a conflict over intergovernmental relations or a moral crusade to bring "equality" (meaning equal protection of the laws) to those in bondage. The twentieth century witnessed an outpouring of legislation that gave new rights to workers, women, and minorities. This has gone so far that social equity, in addition to efficiency, is now a major criterion for evaluating the desirability of a public policy or program.

social indicators Statistical measures that aid in the description of conditions in the social environment (e.g., measures of income distribution, poverty, crime, health, physical environment).

social insurance A benefit program that a state makes available to the members of its society in time of need and as a matter of right.

social responsibility of business The belief that business organizations have a moral and ethical duty to contribute to social well-being; that they have an obligation to society other than seeking a profit in a legal manner. But others, such as the economist MILTON FRIEDMAN, believe the resolution of social problems is the task of governments, not businesses, and managers who so spend money on them act irresponsibly.

social security The popular name for the Old Age, Survivors, and Disability Insurance (OASDI) system established by the Social Security Act of 1935. At first, social security covered only retired private-sector employees. In 1939, the law was changed to cover survivors when the worker dies and to cover certain dependents when the worker retired. In the 1950s, coverage was extended to include most self-employed persons, most state and local employees, household and farm employees, members of the armed forces, and members of the clergy. Today, almost all jobs are covered by social security. Disability insurance was added in 1954 to give workers protection against loss of earnings due to total disability. The social security program was expanded again in 1965 with the enactment of Medicare, which assured hospital and medical insurance protection to people sixty-five years and older. Since 1973, Medicare coverage has been available to people younger than sixty-five who have been entitled to disability checks for two or more consecutive years and to people suffering permanent kidney failure who need dialysis treatment and/or kidney transplants. Amendments enacted in 1972 provide that social security benefits increase automatically with the cost of living. The biggest problem with social security is demographics. In 1950, the ratio of taxpaying workers to pensioners was 120 to 1. In 2030, it will be 2 to 1. This is why social security payroll taxes have risen from 1 percent in 1940 to 7.65 percent in 2002; (6.2 of the 7.65 percent is for traditional social security pensions; the remainder goes to fund Medicare). And that percentage is for employees and employers—so it is double if you are self-employed.

socialism A system of government in which many of the means of production and trade are owned or run by the government and in which many human welfare needs are provided directly by the government. Socialism may or may not be democratic. Socialism is one of the most "loaded" words in U.S. politics. To the Right, it represents the beginnings of communist encroachment on traditional U.S. values and institutions. To the Left, it represents the practical manifestation of the pragmatic and generous spirit that characterizes the United States. Although U.S. political culture countenances limited socialistic measures, it will not tolerate socialistic rhetoric. Thus, the social security program was labeled an insurance system even though its proponents knew that it was designed to be an income transfer program. On the whole, Americans abhor the symbol represented by the word *socialism,* but are very much in favor of limited socialistic measures so long as they are espoused as pragmatic responses to difficult problems. *Compare to* MARXISM; MIXED ECONOMY.

sociological representation Elected or appointed representatives showing the same racial, ethnic, and/or religious characteristics as the people they serve.

sovereign immunity A government's freedom from being sued for damages in all but those situations in which it passes statutes allowing it. The Federal Tort Claims Act of 1946 abolished the federal government's immunity from lawsuits based on torts (civil as opposed to criminal wrongs done to a person). Amendments to the Administrative Procedure Act in 1976 also allow civil suits to be filed against the federal government. *See also* IMMUNITY.

span of control The extent of an administrator's or agency's responsibility. The span of control has usually been expressed as the number of subordinates that a manager should supervise.

special assessment A real estate tax on certain landowners to pay for improvements that will, at least in theory, benefit them; for example, a paved street. *See also* BENEFIT DISTRICT.

special district A unit of local government typically performing a one function and overlapping traditional political boundaries. Examples include transportation districts, fire protection districts, library districts, water districts, and sewer districts. Because special districts are such useful devices, they have been multiplying rapidly. In 1942, only 8, 299 of them existed in the United States; today, there are almost 30,000. They constitute one third of all U.S. government entities.

spillover effects/externalities Benefits or costs that accrue to parties other than the buyer of a good or service. For the most part, the benefits of private goods and services inure exclusively to the buyer (e.g., new clothes, a television set). For public goods, however, the benefit or cost usually spills over onto third parties. An airport, for example, not only benefits its users but spills over onto the population at large in positive and negative ways. Benefits might include improved air service for a community, increased tourism, and new businesses; costs might include noise pollution and traffic congestion.

spin Efforts by an administration or an individual political actor to manipulate the media to contain, deflect, and minimize an unraveling scandal or other embarrassing or politically damaging revelation. The purpose is to keep the situation from spinning out of control.

spoils system The widespread practice of awarding government jobs to political supporters as opposed to awarding them on merit; the patronage practices of one's political opposition. The system got its name in 1832 when Senator William L. Marcy (1786–1854) asserted in a U.S. Senate debate "that the politicians of the United States boldly preach what they practice. When they are contending for victory, they avow their intention of enjoying the fruits of it. If they are defeated, they expect to retire from office. If they are successful, they claim, as a matter of right, the advantages of success. They see nothing wrong in the rule, that to the victor belong the spoils of the enemy."

squatter's rights The right to ownership of land merely by occupying it for a certain period. During the settling of the American West, this was a legal means of acquiring title to land. Today, although squatting is generally not recognized as legal, this has not stopped some urban social activists from squatting in abandoned houses, fixing them up somewhat, and then demanding ownership.

staff 1. The subordinate employees of an organization. 2. Specialists who assist line managers in carrying out their duties. Generally, staff units do not have the power of decision, command, or control of operations. Rather, they make recommendations (which may or may not be adopted) to executives and line managers. The term has its origins with the young assistants of old generals: they were called *staff* because these young aides de camp carried the general's tent posts (or staffs) and ropes. Even today, staff officers are known by the vestigial ropes on their shoulders. But whether military or civilian, public sector or private sector, *staff* seldom refers to a single or even a few individuals. Staff is huge. Staff means personnel, purchasing, legal services, medical services, and the dozens of other support elements of a large organization.

staff out The process that involves soliciting a variety of views or recommendations on an issue so that a decisionmaker will be aware of all reasonable options.

staff principle 1. That a unit of a large organization should be responsible for thinking and planning, for pondering innovations and planning for their implementation. 2. The principle of administration holding that the executive should be assisted by officers who are essentially extensions of the executive's personality and who advise and assist the executive in controlling and coordinating the organization.

staff, chief of 1. The professional head of a state's military or naval forces. 2. The working title for the military officer who supervises the other officers on a commander's staff. 3. The civilian supervisor of an overall management team who reports directly to the chief executive officer. 4. The top aide to a high-level executive. Chiefs of staff have often been criticized for isolating their bosses from those who want to see them and for exercising authority as a de facto deputy even though nobody elected them to that office. A chief of staff was once a rarity and strictly military. No longer. The influence of the German General Staff model is now so pervasive that one cannot walk into a government office without bumping into a chief of staff. Most governors and mayors and county administrators employ them. So do major department heads from police chiefs (yes, the chief has a chief!) to school superintendents. Increasingly, even individual legislators employ them. The point is that a public manager is not very important without one—even if the chief of staff is really not much more than the chief of a few clerks.

staff, general A group of officers in a military headquarters who assist their commanders in planning, coordinating, and supervising operations.

staff, personal 1. Members of an organization who report directly to an executive, rather than through an intermediary, such as a chief of staff. Personal staff members can be relatively low-level secretaries and chauffeurs, or they can be high-level technical experts. 2. The staffs who serve individual legislators either in their capital offices or in home state/district offices, as opposed to the staff of the legislative body or its committees. Personal staffs handle correspondence, publicity, CASEWORK, and local political affairs for the legislators.

staffing One of the most basic functions of management and usually considered synonymous with employment—that is, the process of hiring people to perform work for the organization. Staffing defines the organization by translating its objectives and goals into a specific work plan. It structures the responsibilities of the organization's human resources into a work system by establishing who will perform what function and have what authority.

staffing plan A planning document that minimally (1) lists an organization's projected personnel needs by occupation and grade level, and (2) identifies how these needs will be met.

stakeholder A person or group having a "stake" or interest in a given policy; anyone who might be affected by a pending or implemented governmental decision. The responsible public decisionmaker seeks to obtain the maximum possible stakeholder satisfaction.

standard operating procedures Instructions about how things are to be done under normal circumstances; orders that are valid unless and until countermanded.

standards of conduct A compendium of ethical norms promulgated by an organization to guide the behavior of its members. Many government agencies have formal codes (or standards) of conduct for their employees. Their objective is to ensure that employees refrain from using their official positions for private gain. Typically, a variety of prohibited activities seek to ensure that employees conduct themselves in a manner that would not offer the slightest suggestion they will extract private advantage from public employment. Standards are often part of a state's formal legal code; thus, violations can carry severe penalties. *Compare to* CODE OF ETHICS.

state 1. A political unit having territory, population, and sovereignty over its internal and external affairs. 2. The main actors in international politics. Relations among states form the basis for international society with its system of rules and norms. 3. A component government in a federal system, such as a state government in the United States. 4. One of the fifty states of the United States. In many federal laws, the term also includes the District of Columbia, the Commonwealth of Puerto Rico, and the territories or possessions of the United States. 5. A short form of reference to the U.S. Department of State. 6. An abstract concept referring to the ultimate source of legal authority.

state, department of 1. A state government agency that, among other varied duties, typically maintains official documents, issues licenses for businesses as well as certificates of incorporation, and administers elections. All states have such a department headed by a secretary who is usually elected. 2. The cabinet-level department of the federal government charged with the execution of foreign policy.

state government A subnational government in the United States that consists of its legislative, executive, and judicial branches and all departments, boards, commissions, and other organizational units. It also includes semi-autonomous authorities, institutions of higher education, districts, and other agencies that are subject to administrative and fiscal control by the state through its appointment of officers, determination of budgets, and approval of plans.

state, hollow A reference to the increasing use of third parties, often nonprofit organizations, to deliver social services and constraints (such as privately owned prisons) and act in the name of the state. The state then increasingly ceases to be a service provider and increasingly becomes the manager of a network of subcontractors.

statehouse 1. The building in the state where the legislature meets. A state CAPITOL. 2. A governorship. "Can he [any governor] go from the statehouse to the White House?" is an often-asked question.

state's attorney 1. The attorney general of a state. 2. A local prosecutor (e.g., a district attorney) who represents the state (the people) in a criminal trial.

state's evidence In a criminal trial, evidence or testimony on behalf of the state (the prosecution). State's evidence is what an accomplice to a crime gives to the state in a negotiated effort to obtain a lesser personal penalty for the crime at issue.

states' rights 1. Rights that, according to the U.S. Constitution, have neither been given to the federal government nor forbidden to the states. What remains is the essence of state sovereignty. **2.** A CODE WORD for opposition to federal civil rights legislation, federal land use policies (*see* SAGEBRUSH REBELLION), and other federal policies perceived to be violations of state sovereignty.

statute A law passed by a legislature; legislative-made as opposed to judge-made law.

statute, organic The legislative act that creates an agency.

statutes at large A collection of all statutes passed by a particular legislature (such as the U.S. Congress), printed in full and in the order of their passage.

statutes of limitations Laws that place limits on the time authorities have to charge someone with a crime after its commission; limits on the time someone has to contest a contract in a civil lawsuit.

statutory offense An act that is made a crime by statute as opposed to by common law. For example, statutory rape is rape only because a statute holds that adults who have sexual relations with males or females of a certain age and younger are "automatically" rapists.

strategic 1. Of or relating to strategy. **2.** Necessary to or important to initiate, conduct, or complete a strategy. **3.** Required for a war effort, but not available domestically; thus it is important to stockpile strategic materials. **4.** Of great importance to an integrated plan. **5.** Great range and power in the context of military planning; thus a strategic missile has a nuclear warhead and can hit targets across continents. **6.** Having to do with nuclear war.

strategic management A philosophy of management that links strategic planning with day-to-day decisionmaking. Strategic management seeks a fit between an organization's external and internal environments. All strategic management efforts take an essentially similar approach to planning where an organization wants to be by a target date. These are the features that identify a strategic as opposed to a nonstrategic management approach: (1) the identification of objectives to be achieved in the future (these are often announced in a vision statement); (2) the adoption of a time frame (or "planning horizon") in which these objectives are to be achieved; (3) a systematic analysis of the current circumstances of an organization, especially its capabilities; (4) an assessment of the environment currently surrounding the organization both now and within the planning horizon; (5) the selection of a strategy to achieve both desired objectives, often by comparing various alternatives, by a certain date; and (6) the integration of organizational efforts around this strategy.

strategic plan The formal document that presents the ways and means by which a strategic goal will be achieved.

strategic planning The set of processes used by an organization to assess the strategic situation and develop strategy for the future. The overall strategy chosen is in essence the package of actions selected after analyzing alternatives, assessing the outside environment, and determining the internal capabilities of an organization to achieve specified future objectives through the integration of organizational effort.

strategic studies 1. That branch in the study of international politics that focuses upon the actual or potential use of military force. **2.** A synonym for SECURITY STUDIES. **3.** The study of strategy in the nuclear age that looks not only at the use of nuclear force but also at its nonuse and the threat of its use.

strategy 1. The art and science of developing and using political, economic, psychological, and military forces as necessary during peace and war to afford the maximum support to policies and to promote a favorable outcome. Strategy is basically planning; it is what French General Antoine Henri Jomini in his *Summary of the Art of War* (1838) called "the art of making war upon the map." **2.** The overall conduct of a major enterprise to achieve long-term goals; the pattern to be found in a series of organizational decisions. "Strategy" is derived from the Greek *strategia,* meaning "the art of the general." Until recent decades, the word was mainly confined to its military context. But in the mid-1960s, H. Igor Ansoff (1918–), a mathematician turned business school professor, started producing works advocating strategic planning for better business success. Later he discovered that planning was not comprehensive enough. A broader concept was needed that would subsume strategic planning and go on to encompass implementation as well; this was strategic management. What Ansoff did was revolutionary. It wasn't that strategic leadership was new, but its self-conscious application to business policy was. Ansoff's revolution was confirmed when over the next two decades strategic management almost completely supplanted business policy as a core subject of MBA (and eventually MPA) programs. Strategic management has thus become the modern application of this ancient art to contemporary business and public administration.

strategy, grand 1. The overall strategic policies of a nation or alliance. All military strategy logically follows from this overall national strategy. **2.** Strategy at a higher level than that used for one theater of war or one campaign.

strict constructionist One who believes the U.S. Constitution should be interpreted narrowly and literally. Strict constructionists tend to be against judicial activism and in favor of judicial self-restraint. This is what President Ronald Reagan meant on June 23, 1986, when he said, "The one thing that I do seek are judges that will interpret the law and not write the law." A loose constructionist, in contrast, believes that the Constitution should be interpreted liberally to reflect changing times. Chief Justice John Marshall first made the case for loose construction in *McCulloch v. Maryland* (1819); he said, "Let the end be legitimate, let it be within the scope of the Constitution, and all means which are appropriate, which are plainly adapted to that end, which are not prohibited, but consist with the letter and spirit of the Constitution, are constitutional." The strict versus loose construction construct is highly subjective and has no meaning or consistent application in practice. Even a strict constructionist could be an activist in reversing loose construction. *Compare to* ORIGINAL INTENT.

strike A mutual agreement among workers (whether members of a union or not) to a temporary work stoppage to obtain—or to resist—a change in their working conditions. The term is thought to have nautical origins because sailors would stop work by striking or taking down their sails. A strike or a potential strike is considered an essential element in collective bargaining. Many labor leaders claim that collective bargaining can never be more than a charade without the right to strike. Major strikes have been less frequent in recent years because unions in the public and private sectors have lost a large measure of economic clout and political support. Public employee strikes also have been declining, but for another reason. A great percentage of public sector strikes in the 1960s and early 1970s were over one issue: recognition of the union for purposes of collective bargaining. Because recognition strikes tend to be one-time issues and because many states have in the last four decades passed comprehensive public employee relations laws, public-sector labor strife has been less than it once was. *See also* JURISDICTIONAL STRIKE.

strike force 1. A military force organized to undertake an offensive mission. 2. By analogy, a civilian government effort to attack a problem; commonly used by police and public prosecutors, as in a crime strike force.

strong mayor *See* MAYOR-COUNCIL SYSTEM.

structural-functional theory/structural-functionalism An approach in sociology in which societies, communities, and organizations are viewed as systems; their features are then explained in terms of their contributions (their functions) in maintaining the system. Structural-functional analysis emphasizes the social system at the expense of, or as opposed to, the system's recognized political organizations, actors, and institutions. This approach is generally credited to Talcott Parsons; see his *Social System* (1951).

subgovernments The COZY TRIANGLES/IRON TRIANGLES of congressional committees or subcommittees, agency executives, and interest group lobbyists that often dominate public policymaking in a given area. Subgovernments, with a relatively small number of participants which, as a group, can function pretty much autonomously, are often contrasted with ISSUE NETWORKS—large numbers of people with vastly varying degrees of interest, mutual commitment, and power to influence an issue. Although a subgovernment or iron triangle is a relatively stable unit for purposes of exercising power and political analysis, an issue network is so loose that it almost defies definition.

subnational government State and local government.

substantive law The basic law of rights and duties (contract law, criminal law, accident law, law of wills), as opposed to procedural law (law of pleading, law of evidence, law of jurisdiction).

sunk costs Resources committed to the achievement of an organizational objective that cannot be regained if the objective is abandoned.

sunset laws Laws that fix termination dates on programs or agencies. They require formal evaluations and subsequent affirmative legislation if the agency or program is to continue. Although the purpose of a finite life span of, say, five years is to force evaluation and to toughen legislative oversight, the effect is to subject programs to automatic termination unless the clock is reset. Despite its widespread popularity, such time-bomb evaluation is not without risks. There are limits to the abilities of any legislature's staff to do the kind of thorough evaluation required to make sunset meaningful. Requiring organizations to submit evaluation data for review and to justify their programs may amount to little more than burying the legislature in an avalanche of insignificant paper—something at which agencies have a demonstrated prowess. Furthermore, some agencies, such as police, prisons, and mental health institutions, will be rightly skeptical of the chances of their programs being shut down.

sunshine laws Requirements that government agencies hold their formal business meetings open to the public.

supervisors, board of The governing body for a county government. Membership on the board is determined either by election or by ex officio appointment by other local officials.

Supplemental Security Income (SSI) The federal program that assures a minimum monthly income to needy people with limited income and resources who are sixty-five years of age or older, blind, or disabled. Eligibility is based on income and assets. Although the program is administered by the Social Security Administration, it is financed from general revenues, not from social security contributions.

supply-side economics/Reaganomics The belief that lower tax rates, especially on marginal income, encourages fresh capital to flow into the economy, which in turn generates jobs, growth, and new tax revenue. Because this concept was adopted by President Ronald Reagan and his advisors, it has been popularly called *Reaganomics*, even though Reagan's actual economic policies have been a melange of supply-side thinking, monetarism, old-fashioned conservatism, and even Keynesianism. While economist Arthur Laffer is generally credited with having "discovered" supply-side economics, the underlying premises of it were established almost two hundred years ago by Alexander Hamilton in *Federalist* No. 21. Hamilton argued that: "It is a signal advantage of taxes . . . that they contain in their own nature of security against excess. They prescribe their own limit; which cannot be exceeded without defeating the end proposed—that is, an extension of the revenue. When applied to this object, the saying is as just as it is witty, that, "in political arithmetic, two and two do not always make four." If duties are too high, they lessen the consumption; the collection is eluded; and the product to the treasury is not so great as when they are confined within proper and moderate bounds." George Gilder's *Wealth and Poverty* (1981), sometimes called the "supply-side Bible," is the most comprehensive explanation and justification for Reaganomics.

supremacy clause That portion of Article VI of the U.S. Constitution that asserts that the Constitution, treaties, and laws made on its behalf "shall be the supreme Law of the Land," implying that federal law will preempt state law.

supreme law of the land The U.S. Constitution, laws of the United States made "in pursuance of" the Constitution, and treaties made under authority of the United States. Judges throughout the country are bound by them, regardless of anything in separate state constitutions or laws.

surtax An additional tax, or surcharge, on what has already been taxed; that is, a tax on a tax. For example, if you must pay a thousand-dollar tax on a ten-thousand-dollar income (10 percent), a 10 percent surtax would be an additional hundred dollars.

SWOT analysis A review of an organization's Strengths, Weaknesses, Opportunities, and Threats. This technique is widely used to examine the viability of strategic plans. A SWOT analysis is often undertaken as part of a situation audit, an assessment of an organization's performance in absolute terms or in comparison to a competing or parallel organization.

system 1. Any organized collection of parts united by prescribed interactions and designed for the accomplishment of a specific goal or general purpose. 2. The political process in general. 3. The establishment; the powers that be who govern; the domain of a ruling elite. 4. The BUREAUCRACY.

system, open Any organism or organization that interacts with its environment, as opposed to a closed system which does not. A closed system is mainly a theoretical concept since even the most isolated mechanical system will eventually be impacted by its environment. Even a seemingly closed system such as a thermostat connected to a heater will eventually wear out. Consequently, for all practical purposes all systems theory—especially in the social sciences—is open systems theory.

systems analysis 1. The methodologically rigorous collection, manipulation, and evaluation of data on social units (as small as an organization or as large as a polity) to determine the best way to improve their functioning and to aid a decisionmaker in selecting a preferred choice among alternatives. Norbert Wiener's (1894–1964) classic model of an adaptive system, from his 1948 book *Cybernetics: On Control and Communication in the Animal and the Machine*, epitomizes the basic theoretical perspectives of the systems school. Cybernetics, a Greek word meaning "steersman," was used by Wiener to mean the multidisciplinary study of the structures and functions of control and information-processing systems in animals and machines. The basic concept behind cybernetics is self-regulation—biological, social, or technological systems that can identify problems, do something about them, and then receive feedback to adjust themselves automatically. 2. The development and use of mathematical models as an aid in decisionmaking. But this can be dangerous if nonquantifiable factors are not also taken into account.

systems theory A view of an organization or a society as a complex set of dynamically intertwined and interconnected elements, including its inputs, processes, outputs, feedback loops, and the environment in which it operates and with which it continuously interacts. A change in any element of the system inevitably causes changes in its other elements. The newest thing about systems thinking is theorizing about it as if it were new. But ancients like Aristotle and poets like Shakespeare understood systems instinctively. Perhaps the best poetic description of the human social system is that of John Donne (1572–1631). When he wrote that: "No man is an island, entire of itself; every man is a piece of the continent, a part of the main"; he provided the preamble for modern social science. And when he concluded that "any man's death diminishes me, because I am involved in mankind; and therefore never send to know for whom the bell tolls; it tolls for thee," he explained why everyone had to understand the doctrines of systems theory.

T

Taft-Hartley Act *See* LABOR-MANAGEMENT RELATIONS ACT OF 1947/TAFT-HARTLEY ACT.

tariff A tax imposed on imported products. A tariff is the schedule of duties. A duty, as distinguished from a tariff, is the actual tax imposed or collected. In practice, however, the words are often used interchangeably.

task force 1. A temporary grouping of disparate military forces under one commander to undertake a specific mission. **2.** By analogy, a temporary interdisciplinary team within a larger organization charged with accomplishing a specific goal. Task forces are typically used in government when a problem crosses departmental lines. **3.** A temporary government COMMISSION charged with investigating and reporting upon a problem.

tax A compulsory contribution exacted by a government for public purposes. This does not include employee and employer assessments for retirement and social insurance purposes, which are classified as "insurance trust revenue." Taxes are generally perceived by a public to be legitimate if they are levied by that public's elected representatives. Indeed, one of the causes of, and principal rallying cries for, the American Revolution was that there should be "no taxation without representation" because "taxation without representation" was tyranny. Consequently, practically all taxes at all levels of government are now enacted by popularly elected legislatures. Although Benjamin Franklin wrote Jean-Baptiste Leroy, in a letter dated November 13, 1789, that "in this world nothing can be said to be certain but death and taxes," and Oliver Wendell Holmes wrote in a 1904 U.S. Supreme Court opinion that "taxes are what we pay for civilized society," it remained for Margaret Mitchell to observe in *Gone With the Wind* (1936) that "death and taxes and childbirth! There's never any convenient time for any of them!" *See also* REVENUE GAINERS; TAXATION.

tax abatement/tax remission The relinquishment of a tax that would ordinarily be due. For example, a local government might temporarily abate certain property taxes to encourage the construction of new housing.

tax amnesty A government's forgiving of the failure to pay taxes previously due if they are paid within an announced period. This saves the taxpayer the interest and penalties that would have been due and gains the government far more in revenues than it would obtain through normal enforcement. Since the 1980s, at least thirty states have used tax amnesty programs to increase their income tax collections. The federal government has yet to install a tax amnesty program. Many complain that all such programs are inherently unfair to people who pay their taxes on time.

tax anticipation notes *See* REVENUE ANTICIPATION NOTES.

tax assessment *See* ASSESSMENT.

tax avoidance Avoiding taxes by planning one's personal finances to take advantage of all legal tax breaks, such as deductions and tax shelters. J. Pierpont Morgan (1836–1913) provided the intellectual foundation of tax avoidance when he said, "No citizen has a moral obligation to assist in maintaining the government. If Congress insists on making stupid mistakes and passing foolish tax laws, millionaires should not be condemned if they take advantage of them." *Compare to* TAX EVASION.

tax base The thing or value on which taxes are levied. Some of the more common tax bases include individual income, corporate income, real property, wealth, motor vehicles, sales of commodities and services, utilities, events, imports, estates, and gifts. The rate of a tax to be imposed against a given tax base may be either specific or ad valorem. Specific taxes raise a specific, non-variable amount of revenue from each unit of the tax base (e.g., 10 cents per gallon of gasoline). Ad valorem taxes are expressed as a percentage, and the revenue yield varies according to the value of the tax base (e.g., a mill levy against real property).

tax bracket *See* TAX RATE.

tax collections *See* TAX YIELD.

tax credits The provisions of law that allow a dollar-for-dollar reduction in tax liabilities.

tax elasticity The relation between the percentage of tax revenue raised compared to the percentage of change in personal income. A perfectly elastic tax would always be able to collect the same percentage of the income of its jurisdiction's population.

tax equity Fairness and justice in how taxes are assessed and administered.

tax evasion Taking illegal and criminal actions to avoid paying one's tax obligations. *Compare to* TAX AVOIDANCE.

tax exemption 1. The immunity from the taxation of certain activities and institutions. Exemption may be temporary, such as a ten-year exemption to encourage new housing in a particular area; or permanent, as in the exemptions enjoyed by most schools and churches. **2.** The immunity from the taxation of certain kinds of income, such as child support payments and income from municipal bonds.

tax exempts 1. Land, buildings, and businesses that do not pay taxes because of legal exemptions. **2.** Investments, such as municipal bonds, that are tax free. **3.** Nonprofit organizations that meet legal requirements for tax exemption.

tax expenditure The losses of tax revenue attributable to provisions of the tax laws that allow a special exclusion, exemption, or deduction from gross income or that provide a special credit, preferential rate of tax, or deferral of tax liability. When an individual or a corporation receives a tax subsidy, governments count it as a tax expenditure. *Compare to* TAX LOOPHOLE.

tax extension 1. The expansion of the coverage of a tax; for example, a state sales tax that covered only certain items might be "extended" by new legislation to cover additional items. **2.** Adjusting progressive tax rates so that more people qualify for the highest marginal tax brackets.

tax incentive A provision in a tax law that encourages particular economic activity. For example, provisions for accelerated depreciation encourage businesses to buy new equipment.

tax incidence The effects of a particular tax burden on various socioeconomic levels.

tax increment financing The ability of local government to finance large-scale development through the expected rise in the property tax to be collected after the development is completed. Tax increment financing permits the issuance of bonds according to the expected tax increase.

tax lien Legally executed charges on a property because of unpaid taxes. The lien can result in a foreclosure and tax sale; that is, the property can be forcibly sold to pay the taxes due.

tax loophole An inconsistency in the tax laws, intentional or unintentional, that allows the avoidance of some taxes. An intentional tax loophole is a TAX EXPENDITURE. A tax expenditure for one person is often viewed as a loophole by another. Tax loopholes are perfectly legal; but they have the unsavory reputation of being the handiwork of special-interest lobbyists.

tax rate/tax bracket The percentage of taxable income paid in taxes. This means that the first $10,000 of a person's taxable income might be taxed at a 10 percent rate, and the next $1,000 at a 15 percent rate. This percentage rate is generally called a *tax bracket*.

tax reform The recurrent effort to produce a more equitable tax system at all levels of government. As a process, it is never ending and full of semantic traps — for one person's tax reform often winds up as another's tax increase. Sometimes tax reform is not as much reform as the addition of new kinds of taxes. New things to tax come about by the inventiveness of fiscal experts or by new technology. For example, James Kendall in his biography *Michael Faraday* (1955) tells that when Faraday, one of the pioneers in the development of electricity was first explaining his invention to the British Chancellor of the Exchequer, he was interrupted with "the impatient inquiry: 'But, after all, what use is it?' Like a flash of lightning came the response: 'Why, sir, there is every probability that you will soon be able to tax it!'"

tax revolt A nationwide grassroots movement, heralded by California Proposition 13, in 1978, to decrease or limit the rate of increase possible on property taxes. By 1980, the tax revolt movement forced thirty-eight states to reduce, or at least to stabilize, their tax rates. When California passed Proposition 3 in 1990, which, among other things, doubled the state gasoline tax over five years to pay for new highways, many analysts hailed this as the end of the "tax revolt."

tax shelter An investment in which profits are fully or partially tax free or that creates deductions and credits that reduce one's overall taxes.

tax subsidy A tax advantage designed to encourage specific behavior that furthers public policy; for example, mortgage interest deductions to encourage citizens to buy houses, and investment tax credits to encourage businesses to expand and create new jobs. *Compare to* TAX EXPENDITURE.

tax yield The amount of tax that could potentially be collected. Tax collections are the portion of the tax yield that is actually collected.

tax, broad-based Taxes levied on all eligible taxpayers whether or not they receive benefits from the levy.

tax, capital gains A tax on the profit made on the increase in value of capital assets (such as a house or stocks) when they are sold. Tax rates on capital gains may be lower than for personal income if the assets are held longer than a prescribed period.

tax, corporate income A tax on the privilege of operating a business. To determine taxable income, various deductions can be made for depreciation, capital gains, research and development costs, and so on.

tax, direct/indirect tax A direct tax (e.g., an income tax): a tax paid to a government directly by a taxpayer; an indirect tax (e.g., a sales tax): a tax paid to a third party, who in turn pays it to a government. Article I, Section 9, of the U.S. Constitution holds that "no capitation, or other direct, tax shall be laid, unless in proportion to the census or enumeration herein before directed to be taken." This inhibited the enactment of the federal income tax until the Sixteenth Amendment of 1913 changed the Constitution to allow for direct taxation.

tax, earmarked A tax whose revenues must, by law, be spent for specific purposes. For example, a state gasoline tax may be earmarked for highway construction.

tax, estate The federal and state taxes on a deceased person's property made prior to the estate's distribution to heirs.

tax, estimated That portion of income tax that individuals with other significant income than salaries must declare to the Internal Revenue Service and pay every three months.

tax, excess profits A supplement to corporate income taxes, usually imposed during a national emergency.

tax, excise A tax on the manufacture, sale, and consumption of products such as gasoline and tobacco.

tax, exported A tax paid by nonresidents of a community (e.g., a city wage tax paid by commuters).

tax, flat A tax that charges the same rate to each taxpayer.

tax, income *See* TAX, PERSONAL INCOME.

tax, inheritance A tax, usually progressive, on an individual's share of a deceased person's estate.

tax, license A tax exacted (either for revenue raising or for regulation) as a condition to the exercise of a business or nonbusiness privilege.

tax, marriage Not an actual tax. Under some income tax laws, two-wage earners who happen to be married to each other and file a joint tax return may often pay more in taxes than if they were single and filed separately.

tax, negative income A welfare program in which citizens with incomes below a specified level receive cash payments.

tax, personal income A tax based on the ability to pay; the tax rate is applied against income. All taxpayers have the right to exclude certain kinds of incomes from their gross incomes for tax purposes. For example, interest from state and local bonds is exempt from federal taxation. Thus, a millionaire whose sole income came from investments in such bonds might pay no federal income tax. The taxpayer may also subtract deductions and exemptions from taxable income. Then the taxpayer can deduct a host of expenses if they are allowed by the tax laws: medical care, state and local taxes (if a federal return), home mortgage interest, and charitable contributions. Progressive tax rates are then applied to the taxable income to determine how much tax is due. All states (with the exception of Florida, Nevada, South Dakota, Texas, Washington, and Vermont) have personal income taxes, as do many cities. Residents of Baltimore, Cleveland, Detroit, New York, and Philadelphia, for example, must pay personal income taxes to three governments: federal, state, and local.

tax, personal property Tax on the assessed value of (1) tangible property, such as furniture, animals, and jewelry; or (2) intangible property, such as stocks and bonds.

tax, progressive A tax that has people of greater wealth paying a larger percentage in tax than people of lesser means. Income taxes are often progressive. *Compare to* TAX FLAT; TAX REGRESSIVE.

tax, real-property Tax on land and its improvements; usually called *property tax.* This tax is the mainstay of most local governments; it provides nearly half the revenues that local governments receive from their own sources. To administer a property tax, the tax base must first be defined—for example, housing, land, automobiles. Then an evaluation of the worth of the tax base must be made—this is the assessment. Finally, a tax rate, usually an amount to be paid per hundred-dollar value of the tax base, is levied. Because the value of the tax base will appreciate or depreciate substantially over time, continuing assessments must be made.

tax, regressive A tax by which an individual pays a higher overall percentage of tax than someone who has a higher income. SALES TAXES are examples of regressive taxes. *Compare to* TAX FLAT; TAX PROGRESSIVE.

tax, regulatory A tax levied for a purpose other than raising revenue.

tax, sales A tax on consumption, rather than on income. This favorite of many state and local governments calls for a fixed tax rate, typically ranging from 2 to 9 percent, to be charged on most purchases. Certain items tend to be excluded from sales taxation—for example, medicine and food. The major criticism of the sales tax is equity. Sales taxes tend toward regressivity. To illustrate, a person with an annual income of $8,000 dollars would spend 50 percent of that in direct consumption and might pay a 5 percent sales tax of $200, or 2.5 percent of income. But someone with an income of $80,000 will have a much lower percentage of direct consumption (say 25 percent) and, although that person might pay 5 percent on this amount ($1,000), the proportion of income taken by the sales tax is 1.2 percent—or half that of the lower-income person.

tax, school A local real-property tax imposed by a school district.

tax, severance A tax imposed by more than half the states for the privilege of "severing" natural resources, such as coal, from the land.

tax, shared A tax imposed and administered by a higher level of government that it shares according to a predetermined percentage formula with lower units of government. For example, states commonly collect sales taxes and return a portion to counties and municipalities.

tax, stamp A tax on certain legal documents, such as deeds, when it is required that revenue stamps be bought and applied to the documents to validate them.

tax, transfer A tax on large transfers of property or money, which are made without something of value given in return. Often called a *gift tax*.

tax, unitary A business tax of a percentage of worldwide profits, not just profits earned in the taxing jurisdiction. For example, if a corporation has 20 percent of its payroll, property, and sales in a given state, that state might tax 20 percent of the corporation's worldwide income.

tax, value-added (VAT) A type of national sales tax imposed by almost all Western European countries as a major source of revenue, levied on the value added at each stage of production and distribution of a product; sometimes called a *business transfer tax.* Proponents of VAT in the United States argue that VAT rewards efficiency and, thus, is superior to the corporate income tax in allocating economic resources; it can encourage savings and capital formation because it is a tax solely on consumption; it can help balance-of-payments problems because it can be imposed on imports and rebated on exports; and it can be a major new source of revenue for meeting domestic spending needs, especially social security costs. Opponents of VAT charge that it is a regressive tax; that it is inflationary in that prices to consumers go up; and that it will be an additional tax, rather than a substitute for present taxes.

tax, wage Any tax on wages and salaries levied by a government. Many cities impose wage taxes that have the indirect benefit of forcing suburban commuters to help pay for the services provided to the region by the central city.

tax, withholding Sums of money that an employer takes out of an employee's pay and turns over to a government as prepayment of the employee's federal, state, or local tax obligations.

taxation Government revenue collection. There are major differences between the federal and state-local revenue collection systems. The federal system has experienced a trend toward less diversity; over two-thirds of its general revenue are provided by the federal income tax and the several insurance trust funds (such as social security). State and local revenue systems, in contrast, depend on a greater variety of revenue sources (such as property taxes, income taxes, sales taxes, user charges, lotteries, and federal grants).

taxation, progressive A tax policy in which people in each successively higher income bracket pay a progressively higher tax rate. The federal graduated personal income tax is an example of progressive taxation.

taxes, payments in lieu of Annual sums paid to local governments by tax-exempt organizations. For example, some universities make payments in lieu of taxes to their cities to help pay for such services as trash removal and police and fire protection.

Taylor, Frederick W. *See* SCIENTIFIC MANAGEMENT.

team building A planned and managed change that involves a group of people and is designed to improve communications and working relationships. Team building is most effective when used as a part of a long-range strategy for organizational and personal development.

technocracy A contraction of "technical" and "bureaucracy," which refers to the high-tech organizational environments of the postmodern world.

technocrat An individual in a decisionmaking position of a technoscience agency whose background includes specialized technical training in a substantive field of science or technology. Sometimes used disparagingly.

technology assessment A planning and evaluation device by which the impact of technology in society is judged. It can be used to make an empirical evaluation of the performance and the physical, ecological, political, and economic effects of a particular technology either currently in use or contemplated in the future.

technology transfer 1. The application of technologies developed in one area of research or endeavor to another, frequently involving a concomitant shift in institutional setting (for example, from one federal agency to another). Examples include the application of space technology developed under the auspices of the National Aeronautics and Space Administration (NASA) to the problems of public transportation and weather prediction. 2. The movement of technologies from one nation to another. All governments have been traditionally concerned with restricting the flow of new technologies to potential enemies because of their possible military applications. Technology may be transferred in many ways: by giving it away (technical journals, conferences, emigration of technical experts, technical assistance programs); by stealing it (industrial espionage); or by selling it (patents, blueprints, industrial processes, and the activities of multinational corporations).

technoscience agencies Agencies of the federal government involved in science and technology policymaking. These agencies generate ideas for scientific research and technological development; sponsor research in universities, corporations, and federal laboratories; and direct deployment projects. Examples include the National Science Foundation, the National Aeronautics and Space Administration (NASA), the Department of Defense, and the Department of Energy.

technostructure A term that implies a growing influence of technical specialists in policy decisions. Technostructure is increasingly used as a technical term in the study of science and technology policymaking to refer to the technical decisionmaking structure in private and public organizations.

T-group A training group. The specific understandings of organizational behavior-oriented change processes came out of the sensitivity training (or

T-group) movement that started in 1946 when KURT LEWIN and associates collaboratively conducted a training workshop to help improve racial relations and community leadership in New Britain, Connecticut. During their evening staff meetings, they discussed the behavior of workshop participants and the dynamics of events. Several workshop participants asked to join the night discussions, which eventually led to the initiation and institutionalization of T-group technology. Although the early T-groups focused primarily on individual growth and development, they were adapted for organizational application. T-groups became the method by which organizational members learned how to communicate honestly and directly about facts and feelings. (From the human relations perspective, feelings are facts.) Thus T-groups became a keystone strategy for increasing organizational effectiveness by improving interpersonal communications (e.g., feedback), reducing defensiveness (and thus rigidity), and otherwise helping organizations achieve greater effectiveness through the development of coping strategies. But the T-group needed to be part of a larger overarching methodology. Survey research methodology, when combined with feedback/communication (T-group) techniques, and applied to planned organizational change, resulted in the development of the ACTION RESEARCH model of organizational change—the mainstay of ORGANIZATION DEVELOPMENT practitioners and theorists.

Theory X and **Theory Y** Managerial philosophies premised upon a set of assumptions about human behavior. Douglas McGregor (1906–1964), through his 1960 book *The Human Side of Enterprise,* popularized the contending concepts of managerial philosophy with his now famous Theory X and Theory Y sets of assumptions. McGregor hypothesized that a manager's assumptions about human behavior predetermined his administrative style. Because of the dominance of traditional theory in managerial thought, many managers had long accepted and acted upon a set of assumptions that are at best true of only a minority of the population. McGregor labeled as Theory X the following assumptions: (1) The average human being has an inherent dislike of work. (2) Most people must be coerced or threatened with punishment to get them to put forth adequate effort. (3) People prefer to be directed and wish to avoid responsibility. Theory X sounds very much like a traditional military organization which, indeed, is where it comes from. Although McGregor's portrait of the modern industrial citizen can be criticized for implying greater pessimism concerning human nature on the part of managers than is perhaps warranted, Theory X is all the more valuable as a memorable theoretical construct because it serves as such a polar opposite of Theory Y, which assumes the following: (1) The expenditure of physical and mental effort in work is as natural as play or rest. (2) People will exercise self-direction and self-control in the service of objectives to which they are committed. (3) Avoidance of responsibility, lack of ambition, and emphasis on security are generally consequences of experience, not inherent human characteristics. (4) The capacity to exercise a relatively high degree of imagination, ingenuity, and creativity in the solution of organizational problems is widely, not narrowly, distributed in the population.

think tank A colloquial term for an organization or organizational segment the sole function of which is research, usually in the policy and behavioral sciences. All large governmental entities have think tank operations of one kind or another. However, they are often difficult to spot because they don't wear "think tank" labels. But if one delves behind title phrases such as "strategic planning," "audit and evaluation," and "management and budget," one will often detect thinking. What distinguishes a think tank from an organizational unit with similar responsibilities is its structural independence. This independence allows think tank researchers to advocate policy positions free of hierarchical intimidation. For this reason, the military general staff is independent of line commanders; the urban reform movement of the progressive era got its impetus from independent municipal research bureaus; and the U.S. Air Force created the archetypal think tank, the RAND corporation, as a civilian organization outside the military chain of command. In recent years, there has been a trend toward partisan think tanks. The U.S. tax code encourages eccentrics with enough money to establish foundations that fund research on virtually anything. What was once solely the tool of nations to deal with the great issues of war and peace is now also a vehicle for social reformers and crackpot millionaires.

third sector Organizations that fit neither in the public sector (government) nor the private sector (business); a generic phrase for nonprofit organizations.

third way The acceptance by the political Left in the United States and Great Britain (the Democratic and Labour parties, respectively) of many of the public choice policy prescriptions initially espoused by the political Right.

Third World 1. Countries with underdeveloped but growing economies, and low per capita incomes, often with colonial pasts. The term *Third World* is often used interchangeably with or as a synonym for *LDCs* (less developed countries), *the South, developing countries,* or *underdeveloped countries. Compare* to FOURTH WORLD. 2. The non-Western and non-Japanese world in general. The problem with this conception of the Third World is that it lumps relatively rich states, such as Singapore and South Korea, with poor ones. Now that the Cold War is over and the SECOND WORLD of Eastern Europe and the former Soviet Union is seeking to break out into the FIRST WORLD of industrialized Western societies, the use of *Third World* is being increasingly challenged.

three-strikes law A law designed to take repeat offenders off the streets after three convictions (as in baseball, three strikes and you're out) by sentencing them to life in prison. California enacted a "three-strikes" law in 1994 by a ballot initiative after it was defeated by its legislature the previous year. Twenty-six states now have "three-strikes" laws of one kind or another.

time study A variety of measurement techniques for determining the time it should take a worker to perform a given task.

time-and-motion studies Various techniques for establishing time standards for the performance of manual work.

tokenism In the context of equal employment opportunity, an insincere Equal Employment Opportunity (EEO) effort by which a few minority group members are hired to satisfy government affirmative action mandates or the demands of pressure groups.

total quality management (TQM) A new phrase for quality control in its most expanded sense of a total and continuing concern for quality in the production of goods and services. TQM is hampered by an emphasis on short-term profits (in the private sector) or short-term "looking good" results (in the public sector). The thrust of TQM is to change the organizational culture to one that values long-term, long-lasting effectiveness. *Quality Is Free* (1979) shouts the title of a book by Philip Crosby urging organizations to do their best and focus on the needs of the customers. It's "free" because it doesn't cost more for an individual or an organization to give peak performance. But what does cost is superficial hypocritical quality—the quality that is touted but not delivered. This type of "quality" reduces the perception of an organization's competence in the eyes of its employees and customers.

town 1. An urban entity possessing fewer powers than cities. The powers of towns are strictly controlled by state statutes. 2. The New England town, which combines the roles of city and county; it usually contains one or more urban areas as well as surrounding rural areas.

town meeting 1. A method of self-government, suitable for only the smallest jurisdictions, where the entire citizenry meets to decide local public policy. The town meeting is the governing body for many New England municipalities. 2. A common technique for legislators to keep in touch with their constituents; various "town meetings" are scheduled at town halls, high schools, and other public halls so that legislators can report to constituents and answer their questions.

township A subdivision of a county traditionally having six miles on each side and varying in importance as a unit of government in the sixteen states that have them. Townships in the Midwest are sometimes called *congressional* *townships* because public land surveys in the nineteenth century initially labeled them thus on maps authorized by the U.S. Congress.

trade union A labor organization that restricts its membership to skilled craft workers (such as plumbers and carpenters), in contrast to an industrial union, which seeks to recruit all workers in a given industry.

tragedy of the commons A story illustrative of the principle that the maximization of private gain will not result in the maximization of social benefit. When herdsmen sought to maximize individual gain by adding more and more cattle to a common pasture, the common was overgrazed. The resulting tragedy was that no one was able to make effective use of the common for grazing. The concepts involved with the tragedy of the commons apply to societal problems, such as pollution and overpopulation. Garrett Hardin, in "The Tragedy of the Commons," *Science* (December 13, 1968) wrote that "ruin is the destination toward which all men rush, each pursuing his own best interest in a society that believes in the freedom of the commons. Freedom in a commons brings ruin to all."

training Preparing employees to better perform their assigned duties. A training program is not complete without an evaluation of its effectiveness and usefulness. Although there is a great variety of training formats, almost all will fall into one of the following categories: (1) skills training: teaching specific skills such as typing, welding, and how to work a computer program; (2) coaching: personal instruction whereby an expert oversees the efforts of a learner and provides continual advice; (3) formal or informal classroom instruction: traditional classroom instruction, including courses at nearby academic institutions, whereby groups of employees are instructed (with jurisdictions often providing subsidies for job-related college courses); (4) sensitivity or "T-group" training: assembling small groups of employees to deal with the problems of interpersonal relationships (usually requiring a professional "facilitator" and relying heavily on the willingness of individuals to confront the emotional aspects of their behavior); (5) job rotation: providing employees with differing work activities designed to increase their experience (a variant of this being cross-training, where each job, and thus the entire work of an office, is learned by each employee); (6) special conferences and seminars: meetings of employees or professional groups to discuss and exchange ideas about common processes, problems, and techniques; (7) modeling, games, and simulation training: simulated real-life situations providing employees with various experiences; and (8) exchange and sabbatical programs: taking the individual out of the organizational environment and into a totally different one for a substantial period, several months to a year.

training, laboratory A generic term for educational/training experiences designed (1) to increase an individuals' sensitivity to their own motives and behavior, (2) to increase sensitivity to the behavior of others, and (3) to ascertain elements of interpersonal interactions that either facilitate or impede a group's effectiveness. Although laboratory training and sensitivity training tend to be used interchangeably, sensitivity training is the subordinate term (being the most common method of laboratory training) and the popular name given to almost all experience-based learning exercises. The basic vehicle for the sensitivity training experience is the T-GROUP.

transfer payments Payments by a government made to individuals who provide no goods or services in return. Social welfare programs at all levels of government that provide subsistence income support are transfer payment programs. They are often called *entitlement programs* because one becomes entitled to transfer payments if one meets criteria established by the authorizing legislation.

trial balloon A deliberate leak of a potential policy to gauge public response. The term comes from the meteorological practice of sending up a balloon to test weather conditions. If public response is hostile, the new policy proposal can be quietly dropped (or deflated).

trickle-down theory A basis for government policies that seek to benefit the wealthy in hopes that prosperity, in turn, will trickle down to the middle and lower economic classes. The term was coined by humorist Will Rogers (1879–1935) when he analyzed some of the Depression remedies of the Herbert Hoover administration and noted that "the money was all appropriated for the top in the hopes it would trickle down to the needy."

Truman Doctrine The policy of the Harry S. Truman administration of giving military and economic aid to countries (Greece and Turkey, specifically) seeking to resist "totalitarian aggression." This doctrine became a cornerstone of the U.S. policy of CONTAINMENT.

trust A group of companies that work together to maintain an effective monopoly; this inhibits competition thus raising prices for consumers and profits for the trusts. *See also* ANTITRUST LAWS.

trust funds Funds collected and used by the federal government for carrying out specific purposes and programs according to terms of a trust agreement or statute, such as the social security and the unemployment trust funds. Trust funds are administered by the government in a FIDUCIARY capacity and should not be available for the general purposes of the government.

trustee 1. A person who manages property for another. 2. The role that elected representatives adopt when they vote according to their conscience and best judgment rather than according to the narrow interests of their immediate constituents. This concept was famously expounded by British political philosopher Edmund Burke (1729–1797) in "Speech to the Electors of Bristol" (1774).

turkey farm A government office that performs little work and has slight, if any, responsibility. Government managers frequently find it easier to place troublesome or incompetent employees on turkey farms rather than face the hassle of ADVERSE ACTION proceedings.

turnover The rate at which employees leave an organization—usually expressed as a percentage of all workers who resign or are fired each year.

typology A systematic classification of categories so that they may be more readily analyzed. Typologies are commonly used in the study of public policy and have a long historical tradition. They create neatness out of chaos, make it easier to remember the essence of complex intellectual arguments, and offer the happy illusion that a matter has been settled by our betters and therefore is beyond question. For example, MAX WEBER wrote that there were three pure types of legitimate authority: charismatic (in which the personal qualities of a leader command obedience); traditional (in which custom and culture yield acquiescence); and legal (in which people obey laws enacted by what they perceive to be appropriate authorities). The study of public policy offers enormous scope for the creation of typologies. Textbooks and scholarly monographs sag with lists, categories, and classifications of public policies and ways to analyze them. The study of public policy is a chaotic world that cries out for organization, for definitive classification, and for a unified approach. But this is a cry that will not be heeded. Chaos rules because there is no power—neither U.S. president nor university president—that can tell the scholars of academic disciplines concerned with public policy how to ply their trade.

tyranny of small decisions 1. A system in which individual decisions appear to be rational but the result is the opposite to what was intended, largely because others have made the same or similar choices. *Compare to* TRAGEDY OF THE COMMONS. 2. Recognition that INCREMENTALISM can lock one into a course of action that has unforeseen and damaging consequences.

U

underdeveloped An adjective for the poor countries of the THIRD WORLD. First used in the 1950s, it is now considered mildly offensive and has been replaced by "developing" which seems less judgmental.

underground economy Economic activity that evades tax obligations; work done "off the books," for cash only. Examples of underground economic activity include a medical doctor's accepting a cash payment from a patient and not recording the payment for income tax purposes; a carpenter's doing work for a small business and accepting an in-kind payment, the value of which is not recorded for income tax purposes; and, of course, traditional criminal activity. "Underground" in this context does not necessarily mean secret—except to the Internal Revenue Service.

undersecretary In the federal government, the official next in command after the cabinet secretary. The various assistant secretaries usually report to the undersecretary.

unemployment The totality of persons able and willing to work who are actively (but unsuccessfully) seeking to work at the prevailing wage rate. The unemployment rate is probably the most significant indicator of the health of the economy. Unemployment statistics are compiled monthly by the U.S. Bureau of Labor Statistics.

unemployment benefits Specific payments available to workers from the various state unemployment insurance programs. Unemployment benefits are available as a matter of right (without a means test) to unemployed workers who have demonstrated their attachment to the labor force by a specified amount of recent work or earnings in covered employment. To be eligible for benefits, the worker must be ready to work and registered at a public employment office. Workers responsible for their own unemployment may be denied benefits.

unemployment, cyclical Unemployment caused by a downward trend in the business cycle. It is assumed that those who are unemployed because of cyclical trends in the business cycle will be reemployed when the economy picks up. Cyclical unemployment is inherently temporary.

unemployment, hard-core The unemployment of people who, because of impoverished backgrounds or the lack of appropriate education, have never been able to hold a job for a substantial time. Hard-core unemployment is unlikely to be affected by existing employment opportunities because of the health, mental condition, or education of the hard-core unemployed.

unincorporated area An urban area that has not become a municipality and has no local government structure of its own other than its county.

union 1. A LABOR UNION. 2. The United States, which is a union of its component states. 3. A single-purpose international organization; for example, a customs union. 4. The merging of two or more countries to form one new one. 5. That part of a national flag that signifies the union of two or more states; thus the blue part of the American flag on which are located the fifty white stars representing the fifty states is the union.

union dues Fees that union members must periodically pay to remain in good standing with their union. The dues are used to finance all the activities of the union and its affiliates.

union shop A union security provision found in some collective bargaining agreements that requires all employees to become members of the union within a specified time (usually thirty days) after being hired (or after the provision is negotiated) and to remain members as a condition of employment.

unit cohesion Solidarity within a work group as demonstrated by commitment to common goals, to the organization as a whole, and by the members to each other.

United States Civil Service Commission The central personnel agency of the United States from 1883 through 1978. It was abolished by the CIVIL SERVICE REFORM ACT OF 1978.

United States v. Curtiss-Wright Export Corporation (1936) The U.S. Supreme Court case defining the president's constitutional position in foreign affairs. In 1934, the U.S. Congress adopted a joint resolution authorizing the president by proclamation to prohibit the sale (within the United States) of arms to some South American nations. The president issued such a proclamation. Curtiss-Wright attacked such constraint on its business on the grounds that the joint resolution constituted an unconstitutional delegation of legislative authority to the president. The Court upheld the resolution and proclamation on the grounds that the U.S. Constitution created the "very delicate, plenary and exclusive power of the president as the sole organ of the federal government in the field of international relations" and that, in the international sphere, the president must be accorded "a degree of discretion and freedom from statutory restriction which would not be admissible were domestic affairs alone involved."

United States v. Nixon (1974) The U.S. Supreme Court case dealing with President Richard M. Nixon's claim that the U.S. Constitution provided the president with an absolute and unreviewable EXECUTIVE PRIVILEGE; that is, the right not to respond to a subpoena in connection with a judicial trial. The Court held that "neither the doctrine of separation of powers, nor the need for confidentiality of high-level communications, without more, can sustain an absolute, unqualified, presidential immunity from judicial process under all circumstances." The Court allowed that a limited executive privilege might pertain in military, diplomatic, and security affairs, and where confidentiality was related to the president's ability to carry out his constitutional mandates. This was the decision that in effect forced Nixon to resign as president. *See* WATERGATE.

unity of command 1. The concept that each individual in an organization should be accountable to one superior. 2. The concept that a military unit be led by one commander.

unity of direction The concept that there should be only one head and one plan for each organizational segment.

up-or-out system A career system that terminates individuals who do not qualify themselves for the next higher level of the system within a specified time period. The U.S. military officer corps and Foreign Service are two examples of up-or-out systems.

urban homesteading A local program that gives a family a substandard home in a distressed urban area on condition that the structure be renovated and lived in by that family. Sometimes, these programs provide for low-interest home improvement loans or charge token amounts for the homes.

urban park movement Part of a growing movement in the years after the American Civil War to make cities more beautiful. It sought to create municipal parks designed to appear natural (despite the roadways that wandered through them), waterways situated to provide restful vistas, and well-placed recreational facilities. The leading designer was Frederick Law Olmsted (1822–1903), who designed New York City's Central Park. He, like others who worked on such projects, gave city planning in the United States the elite and somewhat anti-industrial character it was destined to have through the New Deal era. The major premise of the movement was that parks create an environment that help ameliorate the immoral and squalid conditions of urban life occasioned by industrialization.

urban planning The formal process of guiding the physical and social development of cities and their regions. Although urban PLANNING is a highly technical process, it is also highly politicized because the various community interests are always ready to fight for their version of beneficial change.

urban renewal The national program for urban redevelopment, started in 1949 to rejuvenate urban areas through large-scale physical projects. Originally a loan program primarily for housing, it was quickly transformed by political pressures into a grant program for redoing large sections of central business districts and other commercial areas. It has been severely criticized for its uprooting of communities, especially black neighborhoods, and replacing them with commercial developments.

user charges/user fees Specific sums that users or consumers of a government service pay to receive that service. For example, a homeowner's water bill, if based upon usage, would be a user charge. Other examples include toll roads, bridges, and charges to use public swimming pools.

usury laws Laws that limit the amount of interest financial institutions can charge their customers.

utilitarianism *See* JEREMY BENTHAM.

utopia 1. The Greek word meaning nowhere. 2. A model of a society that meets the needs of all of its citizens as they perceive those needs; in their terms, the perfect society. 3. A literary form that posits a carefully designed polity that will, by its character, raise contrasts with reality. While conceptions of ideal societies go back to ancient times, it was Thomas More's 1516 book, *Utopia*, that gave the concept its modern name.

V

veterans' benefits Government advantages available to those who served in the armed forces of the United States that are not available to citizens who did not serve. Veterans' benefits may include government-supplied health care, advantageous home mortgage terms, and pensions.

veterans' preference The concept that dates from 1865, when the U.S. Congress, toward the end of the American Civil War, affirmed that "persons honorably discharged from the military or naval service by reason of disability resulting from wounds or sickness incurred in the line of duty, shall be preferred for appointments to civil offices, provided they are found to possess the business capacity necessary for the proper discharge of the duties of such offices." The 1865 law was superseded in 1919, when preference was extended to all "honorably discharged" veterans, their widows, and the wives of disabled veterans. The Veterans' Preference Act of 1944 expanded the scope of veterans' preference by providing for a five-point bonus on federal examination scores for all honorably separated veterans (except for those with a service-connected disability, who are entitled to a ten-point bonus). Veterans also received other advantages in federal employment (such as protections against arbitrary dismissal and preference in the event of a reduction in force). All states and many other jurisdictions have veterans' preference laws of varying intensity. New Jersey, an extreme example, offers veterans absolute preference; if a veteran passes an entrance examination, that person must be hired (no matter what the score) before nonveterans can be hired. Veterans competing with each other are rank-ordered, and all disabled veterans receive preference over other veterans. Veterans' preference laws have been criticized because they have allegedly made it difficult for government agencies to hire and promote more women and minorities. Veterans' preference was challenged for discriminating against women but was upheld by the U.S. Supreme Court in *Personnel Administrator of Massachusetts v. Feeney* (1979).

veto 1. The Latin word for "I forbid." **2.** Disapproval by the president of a bill or joint resolution, other than one proposing an amendment to the U.S.

Constitution. When the U.S. Congress is in session, the president must veto a bill within ten days, excluding Sundays, after receiving it, or it becomes law without the presidential signature. When the president vetoes a bill, he returns it to the House of its origin accompanied by a message stating his objections. 3. The right of any of the five permanent members of the United Nations Security Council (China, France, the United Kingdom, the United States, and Russia) under Article 27 of the UN Charter to prevent a decision by withholding agreement. 4. The disapproval of proposed legislation by a chief executive who has formal authority to do so.

veto override A legislature's approval, usually by an extraordinary majority, of a bill that has been vetoed by the executive. If the president of the United States disapproves a bill and sends it back to the U.S. Congress with his objections, the Congress may override the veto by a two-thirds vote in each chamber.

veto, absolute A veto that is final because there is no legal way to override it.

veto, item The executive power to veto separate items in a bill. Many state governors have this authority; the president of the United States does not.

veto, legislative A statutory measure that allows the president to put forth a proposal, subject to the approval or disapproval of the U.S. Congress. Either action must be taken usually within from sixty to ninety days. The legislative veto may take the form of a committee veto, a simple resolution passed by either House, or a concurrent resolution. The legislative veto was first provided for in the Economy Act of June 30, 1932, when the Congress authorized President Herbert Hoover to reorganize executive departments and agencies, subject to disapproval by a simple majority of either House within sixty days. Since 1932, several hundred pieces of legislation have included some version of the legislative veto. Until the War Powers Resolution of 1973, the legislative veto was used mainly for executive reorganization proposals. Then the War Powers Resolution unleashed a new conception of the legislative veto. For the first time, it became the only check on major presidential policy initiatives, such as war, as opposed to being an after-the-fact sanctioning of management reforms. In 1983, the U.S. Supreme Court ruled in *Immigration and Naturalization Service v. Chadha* (1983), that the one-house (meaning either house) congressional veto violated the separation of powers and was therefore unconstitutional. The Court reasoned that the congressional veto bypassed the president because he was given no opportunity to sign or veto the measure at hand. The Congress could accomplish the same ends and not violate the separation of powers by using the regular legislative processes to achieve its will; then the president would not be bypassed.

veto, pocket The act of the president of the United States in withholding approval of a bill after the U.S. Congress has adjourned—either for the year or for a specified period. When the Congress is in session, a bill becomes law, even without the presidential signature, within ten days, excluding Sundays, from the time the president receives it.. But if the Congress adjourns within that ten-day period, the bill is killed without the president's formal veto.

vigilantes Citizens who take the law into their own hands and illegally administer what they consider to be justice (by murder, beatings, and so on) to those whom they feel would not be adequately punished by the normal operations of the criminal justice system.

village 1. An unincorporated settlement within a county. 2. A small municipal corporation.

virtual Not real, but resembling something that is real. Thus a virtual organization or a virtual team exists not as a physical presence but only as a network of resources (customers, suppliers, team members) available on the Internet.

vision A view of an organization's future. The purpose of strategic management is to make such a vision a reality.

vision statement *See* MISSION STATEMENT.

Volcker Commission The National Commission on the Public Service created in 1987 to examine the "quiet crisis" in government personnel management. It was popularly called the Volcker Commission after its chairman, Paul Volcker (1927–), former Chairman of the Board of Governors of the Federal Reserve System. The Commission issued a major report in 1989 bemoaning the low quality, low pay, and low morale of the federal service.

voluntarism Actions undertaken freely by individuals and groups for the benefit of others and the society at large.

voluntary sector The nonprofit, independent, or third sector; not part of government or private business.

volunteer A person who provides a service without compulsion or requirement and typically without compensation. However, with the growth of the voluntary sector, the definition of a volunteer appears to be changing. For example, many volunteer ambulance services and fire departments now pay volunteers for their standby time and/or for making runs. These paid persons are still considered to be volunteers, or paid volunteers, so long as their work with the ambulance service is not their primary source of income.

voucher system A government program that issues redeemable vouchers to eligible citizens to purchase services on the open market. For example, housing vouchers have been suggested as an alternative to public housing, and education vouchers have been suggested as an alternative to public education. The idea of using vouchers was popularized by the economist MILTON FRIEDMAN in *Capitalism and Freedom* (1962).

W

wage-and-price controls A government's formal efforts to control inflation by regulating the wages and prices. This is usually done during wartime. The last time the United States had wage-and-price controls was from 1971 to 1974 during the Richard M. Nixon administration.

Wagner Act *See* NATIONAL LABOR RELATIONS ACT OF 1935.

Waldo, (Clifford) Dwight (1913–2000) The preeminent historian of the academic discipline of public administration and the editor in chief of *Public Administration Review* from 1966 to 1977. Waldo first became an influence in public administration when he attacked the "gospel of efficiency" that so dominated administrative thinking prior to World War II. In his landmark book, *The Administrative State: A Study of the Political Theory of American Public Administration* (1948), he asserted that the drive for efficiency has "occasionally served the end of those whose purposes might be regarded as more or less reprehensible if stated in another idiom." Waldo's other major works include *The Study of Public Administration* (1955); *Public Administration in a Time of Turbulence*, (1971); *The Enterprise of Public Administration* (1980).

ward A subdivision of a city, often used as a legislative district for city council elections, as an administrative division for public services, or as a unit for the organization of political parties. A ward is often further divided into precincts.

war on poverty The phrase used by the Lyndon B. Johnson administration for its 1960s Great Society programs designed to eliminate the causes and effects of poverty in the United States. In his January 8, 1964 State of the Union Message, President Johnson said: "This administration today, here and now, declares unconditional war on poverty in America."

warrant 1. In criminal proceedings, a writ issued by a judge directing a law enforcement officer to do something; for example, to search some premises (a search warrant) or to arrest some person (an arrest warrant). Warrants are required because of the Fourth Amendment's assertion that the people be free from unreasonable searches and seizures. **2.** A short-term obligation issued by a government in anticipation of revenue. The instrument (a draft much like a check), when presented to a disbursing officer, such as a bank, is payable only upon acceptance by the issuing jurisdiction. Warrants may be made payable on demand or at some time in the future. Local governments, in particular, have used delayed payment of warrants as a way to protect cash flow.

Washington 1. The capital city of the United States. While Washington refers to the physical location of the federal government's central offices, it is frequently used as a collective noun to refer to the policymaking processes and actors of the national government (e.g., as in Washington said, . . . Washington decided, . . . or it is Washington's policy . . .). It was President John F. Kennedy who said during a November 14, 1961 speech that Washington was "city of Northern charm and Southern efficiency." 2. Washington State, located in the northwestern United States. 3. The District of Columbia, the "D.C." in Washington, D.C., which occupies the same territory as the capital city of Washington. 4. A code word implying vast bureaucracy, endless red tape, and the arrogant use of power. In this sense some political candidates, most notably Presidents Jimmy Carter and Ronald Reagan, have "run against" Washington.

Washington Monument dodge A classic tactic for avoiding budget cuts; an agency is told to cut its budget and announces that the Washington Monument (or something equally popular with the public) will have to be shut down. The uproar that follows sees the cuts reinstated.

Watergate The scandal that led to the resignation of President Richard M. Nixon in 1974. Watergate itself is a hotel-office-apartment complex in Washington, D.C. When individuals associated with the Committee to Reelect the President were caught breaking into the Democratic National Committee Headquarters (then located in the Watergate complex) in 1972, the resulting cover-up and national trauma was condensed into one word: *Watergate*. The term has grown to refer to a political crime or instance of bureaucratic corruption that undermines confidence in governing institutions. *See also UNITED STATES V. NIXON.*

ways and means 1. A government's financial resources. 2. The methods by which a state gains its funds, supplies, and other necessities. The United Kingdom's House of Commons has had a Committee on Ways and Means at least since 1644. The U.S. House of Representatives has had a Ways and Means Committee since 1795. All national tax legislation must originate in the House Ways and Means Committee.

weasel word Any word which serves to make one's views misleading or confusing. Politicians have always had a great fondness for weasel words. President Theodore Roosevelt said in a May 31, 1916 speech in St. Louis: "One of our defects as a nation is a tendency to use what have been called weasel words.

When a weasel sucks eggs it sucks the meat out of the egg and leaves the shell. If you use a weasel word after another there is nothing left of the other."

Weber, Max (1864–1920) The German sociologist who produced an analysis of an ideal-type bureaucracy that is still the most influential statement—the point of departure for all further analyses—on the subject. Weber also pioneered the concepts of the Protestant ethic, charismatic authority, and a value-free approach to social research. *See also* BUREAUCRACY; CHARISMA; LEGITIMACY. For Weber's major works, see Max Weber, *Protestant Ethic and the Spirit of Capitalism,* trans. Talcott Parsons (1904–1905, 1958); H. H. Gerth and C. Wright Mills, eds., *From Max Weber: Essays in Sociology* (1946).

welfare Public financial or in-kind assistance available to citizens as a matter of right if they meet eligibility requirements, such as a MEANS TEST of income or assets below a preset minimum. Welfare is not only for the poor; it can cover a wide range of people of various means. Senator Hubert H. Humphrey provided one of the most eloquent defenses of government welfare programs at the dedication of the Hubert H. Humphrey Building of the Department of Health and Human Services on November 1, 1977: "It was once said that the moral test of government is how that government treats those who are in the dawn of life, the children; those who are in the twilight of life, the elderly; and those who are in the shadows of life—the sick, the needy and the handicapped." Some biblical scholars contend that the commandment "Thou Shalt Not Kill" contained the essence of a welfare program. After all, if a wandering desert tribe did not help those members in need (the ill, the old, the widowed and orphaned), they would surely die. Thus we can conclude that the social provision of welfare services has always been mandated from above —sometimes far above. *See also* ENTITLEMENT PROGRAM.

welfare clause *See* GENERAL WELFARE CLAUSE.

Welfare Reform Act of 1996 The law that abolished the entitlement aspect of welfare by which the federal government "matched" state welfare payments dollar for dollar. The matching funds were converted into block grants with which the states in their fifty varieties of wisdom would decide who was worthy of the new style welfare and under what conditions. In essence, most of the federal strings would be removed, and the states would overall get less than before, but they would have far greater discretion on how to spend it. Now those who are deemed unworthy or undeserving of aid, because they refuse to accept work or educational opportunities, may now be cut off completely. And even if they are highly deserving, they may be cut off if they reach a preset time limit such as two years. The theory goes that if welfare recipients know that funds will run out for them on a certain date, they will be more energetic about finding work or obtaining job training beforehand. The new act was titled the

"Personal Responsibility and Work Opportunity Reconciliation Act" specifically because welfare recipients were generally expected to take more "personal responsibility" for themselves by seeking an appropriate "work opportunity." The traditional welfare office is evolving into a new administrative animal. Massachusetts' Department of Public Welfare is now the Department of Transitional Assistance. Florida's welfare program is now the Work and Gain Economic Self-Sufficiency Program. Indicative of this major change in terminology is the 1998 decision of the American Public Welfare Association (which represents social service agencies) to change its name after sixty-six years to the American Public Human Services Association. Welfare reform may not yet have killed welfare in fact, but it has certainly killed it in name.

welfare state A governing system in which it is a public policy that government will provide extensive economic and social benefits for each of its citizens as a right, not out of charity. The differences between a welfare state and socialism are semantic only.

whistle-blower An individual who believes the public interest overrides the interests of the organization and publicly blows the whistle on corrupt, illegal, fraudulent, and/or harmful activity. Whistle-blowers in our society are not well received. Children have long been taught not to be "squealers." In blowing the whistle, one runs the risk of being ostracized by one's coworkers, of losing one's job, and of being blacklisted in one's field. The Civil Service Reform Act of 1978 provided specific protection for federal whistle-blowers.

white flight 1. The movement of white residents from central cities. It was a common response to public school busing to achieve school racial integration. If they could afford it, whites would tend to move out of the central city and into the suburbs so that their children could attend neighborhood schools. White flight most often occurred when the school population became overwhelmingly black and when bus rides were deemed excessively long. 2. More recently, as in the case of Miami, it is the movement of English-speaking citizens from an area that has become increasingly Hispanic in language and culture.

White House 1. The official residence of the president of the United States. While President George Washington chose the site, John Adams, the second president of the United States, was the first to actually live there. On the day after he moved into the White House, November 2, 1800, President Adams wrote to his wife, Abigail: "I Pray Heaven to Bestow The Best of Blessing on this house, and on All That shall hereafter Inhabit it. May none but Honest and Wise Men ever rule under This Roof!" President Franklin D. Roosevelt had this prayer inscribed over the fireplace in the State Dining Room of the White House. It just goes to show how some prayers are only partially answered. 2. The formal main office of the executive branch of the government of the United States. 3. The modern symbol of the presidency. 4. A building that can speak. Reporters and political commentators frequently state that the "White House said . . . " this or that. The building speaks because it is the architectural embodiment of the bureaucratic institution that is the modern presidency. Thus the building speaks through press releases, news conferences, deep as well as shallow background briefings, and LEAKS. While the President is the main and most desired speaker, there are a few thousand other people who also work there and who give it voice. 5. A complex of buildings that includes the traditional White House, its two wings (east and west), the old Executive Office Building, the new Executive Office Building, and Blair House (an official guest house).

White, Leonard D. (1891–1958) Author of the first U.S. public administration text, in 1926; author of the standard administrative histories of the United States government in the nineteenth century; and one of the most significant voices in the development of public administration as an academic discipline. White's major works include *Introduction to the Study of Public Administration* (1926; 4th ed., 1955); *The Federalists* (1948); *The Jeffersonians* (1951); *The Jacksonians* (1954); *The Republican Era* (1958).

white paper The formal statement of an official or proposed government policy, and its associated background documentation. *Compare to* POLICY PAPER.

wicked problems Problems such as terrorism or poverty for which there are no permanent solutions—only temporary or imperfect solutions. Tame problems, in contrast, are easily defined, decomposable, and solvable.

Wildavsky, Aaron B. (1930–1993) The author of *The Politics of the Budgetary Process* (1964; 4th ed., 1984), which reveals the tactics public managers use to have their budgets passed and explains why rational attempts to reform the budgetary process have always failed. For this classic work alone, Wildavsky would have earned his place in the pantheon of public administration. However, Wildavsky has also made landmark contributions to the study of the U.S. presidency (*see* PRESIDENCIES, TWO), policy analysis, and program implementation and evaluation. Because of the volume, quality, and diversity of his work, Wildavsky is one of the nation's most widely read and influential academic analysts of public affairs.

William Jefferson Clinton v. Paula Corbin Jones (1998) The U.S. Supreme Court ruling that a sitting president could be sued by a private citizen seeking money damages in a civil suit for conduct alleged to have occurred before the president took office. Jones claimed that she was sexually harassed by Clinton while he served as the governor of Arkansas years earlier. President Clinton's testimony about Monica Lewinsky in a sworn deposition in the *Jones* case would set off the political firestorm that led to his impeachment in 1998.

Wilson, (Thomas) Woodrow (1856–1924) The president of the United States from 1913 to 1921. Wilson, who was president of Princeton University (1902–1910) and governor of New Jersey (1911–1913), was also a president of the American Political Science Association; he is considered one of the most influential early voices of both political science and public administration. Wilson's 1885 classic analysis of U.S. national government, *Congressional Government,* found the U.S. Congress to be "predominant over its so-called coordinate branches" with congressional power parceled out to the various congressional committees. It has become customary to trace the origins of the academic discipline of public administration to Wilson's 1887 article, "The Study of Administration," *Political Science Quarterly.* Wilson attempted nothing less than to refocus political science. Rather than be concerned with the great maxims of lasting political truth, he argued that political science should concentrate on how governments are administered. In his words: "It is getting to be harder to run a constitution than to frame one." In this essay, Wilson put forth the then-radical notion that politics should be separate from administration. *See* POLITICS-ADMINISTRATION DICHOTOMY.

work to rule A work slowdown in which all the formal work rules are so scrupulously obeyed that productivity suffers. Those working to rule seek to place pressure on management without losing pay by going on strike.

Workers Compensation Industrial accident insurance designed to provide cash benefits and medical care for a worker injured on the job and monetary payments to survivors for a worker killed on the job. This compensation was the first form of social insurance to develop widely in the United States. Before the passage of workmen's compensation laws, an injured employee ordinarily had to file suit against an employer and, to recover damages, had to prove that the injury was caused by the employer's negligence. The first compensation laws introduced the principle that a worker incurring an occupational injury would be compensated regardless of fault or blame in the accident and with a minimum of delay and legal formality. In turn, the employer's liability was limited, because workmen's compensation benefits became the exclusive remedy for work-related injuries.

workfare A public welfare program that requires welfare payment recipients to work (work + welfare = workfare) or to enroll in a formal job-training program.

working class All who work for wages, usually at manual labor. When the term is used politically, it tends to exclude managers, professionals, and anyone who is not at the lower end of the educational and economic scales.

Z

zero out 1. The total destruction of something. 2. To delete a budget item.

zero-sum game 1. A game in which the total of the payoffs to the players is zero regardless of the outcome. 2. An international political/military perspective that views potential gains for one side as a loss for the other; for one player to win, another must lose. This brings the overall outcome to zero. Once used only in GAME THEORY, the idea of "zero-sum conflict" has gradually gained wider usage.

zoning The process by which local government can designate the types of structures and activities for a particular area. Zoning began in the 1920s to protect neighborhoods from the encroachments of business and industry and to preserve their economic and social integrity; it involves a highly complex legal process, often impacted by local politics.

zoning variance A lawful deviation from normal zoning policy.

zoning, aesthetic A zoning policy operating in the interests of beauty. According to Justice William O. Douglas's majority opinion in the U.S. Supreme Court case of *Berma v. Parker* (1954), "It is within the power of the legislature to determine that the community should be beautiful as well as healthy."

zoning, affirmative Land-use regulations that seek neighborhood development that will benefit the disadvantaged.

zoning, cluster A zoning policy that allows builders to reduce lot sizes below normal standards so that the "extra" land is retained as open space for the community.

zoning, Euclidian A zoning policy that keeps apartments and businesses out of single-home residential areas. This kind of zoning was adopted by Euclid, Ohio, and was the subject of the U.S. Supreme Court case of *Village of Euclid v. Ambler Realty Company* (1926), which asserted that zoning was a valid exercise of local government powers.

zoning, exclusionary A zoning policy that excludes specified types of usages, such as home sites on lots smaller than one acre.

zoning, inclusionary A zoning policy that requires builders to provide (at reduced rates) a portion of new housing units for moderate- and low-income families.

zoning, open-space A zoning policy requiring developers to provide a certain amount of open space, depending upon the size of the project.

zoning, spot Changing the zoning of a parcel of land without regard for the zoning plan of the entire area.